CAMBRIDGE LIB

Books of endu

CU01476774

Anth

The first use of the word 'anthropology' in English was recorded in 1593, but its modern use to indicate the study and science of humanity became current in the late nineteenth century. At that time a separate discipline had begun to evolve from many component strands (including history, archaeology, linguistics, biology and anatomy), and the study of so-called 'primitive' peoples was given impetus not only by the reports of individual explorers but also by the need of colonial powers to define and classify the unfamiliar populations which they governed. From the ethnographic writings of early explorers to the 1898 Cambridge expedition to the Torres Straits, often regarded as the first truly 'anthropological' field research, these books provide eye-witness information on often vanished peoples and ways of life, as well as evidence for the development of a new scientific discipline.

The South-Eastern Bantu

Son of Tiyo Soga, the first black South African to be ordained, John Henderson Soga (1860–1941) was a Xhosa minister and scholar. Like his father, he was one of the first of his people to receive an education in Europe and to marry a European woman. His perspective on his people's history is therefore distinctive. Driven by a desire to record Xhosa traditions before they were lost in a changing world, Soga collected oral histories during his work at mission stations in South Africa, producing this historical survey of three branches of the Bantu family. Including genealogies of the main tribes, and tracing their traditions, beliefs and conflicts, the work first appeared in this English version in 1930, having been translated by the author from his native language. His equally authoritative work of social anthropology, *The Ama-Xosa: Life and Customs* (1932), is also reissued in this series.

Cambridge University Press has long been a pioneer in the reissuing of out-of-print titles from its own backlist, producing digital reprints of books that are still sought after by scholars and students but could not be reprinted economically using traditional technology. The Cambridge Library Collection extends this activity to a wider range of books which are still of importance to researchers and professionals, either for the source material they contain, or as landmarks in the history of their academic discipline.

Drawing from the world-renowned collections in the Cambridge University Library and other partner libraries, and guided by the advice of experts in each subject area, Cambridge University Press is using state-of-the-art scanning machines in its own Printing House to capture the content of each book selected for inclusion. The files are processed to give a consistently clear, crisp image, and the books finished to the high quality standard for which the Press is recognised around the world. The latest print-on-demand technology ensures that the books will remain available indefinitely, and that orders for single or multiple copies can quickly be supplied.

The Cambridge Library Collection brings back to life books of enduring scholarly value (including out-of-copyright works originally issued by other publishers) across a wide range of disciplines in the humanities and social sciences and in science and technology.

The South-Eastern Bantu

Abe-Nguni, Aba-Mbo, Ama-Lala

JOHN HENDERSON SOGA

CAMBRIDGE
UNIVERSITY PRESS

CAMBRIDGE
UNIVERSITY PRESS

University Printing House, Cambridge, CB2 8BS, United Kingdom

Published in the United States of America by Cambridge University Press, New York

Cambridge University Press is part of the University of Cambridge.
It furthers the University's mission by disseminating knowledge in the pursuit of
education, learning and research at the highest international levels of excellence.

www.cambridge.org
Information on this title: www.cambridge.org/9781108066822

© in this compilation Cambridge University Press 2013

This edition first published 1930
This digitally printed version 2013

ISBN 978-1-108-06682-2 Paperback

THE AUTHOR

THE
SOUTH-EASTERN BANTU

(ABE-NGUNI, ABA-MBO, AMA-LALA)

BY

J. HENDERSON SOGA

JOHANNESBURG
Published by the Witwatersrand University Press
1930

EDITOR'S INTRODUCTION.

The present supplement to *Bantu Studies* contains a translation of the Rev. John Henderson Soga's *The South - Eastern Bantu*, made by the author himself at the request of the Editorial Committee of *Bantu Studies*.

The reasons which influenced the Committee in making Soga's *History* accessible in English may be briefly indicated.

1. Up to the present, all instruction in schools for Bantu children has inevitably been based on European text-books translated into the vernacular, or, in the higher classes, studied in the English originals. Such books are naturally written from the European point of view, and educated Natives have not infrequently complained of the " white " bias which, unavoidably, affects more especially the presentation of South African History. This bias appears partly in the accounts of the recurrent wars between Whites and Bantus; and partly also in the comparative neglect of Native tradition and, thereby, of the many happenings which, not having directly affected the Whites, are of purely Native interest. The Rev. J. H. Soga's *The South-Eastern Bantu* is the first considerable attempt made by an educated man of Bantu descent and in touch with Bantu tradition, to present the History of his people in one of the most widely spoken Native languages (isi-Xosa). It will be used in Native schools ; it will be widely read by Natives ; it will keep alive the memory of their

past ; it will help to form their attitude towards
their White fellow-citizens ; it will build up and
strengthen their racial self-consciousness as
Natives. It is, therefore, a *cultural document* of
importance. It is a mile-stone on the road to the
creation of an indigenous literature in the vernacular. Whatever its value as a contribution to
History may be, it has a value as a factor in the
rise of the Bantu peoples in the scale of civilization,
and in the strengthening of Bantu self-respect and
pride of race. As such, the Committee thought
that this book deserved to be made accessible in
English to all who are interested in the effort of
the Bantu peoples to absorb what is of value in
European civilization without cutting off their
roots with their own past.

2. But Soga's work has also some claim to
attention as a contribution to the *history* of the
Eastern Bantu. Not that it brings to light any
hitherto unknown events of first rate importance.
And for the opening chapters, which deal in the
main with matters lying beyond Bantu tradition,
Soga relies frankly on the authority of white historians. But, allowing for all this, Soga's work can
still claim a distinct value as a historical study.
For one thing, it bears evidence, in many parts,
of first-hand enquiry into local tribal traditions.
The author has made many journeys seeking
verification of reports from old Native witnesses.
Thus, e.g., we get a fresh clue to the end of Capt.
Coxon's party (Ch. xx, 384), or a fresh version of
a familiar fact, as in the account of the War of
Ngcayecibi (1877) given by an old Gcaleka councillor who took part in it himself (Ch. xvi, 254)

Again the part played by certain customs in tribal history, e.g. the *isi-zi* custom (Ch. iv, *et al.*), is well brought out. Above all, the author's method of tracing (a) tribal migrations by the locations of the graves of tribal chiefs, and (b) tribal affiliations by genealogies of chiefs, with due attention to the distinction between Great Houses, Right-Hand Houses, and Minor Houses, clarifies and supplements in many details previously existing information. The most important result of the application of this genealogical method[1] is the conclusion that the Zulus are a tribe of comparatively recent origin, and belong most probably to the Lala branch of the Eastern Bantu (Chs. xx and xxii, *et al.*) In spite of their importance at the present day and in the history of the last century, the Zulus appear in Soga's pages as an upstart tribe, not equal in distinction and antiquity to other Bantu tribes.

To this statement of the reasons for the publication of this book in an English translation, may usefully be added two comments in anticipation of possible criticisms :—

First, some readers may complain of frequent repetitions in the pages of this book. These repetitions are undeniable, but they are inseparable from Soga's organisation of his material. And for this organisation there is much to be said, remembering that this book is, in the first instance, written for *Native* readers. Soga divides the Eastern Bantu into three main branches : Abe-Nguni, Aba-Mbo, Ama-Lala, and he deals

---

[1] Certain of Soga's genealogies differ, in some particulars, from the genealogies previously published by Tooke (1883 Commission's report). See also Soga's note in *Bantu Studies Vol. III, No. 1.*

under each branch with the various tribes into
which it splits up in the course of history. It is
inevitable, on this scheme, that, e.g., wars in which
tribes belonging to different branches are involved,
should be mentioned twice, once under each tribe.
A Native reader, interested in his own tribe first
and foremost, would naturally be best satisfied so.

And, secondly, it may be objected that, after all,
we do not get here the voice of a pure Bantu, on
the ground that Soga is of mixed Bantu-Scotch
descent and had a Scotch School and University
education. The facts alleged are correct (see
Biographical Note), but they do not seriously in-
validate Soga's testimony. For, whilst fully
appreciating what he owes to his white mother
and his white wife and his " white " education,
John Henderson Soga has that pride of his Bantu
blood and that sympathy with the lot and the aspirations of his Bantu fellows which his famous
father, Tiyo Soga, wished all his sons to have.
Tiyo desired his sons to regard themselves as
Natives—indeed, in his own word, as " Kafirs,"
a term which had in his mouth no depreciatory
connotation. Soga's book is written in the spirit
of the first of the sixty-two maxims which Tiyo
Soga formulated, under the title " The Inheritance
of my Children," for the guidance of his sons and
daughters through the difficulties of life in general
and of racial prejudices in particular. We cannot
do better than conclude this *Introduction* with a
quotation from that first maxim, in memory of a
noble character and a fine Christian, and in illustration of the spirit in which Tiyo's son has written
his book :— " Among some white men there

is a prejudice against black men ; the prejudice is simply and solely on account of colour. For your own sakes never appear ashamed that your father was a Kafir, and that you inherit some African blood. It is every whit as good and as pure as that which flows in the veins of my fairer brethren, ...I want you, for your own future comfort, to be very careful on this point. You will ever cherish the memory of your mother as that of an upright, conscientious, thrifty, Christian Scotchwoman. You will ever be thankful for your connection by this tie with the white race. But if you wish to gain credit for yourselves—if you do not wish to feel the taunt of men, which you sometimes may be made to feel—*take your place* in the world as *coloured*, not as white ; as *Kafirs*,[1] not as Englishmen....You, my children, belong to a primitive race of men, who, amid many unamiable points, stand second to none as to nobility of character. The Kafirs will stand high when compared in all things with the uncivilized races of the world. They have the elements out of which a noble race might be made !' "

If the earlier investigators had the advantage in time, Soga has the advantage of closer contact with his people and more prolonged research into its tribal traditions. The truth is at least as likely to lie on his side as on that of his predecessors in this field. We must look to future research to clear up the few points of difference, if that is still possible.

R. F. A. H.

---

[1] Tiyo Soga's own italics.

A BIOGRAPHICAL NOTE ON THE AUTHOR.

The author of this book, the Rev. John Henderson Soga, is the second son of the late Rev. Tiyo Soga and his wife, Janet Burnside, daughter of a Glasgow burgess.

Tiyo Soga was the first, and still is the most famous, of the small, but steadily growing, band of men of pure Bantu descent who have received a European School and University education, and then returned to practise their professions in their native land.

Readers of this book who wish to understand something of the background of the author's descent on the paternal side, cannot do better than read the Rev. John A. Chalmers's *Tiyo Soga : A Page of South African Mission Work* (Edinburgh : Andrew Elliot, 1877). Suffice it here to say that Tiyo was a descendant of Gaika chiefs, being a son of Soga, who like his father, Jotello, was greatly respected, both as warrior and as councillor, in the Gaika tribe. Jotello is reported to have been killed at the battle of Amalinde, so frequently referred to in the pages of this book (see p. 157). Soga, though opposed to the war of 1877-8 (see p. 254) and a non-combatant in it, refused to desert the Great Chief, Sandile, and seek a safe retreat. He was killed by Fingo Auxiliaries of the Colonial Army in 1878, whilst his grandson, the author, was at school in Scotland. Tiyo, after receiving the beginning of his education at Lovedale, was taken to Scotland where, after completing his school education, he took the Arts course at Glasgow University, followed by training for the Ministry in the Theological Hall of the United Presbyterian Church. In 1857, he was licensed and ordained by the Glasgow Presbytery of the U. P. C., and returned, with his Scotch wife, to South Africa, where he founded Mission stations, first at Emgwali, in the Stutterheim district, among his own people, the Gaikas, and later at Tutura, among the Gcalekas. There he died in 1871.

Before giving further details of the author, it may be interesting to complete the picture of the Bantu-Scotch family of which Tiyo Soga was the founder, by a brief account of Tiyo's other sons and daughters.

Including John Henderson, there were four sons and three daughters.

The eldest son, William A. Soga, after taking the M.B.C.M. and the M.D. degrees at Glasgow University, entered in Edinburgh upon the Divinity course of the U. P. Church, completed it in 1887, was ordained by the Glasgow Presbytery, and sent out to S. Africa to found the Miller Mission, Elliotdale, Transkei. He was the first Medical Missionary in that field. But finding the demands of two professions, Missionary work and Medical practice, too heavy, he resigned in 1900 from the former and confined himself to the latter, practising at Elliotdale until his death there in 1916. His son, it may be added, has followed his father's profession and is a much respected doctor at Idutywa.

The third of the brothers, A. K. Soga, received his education at the Glasgow High School and the Dollar Academy, Clackmannanshire. After taking Law classes at Glasgow University, he returned to the Cape and is stationed, as an officer of the Public Works Department, in the Kentani district, Transkei.

The youngest brother, J. F. Soga, was a pupil of the same schools as A. K. Soga, and then took the degree of M.R.C.V.S. at Dick College, Edinburgh. As Government Veterinary Surgeon, he took a prominent part in the fight against the Rinderpest epidemic in 1897. He died in 1903.

Of Tiyo's three daughters, the eldest died in 1880; the second is engaged in Mission Work in the Transkei; the third, who went to Scotland at an early age, never returned : she is now a teacher of singing in Glasgow.

John Henderson Soga, the author, crossed the sea to Scotland for the first time at the age of three, for medical treatment of a lameness which was never wholly eradicated. Five other voyages to Scotland followed, for School and University education and for furlough from his Mission work.

He attended Glasgow High School, 1870-3 ; Dollar Academy, 1873-7 ; Edinburgh University (Arts course), 1886-1890 ; U P. Divinity Hall, Edinburgh, 1890-3. He was licensed and ordained in 1893 by the Edinburgh Presbytery, and sent out as Missionary to Bacaland, Mount Frere District, Griqualand East. There he founded the Mbonda Mission, where he worked, 1893-1904, until transferred to the Miller Mission, Elliotdale, in succession to his brother, Dr. W. A. Soga. There he is still working at the present day.

John Henderson Soga's work at School and University was solid but not brilliant. He won no outstanding academic distinction, but in spite of the handicap of his lameness, gained the first medal of his University in Gymnastics. In his proficiency with single stick and boxing gloves, his fellow students thought they could recognise something of the war-like spirit of his ancestors—fortunately well under control.

He married a Scotch lady, Isabella Brown, as did, with one exception, all other sons of Tiyo Soga.

Of his own children, the eldest son has recently taken the B.Sc. degree in Engineering at Glasgow University, while a younger son has completed his school studies at Dollar Academy. The eldest daughter is on the Staff of the Blythswood Institute.

Along with his missionary labours, John Henderson Soga has carried on a literary activity which, especially since 1910, has been very extensive. In that year, he began a series of translations from English into the vernacular, isi-Xosa. He began with *Aesop's Fables*, but this translation has never been published. Of his subsequent translations there have been published :—

1. *The Travellers' Guide from Death to Life*, 1924.
2. *The Work of the Holy Spirit*, by Mrs. Penn-Lewis, 1925.
3. *Our Bodies and How They Work*, by Dr. E. Chubb, 1927.

4. *The Pilgrim's Progress, Part II.* which was brought out by the S. P. C. K. in 1927. The First Part had been translated and published by the author's father, Tiyo Soga, in 1867 (see Chalmers, *Tiyo Soga,* ch. xviii).

In 1924, the author was appointed a member of the Committee for the further revision of the Xosa Bible.   The version endorsed by this Committee is now being issued and has been adopted by the various churches engaged in Mission work among the Xosa-speaking tribes.

John Henderson Soga, like his father, Tiyo, has always been interested in the traditions, customs, and tribal life of his people, on which he has been collecting data since 1880.   These he is now engaged in working up into a book on " Ama-Xosa Life and Customs."   His interest in History was first stimulated by a lecture given to the U. P. Divinity students at Edinburgh, by Mr. Thomas Shaw, later Lord Shaw of Dunfernshire.   The present *South - Eastern Bantu* is the outcome of this interest.

R. F. A. H.

PREFACE.

The original language in which the Manuscript of this book was written is Isi-Xosa. The present translation into English has been prepared by the Author at the request of the Department of Bantu Studies of the University of the Witwatersrand.

While the subject matter of the original has been produced in its entirety, a strictly literal translation has been avoided in order to make the English translation as clear as possible.

The primary object of the book was to place in the hands of the rising generation of the Bantu something of the history of their people, in the hope that it might help them to a clearer perception of who and what they are, and to encourage in them a desire for reading and for studying their language.

It is very noticeable that the Bantu people are losing touch with their own past. Few of the older men are now able to give a reasonable account of the history of the tribes to which they belong, and still less are they able to trace the genealogy of their tribal chiefs with anything like accuracy. The younger men, educated and uneducated, know practically nothing of the history of the Bantu. "Old things are passed away" with them, and " all things are become new." Their present environment, their outlook on the future, has, under the influence of new laws and customs, focussed their attention on matters of life and conduct unknown to their fathers.

The book deals mainly with tribal constitution
and movements, leaving the wider field of customs,
laws, religion, folklore, etc., to others to explore.
The first six chapters are devoted to an effort to
indicate the probable origin of the Bantu race.
In this the writer has had to rely mainly on historical and ethnological sources of information. He has
also attempted to bring some kind of order out of
what appears to many to be a chaotic welter of
tribes, without any clear national cohesion. For
this purpose the Eastern Bantu, i.e., those between
the southern border of Natal and the Cape Province,
with whom this book particularly deals, have been
divided into three main branches :—

    (a) *Abe-Nguni*, (b) *Aba-Mbo*, (c) *Ama-Lala*.

To the English version has been added a chapter
on Tribal and Clan names (ch. vii) and one on the
correlation of Bantu tribes (ch. viii), indicating
its methods and its limitations, together with the
royal salutations of various tribes, and the interdict on the marriage of blood relations, which are
factors of importance in correlation.

Special attention has been given to the compilation of genealogical tables of the more important
tribes, which are of as much interest to the members
of the various tribes mentioned, and possibly to
European students, as the more general matter.

Tradition has been largely relied upon in following out individual and tribal history. Naturally
however, the contact between white and black in
South Africa, made it necessary to include incidents
dealt with in extant history books, but this has been
done as sparingly as possible.

The book will probably exhibit the defects inseparable from a translation from one language into another, where two very distinct idioms have to be reconciled, but apart from these and other short-comings, the author's hope is that the book may provide at least some interest both for the general reader, and for students engaged in the study of Bantu history.

Much encouragement and help which have been accorded the author by Mr. K. A. H. Houghton, Inspector of Schools, are gratefully acknowledged. Thanks are also due to Prof. D. D. Jabavu, B.A., and Rev. M. S. H. Williamson, B.A., B.D., for assistance in the compilation of the Ntlangwini genealogical table and in other ways, and to Mr. Edwin Mpinda for assistance with the Ama-Bele table.

J. Henderson Soga.

Miller Mission,
    Elliotdale,
       March, 1928.

BIBLIOGRAPHY

Some of the publications consulted in connection with this work are :—

Stanford,	*Ethnology of the Egyptian Sudan.*
A. H. Keane,	*Africa, Vol. II.*
W. C. Willoughby,	*Race Problems.*
G. McC. Theal,	*Beginnings of History.*
G. McC. Theal,	*Historical Records, Vols. III. and IV.*
Sullivan,	*Dhow Chasing in Zanzibar Waters.*
F. Brownlee,	*Historical Records.*
J. Bird,	*Annals of Natal.*
A. T. Bryant,	*Zulu Dictionary.*
Moodie,	*Battles, etc., of South Africa.*
H. Drummond,	*Tropical Africa.*
Dudley Kidd,	*The Essential Kaffir.*
W. M. Kerr,	*The Far Interior.*
D. Livingstone,	*Missionary Journeys.*
Victor Poto,	*Ama-Mpondo.*
W. D. Cingo,	*Ibali lama-Mpondo.*
T. B. Soga,	*Intlalo ka-Xosa.*
Jos. Thomson,	*To the Central African Lakes.*
Sir H. H. Johnston,	*British Central Africa.*
Dr. W. Junker,	*Travels in Africa.*
Sir. H. H. Johnston	*Colonization of Africa.*
J. F. Cunningham,	*Uganda and its Peoples.*
G. M. Theal,	*Portuguese in South Africa.*
Emil Holub,	*Seven Years in South Africa, Vols. I and II.*

S. L. & H. Hinde,	*The last of the Masai.*
J. Scott Keltie,	*The Partition of Africa.*
Capt. J. A. Grant,	*A Walk across Africa.*
H. A. Junod,	*The Life of a South African Tribe.*
Cowper Rose,	*Four years in Southern Africa.*
E. O. James,	*Anthropology.*
W. H. R. Rivers,	*Social Organization.*
G. McC. Theal,	*Ethnography and Condition of South Africa before 1505.*
Schweinfurth,	*Heart of Africa.*
J. T. Bent,	*Ruined Cities of Mashonaland.*
Barth,	*Travels in Africa, Vols. I, II.*
Baker,	*Ismalia.*
Galton,	*Tropical Africa.*
G. E. Cory,	*The Rise of South Africa.*
D. D. Jabavu,	*Bantu Literature.*
E. H. Brookes,	*South African Native Policy.*
Holden,	*Kaffir Races.*
T. Rowell,	*Natal and the Boers.*
H. M. Stanley,	*Through the Dark Continent.*
H. M. Stanley,	*How I found Livingstone.*
F. Stretfield,	*Kafirland.*
B. J. Ross,	*Amabali Emfazwe Zakwa-Xosa.*
M. W. Waters,	*Nongqause.*
Henkel,	*Native or Transkeian Territory.*
Ayliff & Whiteside,	*Aba-Mbo.*
S. R. Mqayi,	*Ityala lama-Wele.*
Harris,	*Africa Slave or Free.*

W. C. Scully,   *History of South Africa.*
C. Brownlee,   *Kafir Life and History.*
D. Fraser,   *The Future of Africa.*
Rubusana,   *Zemk'inkomo magwalandini.*
G. Mason,   *Life with the Zulus of Natal.*
Eveleigh,   *Story of a Century,* 1820-
                           1920.

Dower,   *Annals of Kokstad.*
Bokwe,   *Ntsikana.*
Clark Russel,   *Dampier's Voyages.*
Baden Powell,   *Matabele Campaign.*
Wissman,   *Equatorial Africa.*
Sir Godfrey Lagden,   *The Basutos.*
G. E. Cory,   *Rev. Francis Owen's Diary.*
                  Etc. Etc.

ERRATA.

PAGE.	LINE.	
35	14	for *or* read *of*.
39	29	delete *were*.
56	17 and 19	for *Tana* read *Sena*.
164	14	add after *Ndlambe*, " was reported "
174	18	for *adventures* read *adventurers*.
185	6	for *o* substitute *a*.
185	16	for *l* substitute *d* =*ding* for *ling*.
185	6	for *object* read *abject*.
214	11	for *to him* read *him to*.
273	10	for *Zombo* read *Zumbo*.
294	3	for *Mbanqo* read *Banqo*.
302	19	for *whose* read *who*.
302	27	for *young* read *younger*.
303	19	for *head* read *name*.
303	19	for *was* read *is*.
342	6	for *vain* read *main*.
401	33	for *Wusho* read *Wushe*.
465	10	for *Mdungunya* read *Ndungunya*.
428	14	for *no by* read *by no*.
461	19	for *returned* read *retired*.
476	7	for *Mnyambuvu* read *Mnyamvubu*.
476	25	for *Ntsikoni* read *Ntsikeni*.
477	18	for *were* read *was*.
482	4	for *Qiya* read *Qeya*.
487	28	for *latter* read *former*.

CONTENTS.

to meet Xosa chiefs to settle outstanding difficulties, but fails
to meet them.   Reference again made to cession of territory
between Fish and Keiskama rivers.   Sir Charles Somerset
quite right in treating Gaika as paramount of the Gaikas.   Xosas
not always responsible for outrages on the peace of the borders.
D'Urban's accusations against Hintsa.   Sends ultimatum to
Hintsa.   The chief in British camp as hostage, or unjustly
arrested ?   Fingoes " emancipated."   Raid Gcaleka cattle, no
precautions taken against this by the Governor.   Hintsa endeavours to escape, is shot dead at Nqabara.   D'Urban severely
criticised in England.   Lord Glenelg's condemnation of the
Governor.   The Foreign Secretary's Dispatch to Sir Benjamin
D'Urban.   Lord Glenelg's policy severely criticized in South
Africa.

AFRICA

AMA----SHEM

AMA-HAM

AMA----NEGRO

Equator

◯ = Isi-zozo sohlanga
lwa-Bantu.

AMA-BANTU

MADAGASCAR

Congo R.

Tanganyika

Nyasa

Zambezi R.

Sabi R.

Limpopo R.

Orange R.

R. Nile

Atbara R.

Blue Nile

Ama-Galla

Nyanza

SOMALI

Ama-Savi

CHAPTER I

Who are the Bantu?

In order to obtain something like an answer to the question, "Who are the Bantu?" it has been necessary to look into the past and obtain from its history such material as may be a help. Calmet provides us with a starting point, and we make use of his views concerning the entry of the Hamites into North-East Africa, as well as of his dates. It is perfectly well known, however, that other writers give various views on the subject, and differ from Calmet as to dates. The latter, however, is, as has been stated, a sufficient authority to provide a starting point for what follows. The Bible represents Noah as having three sons, Shem, Ham and Japheth. Japheth appears to have been the oldest and the progenitor of the European races, Shem being the second, and Ham the youngest son. The sons of Ham are placed in the following order : Kush, Mitsraim, Phut, Canaan, but in the Rozit ul Suffa (*Asiatic Miscellany*, p. 48, Calmet's *Bible Dict.*) it is written that God gave Ham nine sons, viz., Hind, Sind, Zenj, Nuba, Canaan, Kush, Kopt, Berber, Hebesh, and that on account of their children multiplying marvellously, they were made to speak different languages, and for that reason they were forced to separate, and to form independent communities. There is some doubt as to the identity of the racial descendants of several of these sons of Ham, but the majority may be fairly easily traced. It is stated that—

A

1. Hind was the progenitor of the Hindoos of India ;
2. Sind was the progenitor of the races on both banks of the Indus ;
3. Zenj was the progenitor probably of the races along the Zanzibar Coast;
4. Nuba was the progenitor of the Nubians ;
5. Canaan was the progenitor of races as stated in the Bible ;
6. Kush (?)
7. Kopt was the progenitor of the Egyptians;
8. Berber was the progenitor of the Berbers in North Africa;
9. Hebesh was the progenitor of the Abyssinians.

Notwithstanding that the inheritance of Ham was to be Africa, yet Hind, Sind, Kush, and certain sections of Canaan remained in Asia, the land of their birth. This helps to confirm our knowledge of the existence, at the present day, of powerful Hamitic tribes in Asia. These did not enter into their African heritage. Then again, Asia was appointed as the inheritance of Shem, yet we find Shemites occupying the northern coast of Africa on the sea-board of the Mediterranean and Northern Atlantic.

As regards Canaan, when we study *Genesis*, ix, 25, we note that the Hebrews believed that it was Canaan who exposed his father's condition to Ham, and Noah having found this out cursed Canaan. Others think that Ham was the offender, and Noah believed that by cursing Canaan, the favourite son of Ham, he would the more surely make Ham suffer. Following up a little further the subject of Ham's descendants, we learn that Canaan's eldest son, Sidon, was the progenitor of the Sidonians, otherwise the Phoenicians.   Ten sons of Canaan became the progenitors of ten tribes, the Hittites, Jebusites, Amorites, Girgasites, Hivites, Arkites, Sinites, Zemarites, and Hamathites. The greater portion of all these tribes remained and multiplied in Palestine and Syria, but did not take possession of their African inheritance; that is to say, they remained in Asia.

The Canaanites multiplied greatly, but on account of their wickedness came under Divine displeasure, and God handed over their land to the Israelites, in the time of Joshua (Calmet, *Bible Dict.*)

Before allowing the Israelites to enter into Palestine, Joshua attacked the Canaanites and destroyed great numbers of them, scattering the remnants.   Certain sections of these fled through Asia Minor to Greece, others were driven into North Africa.   We see, then, that the first occupation of Africa by the Hamites took place during the time of Joshua's leadership of the Israelites, before they crossed over Jordan and entered Palestine, 1446 B.C. (Calmet) : 1607 B.C. (Hales).

Now, the tribes which entered into North Africa in the time of Joshua were descendants of Canaan, and from them in the process of time issued the Bantu race.

It is not clear at what period the Shemites entered Africa and became part of its inhabitants. They apparently passed through Syria, crossed the Red Sea, and took possession of Northern Africa.

The general position occupied by the Shemites was along the shores of the Mediterranean Sea, and they settled more especially in the portions of country now known as Tripoli, Algeria and Morocco.

The Hamites, on the other hand, faced south-wards, keeping close to the western shore of the Red Sea, settling along it, and spreading there-from westwards towards North-Central Africa. In these our days the descendants of Ham are recognized in the children of Mitsraim, that is the Egyptians, the Abyssinians, Berber, Somali, Gala, Masai, Huma and so on.

The southern limit of these tribes is the Tana River, which enters the Indian Ocean north of Mombasa. This limit is, however, being gradually over-stepped.

The Bantu Race.

The widely spread Bantu race, which has extended itself over the southern portion of the African continent, is stated by modern authori-ties, who are ethnologists and philologists, to have had its birth-place in the neighbourhood of the Victoria Nyanza, or more precisely in the Tana Basin. Sir H. H. Johnston, on the other hand, suggests the origin of the race to have been much further west. At best, however, this is a matter of speculation.

We would take particular note of the manner in which the country below the Shemites is inhabited. South of the Shemites and central Hamites there is a stretch of country inhabited by Negroes. The name indicates the colour of the skin, and is derived from the Latin *niger*— " black." This race is distinct in many of its human characteristics and in language from the other races of Africa. It is asserted by some that it " is incapable of rising except by miscegenation," but dogmatic statements of this kind are not always borne out by scientific investigation. It is not clear whether or not the Negroes are aboriginal inhabitants of Africa.

If a line is drawn from Cape Verde on the west to the confluence of the Nile and Sobat rivers (W. C. Willoughby, *Race Problems*, p. 15) and from there up the Nile to the northern shores of the Victoria Nyanza, and from that point to the estuary of the Tana river on the east, then this line forms the southern boundary of the Shemites and Hamites and at the same time the northern boundary of the Negroes. The southern boundary of the Negroes has its starting point about the Camerun mountains on the west. From here it stretches over to Zongo, under the great bend of the river Ubangi, whence passing south of Victoria Nyanza it also joins the estuary of the Tana River. The country within these two boundaries is called the Black Belt, and is the home of the Negroes.

All tribes south of this Belt, with the exception of Hottentots and Bushmen, are of Bantu stock.

Ethnologists believe that the Bantu race is not a stock race, like the Negroes, Hottentots and Bushmen, but is the offspring of other races. If we study carefully the land occupied by the Negroes, we will notice that it becomes attenuated towards its eastern limit. Here the Hamites and Negroes are in close juxtaposition, and here, through intermarriage, have produced a new race, to which we now give the name "Bantu." It might be said that this is a mere assumption, but it is, at least, built upon evidence which has led ethnologists to arrive at such a conclusion. That is to say, then, that the Bantu race is a development from the intermixing of Hamitic and Negro blood.

The Eastern Bantu, those occupying the coastal districts, have superimposed upon this a further admixture, that of Arab blood; yet among these tribes, spread along the shores of the Indian Ocean, the mingling of Arab blood varies considerably; some, like the Swaheli, having a larger share while others have less. Furthermore, tribes inhabiting the central portion of the continent of Africa are darker in colour than the tribes along the eastern sea-board, because their blood has been without the admixture of the blood of the lighter coloured Arab.

The Wa-Huma or Wa-Tusi.

The Hamitic influence on the Bantu is maintained to-day in a striking form, though it applies more to the north-eastern tribes than to those further south. It is indicated amongst other things by the fact that among the Bantu tribes in the neighbourhood of the Victoria Nyanza and Mt. Kilimanjaro, the Wa-Huma, an essentially Hamitic tribe, invariably occupy the position of chiefs among the northern Bantu tribes. In this connection, A. H. Keane, in his book, *Africa*, Vol. II, p. 12, remarks " the Wa-Huma . . . . . present some points of great anthropological interest, probably affording a solution of the

difficulties connected with the constituent elements
of the Bantu races in East Central Africa." Speke,
a traveller and famous hunter, "had already
observed that the chiefs of the Bantu nations
about the great lakes were always Wa-Huma, a
pastoral people evidently of Galla stock, and
originally immigrants from the Galla country. . . .
The Wa-Huma, who, under the name of Wa-Tusi,
are found as far south as the U-Nyamwezi
country."

To quote further from Keane, " The Wa-Huma
are also distinguished by their intense love both
of personal freedom and political autonomy, ...
Such is their horror of captivity and a foreign yoke
that those who have failed to maintain their
independence are no longer regarded as true
Wa-Huma." " Traits of this sort would almost
alone suffice to suspect at least a very large
infusion of non-Negro blood in the Wa-Huma
race.   This element we may now trace with some
confidence to the Hamites of North-East Africa
as its true source " (Stanford, *Ethnology of Egypt-
ian Sudan*, p. 10).   The two sources, Negro and
Hamite, from whose union has been produced the
Bantu race are widely different in the essential
qualities, character, and all those attributes which
make for social advancement and racial development.   For, according to many authorities, if we
accept their thesis, the Negroes are of themselves
incapable of civilization and intellectual advancement, unless their blood has had an infusion from
that of more highly developed races.   Hence,
through union and intermarriage between Negro
and Hamitic races, the latter possessing character
and intelligence of a high order, there has issued

from these two sources a race with noble characteristics, courage, love of freedom, and a mental
equipment of no mean order, so that there is no
wisdom, no honour, personal or national, to which
the Bantu race may not aspire.

The history of the races of the world proves to
us that an admixture of blood, instead of being
a disadvantage to a race, is rather of assistance
in its uplift.   We have an instance of that in the
case of the British race, whose blood has undergone a great deal of infusion from other races,
notably from the Angles, Saxons, Celts, Danes,
Norwegians, Picts, Scots, and others, and yet
there is no race under the sun so glorious as the
British race.   It should be evident, then, that
the union of these two races of whom we have
been speaking, the commingling of the two blood
strains of Negro and Hamite which have produced
the Bantu race, have secured to the Bantu a
capacity for development and progress equal to
that of the more advanced Hamite, or at least
greater than that of the less developed Negro, for
their Bantu decendants.

The Zenj.

The name " Bantu " is of modern application.
When Bleek made use of the word " Bantu " as
a comprehensive term for all the dialects of the
inhabitants who formed the largest section of the
people of Southern Africa, he had no intention of
applying it to the people themselves.   Nevertheless, it has been so used, and is adopted as a
generic term to designate the people.   What then
was the name by which this race was known to

those of more ancient times? There is little doubt that all east coast tribes, from Somaliland down to Sofala, were in ancient times called "Zenj." In considering this matter, we note that according to the Scriptures, the sons of Ham were . Kush, Mitsraim, Phut and Canaan, but it is not stated that these complete the list. In the *Asiatic Miscellany*, already quoted, the number of the sons of Ham is given as nine, the third one of these being Zenj. Now we find that this name "Zenj" was applied to the Eastern inhabitants of Africa down to 1154 A.D. That is to say, the term was in use up to that date to indicate the Bantu race.

As is well known, on account of wars and national disturbances in Asia in early times, certain tribes of the sons of Ham entered Africa from the north, and moved southward along the shores of the Red Sea and the eastern sea-board of Africa, forming settlements and taking possession of the country. Theal (*Ethnography of S.A.*, p. 157) says, "In the year 30 B.C., Egypt became a Roman province, and nine years later—in 21 B.C.—an army under Petronius entered Abyssinia, where such success awaited it that Kandake, the queen of that country, was obliged to become a tributary. At that time it is evident that no Bantu were living so far north." This extract is important to us only in that it determines the non-existence of the Bantu so far north as Abyssinia, but though their birthplace was much further south, we find later on that they come under the same racial designation as the Abyssinian, and other Hamites. The term "Zenj" was first applied by early historians to the Hamitic tribes of North-East Africa. Ultimately, however, it was made to include the Bantu further south, probably in recognition of their source of origin— to wit that they were of Hamitic stock.

Writing on the subject of the Zenj, Theal quotes Strabo, traveller and historian, of Amasa in Pontus, who visited Northern Africa, as reporting in 21 A.D. that the country along the west coast of the Red Sea was inhabited by Ethiopians. These people were at that time as at the present day Hamites. Strabo's knowledge of Africa was very limited; consequently, we get nothing from him in respect of the people south of the Ethiopians. It is clear, however, that there were no Bantu tribes known to him or he would have probably mentioned the fact. After Strabo we have no further information about that part of Africa, until 880 A.D. when Abou Zeyd-Hassan of Syraf wrote a book. From him we learn that the inhabitants on the east coast of Africa were called " Zenj," but he does not define their boundaries.

Here, then, we have our earliest notice of the name " Zenj " as applied to the Bantu in those days. It seems reasonable to conclude that this name is derived from that of the son of Ham, and it indicates that the Bantu are of that stock.

Then again, Aboul-Ali el-Masoudi of Bagdad (Theal, *ibid.*, p. 169) who travelled and wrote before his death in 956 A.D. a book containing notes on the Bantu gives the name " Zenj " to the people who lived along the east coast of Africa. He writes about a branch of the Nile as entering the ocean on the east of the African continent— Theal believes this to be the Gulf of Aden. This branch of the Nile, Masoudi says, issued from the great basin of the Zenj, and separated the country of the Zenj from that occupied by the Abyssinians. He continues, "the Zenj proceeded along the channel which flowed from the larger stream of the Nile, and emptied itself into the Indian sea. They established themselves in the country, and spread out to Sofala .... It was there that the Zenj built their capital." Masoudi terms the Indian Ocean "the sea of Zenj," because the coastal tribes were of Zenj stock.

Masoudi is thus describing the country occupied by the Bantu race. It is clear, therefore, that the early name of the Bantu was "Zenj," derived presumably from the name of Zenj, the son of Ham. This name underwent a change and ultimately fell into disuse after 1154 A.D., when an Arab writer, Abou Abdallah el-Edrisi, called the Bantu by the double designation, "Zenj" and "Kaffir." The latter name he applied to them on the assumption that they had no religion. The Arab meaning attached to the word "Kaffir" is much the same as our term "Heathen." Since Edrisi's time, the latter name has superseded the original one, but this also, in our generation, is being discarded for the new name "Bantu," which originated indirectly from Dr. Bleek.

CHAPTER II

Arabs and Portuguese

In dealing with the history of the Bantu, it is impossible to overlook the presence and influence of the Arabs and Portuguese on the East African tribes. In order that we may understand some of the reasons for the migration of Bantu tribes from their original home, it is necessary that we take note of these two peoples, one Asiatic and the other European.

The Arabs were the first to arrive. The actual time of their earliest arrival is not known, for they were already in Eastern Africa when that continent was still regarded as a somewhat mythical land by the white races. They are known, however, to have already possessed colonies on the East coast of Africa during the reign of Solomon, King of Judah, that is about one thousand years before the Christian era.

Our earliest knowledge of the East African Arab in modern times is derived from Portuguese sources about 1500 A.D. At that time both Arabs and Portuguese were carrying on aggressive warfare with the African coastal tribes. Along the sea-board they built villages and towns as centres of commercial enterprise. This they carried on with the neighbouring Bantu, but their chief object was to conquer them and carry them into captivity as slaves. These coastal centres of commerce, beginning from the north and working south, were the following:—Magadosho, Brava, Melinde, Mombasa, Pemba, Zanzibar, Mafiya,

Kilwa, Comoro (islands), Mozambique, Angosha (islands), Quilimane, Sofala, Inhambane, and later on the Zambezi, inland, Sena and Tete.

The commerce in slaves carried on by the Arabs on the sea-board and in the inland districts of the country makes sad reading indeed *of the thousand year old Open Sore*. It is a terrible and frightful record—a story of the release of the worst passions and evil desires of men, let loose upon other fellow-beings, with an abandoned fierceness surpassing that of wild beasts. Murder was the order of the day. Men, women and children were massacred, and the captives sold without regard to the ties of fatherhood, motherhood or offspring; the one ruthlessly torn from the other, as if the bond of love and compassion had no existence. Family on family, tribe on tribe, were often completely swept away, not even an infant being spared; millions upon millions of the sons and daughters of Africa were sent to destruction as if they had been wild animals, simply because they dared to believe that they had a right to live. Some of the harassed tribes, in order to save themselves, even joined the Arabs, and helped in the slaughter of their kindred. As a result of these incessant depredations there was unceasing lamentation, accompanied by the ever-present war-cry.

The Arabs took care to select for their on-slaughts those less powerful tribes which could be more easily overcome, but when desired to attack the more powerful, they sought the assistance of other Bantu tribes. In days not so long passed away the Arabs employed for this purpose the Ma-Nyamwezi, the Wa-Hehe, the

Wa-Gogo and the Masai, tribes which readily lent themselves to that vicious trade. Immediately after capture the slaves were made to carry the Arabs' articles of barter, their munitions, elephant tusks, and anything whatsoever. They were then marched towards the coast, and on arrival at such places as Zanzibar and other towns were as soon as possible put on board vessels and dispatched to Goa on the coast of India, to Arabia, Egypt, Persia, Syria, and Turkey. This inhuman destruction was carried on for unnumbered years, from generation to generation. At the present day even it has not entirely ceased. In 1890, one who was a spectator of the passing of the slave gangs (Pruen, " *The Arab and the African* ") narrates how, during the course of one year, while stationed at Mpwapwa, in what was then German East Africa, he observed about two hundred gangs of slaves passing through that town, on their way to the coast. He estimated the number of slaves to be about 30,000. We are thus permitted to see just a small portion of the open sore which has been and is an ever present source of anxiety and pain to the Bantu tribes of those African regions.

While the Arabs were poisoning the land towards the rising sun, the Portuguese were doing the same on both sides of the continent, east and west. In 1487, an important movement took place in Portugal, which had in view the extension of commerce in East Africa. Before that time they had already firmly established themselves in West Africa. The king of Portugal, in the year mentioned, commissioned Bartholomew Diaz along with certain merchants to examine the coast of Africa. He set sail, rounded the Cape and proceeded along the east coast till he reached what is believed to be the Chalumna estuary, south-west of the port of East London. From there he turned homeward and made his report. Eleven years later, in 1498, Vasco da-Gama followed the same course as Diaz, but advanced much further north to secure, if possible, more detailed information about the country. He proceeded up the coast, touching at Mozambique and Melinde, and after a short rest crossed over to India, following the well known route sailed by the Arab dhows when proceeding to India to dispose of their slaves. The reports of the king of Portugal's emissaries aroused the keenest interest among their compatriots, and an earnest desire was fostered to establish trading stations along the east coast. It became clear, however, that this could not be accomplished until the Arabs, who had for long obtained a foothold on that coast, were driven out. Consequently D'Almeida, a Portuguese officer of standing and admiral of the navy, was dispatched in 1509 to attack and capture the Arab stations. This he eventually accomplished. He destroyed the Arab ships, overcame the people and took possession of their towns. The fruits of this attack were the capture of Sofala, Mombasa, Quilimane, and Mozambique. The Portuguese, further, penetrated inland and established Sena and Tete on the Zambezi river.

The power of the Arabs was, therefore, somewhat curtailed, but that very fact, together with the retention of a few of their stations caused them to expend their fury, disappointment and vengeance on the unfortunate Natives, for whose possession they continued to contend with the Portuguese.

In 1698, however, the Arabs reasserted their power, overcoming the Portuguese and recapturing the towns north of Mozabique. The Portuguese were now as confirmed slave raiders as the Arabs. This raised against them many enemies from amongst the neighbouring Bantu tribes. Indeed in 1570 they brought down upon themselves just retribution, and their name was almost destroyed by the Aba-Mbo and Ama-Zimba. This episode we will touch upon later, when following the movement of these two tribes. While we have mentioned the Portuguese as a slave trading people, yet we do not forget that it is from them that we have our earliest written records of the tribes in their neighbourhood, though of a truth those records show a want of interest and knowledge on their part of the Native peoples. Their maps of those days, considered in the light of our prèsent knowledge, prove that in large measure they were simply fanciful productions and their knowledge of Africa was of the slenderest. Their records make mention of a powerful tribe, occupying the country inland from their coast stations, towards the centre of the continent, and between the Zambezi and Limpopo river. To this tribe they give the name of Monomotapa. They also mention that at that time it was represented by four divisions, which were respectively named, Monomotapa, Tshikongo, Kiteve and Sidanda.

The earliest information the Portuguese give us of this tribe dates back to 1505. According to their maps of that time, the boundaries of this state were set down as the Zambezi on the north, on the south the Orange river, and from thence along a line stretching across country to the region of East London as it now is, and on the east the Indian Ocean, but westward we have nothing definite. Formidable as this tribe was it certainly did not occupy all of that territory. The Portuguese were simply transferring their assumptions of the size of that tribe to paper. The above four tribal divisions they often combined under a common designation, that of the principal section, namely Monomotapa. (Theal, *Beginning of S. A. Hist.*, p. 212, ff). It has been ascertained now that this tribe was really the Makalanga. It is, moreover, the first tribe concerning which we are favoured with any special mention.

Sir H. H. Johnston, who was Commissioner of the district about Lake Nyassa, north of the Zambezi, about 1884 states that he studied with some care this word " Monomotapa," as he found Portuguese references to it very vague. From the Bechuanas he learnt that it was a combination of two words in their dialect, " Mona-matapa," and meant " Lord of the rocks " : and again the Makalanga explain its significance to be " Lord of the mines," but they declare that the two interpretations bear the same meaning. In the Makalanga country are to be found old disused mines variously named Zimbabye, Zimbabwe, Symbaoen and Zemboe, from which in ancient times gold was extracted. Certain authorities

B

aver that it was here that Solomon secured the material for much of his magnificence. The Scriptures tell us that King David gathered a large quantity of gold with which to beautify the temple, and that at his death he left it in the care of Solomon, with instructions that it was to be used for the purpose to which he had assigned it. The building of the temple took seven years and a half. During all that time Solomon was adding to David's gold from his own wealth, being assisted by Hiram, king of Tyre, with his fleet of ships that went out and brought back treasures of many kinds. The question arises :—" Where did these treasures and especially the gold come from ? " Writers who have studied the matter agree, in the main, in suggesting that it came from Africa.

Professor Keane, who is surpassed by none in these subjects, suggests, in reference to the passage in *I. Kings*, ix, 28, where mention is made of Ophir, that this town, or district, which is now understood to have been on the coast of Arabia, was not the site of the gold fields, but rather the place for collecting the gold excavated at the mines, and was also the distributing centre of the gold accumulated. Further, he suggests that Havilah (*I. Sam.*, xv, 7) was actually the country known to us at the present day as Rhodesia, that it was discovered by the early Arabs, and was the scene of their gold-mining operations on behalf of Solomon. Tarshish, again, is believed to have been on the spot where Sofala now stands in Portuguese country. This country (Rhodesia), also, is the one where the Queen of Sheba is supposed to have had her seat of government, and where she obtained her wealth, and probably heard of the wisdom of Solomon from some of her subjects who were workers in the gold mines.

These mines, as we have observed, are designated by the name " Zimbabye." In Si-Kalanga the word means " the court," that is, " the great place," or the place where the paramount chief lives.

Some years ago, 1891, the Royal Geographical Society sent out Mr. Theodore Bent, to make investigations at the site of the Zimbabye ruins. He discovered that the ruins extended over a considerable area, in parts of which the walls were still standing.   These were built of dressed stone, apparently by skilled workmen, and had a breadth of 16 feet at the base with a corresponding height. Within the walls rose a circular tower 72 feet high.   From the character, and great extent of these ruins, as well as from the skilled workmanship of which they show marked evidence, it is clear that Zimbabye was not built by people of the Bantu race, for in Southern Africa no tribe has shown any signs of skill in stone work.

From certain signs it is evident that these structures were anterior to the Makalanga occupation of Eastern Rhodesia. Some of the articles found among the ruins, such as crucibles for melting the gold, flint axes, hammers, pieces of ancient crockery and many others, suggest that the time dated as far back as that of Solomon when these buildings were erected.

CHAPTER III

The Makalanga

In 1505 A.D., the Portuguese first came into contact with the Makalanga. Notwithstanding that there were other smaller tribes near the positions occupied by the Portuguese, yet they do not make any special reference to them, nor do they give us even their names. They had not come into the country to ascertain genealogical facts relating to the tribes. Their main object was to secure for themselves commercial advantages, and incidentally wealth. In a word, they had not come with the purpose of setting forth the history of the inhabitants of the country. They almost entirely ignore even the Makalanga. Yet, though they give evidence of no special knowledge about them, the Makalanga were the one tribe of whom they should have been able to give us detailed information. It is self-evident that the Portuguese of those days did not put themselves to much trouble to get a thoroughly wide knowledge of the people who were their immediate neighbours—where they had come from, their kingdom, laws, customs, or the boundaries of the land under occupation by the Makalanga. They have told us, however, as we have seen, that there were four divisions of the tribe, but they give us no satisfactory information respecting these divisions, nor whether these names, Monomotapa, Tshikanga, Kiteve and Sidanda, were in any sense royal and applied to the various sections as such, or whether they were merely the names of the chiefs controlling the respective divisions.

Modern investigators tell us that each name is that of a division of the Makalanga tribe. Theal in his *Beginnings of S. A. Hist.*, p. 215, maintains that of the Bantu race, the Makalanga had a larger share of Asiatic blood than any other tribe, which may account for their superiority over other tribes in craftsmanship and as artificers. The "great place" of the paramount chief of the tribe was at that time close to Fura mountain, between two rivers that enter the Zambesi from the south, the Singezi and the Mazoe. In Masoudi's time the capital, or great place, was said to be at Sofala, at the south eastern extremity of their country. The Fura mountain was strictly preserved from encroachment, the Makalanga allowing no Portuguese or stranger to set foot on it. The Makalanga were spread over a larger extent of country, both as regards length and breadth, than that occupied by any Bantu tribe at the present day.

Their language is said to have been somewhat like that of the Basuto and kindred tribes. The royal kraals of the Makalanga chiefs were called " Zimbabye " or " Zimboe," and it was here that the law was dispensed and customs introduced and given authority.

Our desire to know more about these things has met with disappointment, because the Portuguese cared nothing about them and left them unrecorded. One custom alone do we hear about, and it is to this effect :—A law was promulgated annually by the principal chief, and issued by his messengers to all parts of the country, that at the new moon, and after official notification, all fires must be extinguished, and not a single live coal allowed to burn. One fire only was to be kept alive, viz., the fire at the court of the Monomotapa, from whence at an appointed time every family throughout the tribe would secure a fire-brand to re-light the home fires. Only the oldest men now living could tell us if such a custom ever existed to their knowledge among the Aba-Mbo or Abe-Nguni. In our day no such custom obtains. During the past hundred years flint and steel were the mediums through which fire was obtained, and these are almost entirely superseded to-day by the household match.

The Portuguese and Makalanga could not for long remain as neighbours without mutual distrust, nor could it be long before, as Natives say, they would be " whistling aggressively " at each other. This soon happened, and the Portuguese ere long realized that they had aroused an opposition that could not readily be put down, though they were not prepared to admit this. It is a simple matter, for such as desire it, to find a *casus belli*, and the Portuguese found it in a proposal to search for certain gold mines believed to exist in Makalanga-land. To enter independent country with an army is tantamount to declaring war. The Portuguese were a proud and patriotic nation—one that had made a great name for itself among the European races by its courage, and especially as a maritime power. They were, therefore, a people to be respected and feared.

In 1569, they decided to force a passage through the Makalanga, in order, if possible, to reach the far distant gold mines of which they had heard reports. A small quantity of gold or gold dust managed annually to reach Sofala, by means of barter, but not in such quantities as to satisfy the cupidity of the Portuguese. Moreover, the people of Portugal, merchants and others, had an exaggerated idea of the wealth of the gold mines in the land of the Makalanga, and so it was finally decided to send a military expedition, and force a way through the Makalanga to the mines.

Barreto's Expedition.

Francisco Barreto was selected as governor over a part of the territory conquered by the Portuguese on the eastern sea-board of Africa, that is between Inhambane and Guardafui. Instructions were sent to him to gather together a force of a thousand men, and he was promised annual reinforcements of five hundred men, besides large financial grants, until such time as the Makalanga were conquered. In November 1571, Barreto set out by ship for Mozambique and sailed up the Zambezi, on his way to Sena, a small Portuguese station on the west bank of the Zambezi, taking with him a considerable force and equipment. It took this force sixteen days on the journey before it reached Sena.

When it disembarked it consisted of seven hundred men, apart from officers, an artillery contingent and slaves. In addition to these were artillery and cavalry horses and a number of mules provided to carry water, and a few camels for heavy burdens.

The first thing this force set about was the building of protective earthworks, and the sinking of a well, but before this latter was completed, word was brought to the commander, that the Arabs in Sena had poisoned the well. One of the Arabs divulged this piece of wickedness to members of the garrison. Work was immediately suspended, and the well was filled up again with earth. Owing to the hardships which the men had to endure, disease broke out in the camp, and men, cattle and horses died at an alarming rate. The Arabs were as a reprisal all put to death, with the single exception of the informer. Notwithstanding that sickness was rife among the soldiers, an advance towards the junction of the Mazoe and Zambezi rivers was decided upon. This point having been reached, the force turned southwards, having lost by then a considerable number, two hundred men having died. Still it moved steadily forward, suffering intensely from the heat and the scarcity of water. In that condition it came face to face with a Bantu army, under the command of a chief named Mongazi. Both armies stood to arms that day, but did not engage. On the following morning the Portuguese selected eighty men to lure Mongazi's army into a position favourable to the Portuguese. The stratagem succeeded. The great army of the Makalanga was led by an old female witch-doctor, carrying a gourd full of charms, which she constantly threw up into the air. This was done in the belief that the Portuguese would be blinded and so reduced to helplessness. Confirmed in its belief of the efficacy of the charms, the Makalanga army advanced to attack the Portuguese. A sharp-shooter had been chosen by the Portuguese to shoot the old sorceress. When she fell, Mongazi's army was temporarily checked; however, it soon came on again with renewed determination. As it approached the Portuguese lines, in close formation, a fusillade of shot and cannonballs was poured into the mass of huddled warriors, and the Makalanga broke and fled. The Portuguese then charged, scattering Mongazi's now disheartened army.

Notwithstanding that Barreto had conquered this section of the Makalanga, his own army was in danger. It was hampered by the wounded and sick, its munitions and commissariat began to fail, while it was yet a long way from its destination—the gold mines. Barreto, however, did not expose his condition to the enemy. Negotiations for the conclusion of peace were set on foot, and terms of peace were finally agreed to. The Portuguese then began a retreat, under terrible hardships and losses. The result of all Barreto's warlike measures and hopes was failure and disappointment. The furthest point reached by him was Masapa, situated at a considerable distance from the goal which he had set out to reach. He returned to his headquarters at Mozambique, empty-handed and in a state of destitution.

The Portuguese, in spite of this failure, were still full of determination to make further attempts to attain their object.

Vasco Fernandes Homem.

Shortly after the abortive attempt of Barreto, another officer, Vasco F. Homem, was appointed to lead another expedition in search of the gold mines. On entering Makalangaland he found the country at war. The divisions of the tribe under the Kiteve and Tshikanga respectively, were at feud. Homem had with him 500 soldiers, besides a large number of. servants and slaves. He first asked the Kiteve to allow him to pass through his country, but that chief feared that if the request were granted, there was a possibility of Homem's joining the tribes beyond him, and thus placing the Kiteve between two enemies. The request being refused, Homem lost no time but immediately attacked and dispersed the Kiteve's forces with his guns and cannon. After several defeats the Kiteve army withdrew, having first despoiled all the grain pits of their contents : they then drove away their cattle, so that the Portuguese should pass through a country bare of everything that would be of use to them, and thus suffer hardship. On the expiry of two days Homem entered into the territory of the Tshikanga. This chief had already heard of the fate which had overtaken the Kiteve's army, and advanced 'to meet Homem with a peace offering. This brave officer, therefore, passed on taking a course somewhat north of that followed by Barreto. The furthest point reached by Homem was a place called Masikesi. Instead of great riches the Portuguese secured only a small quantity of gold. Homem returned practically as unsuccessful as his predecessor. Nevertheless he was not allowed to return without molestation. His whole army fell to pieces through enemy attacks and disease. He reached Mozambique with a mere fraction of the army with which he had set out. It was in a terrible state with sickness and exhaustion. The disappointment of the Portuguese was great at their repeated failure, and the expense involved in those expeditions. They gave up further attempts to reach the gold mines, yet if they had only known it, they were within reasonable distance of the object of their search.

After these aggressive expeditions which had left the Makalanga practically unaffected, the Portuguese concluded peace. They remained on terms of friendship with their powerful enemy. A yearly tribute, however, was exacted by the Makalanga from the Portuguese, and was demanded by the chiefs as a means towards ensuring peace. It is sometimes also called a " gift " to the chiefs, as the latter reciprocated by a gift to the Portuguese. It is clear that the power of the Makalanga was recognised by their enemy, and though war broke out after this, the respective positions of these two peoples were unaffected.

Notwithstanding that the character of the chieftainship of Bantu tribes had much to commend it, yet it possessed within it something that was far from satisfactory, and was one of the causes of the wide dispersion of the tribes. The Makalanga tribe had within its constitution this destructive element, which in due course broke it up into several sections. This was the multiplicity of chiefs, due to polygamy, between whom there was ample opportunity for disputes and jealousy. As a result of this, the Makalanga scarcely exist now as a tribe. There are, it is true, portions of it still existing, though of little consequence, such as the Makololo, the Mashona, the Banyayi, and other small tribes. But the greatness and glory of this once great tribe has gone for ever.

The Makololo, according to Keane (*Africa, II,* 434), were at one time living near the sources of the Vaal river, probably to the south-east of Pretoria. Sebituane, the chief of the tribe, was at the time of Dr. Livingstone's travels in those parts a man of considerable influence, and a friend of Livingstone's. Sometime about 1824, through the pressure of the Boers, who had left Cape Colony, and were seeking pastures new, the Makololo retired and returned to their original home further north. As they proceeded they swept aside and scattered the tribes on their line of retreat, pausing occasionally to strike at the Boers, or the Matebele under Mzilikazi, but nevertheless steadily falling back to the Zambezi. They crossed over to the north side of that river and overcame the tribes settled in that portion of country. Amongst others, they conquered and incorporated the Bahurutse, and re-established the the Makololo kingdom in the neighbourhood of the Kafue river, in what is now Northern Zambezia. Here they absorbed all the smaller tribes near them.

When Sebituane, the old chief, died about 1850, his son, Sikeletu, became chief. His character was inferior to that of his father, besides which he was physically weak, and a sufferer from leprosy.

The next ruler was Mpololo, but treachery and other evils marked his reign. The Makololo kingdom then gradually fell into decay. Its weakness provided an opportunity to the Bahurutse and other oppressed tribes to revolt, and they succeeded in destroying the Makololo power entirely.

*The Mashona (Ma-Tshona or Ma-Swina) and the
Banyayi (Ba-Nyayi).*

These tribes are offshoots of the Makalanga, and
first came into prominent notice with the incursion
of the Boers into their country in 1837. They
were harried by the Boers under Maritz and
Potgieter, but more especially by the Matebele
under Mzilikazi, who in their turn again were
harrassed by Dingana (Dingaan), chief of the
Zulus, whose armies went as far afield as Central
Rhodesia. Mzilikazi was at that time living in
the Marico district, but was forced to move north.
He crossed the Limpopo river, and here it was
that he came into conflict with the Mashona and
Banyayi. The result of all this strife is that,
though individually these three tribes of Makalanga origin still exist, their importance is gone.
On account of the inhospitable nature of their country the Mashona escaped complete destruction.
He who still retains a desire to follow up the Makalanga, may yet find a small section of that once
great tribe living at the confluence of the Zambezi
and Gwayi rivers, on the left bank of the former,
and now in the country of the Bamangwato.

The Aba-Tonga.

Above the Zambezi, amongst other tribes in
that part of the continent, are the Tongas,
generally considered to be a section of the Makalanga. As now constituted, the tribe is evidently
composed of various elements of separate origin.
Junod tells us that at least "two clans came
from the north, the Ba-ka-Baloyi and the Tembe,"
and as their si-takazelo, or royal salutation is
"Nkalanga," there is little doubt but that they

are of Makalanga origin.   This section of Tongas is apparently the earliest of all to migrate into their present position.   Other portions of the tribe indicate the south as the country of their origin, that is Zululand.   According to Junod, vol. I., p. 23, these are the Nkuna, Khosa and Hlabi.

The Baloyi and Tembe, referred to above, are declared by their own historians to be of Banyayi stock.   This latter tribe we have mentioned already as of Makalanga origin, so that the point seems clearly established.   The clans that moved up from the south and became incorporated with the Tonga tribe may be of Lala stock, and if so would be rejoining their own branch of the Bantu race.   When we consider the genealogy of the Tonga tribes or clans, and note that it scarcely in any one of them extends beyond ten generations, we incline to the belief that the latter movements from the south took place after the advent of the Aba-Mbo into Zululand, or, as it then was, into the country of the Ama-Lala.   May the Khosa mentioned above not be an offshoot of the Xosa tribe, which at that date (say 1620) had gone south in advance of the Aba-Mbo ?

The Ama-Lala.

The tribes comprised under this title are numerous and are dealt with as one of the three branches of the Eastern Bantu.   They come under Part III, of this book, and will in consequence not be dealt with here.   Suffice it to say that the tribes inhabiting that portion of country now known as Zululand and Natal, from a period prior to the sixteenth century are designated by the above term, in the conviction that the majority of them are branches of the Makalanga.

CHAPTER IV

Diffusion of Bantu Tribes in Africa

It is evident that when the Bantu tribes had multiplied at the seat of origin of the race, they began to extend eastward and westward of the southern portion of the continent of Africa. Afterwards they spread out to the south. The principal cause of the Bantu tribes multiplying to so great an extent, and at the same time never being able to include themselves under one common racial name, was the custom which produced a host of chiefs, namely *Polygamy*. The male sons of a chief were all chiefs, no matter how numerous they might be. Here, then, were ready to hand all the elements for bickering, jealousy, claims of precedence and strife. In early times the rule of the chiefs was patriarchal. The common people—that is, those who lost their status through the chieftainship becoming extinct—together with all their possessions were accounted as the property of the ruler. While a tribe was small, it could as a whole submit to such an assumption of authority without question. To strengthen and confirm the power and honour of the principal chief many laws, as distinct from customs, were enacted. Yet these very laws, by reason of their multiplicity, brought them at times into conflict with the tribal customs. This might be illustrated by one example.

The border line between law and custom among Bantu tribes is not always very clear, as custom when long established practically becomes law. The *Izi-Zi* custom partakes of this nature.

In one respect, it was a fine for an offence against the chief; in another, it took the form of restitution to the chief, or a forfeit due to him, for the loss by death of one of his people. The mitigation of his sorrow had to be assisted by a gift of cattle, in number according to the importance of the deceased, and it was the bereaved family who made restitution. This so-called "gift" was claimed as a right by the sorely stricken chief. Again, if a wizard was smelt out and killed, all his cattle were confiscated by the ruler. This was a profitable way in which to keep the exchequer in a solvent condition. Whenever it became evident that a chief was on the verge of insolvency, rich wizards began to abound, and it became necessary to thin them out. As a consequence, the fluctuating treasury resumed, for the time being, a stable condition. This *isi-zi* custom had its repercussion on polygamy, for the minor chiefs had to see that the *isi-zi* was collected from such of the families under their jurisdiction as had sustained the loss of one of their number, and that it was handed over to the superior chief. But very often the minor chief believed that he had a prior claim, and if he considered himself strong enough would set at defiance his superior.

These claims, made by the minor chiefs, often caused the tribe to break up into a number of sections through the internecine wars that resulted. Cohesion of the race under such conditions could not be maintained. The tendency was ever towards disintegration. Supreme authority, vested in one individual, had much to recommend it, but it had also much that was productive of dissension among the subordinate chiefs, and between them and the principal ruler. It often needed but a little matter to cause a young chief to turn his assegais against his blood relations. Many unable to endure the laws of the paramount chief broke out into rebellion. To exemplify the occasional effect of the *isi-zi*, in setting a minor chief at variance with his superior, an illustration of a somewhat recent occurrence may be given. Gwadiso, the principal chief of a minor tribe of the Pondos, the Ama-Konjwayo, had under his authority a man called Nzengwa, who had been smelt out as a wizard. He was condemned, and in the evening twilight was thrown over a precipice, named " Ntombi-ne-Ndodana," overlooking the Mtakatyi river. Early the following morning messengers were sent to view the body. They saw nothing. It happened that Nzengwa, as he was thrown over, bounced off the precipice and fell into a deep pool of the Mtakatyi river, and though severely hurt, was revived by the water. During the night, he managed to crawl to the residence of the great chief of that section of the tribe, Nqwiliso. Meanwhile, Gwadiso had confiscated Nzengwa's cattle. The paramount chief, pretending that Nzengwa was dead, though he had him in his care, sent to his subordinate, Gwadiso, for the *isi-zi* due for Nzengwa's death. Gwadiso refused to send it, but instead sent the reply, "I was destroying my own dog." That meant that he was claiming to be an independent chief. It meant more: it meant war.

C

Nqwiliso mustered his army to assert his authority : Gwadiso did likewise to assert his independence.   A fierce battle followed, but in the end the rebellious chief Gwadiso was defeated, and the supremacy of the paramount chief confirmed. The *isi-zi* custom, or an effort to enforce it, was the original cause which induced the Bomvanas to migrate from their home in Natal in pre-Tshaka days, and seek sanctuary in Pondoland.

Polygamy (*Isi-Tembu*).

Polygamy has always been the cause of disintegrating the unity of a tribe. According to custom, chiefs had many wives, and this contributed in no small measure to the importance, indirectly, of the tribe.   These wives, moreover, came from the homes of chiefs and men of importance of other tribes.   They could not, therefore, be treated as of no more consequence than the ordinary possessions of the ruler. The wives themselves, knowing their former important status, could not endure to be just a mere collection of women of no account and without stated rank or precedence.   Besides this, a race of a high order of mentality, such as the Bantu, could not, especially under this custom of polygamy, live just as if they were a herd of cattle.   Hence it became evident that the respective wives must have a declared status, and the various houses in which they were mistresses had to be given names according to their rank. The number of houses would, naturally, be in keeping with the number of wives, but only a limited number were given specific names. Those of special importance were five : (a) the great house, (b) the right-hand house, (c) the support of the great house—" iqadi," from which, in the event of the great house failing issue, the heir would be appointed ; (d) the " qadi " or the right-hand house, from which in the event of the right-hand house having no issue, the heir would be appointed ; (e) the left-hand house, which with some tribes that had no right-hand house took a position corresponding to the latter.

All wives other than those of these specially designated houses simply came under the term " ama-qadi," or " wives of Minor houses," and their relation to the more important houses might be declared or it might not.

A chief's sons when they reached man's estate and took to themselves wives, were not content to live as families simply under parental control. Moreover, when they married, they were each given a number of other families as supporters and thus frequently became strong enough to hive off on their own account and form distinct clans. Sometimes a son who retained affection and respect for his parents, would be forced by circumstances to move off to a distance. In such a case, the invariable excuse given for leaving his father's neighbourhood was that he was off on a hunting expedition. This really deceived nobody, for he set off accompanied by his family and retainers, his cattle and all his possessions. This constant splitting up of families, and the formation of innumerable clans, some of which would develop into important tribes, militated against cohesion and rendered impossible their possession of a racial name, which would include all under a common denomination. For the widespread scattering of the clans, and the lack of a racial name, polygamy is entirely responsible.

Thus Southern Africa became inhabited by clan upon clan, tribe upon tribe, without number, incapable of tracing their own genealogy beyond a few generations, or of knowing with certainty either the name of the original founder of their individual tribes, or the name of the mother tribe from which they sprang.

Polygamy filled the land with tribes without national unity, whose patriotism extended only to the limits of the tribe, and of which, consequently, each one maintained itself by authority of the assegai. Hence, in these days of greater enlightenment and peace, there has been a desire among the members of this race for a specific name, which will combine all tribes of a common origin. This has found expression in the choice of " Bantu " as the racial name. The wisdom of this choice is at least questionable, but apparently it gives promise to endure.

In regard to the right-hand house there are those who assert that this house is of modern creation : that in olden times it had no existence. Some even say it was instituted by Palo in 1702 ; others say by Ngconde, grandfather of the former. One somewhat fanciful story is to the effect that when Palo's councillors were placed in a difficulty as to the status of each of two maidens whom Palo had married, Palo said, in settling the matter, " a person has a head, that is myself, he has also two arms, a right hand and a left hand. Therefore, as concerns these two maidens, the one who is daughter of the more important chief, must be the chief wife, that is, the wife of the great house, and the other will be the wife of the right-hand house."

We know, however, that six generations before Ngconde's time, and eight before that of Palo, Nkosiyamntu, son of Malangana and grandson of Xosa, who reigned about 1575, distinguished between his various houses. There was the great house whose heir was Cira : there was the right-hand house, the heir being Jwara : there was also the Qadi or minor house, the heir being Tshawe, (see Theal, Vol. III, p. 213). It is apparent, then, that the various houses had specific names at a time much earlier than that of Ngconde or Palo. A period of at least 125 years separates Nkosiyamntu's reign from that of Ngconde and about 175 years separates Nkosiyamntu's reign from that of Palo.

In further confirmation of the early existence of the right-hand house, reference might be made to an occurrence in the Imi-Huhu (later Hlubi) tribe. Ncobo, the son and heir to Mtimkulu I, died without issue, having, however, made arrangements to marry Hlubi, a maiden of the Ama-Bele tribe. Radebe, who is designated the son of the right-hand house of the Imi-Huhu, on his brother's death, took to himself the promised bride, in accordance with Bantu custom. The son of this union became heir to Ncobo, of the great house, and not to Radebe's house.

From that distant date, about 1680 or somewhat earlier, to the present time, the two houses represented by these two sons of Mtimkulu I, have been termed the great house and the right-hand house respectively: that would be several generations before Palo's time, and in a different part of the continent from the Ama-Xosa. Consequently, it could not be said of the Imi-Huhu that they derived the idea from the Xosas, who are supposed by some to have originated the idea of a right-hand house. These instances of the existence of the right-hand house might be multiplied by a reference to other tribes besides those mentioned. There is, moreover, nothing to indicate that this institution dates only as far back as the history goes of the Ama-Xosa and Imi-Huhu. It can fairly safely be taken for granted that the establishment of the various houses of a polygamist's family, and their several designations, was of ancient origin.

There are, of course, differences of custom among different tribes, and though this custom, of which we have been taking notice, is universal among Abe-Nguni, Aba-Mbo and Ama-Lala, it is reported that among the Basuto tribes of the northern Transvaal these distinctions are not observed as among the tribes representing the three branches of Bantu just mentioned. Married wives among these Basutos, it is said, have no claims to precedence, the principal wife only having a special status, as mother of the heir. In the event of the chief dying without issue, one of his brothers may through the widow raise up an heir to the deceased chief, somewhat after the Jewish custom mentioned in Genesis, chap. 38. In Mpahlele's country, my informant tells me that the present ruler, Paduli, was born long after Mpahlele's death. The father, whose son he actually is, is called "uncle," not "father," by him. Again in Mpahlele's tribe, the principal wife must be one of Sikukuni's family, from whom Mpahlele obtained his chieftainship, and even if a wife of the chief should be a Matebele woman of high rank, her son can make no claims to the chieftainship. This would indicate that, among certain northern tribes, the position of chief wife is not dependent on the importance of a ruler whose daughter she is, but on relations of supremacy within the tribe. For, though the Matebele were by far the most powerful tribe in those parts, yet a daughter of a Matebele chief took an inferior position to that of the daughter of a chief who was overlord of a tributary tribe.

It might justly be said, in regard to such information, that it enables us to realize the existence of differences between the customs of one and another tribe. Statements concerning the modern institution of the right-hand house are based upon, or rather are a consequence of, the conditions of life imposed on the tribes by the violence of men like Tshaka and Macingwane, chief of the Ama-Cunu, who through jealousy of their sons, whom they feared would in time usurp their authority, had all their male children put to death, as a precautionary measure. Naturally, such measures rendered meaningless all distinctions of rank as between the various houses, and so their names were were in abeyance, until the conditions of life altered. Times of unsettlement with tribes owing allegiance to chiefs of this type were entirely different from times of peace, and from the conditions under which they lived in more normal days.

It should be self-evident, also, that when tribes were migrating and fighting for their existence against enemies encompassing them on all sides, they could only hope to ensure their safety by completely subordinating themselves to the authority of one man, so that when a command was issued, there should be no one who would dare to question it. In times, then, such as these, the word of a chief's son raised in opposition to that of the father would naturally create dissention and division within the tribe, and place it in danger of annihilation. In such circumstances, the advice given by the councillors of the principal chief would be, and was, that all the sons of the chief should be destroyed. During war, therefore, under certain chiefs, and during times of migration, when fighting was the order of the day ideas of precedence, and claims of the various houses to the titles usually assigned to them, were swept aside. When, on the other hand, peace reigned throughout the land, matters of precedence, and the designation of the different houses were as a rule resumed.

After what may appear to be a digression, we must return to the fact which we stated at the outset, that the rapid and extensive spread of the Bantu over Southern Africa was due to polygamy, which gave rise to the existence of innumerable clans and tribes, each possessing within itself the elements of self-government, and to a spirit of independence on the part of the minor chiefs.

Polygamy may increase a population rapidly, but it fails to bind the people together. As the Bantu express it, *isi-Tembu siyandisa, kodwa sizala izikali*, "polygamy enlarges (population) but assegais are its offspring" (i.e. it produces internecine strife).

CHAPTER V

Causes of Southward Tribal Migrations

There are many causes to account for the migration of Bantu tribes from their seat of origin, and from parts later occupied by them, but three may be particularised.

Pressure of Hamitic Tribes.

The first of the causes which induced the Bantu tribes to move away from their birth place, the Tana Basin, may be set down to the pressure exerted upon them by the southern Hamitic tribes. These had become both powerful and numerous, and as they extended southward towards the eastern terminal of the Negro belt, where it assumes its most attenuated form, they constantly came into violent contact with the Bantu. That part of the country, in consequence, was invariably in a state of ferment and unrest. Negroes, Somalis, Gallas, Masai, and others, were ever at variance. Generation after generation all these various elements were carrying fire and sword against each other and against the Bantu, and although these last, naturally, made efforts to maintain themselves against their enemies, the Hamitic tribes were too powerful to be effectually resisted.

Somali, Galla, and Masai swept down upon them ever and again with irresistible force. The conditions of life, becoming intolerable beyond endurance, unsettled the Bantu tribes in that neighbourhood. The Masai especially, more evilly disposed than any of the others, were also nearest to the Bantu. Such doings as raids, robberies, and massacre, were but part of the pressure exerted by the Masai and other Hamitic tribes on the Bantu—a pressure accompanied by unnameable excesses, which produced a widespread state of distress and suffering among such Bantu tribes as were within reach of the raiders' spears. Some tribes were destroyed utterly; others saw hope only in escaping from their surroundings and seeking new homes in other parts of the country. It was generally southwards that they directed their steps, for in that direction alone was the way open. The more powerful tribes might succeed in this enterprise, but they needed ever to be on the watch lest the Masai should overtake and destroy them. Besides, it was necessary that they should have strength enough to force a way through any Bantu tribes that might possibly be in possession of country ahead of them. It is beyond question that conditions of life described above, with daily attacks by their enemies, and atrocities following upon atrocities year in, year out, compelled the inhabitants of those parts to get out of the country. In this state, then, of continual unrest and danger, we have one of the causes which induced the Bantu tribes in the north to move southwards.

Slavery in East Africa.

The second cause for Bantu migration from the north was the slave trade. David Livingstone, missionary and explorer, who before 1860 travelled through North-East Africa, came into close contact with the slave trade ; saw acts of savage cruelty which touched the heart, witnessed the capture and inhuman treatment of human beings destined for the slave markets of India and Europe; wrote to friends in England in very strong terms; and ended by referring to his sense of isolation and helplessness in the midst of it all. He also expressed the pious hope that God's blessing might be granted to him who would heal the open sore of Africa, be he American, English or Turk. What David Livingstone saw, however, was merely the fringe of a traffic whose tentacles stretched from east to west over the continent of Africa, and had flourished for many centuries, in all forms of savage cruelty.

Commerce in slaves existed from very early times through the activities principally of the Arabs. From then until now this diabolical trade was the loadstone which drew Arabs to Eastern Africa, where they built themselves cities and fortresses along the sea-coast, making timely provision for whatever might happen. Their first step, usually, was to gain over the chiefs, and secure from them terms of barter, for they traded in other things besides slaves. When trouble arose between the chiefs of different tribes and their people, the Arab took full advantage of the circumstances, so that it might turn to his own aggrandisement, and when war broke out, he threw in his weight on the side which he guessed would be victorious. In return for his assistance he expected to be paid in prisoners taken during hostilities. As has already been mentioned, from the Tana Basin, westwards under the southern boundary of the Negro Belt, and southwards to the Zambezi the country was inhabited by numerous Bantu tribes from remote times. This

part of the African continent was ever in a welter
of confusion from inter-tribal feuds, but still more
from the marauding incursions of slave raiders.

From time immemorial these conditions prevailed, and in no other part of the continent were
such deeds of violence done as were practised here,
and nowhere else were they surpassed. Some
tribes were swept out of existence ; others, broken
and scattered, yet managed to restore a semblance
of tribal unity again : but naturally, the conditions
of tribal life could never be as they were in times
past. Fierce raiding parties were continually
coming in and going out of this district, like grass
fires fanned by the wind, leaving behind them
blackened ruins, widespread havoc and hecatombs
of victims. These slave raids were not composed
of Arabs only. The Arabs controlled them, but
they made use of certain Bantu tribes in their
depredations, and these carried death and destruction to old and young of their own kind,
sending the living into slavery, and butchering
the wounded—all this to serve their masters, the
Arabs, and to a less extent the Portuguese. They
turned a peaceful country into a wilderness and
barren waste. Those tribes only which by their
courage and strength were a danger to the raiders
were left to inhabit the land : but for these also
there sometimes came a time when the prevailing
conditions became too oppressive, and they were
forced to move to other spheres.

In chapter II, I mentioned the slave gangs on
their way to the coast, previous to transporta-
tion. Such gangs were formed of collections of
miserable beings, captured at different places,
here and there. When the necessary complement

was got together by the slave raiders, the men, in couples, were attached to a forked yoke, the neck being introduced into a fork at each end. Then each end was riveted with an iron bolt, so that the head could not be withdrawn. The same was done to the women, and each yoke was attached to another by a chain, long lines of dejected humanity being thus formed, each individual head carrying some burden or other. None was ever to see its home again.

On all sides were evidences of this terrible trade. The whole country was dotted with the bleaching bones of those who had been shot and speared, and of others who had fallen exhausted by the wayside and been strangled by their captors. In short, the members of these slave gangs met death in all the varied forms which their savage captors could devise. And yet, when we think of the horrors of captivity, we might consider that those who died by the way were better off than those who lived. Day by day the captives saw the sun rise, and saw it set, and this for months together, but it brought with it no hope for them: their portion was a mind disturbed, sad thoughts of what had been, fear for what was yet to come. One hope alone was theirs—that death might come speedily, for the spirit of mercy was dead.

How could it be possible for tribes to remain and live in a country in a state of everlasting ferment ? Impossible.

Livingstone's prayer was answered. The authorities in England sent out ships to patrol the east coast of Africa, capture the slave dhows, and liberate the slaves. Thus did England seek to heal the open sore of Africa. For many years the east coast was patrolled by vessels set apart for that purpose by the Home Government. It was an unselfish and meritorious act of devotion to the highest ethical ideals of the British race, most worthy of the heartfelt gratitude of the Bantu race.

In a book written by Captain G. L. Sullivan, R.N., entitled *Dhow Chasing in Zanzibar Waters*, the author, who was engaged in that enterprise, tells of the widespread nature of the slave traffic, and of the efforts made to suppress it. Sullivan, however, was not alone in this great work. Mention may here be made of the names of a few of those who worked towards the same end on land. There was Baikie, who was stationed at Lokoja on the Niger, towards the west, in 1854; Capt. Lugard, Commissioner of Uganda from 1887 to 1889 ; and the late Sir H. H. Johnston, who was Commissioner beyond the Zambezi. Here he found that the Wa-Yawo (Livingstone's Ajawa) were in league with the Arabs and assisted them in their slave raids. Their determination to maintain the traffic, even against opposition, was so pronounced that it required the Commissioner's very best efforts, backed though he was by force, to overcome them. This, however, he finally accomplished, even to inducing the chief of the Wa-Yawo, Makanjira, to surrender. This tribe was one of the Bantu slave raiding tribes. That was in 1894. For the time being the slave trade was stopped in those parts. The same fine work was being done in other parts, with varying results. It is true that slavery still persists, but it does not flourish as in former times.   The British, in these efforts accomplished what was of immense benefit to the children of Africa.   All this cost immense sums of money, and many lives laid on the altar of sacrifice, in an endeavour to stay this disease   They lie buried in lonely graves, far and wide in North Eastern Africa, in testimony of their answer to the great call which had come to them on behalf of righteousness and love.

The slave trade, the traffic in human lives, was another of the causes, then, for the Bantu migrations southwards.

Internecine Wars.

The third cause was internecine wars.   Polygamy is not blameless for this, since it destroyed sympathy and the bond of unity between relations. These tribes that were constantly at feud, enslaving one another, engaged in mutual destruction and attacked by enemies of other races, were of one kindred, one blood.   Rebellion, quarrels, jealousy, the desire for booty, and mutual recriminations about witchcraft, created an unfailing hatred, which was ever breaking out into open war, and causing daily ruin.   Under these conditions, it could be no otherwise than that brothers should forget the ties of brotherhood.   It is impossible to give a true picture of the miseries of that land and the fears of its inhabitants, who lived in the valley of blood and tears, silent, helpless, facing death every day.   *The whistling of the merciless assegais, was their ever-present nightmare.*

CHAPTER VI

The Ama-Zimba and Aba-Mbo

Our first notice of Bantu races is derived from Portuguese sources. This notice dates from 1487, but more particularly from 1505. It is, however, singularly disappointing that notwithstanding that they lived, from the later date, in the neighbourhood of many Bantu tribes, not one of those early pioneers has given us a thoroughly satisfactory account about them. The information they give is extremely meagre. Perhaps this is due to the fact that the Portuguese came to Africa mainly for commercial purposes. Their real interests were almost entirely bound up with these ; consequently, they concerned themselves very little with historical matters relating to the tribes. Moreover, they apparently placed no great value on anything relating to the aboriginal inhabitants beyond their purchase price, and the material gains to be secured from the sale of ivory and gold. These reasons may account for the very vague accounts handed down to us of the tribes with whom they came into contact. The Portuguese methods of spelling the names of chiefs and places presents difficulties to writers of the present day, so that this fact, added to the constant movements of tribes and the consequent change in the names of rivers and localities, makes the reconstruction of a connected sequence of events impossible.

In 1570, an important occurrence was the means of inducing the Portuguese to give more careful attention to historical information

respecting the Bantu than they had done at any
former period. The occurrence was as follows.
In this year, 1570, two tribes, the Ama-Zimba
and Aba-Mbo, came down from the north,
attacked the Portuguese stations on the Zambezi,
and nearly annihilated them. These tribes, according to Walker's *Historical Atlas of S.A.*, map 2,
were stationed about 1550, south of the great lake
Nyasa. As the Ama-Zimba and Aba-Mbo crossed
the Zambezi about 1575 (*ibid.*, page 6, notes)
they, presumably, at the date 1550 had not left
their homes near the lake. Some distance south
of Nyasa there is a small lake, named Shirwa. It
is also at a considerable distance north of the
Zambezi. Just below this lake the Aba-Mbo lived,
and the Ama-Zimba were alongside of them, but
more to the east. Both tribes were of considerable size. We are unable definitely to say what
the cause was which induced them to move southwards, but from the hatred manifested by them
towards the Portuguese, we feel justified in believing that this hatred was the result of the
ravages committed by the Portuguese and Arabs
in their slave raids.

During the exodus from the land in which they
had lived, these two tribes moved together southwards, facing towards the Zambezi. The Portuguese, at their commercial stations on the Zambezi,
were suddenly confronted with powerful armies,
in numbers as an army of ants. Both the Ama-
Zimba and Aba-Mbo were stopped on their arrival
by the Zambezi river. They were unable to cross,
on account of its breadth, more especially as they
were travelling with their families and possessions.
They touched the river in the neighbourhood of

D

Tete, a small Portuguese station, built on the southern bank of the Zambezi, and consequently, on the side opposite to the approach of these two tribes. They were, in consequence, forced to remain here for some time, mutual dislike between them and the Portuguese marking their stay, The fame of these tribes had preceded them, as from the time they set out on their journey until they reached the Zambezi, they had hewn a way for themselves with their spears through such tribes as stood in their path, none being able to resist them. At length the Aba-Mbo and a section of the Ama-Zimba found a method of crossing the Zambezi. It is impossible to state accurately where the crossing was made, as at the point touched the river was of great breadth, ten times broader, in some places, probably than, for instance, the Kei river at its widest part. In some stretches of the Zambezi in that neighbourhood, it is said that the breadth extends to 1000 yards : there were, however, narrower parts of the river, but these were deep and had dangerous currents.

As has been mentioned, the Aba-Mbo and a fair portion of the Ama-Zimba found a method of crossing the Zambesi, probably by rafts made of reeds, as the Tongas did by floating down the Nkomati, on their way from the Kalanga country to the coast. Those who got over continued their movement southwards, crossed the Sabi river, and settled down for a time between that river and the Limpopo. This position they reached about 1575.

Between the time of setting out from their original homes near lake Shirwa, and reaching the

Sabi and Limpopo, a period of about fifteen years elapsed. They moved very leisurely, resting by the way, probably breaking up the ground and raising crops, then moving on again. Here they must have remained for nearly two generations, parties of them breaking off and going forward on their own account meanwhile, until in 1620 they had reached their final destination, Northern Natal. Those Ama-Zimba who had forded the Zambezi along with the Aba-Mbo, some considerable time later, recrossed to the northern bank and rejoined their countrymen, but before doing so, this section came into conflict with the Portuguese at Tete. Writers of those days do not tell us what the original cause was out of which these hostilities developed, but we know that in 1585 the Portuguese were engaged in a life and death struggle with the Ama-Zimba, the result of which was that the power of the Portuguese on the Zambezi and ultimately along the east coast was practically destroyed. Failing enlightenment by the Portuguese writers on the origin of this war, we seek for first causes in the evils which we know the Portuguese to have been guilty of, namely, the trade in human lives, as well as the setting, by them, of tribe against tribe who hád lived at peace with each other, the purpose being to take advantage of their difficulties, and secure for themselves prisoners whom they could sell as slaves.

References to this war may be found in Theal's *Beginnings of S. A. History*, but it appears that he must have experienced difficulty in arranging the various phases of the war in the order of their sequence. This, however, was probably due to the manner in which the Portuguese chroniclers detailed events.   In an endeavour to unravel the tangle, and take each event in its proper order, it would seem best to relate occurrences as they appeared naturally to follow each other.   The war, apparently, started with those Ama-Zimba who crossed to the south side of the Zambezi, and had not yet rejoined the greater portion of the tribe which had not crossed, but remained on the north bank.   This section of the tribe was under their chief, Sonza.   Alongside of Sonza's Mazimba was a tribe of Bantu under the influence of the Portuguese.   This tribe precipitated events by attacking the Ama-Zimba.   In the subsequent fighting, Sonza's army completely destroyed the attacking force. This involved the Portuguese who immediately armed in support of their friends. Their force consisted of about one hundred soldiers and four thousand of the Ama-Tonga.   Sonza, quite unacquainted with the effect of artillery, made a fatal blunder.   He built a large enclosure, constructed of thorn trees and branches.   Within this enclosure he collected his men, believing that this structure would ensure protection for his force, whereas he was really jeopardising it.   The position was too confined, his men being hopelessly packed together.   On this helpless mass the Portuguese opened a combined fire of all arms.   Men fell in swathes, while cannon belched and muskets poured in a relentless fire. So great was the slaughter, that those who survived sought safety in flight.   They broke through the encircling abatis, shaken and dispirited.   The Portuguese availed themselves of the opportunity given, and made way for their allies the Ama-Tonga to get in amongst the broken Ama-Zimba with the assegai. That was the finish. Sonza's army ceased to exist. It is stated that the Ama-Zimba numbered 12,000 and that their dead amounted to 5,000. That, at least, is the Portuguese estimate.

The Ama-Zimba on the North bank of the Zambezi, who formed the greater part of the tribe, unable to cross and render assistance, looked on at the destruction of their compatriots. They were furious, and immediately sounded the war-cry. The remnant of Sonza's force, at length effected a crossing and joined the main section of the tribe. The long simmering hatred of the Ama-Zimba against the Portuguese, whose conduct had for long been intolerable, was to find expression in a war of revenge, which was to shake Portuguese power, in those parts, to its foundation. The Ama-Zimba now reunited, mustered a formidable army, and set it in motion. It followed the course of the Zambezi eastwards, on its way to Mozambique, in one great force. No attention was paid to the small stations on the river, Tshikova, Nyungwe (Tete) and Sena, as the menace of those had been previously overcome by the Ama-Zimba, consequently they had nothing to fear from them. On reaching Mozambique, the Bantu army found the town was built on an island in the sea. Nothing, therefore, could be effected against it directly, but it was invested by the Mazimba army. On the mainland opposite the town there were fields and grannaries under the protection of a small force of Portuguese, supplemented by a considerable number of slaves, all commanded by a certain Nuno Pereira. The Ama-Zimba fell upon this party and cut it to

pieces, a few only, along with their officer, survived, escaping through the Ama-Zimba to their
friends on the island.

Portuguese accounts state that after the battle
the Ama-Zimba formed camp, cooked and ate the
bodies of those who had been slain.

When we consider that, so soon after leaving
home, it was scarcely possible for the Mazimba
army to have reached such a stage of destitution as
to reduce it to cannibalism, and when we consider,
further, that no quarter was likely to be given,
and that it would be a case of "sauve qui peut"
on the part of the few fugitives who escaped, when
none would stand upon the order of his going;
and, lastly, that the Bantu not being cannibals
by nature, the circumstances scarcely warranted
so great a departure from habitual custom, it is
difficult to give credit to the statement.

After the Mazimba army had destroyed all it
could lay its hands on, it proceeded up the coast,
seeking out the Portuguese trading villages and
towns. Kilwa was its immediate objective. Unlike Mozambique, this town had not the good
fortune to be built upon an island, but, on the
contrary, was in an exposed position. In consequence it was overwhelmed and completely
destroyed with all that was in it.

The Ama-Zimba then passed on leaving a
wilderness behind, and advanced on Mombasa in
the north : a town at the present time on the coast
of British East Africa. The Portuguese citizens
had timely warning of all that had happened at
Mozambique and Kilwa, and made every endeavour to prepare for a stout resistance. No
sooner, however, did the Ama-Zimba set eyes on

the town than they threw themselves against it. The assegai was in evidence and did great execution, but though the town suffered heavily, and was in great peril, it nevertheless managed to maintain its security. The army of the Ama-Zimba had now been constantly fighting, being steadily drained of its fighting strength, month after month, and hampered by its non-combatants, the women, children and cattle, was yet urged forward by its unfailing hatred of the Portuguese, who were regarded with the utmost dislike on account of their offences. Unable to do more than they had done, the Ama-Zimba pressed relentlessly forward with their faces towards Melinde. This was to be their last effort. They reached their destination, weary and in a state of disheartening fatigue. Nevertheless, they made an attack, but it failed completely. Vasconcellos, the Portuguese officer in command, together with his people, and assisted by neighbouring Bantu tribes who had allied themselves to the Portuguese, did not act on the defensive, but met the oncoming forces with a counter attack which proved irresistible. The Ama-Zimba were badly beaten and suffered heavy losses. They then retired. The remnants of their army now faced south again, and made for the Zambezi which was ultimately reached. The Ama-Zimba arrived at the river, '' all that was left of them,'' diminished in numbers and weakened in strength.

Here for a time they settled down.

The Ama-Zimba army was built up again under the supervision of a chief, called Ntondo (Tondo). He was induced to do this by the conduct of Bantu auxiliaries, forming part of the Portuguese

forces protecting the Zambezian stations. These
auxiliaries Ntondo attacked, though it is apparent
that he hoped to involve the Portuguese also.
Ntondo realised that disregard of those tribes that
gave their assistance to the Portuguese, was the
cause of the Ama-Zimba defeat at Melinde, for
instead of crushing these first, the Ama-Zimba
threw their whole weight against the whites, and
in consequence of these tribes acting as reserves
and coming in fresh against wearied troops, the
Ama-Zimba were defeated. On this new occasion,
therefore, Ntondo first broke the power of the
auxiliaries, and confiscated their territory. This
brought the Portuguese into the field. They
expected to repeat the story of Melinde. So
Andrea de Santiago, the commander, collected a
force at Tana of various sorts, Portuguese, mixed
breeds, slaves and several tribes who supported
the Portuguese. Tana was built on an island in
the Zambezi. Santiago proceeded to ferry his
troops over to the mainland by boats. Having
landed them, he began to doubt their ability to
force matters to a successful issue. He immediately formed camp, bestriding a small stream flowing
into the Zambezi. Meanwhile he sent urgent
representations to the commander at Tete, asking
for assistance. In response to this request, the
reply came in the form of all the available Portuguese at Tete, together with coloured troops and
a number of Native tribesmen, being sent to help
him. The stations of Sana and Tete were built on
the southern bank of the river at a considerable
distance from each other, but on the side opposite
to the Ama-Zimba. Encouraged by the knowledge
of the success at Melinde, the Portuguese leaders

hoped to repeat the experience, but they had reckoned without their host, or at least, their reckoning as regards the host opposed to them was at fault.

The Portuguese set their army in motion and advanced towards the position held by the enemy. In their march thither they showed an extreme of carelessness. The Portuguese who formed the vanguard kept to themselves, their Native allies followed some distance behind. The officers in fancied security were carried along in hammocks by their servants, some of the latter carrying their masters' guns. In this formation, the vanguard entered a forest path, was ambushed, and immediately overwhelmed and cut to pieces, the Ama-Zimba rushing in upon it from all quarters, the stabbing assegai doing fearful havoc. Every one of the Portuguese and their attendants, Rosario, a priest, excepted, died here. Rosario was taken prisoner but this was of no avail to him, for he was tied up to a tree, and shot at with arrows until he died.

From that day, the authority of the Portuguese on the Zambezi ceased to count. Such of the Portuguese as remained to garrison the forts at the various stations, having learned of the fate of their main army, made overtures of peace to the Mazimba. Ntondo finally agreed, though at first he apparently hesitated, but he insisted on the condition that, from that day, the Portuguese were to stand aside and not interfere, even by word, with matters affecting Bantu tribes. Following upon that defeat the Portuguese, in that part of the country, remained on sufferance. For generations their authority and power were kept in subjection.   They continued, however, to trade with the surrounding tribes, but subject to the forbearance of the Mazimba.

The Ama-Zimba tribe, as such, is scarcely traceable at the present time.   Like many another famous tribe, it has almost passed beyond human ken.   Circumstances apart from annihilation are often responsible for this.   Identity is frequently lost through a new name being adopted by a tribe, and becoming prominent, submerging the old. This is a common experience with Bantu tribes.

The fact that a tribe at one time so important as the Ama-Zimba should disappear is remarkable. A little thought, however, may bring to light some fact, even though a small one.   It is clear that the Ama-Zimba, after the events narrated above, moved away somewhat from the neighbourhood of the Zambezi, crossed the Revukwe, an affluent of the Zambezi (Kerr, *The Far Interior*, p. 65,) and settled on its western side.   It is believed that they are represented to-day by the Makanga, whose name appears in some modern maps.   The Makanga are said to be of a turbulent character, and this is likely if they are indeed the descendants of the Ama-Zimba.

The Aba-Mbo, whom we left after they had crossed the Zambezi along with a section of the Ama-Zimba, under Sonza, settled between the Sabi and Limpopo rivers from about 1575 till toward the close of the 16th century, when they moved on and reached Natal about 1620, Walker's *Historical Atlas*, p.6.).

CHAPTER VII

Tribal Names of Bantu Tribes

This chapter will be devoted to dealing briefly with several matters, the principal being tribal names. At the outset, however, one or two fallacies might be noticed, since these through frequent repetition have become accepted as facts. With a people, such as the Bantu, prone to believe in the mysterious rather than the actual, it is not surprising that mythical names of chiefs are accepted as real, without question or the least endeavour made to ascertain their actual value.

Tradition,—the transmitting of national information on genealogy, customs or law, from age to age, unassisted by written records, is a broken reed to rely upon implicitly, because of the limitations of the human mind. As a medium of information, it may, in regard to genealogy carry us along for, say, five hundred years with a fair measure of accuracy; but with custom and law, which are subject to occasional changes the period of reliability is much reduced. Hence, this being understood, what value can be placed upon the name *U-Ntu*, and on the two following, —*U-Hlanga* and *U-Zwide?*

According to Bantu tradition, u-Ntu was the first created individual or chief of the Bantu race. It is assumed and stated that at the creation three people were created, viz. the white man, the black man, in the person of u-Ntu, and the yellow man, the Hottentot. Modern accretions are added by Native humourists at the expense of the Hottentot. These tell us that at the creation in the process of forming the human frame, the white man, on whom was expended a good deal of time, was turned out a finished article, so also with the black man: but the end of the week intervened before the Hottentot was completed, and the work was suspended until the following week, when it was found that the clay had hardened. Nothing further could be done, and the Hottentot was left unfinished, as he is to-day,— an incomplete man.

Anthropologists date the genesis of the Bantu race from three thousand to four thousand years ago. If we accept this as likely, then u-Ntu is a long way from the creation, moreover, between him and the chief furthest back on any genealogical table thousands of years intervene, a gap which tradition makes no attempt to bridge. It gives us no supplementary information, such as the name of his son and heir, or his immediate descendants. U-Ntu is merely a personification of the term for the human species, e.g., "isi-ntu or ulu-ntu "— " the human race." From the same root is derived the term " Bantu " — " people," the plural of " um-ntu "—a person, or human being.

Bracketed frequently with the name u-Ntu, as early chiefs of the Bantu, we have " U-Hlanga " (lit. " race,") and " Zwide " (lit. " long country," fig. " wide world ").

The assurance with which these names are mentioned is by no means warranted. Such names as " Hlanga " and " Zwide " are, as we know, more or less common among chiefs in historical times, and were so, no doubt, in earlier times also, but the assertion that these are the names of the progenitors of the Bantu race, without any facts being given in support of it, is not convincing.

Tribal and Clan Names

In introducing the subject of clan and tribal names, it may be noticed that all such names have a plural prefix attached to them. There are about five classes of prefixes used in this connection. These are :—

(a) *Aba* and *Abe*, both plural prefixes of the first class, the latter, *Abe*, being merely a phonetic modification of the former. This modified and softened form is frequently used, e.g., Abe-Nguni for Aba-Nguni, Abe-Sutu for Aba-Sutu, etc.

(b) *Ama*, a plural prefix of the second class. This is the most common of all. It seems more easily adaptable to the greater number of clan and tribal names than other prefixes.

(c) *I* or *In*, a singular prefix of the third class used in a plural sense, as I-Ntlangwini, in connection with a tribe living in the Mzimkulu district.

(d) *Izi*, a plural prefix of the fourth class. This prefix is comparatively rare, few tribes having it. As an instance may be given Izi-Lilangwe or Izi-Langwe, a small tribe in Pondoland.

(e) *Imi*, a plural prefix of the sixth class, and somewhat more common than (d). Examples :— Imi-Dange, Imi-Dushane, Imi-Ganu, etc.

What, then, governs the selection of a clan or tribal prefix ? The answer is, that the selection is governed purely by phonetic requirements. There is no rule determining the use of any prefix attached to the tribal name but that which suits the tongue. It would be phonetically awkward to say, for instance, Aba-Xosa, Aba-Huhu or Aba-Dange. Such a use of the prefixes would not readily accommodate itself to the tongue of a

Native. He would instinctively feel that there was something wrong, for it would be a violation of his phonetic sense.

It is true that etymology as a science is unknown to the Bantu, and there are no phonetic rules laid down by them, as until recently they had no literature. The rules, however, are embeded in the language, and each individual makes use of phonetic rules without having learnt them. The particular dialect in use by a certain tribe exercises a phonetic influence on the form of prefix to be used in conjunction with the tribal name.

In certain cases a chief's name undergoes alteration as it becomes a tribal designation. For instance, the names of Manci and Mnkonde, two chiefs of separate branches of the Ama-Zotsho, are transformed as follows,—in the case of the former, instead of the tribal name becoming Ama-Manci, and the latter Ama-Mnkonde we have excision in the one of the initial syllable, and in the other, of the initial consonant, and the tribal names become respectively—Ama-Nci and Ama-Nkonde. Other examples might be quoted, but the examples given go to prove that the excisions were made in order to make the names amenable to phonetic requirements.

As a general rule the prefix is not a matter of choice, but is subject to what we may call dialectic phonetics.

Families, or an aggregate of families, namely clans, usually take their clan name from a progenitor. It may be the first head of the family, or it may be a son or grandson who specially commended himself to the affection of his people, by his outstanding personality, courage, wisdom or open-handedness. Sometimes it happens that the progenitor of a clan dies leaving no male issue, in which case, in accordance with custom, a relative from another branch of the tribe may be appointed to keep the house " alive." Such a house is called *ixiba* by the Xosas or *isi-zinde* by the Aba-Mbo, and the name signifies an appendage of the reigning house. This house usually, but not always, takes neither the name of the first head, nor of the substitute but of the favourite racing or dancing ox of the former.

This may be illustrated by the case of the house of Tiso, who died without issue. Tiso was the head of one of Tshiwo's minor houses (*iqadi*). Into that house, at the death of Tiso, was placed Langa, a minor son of Palo (principal) son of Tshiwo). Langa, the new head of Tiso's house, however, did not give his name to it, nor was the name of Tiso continued, but the name of Tiso's favourite ox, Mbalu, was adopted as the clan name. Ama-Mbalu, therefore, is the clan name of Langa's descendants.

In circumstances such as the above, this is the common method adopted in the naming of a clan. Occasionally, but very seldom, it happens that though a progenitor has male issue, the clan name is taken not from the chief or his heir, but from his favourite ox. This was the case with Maqoma's clan of Gaikas (Ama-Ngqika.) It took its name from Maqoma's favourite ox Jingqi, and is called the Ama-Jingqi.

Then, again, though also very seldom, adventitious circumstances may determine the name of a clan, e.g. the great Hlubi tribe, whose name is derived from a woman, *Hlubi*, of the Ama-Bele tribe.

At a critical time in the life of what was up to that time the Imi-Huhu tribe, a young woman, *Hlubi*, came from the Ama-Bele tribe as a bride to the heir of the Imi-Huhu chief, and the tribe took her name as its tribal designation : hence the Imi-Huhu are now called Ama-Hlubi. The circumstances are referred to in the chapter on the Ama-Hlubi.

Names are sometimes applied under special circumstances to clans or tribes by enemy tribes, which names may become stereotyped and fixed, as for instance, the term Matebele or Mandebele applied to Mzilikazi's tribe. The original name of Mzilikazi's tribe is Ama-Kumalo, and within the tribe itself this latter name holds sway.

As tribes are merely units composed of a group of clans, bound together by the tie of descent from a common ancestor, it follows that the original clan from which the units of the group are derived, gives its name to the combined unit as its tribal name.

If the study of Bantu history is of any importance, care should be exercised so as not to use tribal names in a haphazard way. This happens even with men of undoubted historical authority. For instance, that prince of Central African historians, Sir H. H. Johnston, sometimes uses the term *Angoni-Zulus* in reference to the Aba-Ngoni or Abe-Nguni of Nyasaland. If the term so used means that the Abe-Nguni are derived from Zulu stock, then it is quite misleading, for the Aba-Ngoni are not Zulus, nor are the

Zulus Aba-Nguni. Both are widely separated branches of the Bantu race. The Zulu tribe is of comparatively recent origin, having only ten generations from the time of the first known chief of that tribe, Malandela, down to the time of Tshaka. Approximately, the date when Malandela ruled would be about 1603, ·if we calculate on 25 years to a generation down, to the date of Tshaka's death in 1828. Whereas, Xosa, the earliest known chief of the Abe-Nguni, according to the same calculation lived about 1535, the difference being about seventy years in favour of the earlier origin of the Abe-Nguni. This, therefore, indicates clearly that the Abe-Nguni are in no sense Zulus, being an older branch of Bantu stock, and consequently cannot have issued from the younger branch. We find the same confusion, the same want of differentiation, in regard to the term Aba-Mbo, which is made to apply, not only to tribes of genuine Aba-Mbo stock, but to others that are distinctly not Aba-Mbo. For instance the Fingos are often designated Aba-Mbo (see Ayliff and Whiteside's book, *Aba-Mbo*). The Fingos themselves have fallen into the same error, and actually believe that they are Aba-Mbo, whereas they have no point of genealogical contact with that branch of Bantu. The Tshaka upheavals are possibly responsible for dislocation of their ideas in this matter.

The Fingos are not Aba-Mbo. The majority of the tribes called Fingo are of Lala or Kalanga origin. This has been pointed out elsewhere in this book. The principal Fingo tribes are Hlubis,

E

Beles, Zizis, and Tolos. Among the Lala tribes there are many not known to the writer—tribes still in Natal, which became merged with the great fighting tribes during Tshaka's regime, or became tributary to those tribes to save themselves from extinction.

Under the designation *Ama-Lala*, which is used here as synonymous with *Ama-Kalanga*, I have included a number of well known tribes in this colony (Cape). Among these the Ama-Hlubi and Ama-Zizi tribes believe themselves to be Aba-Mbo. But there is supporting evidence for my view in a paper by Professor Schwarz of Rhodes University College. In an article appearing in the East London *Daily Dispatch*, of Dec., 1926, under the signature of Professor E. H. L. Schwarz, the statement is made in connection with the Makalanga that, at some indeterminate period, through the attacks of tribes " from the south," there occurred the battle of " Thaba's ka Mambo " (presumably Intaba zika-Mambo), and that the Makalanga nation, as a consequence, became divided into two halves, of which one remained in the north and underwent the most abject slavery, etc. The Basutos and Bechuanas, he seems to indicate, are derived from this section. " The other half," he writes, " went south and east, meeting the Bavenda in the Sebasa, Northern Transvaal, and the Batonga in Portuguese East Africa, and eventually landed in Natal." " They became known as the Ama-Hlubi and Ama-Zizi, and as such took part in much of the early history of Basutoland and Natal. Some still pressed south and became involved in the Kafir wars, etc." This supports my opinion stated elsewhere, independently of the above, that those two tribes *are of Lala or Makalanga origin,* and are *not Aba-Mbo.*

Reverting to the subject of the misapplication of tribal names, we may note that the term Abe-Nguni or Ngoni is sometimes applied by historians both to Mzilikazi's clan, the Ama-Kumalo, and to that of Manukuza, otherwise the Ama-Gasa of Gazaland. It is questionable if there is justification for the application of the term Abe-Nguni to these two tribes. They are indeed related by blood, but the point has to be proved that they are Abe-Nguni tribes.

Sotshangana, or to give him his royal title, Manukuza, was a son of Langa, and younger brother of the great Zwide, chief of the Ama-Ndwandwe or Nxumalo tribe. What the actual relationship is between the Ama-Kumalo, Mzilikazi's clan, and the Ama-Gasa section of the Ama-Ndwandwe or Ama-Nxumalo is not clear as yet. Another chief, Zwangendaba of the Abe-Nguni, now of Nyassaland, with his clan formed part of the military strength of Zwide's Ama-Ndwandwe during Tshaka's wars, but Zwange-ndaba's clan were *at that time* called Abe-Nguni. We have then these three clan names, or tribal names, Abe-Nguni, Ama-Kumalo, and Ama-Ndwandwe or Nxumalo, applied to three branches of the Ama-Ndwandwe army, the names being tribal, not regimental. The Rev J. Dewar, of Maritzburg, to whom I referred the matter for elucidation, expressed the belief that the relationship between the Abe-Nguni of Zwangendaba and the Ama-Ndwandwe of Zwide was political rather than tribal. The application, therefore, of the term Abe-Nguni to Manukuza's section, the Sokulu or Ama-Gasa of the Ama-Ndwandwe, may not be justified, and has probably arisen through the association in war of these tribes and the name of the more distinguished fighting unit has been made to apply to both.

It is in such matters that care should be exercised to designate tribes correctly, so as to avoid confusion, the more so if, as has been said, the study of Bantu history is of any moment.

Then again, the Ama-Kumalo, Mzilikazi's clan is claimed by the Ama-Hlubi tribe to be one of its clans, Kumalo being represented as the son of Mntungwa, an early chief of the Imi-Huhu, now known as Ama-Hlubi. That being so, it is a misnomer to call either Manukuza's Ama-Gasa or Mzilikazi's Ama-Kumalo, by the term Abe-Nguni.

CHAPTER VIII

Correlation of Bantu Tribes

There is no possibility of correlating all Bantu tribes, or even those with which we are familiar, as some have attempted to do, because the formation of a tribe from the main stem (if there be such a thing) may have taken place, say, a thousand years ago, while another, quite as formidable and important to-day, may only have come into being five hundred years ago, and may not be from a main or important branch, but from a lateral or sub-lateral branch. Yet another may even be derived from an offshoot of a lateral or sub-lateral branch. The unlettered human mind is incapable of connecting up under these circumstances, and failing written records on lineage, the task will prove to be beyond the powers of the student of Bantu genealogy.

Correlation can only take place within very narrow limits. We speak and write about the "Main Bantu Stem." Is there, however, such a thing ?

I confess that I occasionally use the term, but in a hypothetical sense, to refer to something which ought to be there, but actually may not be. It requires very little thought on the subject of a main stem to come to the conclusion that it no longer exists. At the time of the origin of the Bantu race a main stem did exist no doubt, but with polygamy in the ascendant, in five hundred years, probably, from the starting point of the race, it would dissipate the main stem, and in its place there would be a multitude of tribes, many of which would no longer be able to trace their connection with the main stem. As time passed, this condition would become more and more emphasized, until to-day he would be a bold man who would assert that a Main Bantu Stem existed. This fact, therefore, if admitted as I believe it must be, will show how impossible, except within extremely contracted limits, it is to correlate all Bantu tribes.

Sometimes we come across genealogical tables which seek to correlate all the principal Bantu tribes existing at the present time in South-Eastern Africa, but these efforts give us what, at best, are merely fanciful relationships.   There are certain prominent tribes which represent well defined streams or branches of the Bantu race: within the limits of each of these streams correlation may be secured, but not outside of them, except in a very few cases.   The Ama-Tonga, for instance, being a branch of the Makalanga, might possibly be able to trace a connection between themselves and the Hlubis and Zizis, etc., which are also of Makalanga origin, but beyond that it is doubtful if they could establish connection.

Let us take the case of a few tribes which, if the data concerning them can be relied on, may be correlated, since the parent branch from which they all sprang is known. I refer to the Ama-Hlubi, Ama-Zizi, Ama-Bele, Ama-Kuze and I-Ntlangwini.   The Ama-Hlubi and Ama-Bele both derive their origin from a common ancestor, Mhuhu.   Mhuhu's heir, Mhlanga, continued the tribal name Imi-Huhu through his descendants down to the time of Mtimkulu I, after which the tribal name became Ama-Hlubi. Mhuhu's other son was Bele, from whom the Ama-Bele got their name. These two tribes can, therefore, be correlated so far. Again, the Ama-Zizi, Ama-Kuze, I-Ntlangwini, and a few other minor tribes, are all derived from a common ancestor, Dlamini. These, then, may be correlated so far, and they may be further correlated with any tribes of Imi-Huhu origin, for Dlamini is a descendant of Mhuhu. As has already been indicated, the Ama-Hlubi and Ama-Zizi both broke off from the Ama-Kalanga tribe, apparently about the same time. Consequently correlation may be effected not only between the two, but possibly also through a common ancestor and member of the Ama-Kalanga with the Makalanga tribe itself. Beyond that it is scarcely possible to prove relationship. It will be apparent, therefore, that correlation of Bantu tribes can only be established within restricted limits. I think it is perfectly safe to say that correlation between Tembu and Xosa, or between Xosa and Aba-Mbo, or between Aba-Mbo and Tembu cannot be secured. They are widely divergent branches of the Bantu race, and their separate origin cannot be dated at the same period of time.

It has been said that correlation can be secured within certain limits. These limits are governed by relationship to common ancestors, who are to be traced by means of the universal custom of the *isi-takazelo* (Zulu) or *isi-buliso* (Xosa), that is, *royal salutations*.

Common ancestors may not be of the same name, but they must be known and accepted as of the same family or tribe. To amplify this point, we would refer to the fact that all genealogical tables have, or may have names of chiefs, representing lateral branches, as well as the main branch of the same family or tribe. It is immaterial, then, for purposes of correlation, whether a royal salutation employed by any clan or tribe be that of a principal or lateral branch, provided relationship can be established between the two. Any tribe or section of a tribe, therefore, whose royal salutation may be traced to any chief in any part of a particular genealogical table, will be known to belong to a definite Bantu stream or branch, that is, either to the Abe-Nguni, Aba-Mbo, or Ama-Lala.

A number of tribes may be untraceable, but that will probably be due to the fact that their salutation is that of a chief of an obscure lateral branch, or of an offshoot of a lateral branch; or possibly of a Basuto or other tribe outside of the scope of the three streams under our consideration. Correlation, therefore, can only apply to clans and tribes belonging to a well defined branch of the Bantu race. Branches of this race being innumerable, and originating at separate points of time, cannot all be brought under one common genealogical table.

If an endeavour is made to secure correlation between the Ama-Lala and either the Aba-Mbo or the Abe-Nguni (Xosa), it will be found to be hopeless, as there is no point of contact between them. The Ama-Lala royal salutations include no names in use by these other branches of the Bantu race, and *vice versa*.

There is one large section of the Ama-Lala, namely the Ama-Ngcolosi, whose salutations, *Bengu* and *Nyuswa*, find no place in the genealogical tables of other prominent Lala tribes, such as the Hlubis, Beles, Zizis, etc. The reason for this may be that the Ama-Ngcolosi are a distinct and separate branch of the Makalanga, while the Hlubis and others represent a different branch, and both these branches may have broken away from the parent tribe at different epochs, and derive their origin from different heads of families— consequently, their salutations would not be the same. Offshoots of the Ama-Ngcolosi, e.g., the Ama-Ngcobo, Nyuswa, Qadi, Osiyane (or Wosiyane), do not use the Ngcolosi salutation *Bengu* or *Bhengu* (Zulu orthography). Instead, they use the salutation *Ngcobo*, the name of the progenitor of these subsections of that great tribe.

To assist in realising the importance of the royal salutations in identifying tribal members of a common stock, we would set forth here various subsections of the Ama-Ngcolosi, giving the salutation of each. Such salutations as are similar at once determine relationship between all tribes and clans using them. I am indebted to Bryant's *Zulu-English Dictionary*, p.250, for these salutations of the Ama-Ngcolosi sub-tribes.

Tribal name.	*Royal salutation.*
Ama-Ngcolosi ...	Bhengu
,, Ngcobo (branch of above)	Ngcobo
,, Nyuswa ,, ,, ,, ...	Ngcobo
,, Langeni ,, ,, ,, ...	Ngcobo
,, Fuze or Funze ,, ,, ...	Ngcobo
,, Ngongoma ,, ,, ...	Ngcobo
,, Qadi ,, ,, ...	Ngcobo

Here then, we have a number of tribes living in different parts of the country, each independent of the other, but whose family relationship is proved by their common salutation, *Ngcobo*. Having established relationship through a common salutation, the next step is to find the tribe from which the older tribal branch (in this case the Ama-Ngcolosi) is derived. If this can be found, together with its sub-branches, the field of relationship will be considerably widened, and whatever the salutations of those sub-branches may be, the point of contact of the two older branches establishes the field within which correlation may operate. This process must be applied in all efforts to establish correlation. Here we need the assistance of the genealogical tables to collect scattered clans and tribes into a correlated system.

For the purposes of correlation, the royal salutation is of vastly more importance than the *tekeza* form of speech. This latter can be acquired by strangers whose own speech is not of the *tekeza* order, and it may be discarded by a tribe whose mother speech was originally of the *tekeza* order. On the other hand, the royal salutation cannot be strictly applied to outsiders but only those who by blood are entitled to it.

Royal Salutations (Izi-Kahlelo or Izi-Takazelo.)

It is important to note the royal salutation adopted by tribes and clans, as this gives an indication of the line of descent of a tribe. The term in the vernacular varies with different tribes, the Aba-Mbo and Ama-Lala calling it *isi-takazelo*, and the Ama-Xosa *isi-kahlelo* or *isi-buliso*. Tribes of a certain Bantu branch, and clans of such tribes, if belonging to the Aba-Mbo or Ama-Lala, generally use the name of an ancestor as a common salutation. It is somewhat different with the Ama-Xosa, who seldom use the name of an ancestor, but instead use that of a reigning chief.

To the initiated, the Aba-Mbo and Ama-Lala salutations are a help towards correlation. *Uku-takazela* means " to applaud," whereas *Uku-kahlela* means " to cast down." The first needs no explanation, the second, however, is derived probably from the old custom of throwing one's self down and approaching royalty on hands and knees. Apart from being used in salutation of a chief, the *isi-kahlelo* may also be applied as a term of courtesy by one individual to another of the same tribe. There is a distinct difference in the form of the royal salutation as used by certain branches of the Eastern Bantu. With the Ama-Xosa the salutation has the " Ah," meaning " Hail," prefixed to the name of the ruling chief, e.g., " Ah, Sandile " = " Hail Sandile," " Ah Sarili = " Hail Kreli." This form with the " Hail " is used only by the Ama-Xosa and such other tribes as have come under Xosa influence. The prefix is always attached to the name of the present occupant of the throne, not as with the Aba-Mbo and Ama-Lala, to that of an ancestor. The *isi-takazelo* of the Aba-Mbo and Ama-Lala does not make use of the name of the reigning chief, but, as has been said, that of an ancestor. For instance, the *isi-takazelo* of the right-hand house of the Bomvanas, an Aba-Mbo tribe, is " Tshezi," the name of a chief who reigned eight generations ago. The Ama-Hlubi, a Lala tribe, have several salutations, that of the principal or royal house being "Mti-mkulu," or "Bungane," or "Ntsele," after chiefs who reigned eleven, twelve, and thirteen generations ago, respectively. The right-hand house, on the other hand, uses the salutation "Radebe," being the name of the progenitor of that house, who ruled ten generations ago.

Then again, the two branches of what are called the Ama-Zulu use different salutations, but the salutations are respectively the names of former chiefs. The two branches referred to are the Ama-Qwabe, the great house, and the Ama-Zulu, the right-hand house, whose name has become all comprehensive of tribes and clans of those branches.

The salutation of the Ama-Qwabe is "Gumede," the name of an ancestor chief, probably father of Malandela from whom issued the two houses mentioned. Accepting that supposition, Gumede reigned about twelve generations ago. The minor house, the Ama-Zulu, adopt the salutation "Nda-bezita." All the smaller branches of those two houses adopt the salutation of the parent house of each, i.e., either "Gumede" or "Ndabezita." This fact helps in the tracing of the origin of a tribe, by giving a clue to the house or tribe from which it has sprung. All tribes whose salutation is "Gumede" or "Ndabezita" are what are now irregularly called "Zulus." This term being the name of a minor house should, strictly speaking, be confined to that house and its immediate branches. Ndabezita is the name of a prominent Bele chief, and the Zulu salutation would seem to indicate that they are of Bele ancestry. The salutation "Ndabezita "* is of somewhat recen origin. Bryant tells us that the earlier salutation of the Zulus was " Lufenu-lwenja." Now, the name of one of the early chiefs of the Imi-Huhu or Hlubi was " Lufele-lwenja," which I take to be the same, though the last syllable of the hyphenated name has undergone a slight change from the Zulu form. Consequently, if this surmise is correct, the Zulus are a branch of the Imi-Huhu, or Hlubi, and a break-off from the Makalanga. They derive thus, according to my divisions of Bantu streams, from the Ama-Lala. Both Lufele-lwenja and Ndabezita are of the Imi-Huhu strain, the former being pre-Mhuhu and the latter post-Mhuhu.

Again, all tribes whose salutation is "Mntu-ngwa" are of the same Imi-Huhu origin. The Ama-Kumalo (of Mzilikazi), the Ama-Nxumalo and Ama-Ndwandwe, all give the salutation "Mntungwa," and some of their lesser clans "Ndabezita," thus indicating that they are off-shoots of the Imi-Huhu, and consequently of Lala or Makalanga origin.

Such salutations as " Dlamini," " Radebe," " Reledwane," " Ndaba " and a number of others indicate very clearly the branch to which they belong. The first is used by all branches of the Ama-Zizi. Therefore, Dlamini being a descendant of Mhuhu, places all Zizis in the same category as Hlubis, Beles, Tolos, and Ntlangwini ; that is to say, they may be correlated under the designation Imi-Huhu, and consequently under the more comprehensive terms of Lala or Makalanga origin.

* Ndabezita as a salutation may possibly be the praise name—isi-bongo—of Ndaba, great-grandfather of Tshaka. If so, this would make the question of the branch to which the Zulus belong obscure,

Tribes which may be correlated under the heading Ama-Lala are the following :—Imi-Huhu (Hlubi), Ama-Bele, Ama-Zizi, Ama-Tolo, I-Ntlangwini, Ama-Zulu, Ama-Qwabe, Ama-Kumalo, Ama-Nxumalo or Ama-Ndwandwe, Aba-Ntungwa, Ama-Ngcolosi, Ama-Ngcobo, Ama-Nyuswa, Ama-Wushe, Ama-Baca and all their sub-clans, besides others not mentioned. For the Wushes and Bacas and also the Ama-Ngcolosi, I have, so far, not yet been able to fix definitely their point of contact with any Lala genealogical table, though they also are undoubtedly of Lala stock.

The origin of the Ama-Xosa, on the other hand is more obscure, as their salutation is confined to the name of the reigning chief, and thus their ancient chiefs are not held in remembrance in the same way as with the other two branches. They are Abe-Nguni, not Ama-Lala or Aba-Mbo, and cannot be correlated with the latter.

There are some sections of Abe-Nguni, of the same stock as the Ama-Xosa, still in Natal, where they remained when the Xosas moved to the south. These are the Ama-Mbayi and Ama-Nzimela, and doubtless there are others. These sections retain the salutation " Mnguni," the name of their common ancestor with the Ama-Xosa. They do not use the distinctive Xosa form of salutation " Ah, So-and-So," but follow the custom of their Lala neighbours and use the ancestral name " Mnguni."

It will be seen from the foregoing remarks that tribal salutations, perpetuating the names of ancient or moderately ancient chiefs, are an important means to the correlation of tribes, and thus help to unify certain scattered branches of the Bantu, which to many seem to have no connection with each other.

Interdict on Marriage of Blood Relations.

In connection with the correlation of clans and tribes, another matter has to be taken into account, that is, the taboo or interdict placed upon the marriage of persons who according to Bantu ideas are related.

The Bantu have been, from time immemorial, strictly opposed to the marriage of blood-relations. The interpretation of the term " blood-relationship " is with them much wider than with most other races. With Europeans as a general rule, intermarriage with cousins is discouraged ; beyond that, however, consanguinity is considered so weak that popular opinion and law make no objection to the marriage of parties so far apart in relationship.

With the Bantu, on the other hand, marriage with members of the same family, however distantly related, is not allowed. Nor is it permitted between members of the same clan, or even of the same tribe, that is with any of the various clans grouped under the larger unit designated tribe. To-day, under European rule, and a different outlook on life, these restrictions are becoming less vigorously observed, but even yet the great majority of men will not marry women who belong by blood to the same tribe, clan, or family.

This custom is very important in determining the existence or non-existence of relationship

between tribes or clans.   For instance, it is sometimes asserted that the Ama-Miya are a section of
the Ama-Zizi (see *Table Ama-Zizi*, by Ayliff and
Whiteside).   It is a simple matter to determine
whether this is so or not, and depends on the
answer to a question.   If you ask a Zizi the
question, "Do you intermarry with the Ama-
Miya?" and you get the answer, "No, we do not,"
you may be sure that they are closely related
by blood.   But if, on the other hand, you get the
answer, "Yes, we intermarry," you may be
certain that the two tribes have no ties of blood-
relationship.   Now, as the Ama-Zizi and Ama-
Miya do intermarry, it is clear that they were
originally of different stock.

The strict manner in which this custom is
observed, is of material assistance in determining
the question of the relationship of clans and
tribes, and, therefore, is another matter to be
considered in connection with the correlation of
tribes.

Ama-Xosa.

J. H. Soga.

CHAPTER IX

BRANCH 1

Abe-Nguni = Ama-Xosa

In the following pages of this book the subject matter will be confined, mainly, to the consideration of the three streams or branches of Bantu inhabiting the coastal regions of South Eastern Africa.

I. The first is that of the Abe-Nguni (Ama-Xosa, and the Abe-Nguni of Nyasaland).

II. The second is that of the Aba-Mbo (the stream which, coming south, reached Natal about 1620).

III. The third is that of the Ama-Lala (who were the first inhabitants of Zululand and Natal, so far as is known. The Lala tribes were already in occupation of that country at the advent of the Aba-Mbo).

The term Abe-Nguni applies particularly to the Xosa tribe, and to others of kindred stock. Before this tribe was called Ama-Xosa, thus perpetuating the name of a favourite, but later, chief, it was called Abe-Nguni, after an earlier chief named Mnguni. There are still a few tribes in Natal, such the Ama-Mbayi and Ama-Nzimela, etc., which are of the same Abe-Nguni stock as the Xosas. When the usual prefix has been added to the chief's name to give it tribal significance, the initial *M* of Mnguni is dropped on phonetic grounds and the name becomes Abe-Nguni.

The term Ebu-Nguni is used by Natives of Natal to indicate the country of the Abe-Nguni or Xosas, which lies west of Natal, hence we find Kropf in his *Kafir Dictionary* saying that the term is used in the locative, and means " in the west, or westward." This is scarcely a correct definition, as no other place except that occupied by the Abe-Nguni or Ama-Xosa is so defined. " Nguni" is not a Bantu term for " west "; the correct term is " entshona-langa "—" where the sun sets." For instance, the Basutos do not call the country of the Bechuanas to the west of them, " ebu-Nguni," nor do any other tribes so designate the country to the west of them.

The term as applied to the country of the Ama-Xosa is due to the fact that the tribe known as Abe-Nguni lived to the west of Natal. That is to say, the inhabitants gave the name to the country, not the country to the inhabitants. Hence, ebu-Nguni is the country of the Abe-Nguni. It is not a geographical position.

The term Abe-Nguni is sometimes used in a sense which is quite unjustified. For instance, A. T. Bryant, in writing about the people of Manukuza, states that the term Abe-Nguni was applied by the Tongas to the Shangaans, Manukuza's tribe, and to all tribes who went north from the south, presumably Natal. There is no justification, to my mind, for using the term in this irregular fashion. If it can be proved that the Shangaans are of the same stock as the Xosas, then there would be an excuse for its use in this way. But, we must remember that Sotshangana, otherwise Manukuza, was the son of Gasa, from whom Gazaland takes its name. Now Gasa was son of Langa, and younger brother of Zwide of the Ama-Ndwandwe or Ama-Nxumalo tribe. Then again, the Nxumalos, like the Kumalos of Mzilikazi, are claimed as of Ntlangwini stock, consequently, if this is correct, the Shangaans are really Ama-Lala, not Abe-Nguni.

In corroboration of this we find that the royal salutation of the Nxumalos is " Mntungwa " and also " Ndaba." Both of these names are those of ancient chiefs of the Imi-Huhu or Hlubi, and these are not of Abe-Nguni but of Lala stock.

The application of the term Abe-Nguni to Manukuza's tribe of Shangaans by the Tongas is, therefore, a misnomer. Its application in this fashion arose, probably, from the fact that Zwangendaba, a chief of a section of the Abe-Nguni who broke away northwards during the time of Tshaka's devastations came into contact with the Tongas about the same time as Manukuza's people did, and the name of the more formidable tribe was indiscriminately applied to both.

It may be accepted with confidence that the Bantu are particularly careful, as a general rule, about the application of tribal names. They do not use them indiscriminately so as to cause confusion. To them the term Abe-Nguni refers immediately and solely to the people of the chief Mnguni. What tribes, then, may be comprised under the term Abe-Nguni ? The answer to that question is, that two great tribes only, with their many clan divisions, the Ama-Xosa and the Abe-Nguni of Nyasaland, correctly speaking, come under that designation. A few other tribes still in Natal, whose salutation is " Mguni," are also comprised under the same name.

From the very outset we are met with the difficulty of locating the *original home* of the Abe-Nguni, and of identifying the tribe from which they broke off. It is, however, apparent that they were in Northern Natal prior to the advent of the Aba-Mbo in 1620 (Eric Walker, *Historical Atlas*, p. 6).

Indications point to their having an admixture of Arab or Portuguese blood. As a tribe, the Xosa section at least, they stand pre-eminent among the tribes south of Natal, for pride of race, manly bearing, haughty demeanour and courage.

They are lighter in colour than the majority of the surrounding tribes. Some writers ascribe this to Hottentot blood, but their facial characteristics give a denial to this theory. Their appearance, physique, and bearing would have suffered from amalgamation with an acknowledged inferior race.

The original home of the Abe-Nguni is difficult to determine, and is necessarily a matter of conjecture. We know where the Aba-Mbo came from, but we are uncertain as to where the Abe-Nguni came from before they entered Natal. The probability is that they came from somewhere on the north-east of the continent. Dohne, the well known German missionary of Stutterheim, visited Natal in 1852 and came in contact with " a small section of Ama-Xosa that had been left behind." Theal says concerning these people " these tribes, he (Dohne) believed to have come from the Mozambique coast," "but," adds the historian, "of course he knew nothing of the invasion from the north-west, and the terribly destructive wars towards the close of the 16th century, of which the Portuguese on the Zambesi have left records."

It is strange how the theory of a north-west origin of the Xosas persists without any real evidence whatsoever. Dohne's opinion, as that of one who had met with Abe-Nguni 300 to 400 miles nearer to their original home than the Ama-Xosa, their relatives here, is worthy of respectful consideration. He would get the idea from the people themselves. Then again, the "destructive wars" referred to in the above quotation, were undoubtedly those of the Ama-Zimba and Aba-Mbo, who broke the power of the Portuguese in East Africa. These may justly be termed East African tribes, and this goes to support Dohne's belief of an East African origin for the Ama-Xosa.

For centuries before the advent of the Aba-Mbo in Natal, national upheavals were taking place in middle-east Africa, and along that coast Arabs and Indians were carrying on trade, and forming connection with the surroundings tribes, as did also the Portuguese at a later date. It is not at all unlikely that as a result of tribal dislocations, the Abe-Nguni broke away and took the only open road to the south. It is possible that they were a section of the Ama-Zimba, a tribe in fairly close contact with the coastal Arabs and Portuguese. The time of Xosa's reign coincides fairly well with that of the Ama-Zimba attacks on the Portuguese stations on the Zambesi, or with the time of the settlement of the Aba-Mbo between the Sabi and Limpopo rivers. Nothing definite, however, can be asserted about this at present. Perhaps the future may, by some fortunate chance, or documentary evidence, Arab or

Portuguese, give us something more tangible. It is clear, at least, that the Ama-Xosa entered Natal before the Aba-Mbo, but it may not have been much before the latter.   In further reference to the original home of the Abe-Nguni or Xosas we find such authorities as Willoughby, *Race Problems in the New South Africa,* p.37, writing to the effect that the Ama-Xosa and Aba-Tembu and Ama-Hlubi are sister tribes which entered South Africa by force; that they came from the west coast subsequent to 1600, A.D.; and that the Ama-Xosa and Aba-Tembu fought with the Hottentots, overcame them and took their women as wives.   These statements, however, are not apparently surported by facts on which we can take secure hold.   If, as is asserted, these tribes brought with them some words common to the tribes on the west, it is a pity we are not informed what they are.   In any case, when we consider that the Bantu language is universal south of Victoria Nyanza, even though dialects differ, there must be, and are, words common to tribes on the west, east, north and south.   There should be nothing surprising in that.   But what does surprise is that a theory of the original home of the Xosa and Tembu tribes should be built on so slender a foundation.

In connection with this western theory, it may be pointed out that an immense area of country would have to be traversed by tribes crossing the continent from west to east, constant opposition encountered, and a daily appeal to arms against tribes prepared to dispute the way.   Few, if any, tribes could endure the depletion of their numbers under such conditions, and survive.

The statement that these two tribes are sister tribes is only true of them in that they are both of Bantu stock, but they are not closely related for all that. They are of totally different branches of the race.

Again, as has already been stated, the first contact of the Ama-Xosa with Hottentots took place in Pondoland (see chap. 7) about 1650. This would apply also to the Tembus, a branch of which tribe moved south from Natal to Pondoland about the same time as the Xosas. There is no acknowledgement on the part of the latter tribe that Hottentot women were incorporated wholesale into the tribe. Reference to this subject will be made later on in this chapter.

The Abe-Nguni dialect of the Bantu language differs materially, not perhaps in its structure, but rather in its intonation and accentuation, from the *tekeza* group. There is no reason to believe that the Xosa language has undergone any change of structure or pronunciation from its original form. There is no indication that the Xosa ever used the *tekeza* form of the Lala tribes, or the *tsefula* form of the Bacas, or the *ngingiza* of the Hlubis. The Xosa language came down from old time in the form in which we find it to-day. On account of the striking character of Si-Xosa it is impossible to class the Ama-Xosa with the *tekeza* group of tribes, or in a less degree with the Aba-Mbo tribes.

The Ama-Xosa (*Abe-Nguni*.)

Before this tribe reached Natal, and for a considerable time during its stay there, it was known as the Abe-Nguni, not as the Ama-Xosa. Indeed, by the other tribes in Natal, this tribe even to the present day is more frequently spoken of as Abe-Nguni than as Ama-Xosa.   M. M. Fuze, in his book *Abantu Abamnyama*, says, "the great tribe of Mnguni set out westwards (from Natal). . . . . This is the Mnguni who was father of Xosa, indeed the latter would appear to have been his first born."

There is no record of how Xosa so distinguished himself, that the tribal name Ama-Xosa to-day has largely superseded that of Abe-Nguni within the tribe itself.   It is not even clear that Xosa was the chief who led his Abe-Nguni into Natal, though this is presumably the case.

In considering this tribe alone, it will be seen how once famous names are superseded by the names of chiefs of later fame, and these by others later still.   The great name of Mnguni, though still recognized as all-comprehensive of tribes which derive their birth from him, has largely fallen into abeyance in favour of that of Xosa. Then, again, at the present day the names of two chiefs, Gcaleka and Rarabe, are gradually superseding that of Xosa in general use, and so it goes on, Rarabe's name being superseded by that of his grandson Ngqika (Gaika).   This constant change of tribal name would soon cause confusion or even complete loss of the identity of a tribe to those not familiar with these facts.

The term Ama-Xosa is all comprehensive of that section of the Abe-Nguni who are descended from Xosa.   The Ama-Xosa are subdivided into several sections, the principal or best known being the Ama-Gcalekas (Galekas) and the Ama-Ngqika (Gaikas).   When we speak of the Ama-Gcaleka, we refer to those branches of the Xosa tribe that derive their origin directly from the chief Gcaleka, son of Palo. In like manner, when we speak of Gaikas we refer particularly to those branches of the Xosa tribe directly descended from Ngqika, son of Mlawu and grandson of Rarabe.

Then again we have the term Ama-Rarabe. This refers not only to Rarabe's immediate descendants, such as those of the house of Ndlambe and Nukwa sons of Rarabe, but also to the Gaikas, through Mlawu, great son of Rarabe. At the same time, there is this distinction to be noticed; the Ama-Ndlambe and the descendants of Nukwa (Ama-Ntsusa), brother of Ndlambe and Mlawu, are *not* Ama-Ngqika (Gaikas), but are strictly speaking Ama-Rarabe, while at the same time the Gaikas are also Ama-Rarabe.

Then, again, those tribes that first came into conflict with the colonists at the Fish river about the middle of the 18th century, namely the Ama-Gwali, Ama-Ntinde, Ama-Mbalu, and Imi-Dange, while they are Ama-Xosa, are neither Rarabes, Gcalekas, nor Gaikas, strictly speaking, as they were formed before these latter had any existence at all, and the Ama-Xosa had not yet any important sub-divisions.

There are two great divisions into which the Gcalekas are separated for warlike purposes. These are the I-Ntshinga and the I-Qauka. In time of war, as in peace, both divisions were under the supreme direction, as Commander-in-chief, of the paramount chief. Each division has its own general, under each of whom are subordinate officers, usually chiefs of sub-divisions of the tribes. When war is imminent the war-doctor is called upon to doctor the warriors and make them invulnerable. The methods adopted by the war-doctor (i-tola) may be given in detail at this stage.

The War-Doctor.

In all tribal wars the presiding figure who prepares the army, and instils into it courage and a determination to conquer the enemy, is the war-doctor. When war is imminent, the "tola" or war-doctor is commanded to repair to the Great Place. The whole tribe is also warned and required to come armed. All having arrived, dancing commences, and war songs are sung. This lasts for the greater part of a day. After this, fires are lit in which medical herbs are roasted and then eaten; part of them, having been prepared by fire, are powdered and mixed with other preparations and the gall of slaughtered cattle. The doctor then proceeds to take a small portion, which he places in the mouth of a warrior. The latter then leaves the ranks and dances facing the sun. Another is taken from the ranks and then another, and the process is repeated until the whole army has been individually attended to. In so great a work the doctor has to be assisted by acolytes.

This stage having been accomplished, the warriors sit down in their ranks, and on the forehead of each is painted a black mark.

By this time, it is late in the evening, but none may go home to rest; all must sleep in, and about, the cattle kraal of the Great Place.

Next morning, the army is taken to the river, the doctor going in advance. Arrived there, the warriors are all required to enter, medicine is then poured into the water, and all must wash.

This part of the ceremony is performed by men in batches, as no ordinary river could, at one spot, accommodate simultaneously the whole army.

Having performed its ablutions the army returns to the Great Place, and dancing is resumed. Meanwhile, the doctor and his assistants, move in and out among the warriors, placing a charm round the neck of each man to render him invulnerable. After this, if there is no immediate prospect of battle, all disperse to their homes to await orders; but if the enemy is near, the warriors are addressed by the chief, the various divisions are arranged, and selected commanders appointed. The army then advances against the enemy.

The commander-in-chief, before engaging the enemy, addresses the assembled warriors, informs them of the cause of the war, indicates the principal objective and requires of them implicit obedience to the generals and officers placed over them.

The Dedesi.

On the arrival of the Aba-Mbo, 1620, in the Wakkerstrom District of the Transvaal, and the north eastern point of Natal, the Ama-Xosa or Abe-Nguni are said to have been living at the Dedesi, said to be a small tributary of the upper Mzimvubu or St. John's river, which issues from one of the spurs of the Drankensberg mountains. They had settled down here before the Aba-Mbo came.

During the winter of 1926, the writer made a journey to the upper reaches of the Mzimvubu, with the express purpose of locating this stream, but none of the present residents of those parts could identify it. This is not to be wondered at. For about two hundred years after 1650, approximately from the time of its evacuation by the Ama-Xosa, this part of the country was uninhabited, and was within what was later called No-man's-land, which name it retained until about 1860, when the Griquas were transported from Griqualand West, took possession of it, and renamed it Griqualand East. For two centuries, then, the country was without a population: consequently on its re-population a new set of names was given to all the streams thereabouts, and these were mostly Griqua names. The locality is said to be near the spot where Langalibalele, the Hlubi chief, crossed the Drakensberg mountains when he endeavoured to escape the forces sent after him by the Government of Natal. This incident is referred to elsewhere. Other tribes who are said to have been neighbours of the Ama-Xosa in those parts are the Pondos, Pondomise, and others. These others were probably the first of all to occupy that country, namely the Ama-Tolo on the upper Ilovo. Beyond them, and further east, were their relatives, the Ama-Zizi, at the Mtshezi. Above the Zizis, on the upper reaches of the Mzinyati (Buffalo river), and partly on the Ndaka, were the Ama-Bele. Beyond the Beles were the Ama-Hlubi. The Hlubis were neighbours of the Beles on the upper Buffalo river; they also occupied both sides of that river from the point of contact with the Beles, right down to the junction with the Blood river. During the latter half of the 17th century the Xosas set out from the Dedesi for the mouth of the St. John's river. Having reached this point and crossed over to the west bank, they settled down. At that time, Xosa's name was beginning to supersede that of Mnguni, but some sections of the tribe that did not leave Natal at that time, and some of which remain there to the present day, still call themselves Abe-Nguni and not Ama-Xosa, though they acknowledge the relationship. The fact that from the time of the Aba-Mbo entry into Natal, tribes of Abe-Nguni allied themselves to them, and fought their battles, seems to indicate the probability of these two tribes having come down together from somewhere in the north, possibly from the Zambezi or even beyond it, and that the Abe-Nguni, whose arrival in Natal was apparently somewhat prior to that of the Aba-Mbo, constituted, as it were, the vanguard of that great southern movement. But, as the Xosas are not Aba-Mbo, I favour the opinion that they may have been of the Ama-Zimba tribe which moved southwards together with the Aba-Mbo; if not, then of some East Coast tribe that moved down simultaneously with them.

Alleged incorporation of Hottentots in the Xosa tribe.

The statement sometimes made that the Xosa tribe has a large admixture of Hottentot blood in its composition is not strictly correct.

One writer of repute (Theal, *Beginnings of S.A. History*, p. 298) writes about the "incorporation

of the Gonaquas (Hottentots) in the Xosa tribe "
as having "recently taken place" (see also
Willoughby, *Race Problems*, p. 37). No
general incorporation of Hottentots, however,
ever took place within the Xosa tribe. This is
corroborated by the Ama-Xosa themselves.
There is a semblance of reason, however, for the
statement, as it may refer to the admission by
courtesy of the Ama-Gqunukwebe tribe into that
of the Ama-Xosa. It is true only of several
clans of so-called Ama-Xosa that they bear
distinct traces of Hottentot blood. Their origin
is ascribed by the Ama-Xosa either to Hottentot
progenitors or to union with Hottentot women.
These clans are the Ama-Gqunukwebe, the Ama-
Sukwini, and the minor branch of the Gqunukwebes, the Ama-Nqarwane, but none of these clans
has any place in the genealogy of the Xosa tribe.
They are, one and all, regarded by the Xosas as
of alien origin, not of true Ama-Xosa stock.
The assertion, sometimes made, of wholesale
capture of Hottentot women and their absorption
by the Xosa tribe is not substantiated by tradition
or history. In the article on the Ama-Gqunukwebe in the following chapter, it will be noticed
that the origin of this tribe was due to Kwane,
a councillor of Tshiwo, chief of the Ama-Xosa,
who ruled about 1685, on the west side of the
Umtata river. To what clan of the Ama-Xosa,
if to any, Kwane belonged is not known, so far
as I can find out. Councillorship may be, and
frequently is, granted to members of tributary
tribes. Kwane had, as the official executioner,
secreted a number of persons who had been
" smelt out," and saved them from execution.

At the time, as far as can be ascertained, the Gqunuqwa tribe of Hottentots occupied the almost almost impenetrable country about the Mgazi and Mgazana rivers, west of the St. John's river, and extended well on to the east bank of the Umtata river. These Hottentots were neighbours to the Ama-Xosa. This piece of country occupied by the Hottentots provided a sanctuary to fugitives from " justice." Here it was, and among these Gqunuqwas, that Kwane hid condemned wizards. These fugitives, through inter-marriage with Hottentot women, produced the foundation of the Ama-Gqunukwebe tribe, as their name indicates. The tribe still bears traces of its Hottentot origin.

The Ama-Xosa are physically on a par with the very best of Bantu tribes, and their personal appearance is superior to that of any other of the South-Eastern tribes. Had there been a considerable mixture of Hottentot blood in their composition, it would have manifested itself very distinctly in their features and physical build, but such has not been the case. The Hottentots were regarded as inferior beings, and a proud people like the Ama-Xosa, who have ever been strict in the selection of their wives, would not, and did not, readily ally themselves with inferiors.

Clicks in Si-Xosa.

History informs us that the Hottentots for many centuries lived in close proximity to the sea coast. From about Walfish Bay on the west of the African continent, which was their extreme northern limit, they extended southward to the Orange river mouth, and followed that a considerable distance inland to the eastward. Then, from the river's mouth, they continued along the coast, doubled Cape point, and extended eastward as far as the coast of Pondoland. I can find no traces of Hottentot extension beyond the St. John's river. They seem never to have been far from the sea. There are no traces of them inland, except in the case of Hintsati's Hottentots who occupied the territory now known as Somerset East, amongst whom the fugitive Xosa chief, Gwali, sought refuge about 1710. Another case is that of the Hottentots of Hoho, a chieftainess whose headquarters were at Xaxazele hill, in the Stutterheim district. When, therefore, we consider that the first contact of Ama-Xosa and Hottentots took place when the former reached the sea coast near the St. John's river, where they met the Gqunuqwa and possibly Damaqwa Hottentots, approximately about 1650, and that the Ama-Xosa already possessed the clicks, some other source must be found for these alien accretions to the Bantu language. The x click occurs in the name of Xosa, who lived not later than 1535; the c click occurs in the name of Cira, great grandson of Xosa, about 1600, and also in that of Cedume, a Tembu chief who lived about 1575. The q click is contained in the name of Qwambi, minor son of Tshawe, circa 1600. We have then three clicks traceable along the line of Xosa and Tembu chiefs to a period antecedent to the contact of these tribes with the Hottentots. The Bushmen were not, as was the case with the

Hottentots, limited to a definite coastal area, but were spread over the greater part of central and southern Africa, occupying the uplands in preference to the sea-board.

Contact with Bushmen came much sooner to the Bantu than contact with the Hottentots. The language of the Eastern Bantu tribes, for some reason, seems to be more affected by these harsh sounds than is that of the more central and western tribes. The indications suggest the probability, we might almost say the certainty, that the Bantu derived these phonetic additions to their language from the Bushmen and not from the Hottentots.

Succession to Chieftainship.

It is no part of the writer's intention to deal with tribal customs in this book, but where it seems necessary to do so, they are touched upon lightly. As a corollary to the subject of the status of a chief's wives, it seems fitting to refer briefly here to the custom of succession to the chieftainship. To this is added a few remarks on the chief's exclusive privilege of a free gift of cattle (um-Qolo) on his accession. The status of the principal wife of a chief is usually declared (ukutetu a) during the chief's life-time. The court of councillors along with the chief, determines which of his wives is to be the principal, and mother of the heir. In the event of the principal wife failing to have male issue, a male child is transferred from the minor house attached to the great house (iqadi lendlu enkulu), and placed

G

in the care of the principal wife, who adopts the child as her own son, and heir in succession to his father.

The right of succession having once been declared, is rigidly observed by the tribe. Even if the declared heir is unsatisfactory, he is endured as long as possible. The declaration is seldom overturned by legal means, but the influence and power of a chief, once he becomes ruler, may be frittered away by his own unworthy conduct. He may be forgiven much, but never for meanness and want of open-handedness. Gifts to individuals who wait on the chief and give him personal service as well as frequent slaughter of cattle to entertain people of the tribe, are mighty influences in giving stability to the throne. Neglect of these is often the most potent cause of a chief losing his influence and the affection of his people, and though no public declaration may be made depriving him of his position, yet if the chief of the right-hand house, or indeed any other house, is above all things open-handed and ever ready to entertain, he gradually, designedly or not, gains over to his house many of the adherents of the principal chief. When this state of affairs becomes very obvious, it then becomes a matter for the arbitrament of the sword, and as by that time the numbers of the more popular chief have largely increased through defections from the reigning house, the issue is seldom in doubt. Thus a legally appointed and declared chief may be deprived of his position through his meanness, and an inferior arise and rule the tribe.

Um-Qolo.

It is true of Bantu chiefs, as it is of the rulers in civilised countries, that, "uneasy lies the head that wears a crown," even though, with the former, the crown is merely a metaphorical symbol. Bantu rule is by no means an absolute monarchy, for it is subject in certain measure to popular will. For instance, certain prerogatives of a chief may at times meet with tribal opposition, expressed through the chief's councillors. One of these exclusive privileges is the um-Qolo, or free gift of cattle to a chief. It is called a free gift, but it often partakes of the character of a levy.

When a young chief is installed as ruler, with the impetuosity of youth, he desires to signalise his accession by some noteworthy action. This usually takes the form of picking a quarrel with some other tribe, with a view to war. It is necessary that he carry the people with him in this, but as they are the principal sufferers, he does not always get the support he needs. Even with undisciplined armies, a certain measure of the "sinews of war" is required to keep the warriors fit for the coming struggle, and for a time to keep things going. Cattle represent the sinews—they are the tribal treasury on which the chief draws. Hence the value of the um-Qolo. The um-Qolo, however, does not always connote war, but the tribe is always anxious when it is announced, lest it should issue in some unlooked for and dangerous adventure on the chief's part. Immediately after the young chief's accession, word is sent throughout the tribe, that a free gift of cattle is required for the chief.

All families are expected to give a gift of at
at least a beast ; the more wealthy according to
their wealth. No definite number, however, is
demanded, and whatever is given will be accepted,
without question, nor will a detailed statement of
individual gifts be made. The cattle are brought
before the chief in herds of various size, and the
announcement is simply made in regard to each
lot, "these are from such-and-such a clan."

An assembly of the tribe takes place at headquarters on the day when the cattle are to be
presented. Numbers are then slaughtered for the
entertainment of the people, others are given as
gifts from the chief to certain sections of the
people, and a few to single individuals in the
chief's favour. The remainder are retained by
the chief for his own use, and to further any
project which he may have in mind. If the
project is an unnecessary war, the people are
most likely to veto the proposal, and the chief
has to bow to the will of his subjects.

CHAPTER X

The Ama-Xosa—Approximate Dates

When we consider the number of chiefs of a certain line, and we are fortunate enough to have a known date applicable to any point in that line, we may arrive at something like a fair approximation of the date when each chief ruled. Some authors make their calculation on the basis of 30 and some 40 years to a generation. The former number is used along with the eldest son, and the latter along with the heir. The difference is that those who use the latter number have in view the fact that the heir is seldom the first-born, and is often born many years after the eldest son.

Others again calculate on a basis of 25 years irrespective of any of the above considerations.

This last is the basis used everywhere throughout this book. It is remarkable, when working with known dates, how fairly accurate the calculations are under this system, but I believe it would be less reliable than the other methods mentioned for an extended period, that is, say, for a period of 25 or 30 chiefs. Fortunately, concerning the Ama-Xosa we have the authentic date 1686. This represents the year of the wreck of the *Stavenisse* on the Pondoland coast. The survivors in their effort to reach the Cape overland passed through several tribes, one of which, the Ama-Xosa, we are told, were under the rule of a chief, Togu. Here, then, we have a starting point from which to follow the genealogical line either backwards to the earliest known chief, or forward to historical times. It is almost certain that Togu at this date was near the end of his reign, probably within a couple of years of it. He died and was buried at the Qokama, on the east side of the Umtata river, in what is now the Ngqeleni District of Pondoland. Togu's father, Sikomo, who died and is buried at Cumgce (Buntingville) in Pondoland, probably ruled about 1660. Ngcwangu, Sikomo's father, is said to have been buried near the St. John's river; his rule would be about 1635. His father, Tshawe, would rule about 1610, and be preceded by his father, Nkosiyamntu, about 1585; his grand father, Malangana, about 1560; his great grandfather, Xosa, 1535; and Mnguni about 1510. The advent of the Aba-Mbo into Natal, in 1620, would coincide with the reign of Tshawe among the Xosas, or Aba-Nguni, the older name by which the tribe would then be known. It is peculiar how some names are handed down to posterity, without accompanying information as to the characters or achievements of the individuals named. Such is that of Xosa, of whom nothing is known but the name. It sometimes happens that a turning point in the history of a tribe, or a circumstance of importance affecting the tribe, not directly due to the reigning chief, brings his name into prominence, so that it lives, when the names of more worthy individuals sink into oblivion. A more useless chief than Gcaleka never ruled over the Xosas, and yet through the accident of the tribe being split up into prominent sections, his name is likely to live to the end of the Xosa tribal life. Xosa's son and heir was Malangana of whom nothing is known beyond the fact that his son and heir was Nkosiyamntu. A curious fact is that though the leading chiefs were polygamists by conviction and practice, yet concerning one after another we have no record of issue, save the heir. It may be that the explanation is to be found in the loss of all trace, or even the extinction of, the clans formed by a chief's sons. This, however, is difficult to credit.

Killing off the sons of a chief.

What seems a more probable explanation is that it may be due to the enforcement of a law which was common with Bantu tribes, in times of great tribal danger. I refer to the law requiring, in war time, the slaughter of all the sons of a ruling chief save the heir, who would, in any case, be a mere child when his father was at the height of his power. It will be readily understood that when a tribe was compelled to leave its birth-place, and seek a new home, it did so at the peril of its own existence. It had to clear a passage through tribes, sometimes very powerful, which opposed its advance. There were enemies on every hand, ready to take advantage of any sign of weakness, and to use to the full the opportunities presented by any internal disruptive forces. There was, therefore, but one way for a tribe to preserve its identity under war conditions, and that was, to cause all the sons of a chief to be put to death, one only excepted. There would then be less likelihood of a chief's order being disobeyed, and the tribe riven to pieces through the ambition of a son. This law held during war time, but as a state of war was a fairly normal one at certain times, and existed for long periods, it occasionally was carried over even into the peace times that followed, but in most cases when the necessity for its use was past the law was repealed. This law is quoted, not because there is any certainty of its being in operation during the times of which we write, but rather as a known law, which might, if in operation, account for a seeming dearth of sons and their clans. There is no record of Xosa or Malangana having a right-hand house, or a minor house (*i-qadi*), and yet the custom of naming the houses of the various principal wives of a chief must have been immemorial. Nkosiyamntu, the son of Malangana, is an exception in a long line of chiefs whose sons cannot be traced. He was probably a man of more refined instincts than his predecessors, for he preserved at least three of his sons. His heir of the Great House was Cira, and of the Right-Hand House, Jwara, and of the qadi or Minor House, Tshawe; at the same time, it would appear as if the rule regarding the slaughter of a chief's sons was still regarded by the tribe as part of the tribal customs, since Tshawe's mother had to flee with her young son to her own people, where he was brought up, and trained to a miliitary life.

Tshawe.

Amongst his mother's people Tshawe was a favourite on account of his courage, and when he attained manhood was granted, in accordance with custom, a considerable number of retainers, who formed the nucleus of a tribe. After a time, probably desiring to distinguish himself, and considering himself sufficiently strong, he collected all his people and set out ostensibly to visit his father Nkosiyamntu, though he probably knew that his father was dead. As he proceeded, numbers of broken men from other tribes joined him and he reached his father's place to find the heir, Cira, in power. For a time he settled down, no sufficient excuse presenting itself for the trial of strength which he contemplated with his elder brothers of the Great, and Right-Hand Houses. Wars, however, were easily started in those irresponsible days. A subject of dispute, however small, was enough to start a conflagration. On a certain day a general hunt was proclaimed, and all sections of the tribe joined in. Tshawe was successful in killing a blue-buck antelope, and, following the usual custom, the principal chief, Cira, required that a certain portion should be reserved for him. This Tshawe refused, on the plea that the animal was too small. Cira replied that it was old, as it had horns. But Tshawe's refusal was final, and the setting at naught of the great chief's demand could only be squared by an appeal to arms. Cira returned home in high dungeon, and immediately set about preparing his men for war, as the only way to wipe out the insult he had received. He asked for the assistance of Jwara, chief of the Right-Hand House, and this was given. Tshawe was not behind-hand with his preparations, and the battle was shortly joined. During the course of the fighting which was going against Tshawe, he sent to the neighbouring tribe of Pondomises for assistance, and the clan of the Ama-Rudulu of the Imi-Haga section was sent. These being fresh warriors, and in numbers considerable gave the advantage to Tshawe, who completely overthrew his elder brothers, and usurped the chieftainship of the Xosas. It is Tshawe's house, the minor house (iqadi) of Nkosiyamntu, which has ever since ruled among the Xosas. The greater part of the Ama-Rudulu remained with Tshawe and did not return to the Pondomise ruler, and have been incorporated into the Xosa tribe under the name of Ama-Ngwevu, They were evidently veterans, and in recounting their exploits during the battle, were spoken of by the Xosas as "these grey beards" —"i-Ngwevu," and the name stuck.

Cira ignobly elected to stay under the usurper's rule, but his authority was gone. Jwara, chief of the Right-hand House had, however, refused to "bow the knee" to his younger half-brother and went off with a certain following to seek a new home. He left behind him, nevertheless, his son and heir, Mazaleni, who remained with Tshawe, and acted as spokesman of the tribe. As blood "speaks," the Ama-Cira are still recognized as a royal clan, though they are now broken and hold no position of authority in the Xosa tribe.

Ixiba.

The question arises, "Where did Jwara go to, when he left to seek a new home?" The story is an old one dating as far back approximately as 1620 or thereabouts, and consequently, tradition has by now variations of the same story. It is said that Jwara went off to his mother's tribe the Ama-Bele, and was there received and given rank as chief, since he was known to be such. This can only be done in one way, if the claims of various heirs are not to be interfered with, that is, by placing such a man in the kraal of a deceased chief, whose sons have already been provided for. He then becomes what is known as *i-xiba Lakomkulu.* Kropp's definition of Ixiba is :—" A grandfather's place given by a father to an inferior son." Supposing a great chief dies and his heir occupies the throne, he becomes the paramount, but his father's other sons have probably all secured positions in the prospective houses in which they were born and none of these may be available. None is available, as a rule, in the grandfather's house for the reigning chief belonged to that house, and now has formed his own, leaving his father's house without a male representative. In order that the grandfather's house should not become extinct, the new chief appoints either an inferior son of his own if such is available, or, if not, an important individual, who even though he is not a chief may be put into that house and becomes an appendage of the reigning house, under the designation "ixiba la-komkulu"—"the grandfather's house attached to the reigning house."

Jwara is, therefore, supposed to have become " Ixiba " of the Ama-Bele ruling house of that day. The Ama-Jwara are very numerous among the Beles. The Xosa tradition is that Jwara went and settled among the Beles. The Bele tradition on the other hand reverses the order, and states that Jwara was one of their chiefs, but went over to the Xosas. Against this latter view, however, is the fact that in the genealogy of the Beles there is no chief called Jwara, whereas there is such among the Xosas.

It is not disputed that Jwara found a resting place among the Beles, for the Beles acknowledge the presence at one time among them of a chief, Jwara. To restate the position :—(1) There is no doubt that Jwara was Right-Hand son of Nkosiyamntu, chief of the Ama-Xosa. (2) There is no doubt as to his having left on Tshawe's accession, as he refused to come under the latter's authority. (3) Nor is there any doubt that he left a section of his tribe among the Ama-Xosa under his son, Mazaleni ; (4) nor that a large number of Jwaras are still to be found among the Ama-Bele.

The weight of opinion inclines to the belief that the Bele Jwaras are of the same stock as the Xosa Jwaras.

We have instances of the placing of individuals, even aliens who had no pretensions to chieftainship, in the *ixiba*, and whose descendants through that circumstance have become incorporated into the body of the tribe. There is the case of Jekwa, one of a few Europeans who were wrecked off the coast of Pondoland during the reign of Matayi, chief of the Ama-Tshomane. Puta, father of Matayi, died about 1735 or '40, and his son, Matayi, ruled in his stead. As the grandfather's house had no male representative alive, his son, Matayi, placed the European, Jekwa, in Puta's kraal to keep the house "alive." The descendants of Jekwa are the Abe-Lungu (Europeans), a clan living in Bomvanaland to-day, but according to Bantu reckoning, they are *ixiba* of the Ama-Tshomane. We find this custom of common occurrence among Native tribes. We might quote one other instance. Palo, great chief of the Ama-Xosa had an uncle, Tiso, a younger half-brother of his father, Tshiwo. Tiso died without issue, and Palo placed his own half-brother, Langa, of the iqadi (minor house) in Tiso's house, to raise up seed to the latter. Langa's descendants did not take Tiso's name, however, nor that of Langa, but that of his favourite ox, Mbalu, and the clan is called by the ox's name, Ama-Mbalu. The Ama-Mbalu are, therefore, Palo's ixiba.

Xosa Movement from the Drakensberg towards the Sea.

This movement took place somewhere about 1660-70, for that time corresponds with the reign of Sikomo, who is supposed to have led the Xosas from the Dedesi to the sea. He died at Ntumbankulu (T. B. Soga, *Intlalo ka-Xosa*, p. 18) in Pondoland. The graves of the chiefs who ruled previous to Sikomo are unrecorded, which leads to the belief that they died either at the Dedesi, under the Drakensberg, or in days anterior to the Xosa entry into northern Natal. About the time of this Xosa movement towards the coast, other tribes, such as a section of the Tembus and the Pondomise, moved in the same direction. The Pondos had already set the example, and were located east of the St. John's River. We find from the records of survivors from the Dutch ship *Stavenisse*, which was wrecked on the Pondoland coast in 1686 somewhere about the Mtamvuna River, that in their endeavour to reach the Cape overland they met with several tribes whom they

named. Though their spelling is archaic yet we
are able to recognise who these tribes were. A
few of the survivors reached Cape Town after
much suffering, and were brought before P. de
Galiardi, assistant to the Governor Simon van der
Stel. It was elicited from them that coming south
they encountered Embos (Aba-Mbo), Maponto-
mouse (Mampondomise), Maponte (Mampondo),
Matimbas (Ba-Tembu), Maligryghas (probably
Ama-Riligwa or Hottentots), and Magossebe (Ama-
Xosa). We meet here with an unusual suffix,
"-ebe," as the terminal to the name Magoss*ebe*.
This same suffix is found attached to the name
Gqunukw*ebe*. It is either some obsolete form of a
Bantu tribal suffix, or is of Hottentot extraction.
Students of the Hottentot language may be able
to state its significance. It is no longer in use in
connection with the name Ama-Xosa but still
exists with that of the Ama-Gqunukwebe. We
find it also in place names such as Nxukw*ebe*—
Healdtown, Mgqokwebe—Burnshill, and Qwebe-
qwebe—Main. The period embracing the names
of the Xosa chiefs, Mnguni, Xosa, Malangana,
Nkosiyamntu, Tshawe, Ngcwangu and Sikomo,
is singularly meagre in traditional information.
Little is known of the individuals mentioned, or
of their rule and the incidents of their reign.
Connection has been established in one or two
cases through research, by re-establishing identity
between tribes whose point of contact with their
progenitor was lost, e.g., such tribes as the Ama-
Qwambi whose origin is derived from Tshawe ;
the Ama-Nqabe, believed to have originated from
Sikomo ; and the Ama-Togu, a small tribe,
mainly to be found among the Pondomise, which

is Ngconde's "ixiba," that is, the issue of a minor son or younger brother of Ngconde who was placed in Togu's house after his decease.

Togu 1686 :—From the time of this chief down to modern times tradition is more generous. Togu's place in the list of chiefs will be seen in the Ama-Xosa table. We might, however, set forth here the table of an offshoot, or as it is called " ixiba," from him thus :—

Togu	("ixiba")	
Ngconde	Tshantshalaza	(Right Hand)
—	Mguzulo	Nonyoba
—		Jima
	Kolofile	Nontshiyi
	Mqengqwa	Lizo
	Pitshi	Gimbela
		Matwebu.

The *Stavenisse* survivors tell us that they received much kindness from Togu, chief of the Ama-Xosa (Gossibe). This information fixes definitely for us a date when Togu ruled, but research reveals the fact that the date 1686 coincides with the last years of his reign. After this time, events may be assigned dates with a certain measure of assurance. As we have said, Togu is buried at the Qokoma, Ngqeleni District, Pondoland, about 20 miles inland from the sea, and it must have been hereabouts that the *Stavenisse* people met him. His son, *Ngconde*, 1695, was still a young man when he succeeded his father. His grave is still further inland, namely at Buntingville or Cumgce, the distance from which place to the town of Umtata is probably about 15 miles. There are two known sons of Togu, his great son and heir, Ngconde, and a minor son, Ziko. Ziko is sometimes called by the "isibongo" (praise name) of Gando-we-Ntshaba. This latter praise name is also erroneously given to Ngconde who was Ziko's half-brother and successor to the chieftainship on Togu's death. Ziko's clan is called the Ama-Kwayi. This needs explanation. The Ama-Xosa abhorred anything in the nature of incest, the marriage of blood-relations coming under that category. It is said that Tshiwo, heir and successor to Ngconde, took a great fancy to one of Ziko's daughters. She would be, presumably, a half-cousin according to European notions; but according to Xosa ideas she was Tshiwo's sister. In spite of the natural prejudice against such unions, Tshiwo married the girl, and as a consequence Ziko's clan were reduced to commoners. This reduction of a royal clan to commoners was a Xosa legal artifice to square the law and save the reputation of a chief, who according to Bantu notions could do no wrong. This lowering of the status of a clan is call *uku-kwaya* —to "degrade." Ziko's clan, therefore, became known as the Ama-Kwayi. *Ngconde's* principal son and heir was Tshiwo; his right-hand son being Mdange who had a younger brother by the same mother called Jemose. Ngconde's son of the Left-Hand (*ikohlo*) House was Ntinde, father of the Ama-Ntinde clan, which has resided in the neighbourhood of King William's Town for the last one hundred years. Ngconde's minor house (iqade) had two sons, Ngwema who proved unsatisfactory and was displaced by his younger brother, Hleke.   His clan is called the Ama-Hleke, and resides mainly about Pirie Mission some miles west of King William's Town.

Tshiwo, Ngconde's heir, became chief at an early age.   His eldest son, not the heir, but head of the Right-Hand House was Gwali, of infamous memory.   Palo was Tshiwo's heir, but was born after his father's death in 1702 and was during his minority placed in the care of his uncle, Mdange.   An attempt was made by Gwali to usurp the heir's place as chief of the Ama-Xosa, but Mdange and Palo's councillors frustrated the plot.   In the ensuing fighting in an endeavour to assert his claim Gwali was badly beaten, together with his uncle of the Left-Hand House, Ntinde who had joined him.   In consequence both fled with their people.   The fighting took place between the Umtata and Bashee Rivers.   The fleeing clans did not settle down until they reached Nojoli, Somerset East.   Besides Palo, the heir, and Gwali of the Right-Hand House, Tshiwo's son of the Minor House (iqade) was Tiso.   This son died without issue, and in time Palo placed Langa, his own son and head of his minor house in Tiso's house.   Langa had sons and was able to raise a clan for this house, which became known as the Ama-Mbalu, after the name of Tiso's favourite dancing ox.   The clan, therefore, did not take either the name of Tiso or that of Langa, but of the favourite ox, Mbalu, which was regarded with so much veneration that it was recognized as occupying the place of a son to the dead chief.

H

The Ama-Xosa under Tshiwo never settled west of the Bashee, but occupied the country between the Umtata and Bashee Rivers. Tshiwo's grave is at the Ngcwanguba, a few miles west or south of the Umtata River. He died while away from home at a hunt, but his body was brought back and buried at his kraal. A forest of considerable size and a land-mark, called the Ngewanguba forest, has grown up around the grave. The original shrubs (imi-lenya) growing on the grave multiplied, through the protection afforded to a chief's grave, until a respectable forest is the result.

Ama-Ndluntsha—" The Adherents of the new House."

Tshiwo had a number of wives, and consequently an equal number of royal kraals, one to each wife. As we have seen, there are five principal kraals, the Great House, the Right-hand House, the Minor House attached to the Great House, the Minor house attached to the Right-Hand House, and the Left-Hand House. All others after these are simply called minor houses (Ama-qadi—"supports"). It is related that the last wife to be married by Tshiwo was Noqazo. As all available names declaring the status of Tshiwo's houses had already been allotted, there was no name for Noqazo's house. It was simple designated the New House (Kwa-Nluntsha). Noqazo had no male issue, but, contrary to the usual custom, she was waited on and given personal service as if a chief. Broken clans, especially those whose line of chiefs had died out, or whose

condition had changed from the royal clans to
cómmoners, gave in their adherence to her, and
are called in consequence the adherents of the
New House (Ama-Ndluntsha). The principal of
these are the Ama-Cira, whose position was
usurped by Tshawe; the Ama-Bamba, the Ama-
Nkabane, and others. Though Noqazo died
about the middle of the eighteenth century, these
clans still keep up the pretence of a royal court.
At stated times a curious ceremony is observed
by them. A general meeting of the Ama-Ndluntsha is summoned by the Queen's Councillor,
though she is no longer in the flesh. The meeting takes place in a large hut, and to keep up the
pretence of the Queen's presence, one of the
pillars of the hut is selected. A woman's hand-
kerchief is twisted round the pillar at about the
height of a woman's head from the ground.
Below this is wound a breast covering "incebeta"
adorned with beads, and below this again a
woman's leather skirt. The Councillor then
announces that her royal highness has called this
meeting together in order to lay before it the
following matters. Each announcement is preceded by the words, "Iti inkosi!"—"the chief
say," and the item of information follows. This
particular custom is still observed, and has been
for the past one hundred and seventy years. The
Councillor is chosen sometimes from one clan,
at other times from one of the others. At present the Ama-Ndluntsha are split up into two
sections, each with a Councillor. One is in the
Willowvale district under the charge of Boza of the
Ama-Bamba, and the other is in Bomvanaland at

the Mngazana under Msasa, son of Mampangashe of the Ama-Nkabane.

Ama-Gqunukwebe.

In Tshiwo's time the Ama-Xosa had as neighbours the Gqunuqwa clan of Hottentots, some say the Damaqwa also. These tribes though neighbours were independent of each other, but lived on terms of friendship. It should be remembered that the Ama-Xosa under Tshiwo occupied the country between the Umtata and some of the outposts reaching as far west as the Bashee, but none crossing over the latter. It was only during the reign of Tshiwo's son Palo, that the Bashee was crossed. The country, then, in occupation during Tshiwo's time was the birthplace of the Ama-Gqunukwebe, not as some assert the district west of King William's Town. The birth of the tribe is variously related, but though the stories differ in details the general facts are correct, namely that this tribe took its rise in Tshiwo's time. That would be, to assign a date, about 1700 A.D. The country occupied by the Gqunuqwa (Gonaqwa) Hottentots was that inaccessible and difficult district, the Mngazi, just west of the St. John's River, and near the coast.

One story states that a councillor of Tshiwo's, named Kwane, was also what might be termed Lord High Executioner. Wizards, after they had been smelt out and convicted, were handed over to him for execution. Instead, however, of carrying out his orders to the letter, he was in the habit of confiscating on behalf of the chief all their cattle, but sparing their lives and secreting their persons. It is evident that the inaccessible country of the Gqunuqwas provided a suitable sanctuary. Here from time to time he settled these victims of superstition, together with their families, and after a number of years working on these lines had accumulated a formidable fighting force. It happened that on one occasion Tshiwo was engaged in one of the many internecine conflicts, and sorely needed help. At the critical period Kwane appeared with a strong force in support of his chief. When the battle was over he presented his men to the chief, at the same time informing him that these warriors were the wizards and their sons, whom Tshiwo had handed over to Kwane for execution, but that instead of putting them to death he had saved their lives for such an emergency. Tshiwo commended his wisdom and there and then appointed Kwane as chief over them. During their stay among the Gqunuqwas many of the males married Hottentot women, and it was a very mixed race that came to Tshiwo's assistance. These are the people who formed the Ama-Gqunukwebe tribe, and to this day are spoken of by the Ama-Xosa as Ama-Lawu or Hottentots. On account of its peculiar origin, while allowed to live alongside of, and on friendly terms with, the Xosa tribe, the Ama-Gqunukwebe tribe had always been regarded as of alien origin. Nor has it ever had a place assigned to it within the body of the Xosa tribe.

On account of the intricate nature of the country about the Mgazi, already referred to, Tshaka's forces in a raid on the Pondos could make no impression on them, and were compelled

to return to Natal leaving the Pondos uncon-
quered. The name Gqunukwebe to my mind
appears to be derived from that of the Hottentot
tribe, Gqunuqwas (Gonaquas). Another version
of the origin of this tribe is to be found in a book
by Cowper Rose, an officer of Engineers, who
went through some of the fighting which occurred
in the neutral territory between the Fish River
and the Keiskama. The book was published in
1829. We would quote his own words, the
narrative being doubtless taken down from the
lips of some old Xosa historian. He says:—
" In the reign of Tshiwo . . . . the Gqunukwebe
ancestor, Quaani (Kwane) was a great soldier and
favourite, and to him and one other the execution
of the chief's orders was intrusted; these orders
were often tyrannical—destruction of whole
kraals, the seizing of cattle, and the massacre of
their wretched owners,—and Kwane evaded
them, by sending some of the cattle to the chief,
and concealing the families in a far distant part
of the country, remote and shut in by mountains.
This had continued for some years when suspicion
arose, and the other captain asked him whether
he always obeyed the commands of his chief; and
on finding that he did not, they quarrelled and
Kwane left the kraal of Tshiwo, and told his
enemy that he went to gather his people together.
He was absent for many days, when one night
Tshiwo's favourite queen was surprised by his
entering her hut, and giving her the following
instructions: " At the dawn of day go to
Tshiwo's, and then look to the hills, and you
will see my warriors." The queen followed his
instructions, and as she looked towards the hill,

she exclaimed, "What do I see, is it mimosa bushes? they grew not there yesterday!" She looked again, and cried out that they were armed men come to surprise them, and Tshiwo was sorely disheartened. Then Kwane came down with a hundred young men, with their shields and assegais, and their war plumes, and Kwane and his warriors kneeled before the chief, and laid their arms at his feet, and then followed the aged men, and then aged women and the children and cattle, and Kwane said to Tshiwo, "These are the people you ordered me to destroy, behold, I have saved them." And Tshiwo took unto himself a portion of the people and of the cattle, and gave the remainder to Kwane, and bestowed on him a territory on the sea-coast of 70 miles in length (?), and 12 miles in breadth, and said unto him, "I adopt you as a son, you are now of the Ama-Tshawe (clan of the Chief), and should a son of mine raise his assegai against you, raise yours against him, for you are his equal" (*Four Years in Southern Africa,*" p. 148—50).

The Ama-Gqunukwebe tribe, or clan as it then must have been, was one of the first to move west during Palo's time, and probably accompanied the Ama-Gwali and Ama-Ntinde in their flight after the former's abortive attempt to usurp the chieftainship.

CHAPTER XI

The Ama-Xosa—Chief Palo

According to custom among the Ama-Xosa, when a ruling chief dies, leaving an heir who is an infant or a minor, as was the case with Palo, the child was usually placed in charge of an uncle. This custom was observed in this instance, Mdange being appointed regent and guardian of the infant heir. Mdange was half-brother of Tshiwo, Palo's father, and was, moreover, the head of the Right-Hand House of his father, Ngconde. He was the proper person, therefore, to have charge of the infant, and to safeguard the interests and the training of the child so as to fit him for the onerous duties which in time, as chief, he would have to assume.

Palo was born in 1702, the year in which his father died. The position of an infant heir, "most ignorant of what he's most assured," is one of considerable anxiety. Oppression and ill-fortune go hand-in-hand with such a child. These conditions develop in some natures a spirit of inflexible harshness and cruelty, as was the case with Tshaka. They grow up Ishmaelites, their hands against all men, and all men's hands against them ; refusing to listen to reason once the bonds of control are removed from them, because the finer instincts have been crushed and withered by the harshness of their upbringing. And yet in others these adverse circumstances, where they touch finer natures who have the sympathy and support of wise guardians and generous instructors, often

Ama-Nqabe nama-Gcina.

Nqabe

Bedla

Ndimande

Rt H.

Mtshoni

Rt.H

Ama-Ninwayo

Ninwayo

Mpulana — Ama-Gcina — Gcina — Gwangwayo

Lungxoko — Tyópo — Xwarube

Left H. — *Rt.H.*

Kånjwa — Mbingwa — Mpangele

Danò — Gomatana — Gecelo

Tabåse — Qila — Malangeni

Rt.H — Mbangwa

Gayiya — Xwangu — Vezi

Mazolisa — Nqwili — Mjanyelwa

Sandile — Langa

Sitùnzi — Mgqunywa

Mrazuli

J. H. SOGA.

enhance the beauty of the inner nature, and the early loss of a parent is not so marked in its effects.

From his earliest years Palo gave evidence of possessing the elements of a fine character and temperament, which was fostered and confirmed by the wise guidance of his father's councillors. Consequently, he grew in favour with the Xosa tribe, as the years advanced. But, notwithstanding, an effort was made to wrest his birth-right from him, 'ere he came to the throne. Gwali, the first-born, but not the heir, of Tshiwo, who was the senior by a number of years to Palo, sought to usurp the chieftainship. He was head of the Right-Hand House, but had designs of securing a still higher position. This becoming evident, war threatened, and the greater part of the tribe determined to uphold Palo's rights. Gwali together with Ntinde, head of the Ama-Ntinde, collected their forces with a view to settling the matter with the assegai, but before the battle was joined they realized that their prospects of success were hopeless, and that only one course was open to them—flight. Their evil design could not be overlooked : it was unpardonable.

At this time, the Ama-Xosa were occupying the country between the St. John's river, where they had outposts, and the Bashee, their extreme western limit. With no clear notions of their destination, but with the sole object of placing distance between themselves and Palo's forces, the Ama-Gwali and Ama-Ntinde together with the newly organised Ama-Gqunukwebe clan, crossed the Bashee in flight—to the south-west. In succession they crossed the Kei, the Buffalo and the Keiskama, in forced marches, and finally the Fish River where Somerset East now stands. Here they thought to settle down.

The regent, Mdange, about 1715 marshalled Palo's forces, and selected a special punitive body of warriors and followed on the trail of the fugitives. He came into contact with the Ama-Gwali at Somerset East, where they were under the protection of Hottentots. The Hottentot chief, Hintsati, prepared to do battle on behalf of Gwali. Mdange having crossed to the west bank of the Fish River immediately attacked the combined forces. The Hottentots fought well, but the Ama-Xosa had not come thus far to retreat with their task unfulfilled. They, therefore, pressed the attack and finally overcame the Hottentots and Ama-Gwali. In this battle, Hintsati, the Hottentot chief was killed, and large numbers of his tribe's cattle were seized. Gwali escaped, however, and fled still further south. It would appear that when the fugitive Ama-Ntinde crossed the Buffalo they separated from Gwali and settled between that river and the Keiskama, with the Ama-Gqunukwebe along the coast below them. They, in consequence, were out of the direct line of the march of Mdange's force and escaped being involved in the battle. Having accomplished its object, Mdange's force returned homewards, but the Hottentots still had some fight left in them, and before Mdange reached the Keiskama River, they were upon him, but were beaten off. Nevertheless the Hottentots continued to harass the Ama-Xosa and attacked the latter, as they forded the Keiskama, like a hive of bees. They met with little success until Debe Nek was reached. Here they managed to recapture some of their cattle, but leaving the majority in the hands of the Ama-Xosa, then retired home.

Mdange had taken a fancy to the country traversed by him, so that, at a later period, he got leave from Palo to settle his section of the tribe therein. In 1736 (Theal, vol. III., p. 102) Palo, now in full control of the Xosa tribe, was stationed at the Tongwane, a small stream east of the Toleni stream, which flows into the Kei River. The land bordering the Kei here is on both sides of that great river less precipitous than elsewhere, for a considerable distance either upwards or downwards. Here the passage of the river was comparatively easy, and this was, in consequence, in those days the main crossing for hunting parties of Europeans with their wagons. It would seem that at Palo's kraal at the Tongwane occurred the unfortunate attack by the Xosas on the party of Hubner, the hunter. It is not necessary to enlarge upon this incident, as it has been fully related by historians, but one or two points might be noted. From the movements of Hubner's party, it will be realized how far north-eastwards hunting and other expeditions penetrated with impunity into native territory. This party went as far as Mtata River, passing through tribes of Tembus, Hottentots and Xosas. On this occasion, however, something happened which has never been stated, namely, what caused the attack. It is also the first occasion we know of when blood was spilt through the meeting of white and black in South Africa.

Another point of interest is that Hubner's
expedition met with three Europeans, Thomas
Miller, Henry Clark and William Bilyert, survivors
from some nameless wreck which was wrecked
on the Pondoland coast, who were living amongst
the Natives, and showed no inclination to be
rescued. But to return to Palo. It has been
mentioned that he was beloved by his people,
and in all tribal matters gave the utmost respect
to the opinions of his councillors; but a time
came when his father's councillors to whom he
adhered, died out and he was left with younger
men less wise, and of less reliability perhaps. In
any case, a disruption of the tribe took place
during his reign. His heir, Gcaleka, when he
came of age, was instigated by his young
councillors to claim control of the tribe, although
his father, Palo, was still in the vigour of body
and mind. Rarabe, the Right-Hand son of Palo
and his father's favourite, opposed the heir's
pretentions, and war followed. It would seem
that the issue was unfavourable to Gcaleka, for
though his section of the tribe was the more
numerous, Rarabe was his superior in courage
and strategy. Victorious as he was, Rarabe
perceived that the future condition of the tribe
would be one of constant quarrelling and unrest
and possibly destructive warfare. He, therefore,
decided to cross the Kei, and put that river
between himself and Gcaleka. Palo decided to
follow the fortunes of his Right-Hand son, and
crossed the Kei with him in search of a new
home. Rarabe formed a number of royal kraals
one of which was at the Izeli near King William's
Town. After this, Palo was not much in evidence

and did not take any further outstanding part in the control of the Xosa tribe. He died in 1775 at the Tongwane, his old headquarters before the division of the tribe, to which place he appears to have gone in his old age. He was at his death aged about 73 years. So he passed to the land of the spirits of his fathers.

Langa.

This chief was the head of one of Palo's minor houses. When Tiso, a younger half-brother of Palo died, Langa was installed in his house. He was an unusually active man, a great hunter of the larger wild animals, elephants, lions and so forth; a man of restless spirit and unbounded courage. These characteristics commended themselves to the more ardent spirits among the young men, and numbers drew to him, young men of kindred spirit, ready to engage in any enterprise that called for courage and strength. A man of Langa's stamp never lacks a following, and it is generally composed of the most vigorous elements of the tribe. Langa's descendants did not take the name of Tiso, or that of Langa as the clan name, but that of Tiso's favourite ox named Mbalu, hence that clan is called the Ama-Mbalu. Subsequent to the flight of the Ama-Gwali and Ama-Ntinde, Langa resided with his brother Palo's tribe, the Ama-Xosa, in the country between the Umtata River and the Bashee, then the spirit of adventure decided him to strike out for himself. Somewhere about 1740, while in the prime of manhood he collected his followers and followed in the footsteps of the Ama-Gwali,

Ntinde, Gqunukwebe, and the Imi-Dange, who some years before had also gone south-west, and settled on the Fish River. These clans of the Ama-Xosa, it should be noted, were settled on the Fish River, some as early as 1703, and were the first tribes met with by Dirk Marx, in 1755, who had been sent by Governor Ryk Tulbagh in search of possible survivors from vessels wrecked on the east coast. These, moreover, were the independent Xosa tribes that came into conflict with the Europeans. They were pre-Gcaleka and pre-Rarabe. Not until 1818, or one hundred and fifteen years later, did the Gaika or Ndlambe tribes, to whom the former paid no allegiance, fight Europeans.

Langa and his Ma-Mbalu got mixed up with the conflicts at the Fish River boundary. It would have been too much for this ardent spirit to sit still while others were enjoying themselves. Even after he had passed the "allotted span," he was to be found on the war trail. When Langa was about 75 years old, that is in 1779, he crossed the Fish River, which had been declared the boundary between the two races, together with the Imi-Dange under Mahote. The actual cause for this inroad is obscure, for, as Theal observes, there was much difference of opinion on the subject. Some asserted that a certain William Prinsloo of the Boschberg, on finding a man of the Imi-Dange stealing a sheep of his, not only shot the thief, but raided the cattle of the Imi-Dange in order to reimburse himself. Others assert, it was the son of this man, Marthinus, who, with a commando, disregarded the proclamation of the Governor, which stated that no

European was to cross the boundary into Native territory; that this commando attacked the Ama-Rarabe, killing one of their number. Others again, lay the blame on Kobe, a son of Titi of the Ama-Gwali, who was one of those who had agreed to recognise the Fish River as the boundary, and yet crossed over into Colonial territory and was hustled and severely handled beyond what the offence merited. When Langa saw the preparations of the whites for war, he made his peace with them. Ten years later, however, 1789, the old warrior, then 85 years old, sharpened his assegai and again crossed the boundary into Colonial territory. Whatever matter was in dispute, was again on this occasion settled amicably. This was Langa's last appearance as a warrior. He died, being well on for ninety years of age.

CHAPTER XII

The Ama-Xosa—Chief Rarabe, 1722-1787

Rarabe, son of the Right-Hand House of Palo, was born about the year 1722 and died in 1787, A.D., being about 65 years old. By birth, he was senior to Gcaleka and others by several years. He early exhibited a strong personality, being a man of public weight, wisdom, and superior courage. When Gcaleka reached young manhood Rarabe was already in his prime. For common-sense and physical courage he was far and away the superior of Gcaleka. Although his father had given him control of the Right-Hand House, he maintained a filial respect for his father's authority. Thus he lived on excellent terms with Palo, by whom he was greatly beloved, and under their rule the people prospered. But when Gcaleka emerged into manhood after the customary rites of circumcision, signs of restlessness and division became apparent in the tribe. This youthful aspirant to power considered himself quite capable of controlling the Great House, although Palo was still physically fit. This led to bickerings and faction fights which brought the assegai into play, resulting in the permanent division of the Xosa nation. In these disturbances Rarabe supported his father's cause, and although Gcaleka had the larger following of tribesmen he was beaten by Rarabe. Nevertheless, his position as heir-apparent was not disturbed, but the social relations of the tribe under these conditions were seriously altered. It, therefore, became clear to Rarabe

that a state of hostility, which might at any time
lead to affrays and the use of the assegai, was
intolerable.   He, therefore, turned his eyes toward
the West, or in other words, across the Great Kei
River, and prepared his section of the tribe to
remove to a new country, his father Palo being in
favour of this step. Having made all arrangements,   he burnt his huts and moved in the
direction of the Lwalwa Drift on the Butterworth
River, and crossing this, he made for the Buffalo
Drift in the Kei.   Arriving here, he was at once
intercepted by the Hottentots who occupied the
country on the further bank, and who were
determined   to prevent the Ama-Rarabe   from
crossing into their country. The opposing forces
met at the drift, and the Ama-Rarabe found it
difficult to contend with two enemies in the shape
of the current of water and of the assegais of those
who defended the opposite shore.   The Kei was
thus dyed red with the blood of the heroes who
found in it a watery grave, but in spite of this
the passage was pressed by the Chief Rarabe who
urged on his men to valiant deeds.   Eventually,
through his resolute example the vanguard touched
ground, and rallying together they fell upon
the enemy with their assegais and as reinforcements continued to arrive, forced the passage.
The whole army having now crossed, the
Hottentots were driven back, and their chief was
killed, upon which they scattered and fled
retreating in the direction of their stronghold at
the Xaxazele.

Having effected the crossing of the families and
stock of the tribe, Rarabe determined to follow up
the Hottentots, not because he was anxious for

J

further bloodshed, but as a matter of precaution against further reprisals. His army marched toward Xaxazele and, arriving there, he opened communication with the Hottentot Queen, Hoho, whose husband was slain at the Kei Drift. An amicable arrangement was concluded, by which all the rights to that part of the country lying between the Keiskama and Buffalo Rivers were granted to Rarabe by purchase, including large tracts of forest lands on the Amatole Mountains, and the conspicuous hill called Hoho between Middledrift and King William's Town. It is said that Rarabe's authority was felt as far as the Great Fish River, although the tribes of the Ama-Gwali, Ama-Ntinde, Ama-Mbalu, Imi-Dange and Ama-Gqunukwebe who had previously occupied the country, refused to submit to the rule of the Ama-Rarabe, because they had assumed their own independence for so many years that extraneous control would be irksome to them, and, moreover, they had migrated before the causes which divided the principal Houses of Palo had occurred. These are the tribes which were at constant feud with the Europeans. Certainly, they were not under the authority of the Right-Hand House, rather should they be included under the Great House, but they, for the time, were not concerned about that. About the year 1779, when the Imi-Dange, the Ama-Mbalu and other lesser tribes which crossed the Great Fish River, came into conflict with the whites, Rarabe sent word to the Boers dissociating himself from these disturbances, and declared himself neutral and stating that these sections were acting independently of his authority. He had no quarrel with the whites and desired none.   It was different, however, with the tribes with whom he was at war.   Rarabe had married a Tembu woman, a daughter of Ndungwana, belonging to a lesser house of Nxego, eldest son of Bomoyi.   Tembuland was then under the Chief Ndaba, who was a hasty and irritable man, and never satisfied except when fomenting trouble, although he was not renowned for personal courage.

Rarabe was solicited by the Ama-Ndungwana to assist them in a quarrel between them and Ndaba, in which blood had already been shed. The son of Palo was quite willing, and as a result of his intervention Ndaba was defeated.   He thus became the bitter enemy of Ndaba, all of whose cattle had been seized by Rarabe.   Sometime after this trouble Ndaba visited Rarabe to make peace with him.   Rarabe was then living westward of the Buffalo River.   But Ndaba delayed and tarried under the protection of Gcaleka who lived at the Izeli near King William's Town.

By peaceful overtures Rarabe endeavoured to induce him to cross over to his side of the river, and he restored some of the cattle he had seized from Ndaba, to provide for his sustenance.   But instead of reciprocating these advances Ndaba was seized with vague alarm and fled back to his own country, regarding Rarabe henceforth as a pronounced enemy.

The motives which actuated Ndaba are obscure. Whether or not he sought a cause for revenge is not clear, but he solicited in marriage a daughter of Rarabe, and as dowry sent a miserable hundred head of cattle, showing in this way his contempt for the Xosa chieftain.

Such an insult could not be lightly borne by Rarabe, whose remedy for such wounds was the assegai. He at once entered Tembuland to remove the affront and forthwith fell upon Ndaba, scattering his tribe and seizing all his cattle. But at the affair of the Ngxogi on the Xuka River, Rarabe was struck by an assegai, fatally wounded, and died.

This was about the year 1787 when he was sixty years of age. He left the tribe united, and in good order, with its laws and customs an honoured tradition, and Gaika, his grandson, when he came to the Chieftainship, found the Ama-Rarabe firmly established as a legacy from his grandfather.

He had steadily maintained peaceful relations with the Europeans down to his death, and the First Kafir War, so-called by the whites, was with the Ama-Gwali, Ama-Ntinde and Imi-Dange, and those lesser tribes which as we have already seen, were semi-independent, and were not amenable to the laws or authority of Rarabe. And thus Rarabe died in the affair at Ngxogi with Ndaba's Tembus.

His grave is pointed out by some at the Amabele near Emgwali, close to Dohne. The year 1787 marks the date of his death.

The First Kafir War with Europeans (1779).

Those tribes which had broken away from the main body of Xosas after the death of Tshiwo traversed the country till they arrived at the Great Fish River. These were the Ama-Gwali of the Right-Hand of Tshiwo; the Ama-Ntinde of the Left-Hand of Togu; the Ama-Mbalu representatives of the Minor House of Tiso, and the Imi-Dange of the Right-Hand of Ngconde. At the Fish River they encountered the whites in 1757, and they were already established there when the Boers came up from the Cape. At that period the country was inhabited by the Hottentots, who were pushed aside by these two races, until the name of Hottentot was submerged. Rarabe followed after a long interval of time, and abode in a part of the country purchased from Hoho.

Although these tribes showed a formal recognition of Rarabe's superior chieftainship, they were not under his laws. When, however, they got into difficulties with the whites, they were wont to describe themselves as people of Rarabe, but this was only lip-loyalty.

South of the Fish River the Boers were in occupation, under Governor van Plettenberg. They lived principally as stock-owners, and their herds of sleek cattle excited the Xosas' cupidity, so much that they could not refrain from raiding them. The Boers accused the Xosas of thieving, while the Xosas retaliated by likewise accusing the Dutch of a similar predilection for stock grabbing. And so it went on.

The real origin of these conflicts has never been explained. But there is a story to the effect that a certain Boer, named Marthinus Prinsloo, crossed the Fish River and entered Kafirland in spite of the law against such intrusion. He was accompanied by a party professedly bent on purchasing cattle. A dispute arose between them and the people of Chief Rarabe's kraal, in which one of the tribe was killed. (Theal, *Vol. iii.*, p. 243). Another story says that Kobe, a son of Titi, Chief of the Ama-Gwali, who was one of those who was a party to the Fish River being recognised as the boundary between them and the Boers, crossed over on a certain occasion to the Boer side, and was at once forcibly ejected in a manner which was altogether unreasonable in its harshness. (The latter would appear to be the more reliable account, for Rarabe never was at war with the whites; moreover these encounters were common with those semi-independent tribes already referred to above). Whereupon the Ama-Ggwali under Titi flew to arms. They were at once joined by the Ama-Ntinde under Ciko, son of Mbange, their Chief; similarly the Ama-Mbalu under their Chief, Langa, a courageous old warrior, son of Palo; and the Imi-Dange under Mahote, son of Mdange. The spark was alight; the war-cry resounding on all sides.

The Boers raised two Commandoes under Joshua Joubert and Pieter Ferreira. They met the Imi-Dange, and Mahote was driven back, although he did not at once retire to his own side of the boundary. Upon this the Boers sought to discuss terms of peace. The Chief Langa consented, and retired with the Ama-Mbalu to his side of the line. The other tribe, however, refused to accept terms of peace, and hostilities were renewed; the Hottentots on this occasion assisting the Dutch.

After two months of this warfare the Ama-Ntinde, Ama-Gwali, together with the Imi-Dange were defeated, and driven over to their own side of the river. Messengers were dispatched from both contending parties, and the boundary question was raised afresh. The result of the conference was that the Fish River was declared to be the agreed boundary, and no doubts were to be entertained about it in future. The agreement was put in writing, but it soon became apparent that it would be honoured more in the breach than the observance.

This war ended in the winter of 1781.

The Second Kafir War (1789).

After a peace which was maintained for eight years, the Second Kafir War broke out. Rarabe was already dead some two years when it began, and the House of Rarabe was controlled by the regent, Ndlambe. The Dutch occupied the Cape under their Governor Cornelius Van der Graff. This war, like the previous one, was with those lesser tribes who had been engaged in the first war, except that, on this occasion they were assisted by the Ama-Gqunukwebe.

All alike were hostile to Ndlambe, being altogether opposed to him, and seeking to maintain their tribal independence under their own chiefs. In the war of 1757, the chief Langa had been the first to come to terms of peace with the Boers, but on this occasion was the first to begin the war. This son of Palo, who was renowned for his prowess in the hunting field against wild beasts such as the elephant, the buffalo, and the stronger antelopes, was more courageous and determined than most, and although he was now about 77 years of age, he felt himself equal to the occasion.   He was assisted by those semi-independent tribes already mentioned, among whom were the Ama-Gwali, whose chief Kobe had on a former occasion been so unmercifully treated as to precipitate the first war.

The Dutch Government at the Cape was averse to assisting the Boers with men and material, believing that the Boers on the boundary were themselves responsible for the unsettled state of affairs.   Thus, the main brunt of this war was borne by the Boers who lived adjacent to the border.   On the approach of the armies of the Ama-Mbalu and Ama-Gqunukwebe, the leaders of the Boers called a truce and endeavoured to bring the Chiefs to a council, in order to discuss and, if possible, remove the causes of the recurring boundary disputes.

The council was agreed to, but the leading chiefs of the Xosa did not attend in person.   At this conference the question put forward by the Boers was: "Why did the Ama-Mbalu and Ama-Gqunukwebe cross the Fish River which was the settled boundary, and seize Boer stock, and murder Boer poeple?"   To which the Xosas replied, that the territory which they had occupied between the Fish River and the Kowie was theirs by right of purchase, having been bought from one Ruiter, a Hottentot Chief who was then in possession, for which reason they refused to surrender their right to it.

The Boer Commissioner, Wagener, urged the Xosas to renounce their claim to the territory, promising to restore the purchase price.   This offer was refused and negotiations fell through, thereupon Wagener, taking his leave of them, remarked that if the facts were as stated, the Xosas might continue in occupation, until such time as the will of the Governor, after he was made acquainted with the results of the conference, was declared.

By this time the Chief, Ndlambe, had firmly grasped the reins of Government of the Ama-Rarabe. The Boer leaders now referred their disputes to him. Ndlambe replied that, for his part, he desired that the Boers and Xosas should live together in peace, but he shrewdly concealed the fact that he had no authority over any of the tribes, other than those of his own particular section. Moreover, there were lawless Boers who did not respect their own Government's efforts to prevent them from crossing over the Fish River. These disregarded the law, in order that they might engage in free trade in cattle. With them Native life was cheap and, therefore, they constituted a dangerous element on the frontier.

The historian, Theal, records one dastardy deed resulting from this spirit among these Boers. He relates how, in the year 1781, a Dutch Boer, named Adriaan van Jaarsveld, demonstrated this spirit of holding Native life cheaply. He went among the Ama-Ntinde with a commando, and at a friendly meeting with these unsuspecting people, van Jaarsveld threw some bits of tobacco among them, and while they were engaged in scrambling for these, he suddenly opened a destructive fire upon them with tragic results.

The incident lives in the memory of the Ama-Ntinde to the present day, and it created among the Xosas a feeling of bitterness which destroyed their faith in the whites.

On the retirement of Commissioner Wagener, the Governor appointed H. C. Maynier in his stead. The new commissioner was a strong supporter of the view of the authorities, that peaceful relations should be maintained with the Ama-Xosa, for although these disturbances on the border were dignified with the name of "wars," they were at their worst only in the nature of forays.

Nevertheless, neither side was willing to renounce its claim to the disputed territory. Thus the situation continued to present an insoluble problem, irresponsive to any treatment. These struggles over the boundary question, and also the land and cattle, became the settled condition of the Boer and Xosa relations, year after year, neither side agreeing to concede anything to the other, and eventually leading to the third war between these races.

Ndlambe was still regent over the Ama-Rarabe, and at length he was also involved in the struggle, as will be shown later under the notes referring to Ndlambe.

The English and the Transference of the Government at the Cape, 1795.

It was during this period that the French with the assistance of their allies, the Spaniards, were striving to secure the suzerainty of Europe and both declared war against England. Holland, which sympathised with the Cape Dutch, was in the throes of an internal revolution which divided

the country. The supporters of the House of
Orange favoured an alliance with the English.
Thereupon the French invaded Holland in the
interest of those who supported their own pro-
paganda. The Prince of Orange was forced to
seek asylum in England from whence he wrote to
the Cape Dutch urging them to hand over the
control of the Colony to the English. To this
the Dutch authorities demurred, notwithstanding
their friendly relations with the Prince.

Upon their refusal, the English sent out a fleet
of warships and an army of over 3,000 soldiers to
occupy the Cape by force. The army landed at
Simonstown, in close proximity to Cape Town.

The Dutch Governor, Sluysken, aware of the
weakness of his position, attempted, nevertheless,
to offer resistance, which, being too weak, availed
nothing, and the English took over the control of
the Cape.

Later, in 1802, peace was declared between the
French and English. The peace terms contained
a clause which stipulated that "The Cape should
be restored to the Dutch." The stipulation was
observed, and the Colony restored to the Dutch
in 1803. But during the same year hostilities
were renewed between the French and English,
with Holland aiding the French. This resulted
in the English annexing the Cape in 1806—since
when it has continued under their authority.

Thus all wars which occurred after 1806 have
been between the English and the Xosas, for the
Boers were now subject to the former.

The regency of Ndlambe was also contemporaneous with these events.

CHAPTER XIII

PART I

The Ama-Xosa—Chief Gcaleka, 1730-1792.

Gcaleka, the prince royal and successor to Palo, was born about the year 1730 A.D. and died about 1792, his older brother, Rarabe, of the Right-Hand House, being a youth of about eight years of age when Gcaleka was born. This prince reminds us of the adage, "Greatness is not achieved by mere force," for while he was heir by right, yet he attempted to seize the reins of authority before they were handed over to him with his father's consent. The name of Gcaleka is indeed widely known, not, however, because of any worthy achievement on his part. His fame principally rests upon the transmission of his name to the Great House of Xosa. This was accomplished at the expense of splitting the tribe into two divisions.

In its descent from Xosa to Palo the tribe was an undivided unity, one in language and name, viz. Xosa. To-day, after Gcaleka's appearance on the scene, the Xosas are described by two names, the Ama-Gcaleka and the Ama-Rarabe, or otherwise Gaikas. This was brought about by his ambition to usurp the reins of government from his father, while still a youth, although his father was only about fifty years of age at the time. In our historical notes on Rarabe we touch upon this point as relating to a war which cleft the Xosa tribe into two sections. It may be said that Gcaleka was not singular in his action in this respect, because

the Chief Gwali was defeated in a similar attempt
to wrest authority on his own behalf from Palo,
and moreover the Ama-Ntinde, Ama-Mbalu, and
Imi-Dange had divided the tribe by assuming an
independent attitude.   That is, of course, true,
but those clans were lesser branches of the tribe,
and their departure did not affect the union of the
tribe in the same manner.

On the other hand, Gcaleka, although then by
right the heir, attempted to seize the reins of
government before they were delivered over to
him, and but for that action the Right Hand-
House of Rarabe would not have separated itself ;
it would have remained to strengthen the tribe as
its main support.   Gcaleka, on his part, developed
no great or worthy record as a chief or as an individual, but, as already stated, he was a founder of
discord, division, and bloodshed, and his most
distinguished action was that which has already
been recorded of him, viz., he was a divider of the
House of Xosa, and a shedder of blood in that
ignoble cause.   And when he had succeeded in
assuming the reins of government, he produced
no evidence to show that he was worthy of ruling
so great a people.

There were other reasons which tended to injure
his reputation among his own people.   First, he
was unfortunate in his mother.   His mother was
a termagant, respecting neither old age nor youth,
and given to reviling everybody in her tantrums.
People, therefore, avoided the Great Place, and
those who went there were only forced by compelling circumstances to do so.   Secondly, Gcaleka
assumed the office of a witch-doctor, a circumstance which greatly alarmed the people, who

perceived that the chieftainship and wizardly could not be reconciled in one person, that the combination was a real danger in one who held the kingship. The dual role which gave him authority to rule the people, and also at the same time to " smell them out " and kill them, was too dangerous a pair of twins to be in charge of one individual.

It became very clear to the people that once the Chief had graduated into a full-fledged witch-doctor, there would no longer be peace in the realm. The Ama-Gcaleka were therefore fearfully exercised over this ominous and unprecedented circumstance.

Gcaleka as Witch-Doctor.

It is related that Gcaleka graduated as a fully qualified witch-doctor at the Ngxingxolo, on the Kwelera River near East London. On a certain day, a large hunting party accompanied the Chief to hunt, and during the hunt Gcaleka was seen to disappear into a large pool of water at the Ngxingxolo. Only one person saw him, named Mtukutu, son of Konzo, and grandson of Nxuba of the Amangwevu clan. When he observed the Chief disappear into the pool, Mtukutu stopped those who were approaching the place where the Chief had disappeared, and ordered them to go back. He accompanied them back to the Great Place. Arrived there, he gave instructions that a certain hut should be swept and prepared for the Chief's reception, and that nobody was to approach or enter it. Later, on another day, the people went to the place where the Chief had disappeared, driving before them a herd of cattle. Arrived at the pool, a black and white spotted cow separated from the herd and entered the water. The diviners affirmed that it had gone in to pacify the Ancestral Spirits. After a time it reappeared, and coming out of the water lay down at the spot where Gcaleka had disappeared, upon which it was immediately seized and slaughtered as a sacrificial offering. A miracle then happened, for the meat moved, and disappeared into the pool, and piece after piece of the flesh went down into the water without a hand being seen to move it. The butchers helped themselves to a portion of the meat which they roasted and ate, leaving a portion which was near the brink with the skin, at the same time uttering the incantation ;—"Here is our meat offering, give us other Councillors," meaning those who dwell in the river. So the story goes. Whereupon a portion of the meat which had disappeared was cast up by the water-spirits, and moving on the surface wriggled on to the bank. This meat was accepted gratefully by the people and a large piece was roasted, but before eating it, they passed what remained of the cow into the water hole, where it disappeared while they exclaimed :—"Give us more Councillors." There was also a reed basket of tobacco from which the butchers smoked before placing it above the hole. The basket was rent, and portions of tobacco were conveyed by unseen hands into the water hole. A small lot of tobacco which remained in the basket was moved toward the owners of the basket who divided the tobacco among them, Kafir-corn, mealies, pumpkins, and sweet-cane were also placed above the hole with the same result. All disappeared into the pool. After which the whole skin moved into the water, and the people departed 'leaving Mtukutu and Bala of the Mpinga clan behind.

When the butchers departed, the Chief emerged from the water at the spot where the skin had disappeared. Again he disappeared, but after a brief interval, during which the waters were in turmoil, the Chief reappeared and came out. Mtukutu hastened to receive him and caught hold of him, but the chief pulled him into the pool and both disappeared together. Shortly afterwards, they came out of the water, smeared with white ochre, the chief being supported by Mtukutu, for he was staggering as a result of his interview or association with the water gods. Mtukutu being joined by three men was assisted in taking the Chief to the waiting crowd, who at once surrounded him and those who came out of the river with him, and started a chant in honour of Gcaleka. Thus they moved homeward, and arriving there entered the hut which had been prepared for him. The Chief was placed in camera behind a reed mat. Doctors were then sought to prescribe for him because he had come from among the gods of the water. Two doctors arrived, viz., Buyo, of the Mpinga clan, and Wayiza of the Mvulane, who prescribed for the chief so as to remove the trembling fit which was the result of his association with the water-spirits. He was then baptised or initiated into the fraternity of doctors by being anointed with some white infusion of herbs.

In this manner the Chief Gcaleka became a fully qualified doctor. At the Great Place, where many people assembled as the custom was, the unsuspecting people would often be alarmed by hearing Gcaleka say: "Arrest that person," and again, "Seize that person," and so it went on, the victims being thrown over a precipice by the command of their own chief. This precipice is at the Mlinyana, close to Komgha River where it enters the Kei.

Things went on in this manner until the death of Gcaleka; his court was abhorred, because no questions could be asked, for the people were done to death by their own chief, who had the disposal of their lives.

It might just be added that apart from his doctorship, which terrified his people, Gcaleka produced nothing favourable to his rule. His name is chiefly distinguished in that, when he assumed the chieftainship he broke the House of Palo into two; viz., the Ama-Gcaleka and Ama-Rarabe.

That is all, and nothing more.

The Chief Kawuta (1760—1820).

The Chief Kawuta, great son of Gcaleka, became sovereign of the Xosas in 1792. There is nothing of importance to record of him, except that during his regime peace reigned throughout the land. Tradition records only one story of him, which relates to a holocaust of dry bones of people who were the victims of Gcaleka's wizardry.

The story describes how the House of the Ama-Giqwa was raised to prominence. On a certain occasion a hunting party which included the Chief Kawuta and his party, went out to the

K

chase. During the progress of the hunt, a large party of the hunters arrived at the Mlinyana or Mauze where was the precipice over which those accused of witchcraft had been thrown. With the Chief's party was a young lad, the Chief's pipe bearer, named Ngqila, son of Tshenco, of the Ama-Giqwa clan, and as they came suddenly upon a heap of human bones, the boy enquired of Kawuta, "Your Excellency, what are these bones?" The Chief replied, "These are the bones of those destroyed by Gcaleka for sorcery." The boy, Ngqila, then enquired if the Chief of the Giqwa's had also been thrown down there by Gcaleka? Kawuta remained silent for the time, in thought. But on their return home he assembled the whole tribe and the youth was summoned. When he arrived, the Chief addressed the assembly saying, "Interrogate this lad as to what he enquired of me as we sat below the precipice of the Sorcerers." The question was asked, and Ngqila answered, "I was asking what that multitude (of dry bones) represented." Upon considering this answer, the reply of the assembly to Kawuta was, "Your Excellency, this youth is predestined to rule the House of Ntshingeni and thus be your commander-in-chief." The Chief replied, "So be it. One who dared make such an enquiry is worthy to command, and guard the interests of my people." The boy's relatives thereupon asked who would milk the Chief's cows, as was this boy's duty? The Chief replied, "Other members of the Ntshinga." "Come forward, Ganya," said the Chief, addressing one of his councillors. "Here are the representatives of the Qaukeni, henceforth you will exercise authority over them."

In this manner Ganya was raised to the Chieftainship over the Qauka. Kawuta further remarked, " If Ngqila, at his age, has the brains to think, and the heart to commiserate, with those condemned for witchcraft and to enquire about them, he already proves himself fit to assume the honour conferred on him, when he reaches manhood, and to rule the House of Ntshinga."

For war purposes, the Gcaleka tribe is divided into two great sections named, respectively, the Ntshinga (i-Ntshinga), composed of the majority of clans having royal blood; and the Qauka (i-Qauka), composed of general community clans. Thus were officers this day appointed to be the heads of the two sections mentioned.

The two sections, viz., the Ntshinga and Qauka, are of equal rank and hold separate commands.

The genealogy of the Ama-Giqwa may be given here :—

Ngesabe		
Solawukazi		
Somabolowana		
Totywayo		
Wuhle		
Pelu		
Ndweshe		*Rt. Hd.*
Nkosana	*Rt. Hd.*	Mondiso
Jikijwa	—	
Tshenco	Bam	
|	Nqakwe	
Ngqila	Mabula	
Gige		2. Tyila
Kwaza.	2. Yena	
Sijako	Maki	
	Feni.	

CHAPTER XIII

PART II

The Ama-Rarabe—Chief Ndlambe (1755-1828)

Ndlambe was Rarabe's son next in rank to the heir, Mlawu, of one mother, together with a younger brother, Nukwa. Nukwa was father of Gasela. The great son of the Right-Hand House of Rarabe was Cebo.

When Rarabe died (1787), Ndlambe was made regent for Gaika, whose father, Mlawu, died while still a young man. Ndlambe's status has always been indeterminate. He occupied a position *sui generis*. He grew up together with Mlawu, and both married and had children about the same time, but Mlawu predeceased Rarabe, their father. Mlawu, however, left heirs, viz., Gaika, of the Great House and Ntimbo of the Right-Hand House. We have seen that the Right-Hand of Rarabe was Cebo, and the Right-Hand of Mlawu was Ntimbo. Cebo died in his youth, without issue. His house was thus bereft of heirs.

These two, Gaika and Ntimbo, during their minority were placed under the guardianship of Ndlambe. The reason, therefore, why Ndlambe's status has ever since remained undefined was that, as guardian of the Great House of Rarabe, he hoped that, as the tribe became accustomed to his rule, it would throw its weight in his favour, and that thus he would secure the overlordship of the Ama-Rarabe. He had the attributes of chieftainship well developed, but he failed in great part to capture the hearts of the Xosa people. He might, but for this ambition, have been confirmed as Chief of the Right Hand on the death of Cebo, for when the Councillors of Cebo approached him and asked him to assume control of Cebo's house, he turned a deaf ear to their solicitations : then, seeing that he was indifferent, they asked him to appoint one of his own sons to that House. Thereupon he appointed Mdushane, who thus became the representative of the Right-Hand House of Rarabe, as successor to Cebo. Moreover, the Right-Hand of Mlawu, Ntimbo, died without male issue ; hence, Gaika, when he had a family, filled the position by appointing Anta, his own son, to revive the House. We have seen that the Right Hand of Rarabe was placed under Mdushane, and that of Mlawu under Anta. The result was that when Gaika took over the sovereignty, Ndlambe was left with his status undefined. Thus, those who affirm that he represents the Right Hand must not overlook the facts, as there is no record of Mdushane being ejected in favour of Ndlambe, nor yet of Anta having surrendered his position to Ndlambe.

It is true that Anta was later elected spokesman of the House of Sandile, but this was long after Ndlambe had ceased to give trouble. Ndlambe continued to rule the House of Rarabe for upwards of twenty years, wisely, and extricating the tribe from many complicated situations with consummate judgment, especially those which threatened the peace between Xosas and Europeans.

He was a cautious ruler and weighty in counsel, although his own personal ambitions were never fulfilled. In time, there developed an estrangement between him and Gaika, which continued till death divided them.   During his regency, all the tribes westward of the Great Kei River were under his authority, except those lesser nomadic tribes (the Gwalis, Ntindes, Mbalus, and others), already mentioned, who preferred to conduct their affairs much as they pleased, although during Ndlambe's regime they dissembled by assuming a a lip-loyalty to him.

Concerning Mdushane, some regard him as Ndlambe's eldest son, others say Mhala, others again Mqayi.   Only the Chiefs themselves could unravel these old disputes of ancient rank and heredity, but we do not forget that Mdushane quarrelled with his father for divorcing his mother, and Mdushane, therefore, leant more towards Gaika's side. Nor was Mdushane to be held in light esteem, because he soon exhibited traits which proved him to be a man of outstanding ability and, as a Chief, superior to all his contemporaries among the Xosa chiefs of his day.   He possessed foresight, wisdom, and zeal, and was altogether a superior man.

The Councillors of Ndlambe, perceiving this, endeavour to reconcile father and son, and their efforts were successful.   The result of this was afterwards apparent, when in a subsequent conflict at Amalinde, Mdushane brought up a strong contingent of his followers on the fatal field of Debe Nek.   Both by reputation, and because of the general confidence in him, he was elected Commander-in-chief of the allied forces engaged on that disastrous day which proved so fatal to the Gaika.   Mdushane died while still in the prime of manhood.

In Maclean's *Compendium of Kafir Laws and Customs*, one of the narrators mentions that

Ndlambe's son, who was eligible to succeed his father died during Ndlambe's lifetime. And because during that time Ndlambe was subject to Gaika, it was mutually agreed between them that during Ndlambe's lifetime his successor must be named. Now Umhalla's mother was a concubine of Ndlambe's, and there was no other heir to the Great House, excepting perhaps Dyan, who was Umhalla's elder brother and who was in charge of his father's House. But Dyan was a listless and irresolute fellow, and Umhalla who happened to be sick took advantage of that circumstance to call in the witch-doctors, and Dyan was "smelt out." Dyan was privily informed of his danger, and his irresolution was instantly succeeded by remarkable activity. He decamped immediately, not even taking time to collect his cattle, and left everything behind him.

Doubtless he had presentiments of the Sorcerers' precipice at the Nxaruni, and he disappeared into the dark never to be heard of again. Uqayi, another member of the Great House of Ndlambe, was considered of small account, because he was not only of a peaceble disposition, but was too friendly inclined to the Europeans. It was in this way that Umhalla succeeded Ndlambe.

The Third Kafir War—1793.

Affairs were in this position in 1793, with Ndlambe scheming to oust Gaika and to secure the overlordship of the Ama-Rarabe. He at length contracted an alliance with the Boers, and accordingly raised a force and fought for them against his own kith and kin, the Ama-Mbalu of Langa, the Ama-Gqunukwebe of Cungwa, and the Ama-Ntinde of Ciko, and routed them, taking Langa prisoner. Besides this, Ndlambe assisted Lindique, a prominent Dutchman, whose Commando had declared war against the other tribal divisions of the Xosas.

Thus, White and Black, formerly divided, now made common cause and, surrounding the Xosas, seized 800 cattle of which Ndlambe received 400, and the remainder of the booty fell to the Boers, in reprisal, so the latter asserted, for cattle previously seized from them.

It was clearly evident that Ndlambe by his alliance with the Boers sought their favour, in order to gain their assistance when the time came to oust Gaika from the sovereignty of all the Ama-Xosa. And yet, it was the same Ndlambe who accused Gaika afterwards, on the occasion of the defeat of the Gaikas at the battle of Amalinde, of soliciting the aid of the whites.

These recurrent affrays, which historians have dignified by the name of wars, represented the " Third War " which occurred between the Xosas and the Dutch. After it an armed peace succeeded between Whites and Blacks, dating from 1793 to 1818, during which there were frequent breaches on the border line, and armed encounters, until a change of Government was effected at the Cape, whereby, as we have already seen, the English seized the Cape from the Dutch, and thus inherited the troubles which related to the vexed boundary question.

The Governor, Lord Charles Somerset, paid a personal visit to Gaika, at the Ncwenxa, Gaika having now taken over authority ; and certain measures were agreed upon with regard to the boundary question : they were, however, fruitless.

But there was one important result which emerged out of their conference, for Lord Somerset had recognized Gaika as Sovereign of all the Xosas. It came about, therefore, that when, later, Gaika was assailed by a confederacy of the other chiefs, he appealed to the Whites and obtained their assistance. And so it was, that after the battle of Amalinde, near Debe, when Gaika was overwhelmed by Ndlambe, the Europeans came to Gaika's assistance and prevented his total destruction ; whereupon Ndlambe, in great fury, turned upon the Whites and attacked them at Queenstown, the result of which action was that Ndlambe's power was completely destroyed.

It thus came about that whenever a war occurred between Gaika and Ndlambe, the Europeans having once become involved, it was assumed that the Europeans would always be the allies of Gaika. Henceforth, Ndlambe was regarded as the principal offender in subsequent conflicts with Gaika, and the mutual hatred of these two chiefs, whose careers were contemporaneous, ended at length in the tragedy of the battle of Amalinde.

We shall now consider the character of Gaika, and touch on the battle of Amalinde, before turning to other subjects.

Chief Gaika (1775-1828).

Gaika, eldest son of Mlawu, and grandson, therefore, of Rarabe, was placed under the guardianship of Ndlambe on the demise of his father. He occasionally visited the Chief Kawuta, where he met, and formed a friendship with, Hintsa, although there was a disparity in their ages : for Gaika was about 15 years old when Hintsa was born. The representative of the Right-Hand of Mlawu was Ntimbo, who died without an heir, so that a minor son of Gaika, Anta, was appointed to preserve that House. Between Gaika and Ndlambe strained relations soon arose, for more reasons than one, and for which both were to blame. Probably, when Gaika came of age, he observed that Ndlambe was seeking to usurp his authority, and doubtless his councillors had hinted to the same effect ; consequently, their mutual relations resembled those of the snake and the frog. Gaika's personal conduct was that of a freelance, showing little respect for the family proprieties observed by those of his rank, and so indifferent to the claims of relationship that he contracted an incestuous liaison with one of his uncle's (Ndlambe's) wives, the beautiful Tutula, a daughter of Dibi, which shocked the people. This was one of the main reasons which led to the affair at Amalinde, for this conduct gave Ndlambe strong cause against him and brought over many of the Xosa nation to Ndlambe's side.

In the year 1817 Lord Charles Somerset met Gaika, as a result of which meeting Gaika was forced to cede to the Government the territory lying between the Fish River and the Keiskama, an arrangement which greatly offended the Xosas, and out of which Ndlambe took care to profit personally, although he also had had similar relations with the Europeans in the years gone by.

This famous Conference had an important sequel in the so-called "War of Hintsa," which gave

Lord Glenelg, who was then Colonial Secretary in England, occasion for strong comment to this effect:— that Lord Somerset made terms with Gaika about land which did not belong to him, but to the Xosas as a whole, and moreover that Gaika was not the Sovereign Chief of the Xosas, and had not, therefore, any authority to alienate their land.

These sentiments were expressed sometime after the conference had been held, that is, after the invasion, by Sir Benjamin D'Urban's forces, of Hintsa's country. Lord Glenelg pointed out that these disturbances originated from such methods and practices as those in which Sir Benjamin D'Urban had been engaged.

While Gaika can be justly accused of unconstitutional methods, he did one notable thing which proved favourable to the Xosa nation,—he abolished the impure Custom of u-Pundlo (see Maclean's *Compendium of Kafir Laws and Customs*) This custom was revived by his son, Sandile, about the year 1845, after Gaika's demise.

As has already been observed, Gaika lacked the principles which govern honourable conduct. He was rude and outspoken in his language and behaviour, and reckless of evil consequences, comporting himself in a manner which often grieved his relatives; but at the same time, it is well to remember that the higher the rank the greater the temptations, some of which are not common to ordinary folk, and thus chiefs are peculiarly exposed to disgrace. As Chief of the Ama-Rarabe he encountered great trials and troubles, with the result that he became addicted to European drink, believing doubtless that in this way he would find ease of heart. But what above all estranged many hearts from him, and caused his people to ally themselves with Ndlambe, was the agreement he concluded with Lord Charles Somerset. For a Governor to dare to settle matters of the highest importance to the Xosa nation, and that with a prince who was only representative of the Right-Hand House of Palo, and by so doing to close permanently the door against Ndlambe's hopes for the Chieftainship, was to implant a lasting grievance, and was bitterly resented by Ndlambe.

The pot of Ndlambe's grievance was now boiling over. Moreover, the pride of Gaika had alienated those chiefs who might have helped him. Both Kawuta and Hintsa in the matter of Amalinde sided with Ndlambe because, as was alleged, they were shocked at the scandalous conduct of Gaika and Tutula, and felt that this son of Mlawu deserved punishment. But others say that, when this scandal was reported to the Gcalekas, Kawuta merely denounced Gaika, but Hintsa took his side. One thing is clear, that all branches of the Xosa nation condemned him and held him in aversion, and this was proved later. On the day of the battle of Amalinde, which was fought between Gaika and Ndlambe, the Gcalekas joined forces with Ndlambe, so likewise did the Imi-Dushane, the Imi-Dange, the Ama-Gqunukwebe, the Ama-Hleke, and other branches of the House of Xosa. Thus Gaika stood alone, without a single advocate, unsupported in this battle by those clans who placed loyalty before all else.

The Battle of Amalinde, 1818.

Some battles have been fought for trivial causes: the War of the Axe, for example, because the Chiefs refused to hand over a thief who had taken refuge with the tribe. The war of Ngcayecibi arose out of a refusal to produce beer at a drinking party. But this affair of Amalinde, although it was only a battle, and not a war, was brought on by substantial reasons.

The bitterness long nursed by Ndlambe against Gaika found expression on the Debe Flats. He had never forgiven the insult to his House at the hands of Gaika, or his disgraceful mesalliance with his wife, the daughter of Dibi ; a scandalous affair, which not only discredited the son of Mlawu himself, but revolted the mind of the whole Xosa nation. Besides this, public feeling deeply resented the agreement with the Governor, which placed Gaika above all the other Chiefs, thus degrading the status of the Great House of Gcaleka.

All these considerations combined to arouse the wrath of the Ama-Xosa, and it needed only a spark to set the flames of war alight. Gaika himself applied the spark. It is related that in 1818 the whole country was suffering from a severe drought, and the country occupied by Gaika was scorched and the rivers dried up. The stock had nowhere to graze. About this time Gaika contemplated paying a visit to his uncle Ndlambe, who then resided in the neighbourhood of the Buffalo and Peelton Rivers, Gaika then being at the Keiskama. Before he arrived at Ndlambe's kraal, he was surprised to find green pastures and grass growing luxuriantly upon which Ndlambe's cattle were grazing. Here also Kawuta had feed-kraals in charge of Hintsa, who was overseer of the royal herds at this period. Gaika immediately returned home upon observing this wonder, without seeing Ndlambe. He came back with his own herds of cattle, and acting on his own authority he proceeded to graze on his uncle's pasturage, and to drive Ndlambe's herds away. There was consternation among the herdsmen; both sides immediately attacked each other; and a free fight ensued in which the herdsmen of Ndlambe and Kawuta were driven off. They reported to their masters what had happened. The matter was then taken up by the Gcaleka tribesmen. At this time Kawuta died, Hintsa was just entering into manhood, and the Gcaleka tribe was placed under the regency of Nqoko, of the Ama-Mbede, one of the minor houses attached to the Great House.

In order to remove the supposed insult, the regent began to make preparations for war. When these were completed, he set his warriors in motion. From near the Kei River they proceeded towards Keiskama to punish Ngqika (Gaika). The latter was informed of the warlike intentions of the Gcalekas and of their approach. He immediately collected an army and awaited the arrival of the Gcalekas, who were under the command of Nqoko, the regent. The opposing forces met in the neighbourhood of Hoho mountain, one of the Amatole range. In a very short time the Gcalekas gave way and retired homewards, fighting rearguard actions all the way. Back they were driven, till they reached the

Dwesa forest, the Gaikas hot-foot on their track. Having reached this point, the Gaika army saw herds of Gcaleka cattle grazing below the forest, on the low-lying ground bordering the sea-shore. A party of Gaikas under Mpaku of the Ama-Qwambi clan was sent through the bush to intercept and capture the cattle. This they accomplished. Ngqika then sent a messenger to Hintsa, the young chief, asking for a meeting, and promising the latter a safe-conduct. Hintsa came. When he was seated, Ngqika addressed the fallen Hintsa in these words, "My elder brother's child, why have you come against me armed, in a matter that affects Ndlambe and myself alone? You, the representative of the Great House, making war upon me, your Right Hand! Why have you done this? Here I hand you four assegais (*intshuntshe*); they are the heritage of the Xosa tribe. Let them be a symbol of peace between us. Let this matter be ended. It is late, already dark, we will speak further in the morning." They then separated. During the night, Hintsa's councillors, fearing for the safety of their chief, came to him and said, "Ngqika is plotting mischief, your life is in danger, let us depart secretly with you." Hintsa agreed to this. On the following morning Ngqika was informed that the Gcaleka chief had fled. The Gaika chief was much upset. "I am disappointed," he said. "Why has Hintsa done so undignified a thing? Men of Rarabe, set free those captured cattle, let them go, I am disappointed." Hintsa's want of trust in the Gaika chief, his fear and flight indicated too clearly that matters were not settled, and that a state of war would continue to exist between Hintsa and himself. Ngqika had gauged the situation correctly.

The Gcalekas were deeply mortified, that they, the Great House of Xosa had been beaten by the Right-Hand House, and they feared that the lesser house would usurp the power and be masters of the whole Xosa tribe. This they could not endure, and were determined to prevent it if possible. They knew that Ndlambe was at "daggers drawn" with Ngqika and that circumstance afforded them their only hope. Messengers began to pass between Hintsa and Ndlambe to the great joy of Ndlambe, for now, he believed, would his dreams of becoming the principal ruler of the Ama-Rarabe be fulfilled. Arrangements to act in concert against Ngqika were completed. This, then, was the cause which brought the Gcalekas into the fight at Amalinde as allies of Ndlambe. Alone, the Gcalekas could not have succeeded against the Gaikas: single-handed, the Ndlambes dared not face the Gaika spears, but this combination would be more than a match for them.

As we have seen, there were several reasons which made for war between the Ndlambes and Gaikas. There was the charge of incest against Ngqika; there was the insult offered to Ndlambe through the treatment of his herdsmen; there was also the desire of Ndlambe to wrest the chieftainship from Ngqika : but the spark which lit the fire was the injured pride of the Gcalekas, and their fear of being superseded by the lesser house, which induced them to add their strength in support of Ndlambe.

The other tribes, viz., the Ama-Ntinde, Ama-Mbalu, Imi-Dange and Ama-Gqunukwebe, which had hitherto maintained an independent attitude, now associated themselves with the Gcalekas. Gaika was thus isolated and stood alone.

At this juncture, Nxele, whose other name was Makanda, a son of Balala, appeared and stirred up the war spirit. He was a member of Ndlambe's tribe, and lived at the Qagqiwe near the sea in the district of Uitenhage. Here there was a Hottentot Mission in charge of Dr. Vanderkemp (in Xosa "Nyengana.") Nxele attended the services, and was impressed with what he heard, not because he was converted, but because, like Simon Magus of Scripture story, he perceived that he could profit by it and add lustre to his name. And the particular sermon which attracted him was about the Resurrection from the dead. He turned the trend of this sermon to his own deceptive purposes, for he was a subtle orator and brainy withall. He then left Uitenhage and returned to Ndlambe's country.

He immediately proclaimed himself, asserting that he was the Son of God, who was sent with a message to Ndlambe to the effect that he would raise the dead on a certain day. Such an extraordinary miracle had never before been heard of among the Ndlambe tribe. Had ever such a thing been heard before even among the Xosas themselves ? Nevertheless, at a later period, the Chief Kreli built upon this foundation the prophecies of Nongqause and Mhlakaza. On this occasion, this son of Balala beheld himself enriched in a twinkling. Cattle came pouring in long lines to secure this blessing to the people—the raising of their dead relatives

L

for whom they mourned.   A day was appointed by
Nxele who summoned every living soul to Gompo.
Arrived there, he ordered each person of the expectant assembly to hop on one leg, and to exclaim
"Tayi, Tayi."   At the same time, Nxele continued
working up the excitement, until the fateful day
appointed for the resurrection arrived, and with
straining eyes and heaving breasts the expectant
crowds stood rooted, staring in the expected
quarter.   There is a Xosa saying that "No genius
can lick his own back."   In spite of Nxele's most
strenuous exertions and antics, the dead refused to
rise.   The sun moved on its round, while he
frenziedly cried and shouted to his gods, "Tayi."
But the sun moved on relentlessly to its usual
setting because forsooth it was no party to the
agreement and had not been consulted.   All hope
was now abandoned, and the people returned to
their homes dejected.

People who are nurtured on ancient superstitions
and worship, when deceived, are prone to despair.
And yet although the failures of the witchdoctors
are clear and proclaim the fact with a loud voice,
nevertheless it is hard to disillusion the people, or
to induce them to blame such false prophets as
Nxele, even though they realise the failure of their
false doctrines.   The reason for this was that the
Chiefs gave witchdoctors or prophets their protection, as being useful agents of the Great Place.
These deceptions are conceived through, and spring
out of, the associations of the Chiefs with the
witchdoctors.

While the nation was still perplexed by these
events, and at the same time living amidst vague
rumours of coming trouble, there arose from

among the Gaika tribe a man who spoke in un-
accustomed ways, Ntsikana, son of Gaba of the
Ama-Cira clan. This individual denounced the
war which he could see was being fomented by
Nxele. Now, there are European writers who say
the object of Nxele was to arouse all the Xosas to
fight the Whites and drive them to the sea from
whence they came. But this is not what the
Xosas say. They hold on the contrary that what
Nxele had in view was to arouse the Ndlambes to
destroy the Gaikas. The idea of war with the
Whites only occurred to their minds after being
defeated by Gaika, who obtained European assistance in strengthening his claims against Ndlambe.

Ntsikana was a convert to Christianity under
the ministrations of the Rev. Williams, and like
one inspired he did his utmost to turn the Gaikas
from the idea of engaging in war with Ndlambe,
and from all the preachings of Nxele. He even
sent Ncamashe, one of his neighbours, to Gaika
with a message saying, "Abandon all thought of
war with Ndlambe, otherwise you will bring
down upon yourself fearful retribution, the nature
of which I cannot describe, but I see the heads of
the Gaikas being eaten by ants."

Shortly after the return of Ncamashe, word
came from Gaika saying, "Our cattle are already
seized by the Ndlambe warriors," to which Ntsikana replied, "Do not attempt to recover them."
But the message crossed another which reported
that Ndlambe's army was on the march, and
observing that the Gaikas still hesitated to listen
to him he said in despair, "If you insist upon meeting them, beware lest the enemy entice you; do

not follow them up, because you will fall into a dangerous ambush."

When Ntsikana's messenger took this message to the Chief, there was a man present, named Manxoyi, one of Gaika's Councillors, who spoke with contempt of Ntsikana's message. And so he was the man who was mainly responsible for the calamity which befell the Gaikas, by advising them to ignore the council of Ntsikana which said, "Beware! if the enemy seeks to draw you on, do not follow them, because you are being led into a dangerous trap."

On the morning following the capture of the cattle by the army of Ndlambe, and before sunrise, Gaika's army left the Tyumie and marched in the direction of the Debe. When it reached the ridge of the Debe the army of Ndlambe came into sight, encamped on the plains beneath them. The Commander-in-Chief was Mdushane, son of Ndlambe, and of the Right Hand of Rarabe. The Gaika forces were under the command of Maqoma, eldest son of the Right-Hand House of Gaika, and still a youth. The Ndlambe army was reinforced by the Gcalekas, and with them were associated those lesser branches or semi-independent tribes already referred to, who on this day renewed their allegiance to the Great House from which they had long been separated.

Instantly, upon the appearance of the Gaikas, Mdushane attacked the younger bloods on both flanks as they pressed forward. It became at once apparent that the Gaika army was outnumbered. There was, however, on its part no hesitation. Soon the assegai was busy cutting, slashing and stabbing, until a momentary pause ensued in which the combatants separated and halted, facing each other in a state of uncertainty. This gave an opportunity to the older veterans, who sprang forward, and once more the conflict was renewed with terrible fierceness, men falling on all sides as kafir-corn falls before the reapers. It was here that Maqoma distinguished himself. Although it was the first engagement in which he had fought, he led his warriors right into the heart of the fighting enemy. But it was of no avail; the Gaikas were surrounded and Maqoma fell, only to rise again covered with wounds. Signs of wavering now became apparent in his army, and he drew off.

It was at this juncture, that the bravest of the Gaikas fell like leaves on the fatal plain of Amalinde. But it was not an inglorious flight, for the defeated army retreated fighting, turning many times to beat off the enemy who pressed too closely on their heels, seeking to obliterate the name of Gaika. For the first time in their history, misfortune befell the famous tribe of the Gaika. Some families lost all their men folk, for they had fallen on the plain of Amalinde at the Debe. As Maqoma's army retreated, darkness was setting in, upon which Ndlambe's men turned on the wounded and slaughtered them with their assegais, exclaiming that in this way they were putting an end to the name and pretentions of Gaika.

Next morning, the remnants of Gaika's army laboured home, and then the greatness of the catastrophy which had befallen the tribe was at once apparent. There were few kraals that did not lament some male relative, young or old, slain on the Debe plain. And the lamentations of the women-folk—words fail to describe a sorrow like that of Rachael weeping for her children.

The Raid on Grahamstown, 1819.

After the battle of the Amalinde, Ndlambe was elated at defeating Gaika, and sought occasion to revenge himself on the Whites for protecting and assisting Gaika, both before and after the affair of Amalinde. He also conjectured that his long cherished ambition to succeed to the chieftain-ship of the Ama-Rarabe, was now within measurable distance of being fulfilled. By weakening the power and authority of the Europeans, who constantly interfered in the affairs of the Xosas, he would stand to profit.

One of his plans, therefore, was to cross the border suddenly and to take the Whites by surprise. Crossing the Fish River, he plied his assegais ruthlessly, and those Europeans on the border who failed to find places of refuge were indiscriminately slaughtered or scattered. He then made a diversion to Grahamstown, accompanied by his favourite medicine-man, Makanda (Nxele), and a strong force of mixed adventurers from the diverse clans already mentioned, which force was "doctored" according to custom by the Chief's medicine-man, who deceived them by saying that "the bullets of the Europeans would be turned into water through his arts." On arrival in the neighbourhood of Grahamstown, word was shouted to the Whites that "we shall breakfast with you in the morning." To be brief, they attacked at day-break, but things went badly for Ndlambe, who was defeated by the English and the Hottentots and retreated home. It was plain that victory was not to be his, for the bullets did not turn to water. Nxele, the genius of this movement, then surrendered himself to the Europeans. He was sent as a prisoner to Robben Island, near Cape Town, by the Governor. There one day, essaying to escape to the mainland, he seized a rowing boat which, however, turned turtle when he was some way from the land, and he was precipitated into the sea. In this manner the son of Balala died.

The power of Ndlambe was shattered, so much so that the government took the opportunity to rearrange the boundary between the Europeans and the Ama-Xosa. The Xosas were removed from the country lying between the Great Fish River and the Keiskama, making the latter river the boundary of the Ama-Xosa, and the former that of the Europeans. The country between was to be vacated and remain a Neutral Territory upon which nobody was permitted to reside.

The Emancipation of the Slaves at the Cape, 1834.

The English, as did other nations, examined the question of slavery with patience and sincerity. England herself had participated in the traffic and owned thousands of slaves in her several Colonies. The Dutch of the Southern Continent of Africa also were large holders of slaves. Thus, when the Government changed hands from the Dutch to the English, the new administration inherited slavery from its predecessor. About this time, a great anti-slavery movement arose in England. Wilberforce, whose name is immortal, stood alone for a time in his advocacy of emancipation. In the teeth of the most stubborn opposition, he persisted in demanding the abolition of slavery. He held that "the right to buy and sell the bodies and souls of other people should be legally abolished by Parliament." At length Parliament was convinced as well as the public of England, who adopted the views of Wilberforce and by a decree of Parliament abolished slavery. There were thousands of these miserable people in the service of the Dutch in 1834, and these were now released. In consideration, however, of the expenses incurred by the slave holders, the English Government decided to purchase their interests in their slaves and it set aside one and a quarter million pounds (£1,250,000) as a solatium for the loss of their property, but not as restoration of all the expense incurred by the owners.

These latter were by no means satisfied with this arrangement. Claiming full compensation and considering themselves unjustly treated by the English authorities at the Cape, they made it a perpetual grievance, which ultimately led them to sever their connection with the English Government, and to trek northward. But we need not follow their movements during the years 1836-40; it will be sufficient to note that they did not all remove *en bloc* from the Cape, but in parties, some of which were large, others small. Abandoning the Cape, they crossed the Orange River. Some of these people settled in the Transvaal, and others in the country now called the Orange River Colony. Others, again, moved north across Basutoland, seeking new homes beyond the Tugela River. Thus they sought to throw off the yoke of England.

It is well for us to understand that the genesis of the movement for emancipation in England was in great part of a religious and evangelical character. Sir Benjamin D'Urban, who came out as Governor of the Cape at this period, was doubtless influenced by this spirit which inspired in him a hatred of slavery, and for that reason he was easily moved to eagerly accept stories which were circulated by rumour, to the effect that slavery existed among the Gcalekas. This point will be touched on when we come to refer to the war of Hintsa. My object is to ascertain the reason which led Sir Benjamin D'Urban to the belief that the Fingoes were held in slavery by the Gcalekas, and his prompt acceptance of the statements of others to that effect. I am of the opinion that the hatred of slavery overseas made such an impression on him as to impart a bias to his attitude in regard to the condition of the Fingoes. And while on this subject of the Governor, I may as well remark that he enjoyed the greatest esteem among the Europeans of this country, and even down to the present time his name and memory are cherished by them. Nevertheless, a careful examination of his career presents clear evidence that as an individual his was not a strong character.

The Ama-Rarabe or Gaikas.—Maqoma, 1834.

Maqoma, eldest son of Gaika of the Right-Hand House, was born before Sandile, the heir of the Royal House. He was born about the year 1800. His mother was a daughter of the Ama-Ngqusini clan, and her name was Notonto. Maqoma belonged to the House of the Ama-Jingqi, so called after his favourite ox. At the time of the battle of Amalinde he was a youth recently emerged from the rites of circumcision. Colonel Maclean, the magistrate with the Ama-Ndlambe, says of him at that time : "Maqoma is admitted by everybody to be an orator above the ordinary, and a warrior unrivalled among his Xosa compeers." The only one who could approach him in martial skill was Mdushane, son of Ndlambe. By this we mean that Maqoma stood in a rank alone for courage and as an orator. Sandile was born when Maqoma was already a young man, because at the time of the death of their father, Gaika, the heir was taken to Maqoma to be reared by him. Now, while the training of a Chief to discharge the duties devolving upon those of his rank in Society is an arduous and important task, it cannot improve those who have not the brains to understand and assimilate it. Sandile during his lifetime never proved himself to be one who had the advantage of being trained under a man of energy, an orator, and an unusually brave soldier. It may have been that, by nature, Sandile was of a quiet disposition ; besides which he was a cripple from infancy, an infirmity which prevented him from engaging in manly sports and other feats of strength.

Maqoma was mightily opposed to the arrangement concluded between his father Gaika and Somerset, by which the country between the Fish River and Keiskama was ceded to the Europeans. He regarded this action as one of the fruits of the unjust methods practised by the Whites to deprive the Ama-Xosa of their heritage. A previous agreement with all the tribes had established the line of the Fish River as a perpetual frontier, which should not be violated by either European or Xosa. Instead of respecting this, the Government had since settled Bastards and Hottentots in the neutral territory, the result being that both Europeans and Natives trespassed and found an asylum there.

Maqoma, who noted these conditions, felt himself also entitled to enter the Reserve, and he established himself at the head waters of the Ncwenxa stream. Soon his cupidity was aroused by the herds of cattle belonging to the Settlers living near the boundary. These he seized and took home. European Commandos were then sent out against him. Mutual raids and pillagings followed. These conditions prevailed until the country was irremediably disturbed. Thereupon, the Europeans determined to oust him altogether from the ceded territory. This was done. But the treatment which first permitted him to settle thereon, and afterwards drove him therefrom, irritated him and, as his countrymen say, "licking his wounds," he awaited an opportunity to revenge himself.

He plotted with the chief of the House of Ngca-ngatelo to bring on the war of 1834, quite unaware that the result would be to implicate Hintsa, far away across the Butterworth River among the Gcalekas. By the month of November of that year their forces were prepared to take the field, and in December they opened the war. Their army was twelve thousand strong. (Lucas, *History of S.A.*, p. 156.) This invasion included all the territory from the Winterberg (Nkonkobe) to the sea.

Such an extensive movement, carried out with consummate strategy, had hitherto been unknown. The suddenness of this rising took the country by surprise, so much so that even the missionaries and the traders living among the Xosa tribes were ignorant of it, and awoke to its reality too late.

The armies rendered the whole country between the Mandi and Port Elizabeth uninhabitable. The order of operations was as follows:—Maqoma's army crossed the Ncwenxa below Fort Beaufort; Tyali's impi sprang north; Mhalla, Nqeno, Siyolo and Botoman, together with the Ama-Gqunukwebe, crossed the Fish River by several drifts. All wars have some starting point, even when they have been long hatched and prepared. In this war it was the head of Xoxo, son of a lesser house of Gaika. It happened in this way. A small patrol of soldiers, commanded by William Sutton, was sent out to destroy a new kraal which was being erected by some of Tyali's people, the Imi-Ngcangatelo, on a ridge between the Gaga and Mankazana. Arrived there, they burnt the huts, and seized sundry cattle, which as it happened, belonged to Tyali. On their retirement the soldiers were followed by Tyali's younger brother, Xoxo. On his coming up with them, shots were immediately exchanged. It was here that Xoxo was wounded in the head, although not seriously; but because the blood of a chief had been spilt, the war cry resounded on all sides. Thus it came about that the armies of the Ama-Xosa invaded and devastated the country as already described. We said that the Missionaries inside the cordon were taken unawares, but they were not harmed. The Rev. John Brownlee, father of Hon. Charles

Brownlee (Xosa, Napakade) who was prosecuting his work as a Missionary with the Ama-Ntinde, was well treated by most, but certain of the wilder spirits decamped with his cattle. For this reason among others, he decided to remove with his family and with a certain trader who was in ill-favour with the Ama-Ntinde and had taken shelter with the Missionary. They made for Wesleyville. Sutu, mother of Sandile, took them under her protection, with other Europeans who were shut up in Kafirland by the war. When the rumour of this conflagration reached Cape Town, Sir Harry Smith left Cape Town hurriedly on horseback, and arrived at Grahamstown about the end of 1834. In the following months he had pushed the Xosa impis back; driving them over to their own side of the Keiskama. And then he made preparations to invade their country. He made agreements with certain other tribes to assist him, such as the Tembus who would come from the North, the Pondos from the rear, and likewise the Basuto in the centre-rear. The Paramount Chief himself was in Gcalekaland, remaining neutral. This, however, did not help him, for the Basutos entered his country and seized his cattle. It must be remembered that this war was begun by the Gaikas of Maqoma and Tyali, and by the other tribes bordering on the Keiskama, viz., the Ama-Mbalu, Ama-Ntinde and Ama-Gqunukwebe, which were in league with those chiefs in this undertaking.

The Gcalekas, on their part, had nothing to do with this war, and yet the Governor determined to implicate them in it. By the defeat of the tribes of Maqoma and Tyali and their allies the war should have virtually ended. But it was not so. In the month of February, 1835, the Ama-Rarabe had already been overcome. Sir Benjamin D'Urban then sent an ultimatum to Hintsa, the tenor of which was, first, that he surrender the plunder which was secreted in his country by the Ama-Rarabe, and, secondly, that " Hintsa should desist from helping the Ama-Rarabe." With regard to the first matter mentioned, the Governor did not discriminate between those cattle which had been taken to Gcalekaland legitimately, and for safety, by the more peaceful sections among the Ama-Rarabe who desired to avoid war, and the booty of those of the enemy who engaged in the war. With regard to the second matter, it is not clear why it was affirmed that Hintsa assisted the Rarabes. It was not justifiable to enter Gcalekaland because of the actions of irresponsible individuals who acted in despite of the laws, and were really adventures acting on their own.

The Gcaleka nation did not sharpen their assegais in preparation for war. Let us, however, turn from this digression, for this subject is dealt with in its own place. On his return from the country of the Gcaleka, Sir Benjamin D'Urban met Maqoma and the chiefs of the Ama-Rarabe at the Keiskama to arrange terms of peace. At this Conference, the Chiefs put their mark to the paper of conditions and agreed to come under the wing of the Government of the English, and to respect the laws and proclamations of the Whites, and on the other hand, the Native Laws and Customs were not to be interfered with. They also agreed to surrender their arms, and also to pay a tax of one good ox per year. On the European side, it was agreed that they should protect the rights and interests of the Xosas, and secure the Gaikas' territory between the Great Kei River to the East and the Tyumie to the West.

To return to Maqoma, this Chief had long held a prominent place among the Xosa right up to the time of the War of the Axe. For a long time he was not on good terms with Sandile, being estranged by mutual jealousies.

Consequently, on account of their disagreements, Maqoma refrained from joining in the War of the Axe. He came out as a neutral, and the Government gave him a place on which to live at Lovedale with his family and retinue during the time of hostilities. But owing to his ungovernable temper and general cruelty to his womenfolk, more especially when under the influence of the white man's fire-water, he was a thorn in the flesh to Calderwood (Xosa, Kondile) who was Magistrate of that district. Maqoma's wives numbered twenty-six, and his children fifty-two, and all the expenses connected with them were borne by the Government during the progress of the war.

Theal describes a painful action by Sir Harry Smith, after his return from India, where he received honour for his courage at the battle of Aliwal. He arrived in this country about the close of the War of the Axe, carrying his honours proudly and swelled up with self-importance. He was now returning as Governor to which post he had been appointed. He was worshipped by the Whites, who on his arrival at Cape Town welcomed him with great enthusiasm. From Cape Town he went up to Port Elizabeth and was received with similar marks of welcome. Amongst the crowd who assembled on his arrival Smith recognized Maqoma, and calling him over to him denounced him in unmeasured terms for daring to fight against the Europeans (which he had not done in the late war). Not satisfied with that, he put his heel on Maqoma's neck using contemptuous language, to his own disgrace and belittlement. Certainly his admirers may praise Sir Harry Smith, but by this action towards a brave man, who feared nothing under the sun and who was now a subject of the White Government, Sir Harry Smith lowered himself in the eyes of right-thinking men who considered his action discreditable and contemptible. It is most regrettable that, while Maqoma was endowed with admirable gifts, he permitted himself to become the victim of foreign liquors which debased him. In this respect he took after his father Gaika, who imagined that he would find relief in drink from the cares, sorrows and anxieties, brought about by his difficulties with his white neighbours.

In the war of Mlanjeni, Maqoma again took a prominent part and distinguished himself by his courage, of which tales are still told to-day, especially of the fight at Burnshill. His name was a terror to his enemies, but among his own people his was a name to conjure with. In the Cattle Killing he stood whole-heartedly on the side of the converts to that strange delusion, and when it had passed, he was arrested and sent a prisoner to Cape Town. After a time, he was again released and determined to return to the Ncwenxa, his former home, but he found the land already parcelled out to the European settlers. At this disappointment he was very wroth, and he made so much trouble about it that the European settlers and frontier men were alarmed.   Correspondence passed and repassed between them and the Governor, until the authorities fearing further mischief, again had him arrested.   This time he was deported to Robben Island after the manner of Makanda (Nxele).   He never saw his native country again.   He lived there for 17 years and died in 1874 full of years.

M

CHAPTER XIV

The Ama-Gcaleka—Hintsa (1790–1835)

Hintsa was eldest son of Kawuta, and Nobuto was his mother. His mother is said to have been a daughter of Tshatshu, whose father was Xoba and grandfather was Tukwa of Tembuland. The first wife of Hintsa was Nomsa, mother of Kreli, (Xosa, Sarili), and his wife of the Right Hand was Notonto, mother of the chief Ncapayi. We have already referred to the fact that, as a lad, Hintsa was placed in charge of the herdsmen of the royal herds of Kawuta, at Ndlambe's feed-kraals. The battle of Amalinde was fought when he was a young man. We meet him again as nominal Commander-in-Chief of the forces of the Gcalekas in 1834, the fighting general being the Regent, Nqoko. In the following year he was made *particeps criminis* in the war against the Ama-Rarabe, in other words, against the Gaikas, which was afterwards designated "the War of Hintsa." The Qauka, and the Ntshinga, the two divisions into which the Gcalekas were divided for war, had not been called out, nor had the Ama-Velelo and Tsonyana sharpened their assegais, for Hintsa, the Chief, had declared himself neutral. The war started, or was hatched, in territory adjacent to the Fish River. In the official reports it was described as the Sixth Kafir War. In the chapter referring to Maqoma, we made mention of a standing grievance which irritated the Xosas, viz., the alienation to the Europeans, with Gaika's consent, of the territory lying between the Keiskama and Fish Rivers.

This gave rise to border reprisals in which cattle were extensively plundered by both sides. While this was happening, word came to the effect that the land between the Keiskama and Tyumie was to be handed over to the Xosas by the Government. Whether this was an official pronouncement or not, is not clear, but the historian Theal says of it that Dr. Phillip was the bearer of this news to the Kafirs. But in whatever manner the report came, it had the effect of appeasing the ferment in the Xosa mind for the space of two months. But when the promise was not fulfilled trouble again arose. The Xosa hosts of Maqoma and Tyali got moving, crossed the Fish River and entered into European Territory. The lesser, semi-independent tribes also crossed at several points, extending from the neighbourhood of the Nkonkobe (Great Winterberg) to the sea, and the war fluctuated between the combatants, both sides encountering successes and defeats. At length the Ama-Xosa army was forced back to the Amatole Forests and the Fish River by Lieut. Col. Henry Somerset, and was hemmed in there by the European forces, under command of Colonel England, with two thousand men. While it was thus surrounded, the Governor (Sir Benjamin D'Urban) set out for Gcalekaland with a large force under Sir Harry Smith and thus carried the war into Gcalekaland, Hintsa's country.

Fingo "Emancipation." Slavery?

For ninety-three years, that is, from the date of Hintsa's death in 1835 to the present, 1928, the condition of the Fingoes who sought sanctuary in Gcalekaland has been falsely represented as slavery.

Colonial historians have been content to accept the misrepresentation as fact, and the general public has not worried over the matter, but has accepted without question what has been served up to it.

In justice, however, to Hintsa and the Gcalekas, the misrepresentation should not be allowed to pass any longer without protest.   As an indication that searchers after truth are not satisfied about the matter, the question is being asked to-day, "Were the Fingoes really slaves under Hintsa?" The answer is a categorical denial,—"Fingoes were in no sense slaves under Hintsa."   In the terrible war waged between Tshaka and the Ama-Ngwana led by their redoubtable chief, Matiwana, the Ama-Hlubi became involved.   Tshaka retired after having driven the Ama-Ngwana over the Drankensberg.   Shortly afterwards Matiwana returned, and attacked the Hlubis who had acted treacherously towards the Ama-Ngwana.   The impact was so terrible that the Hlubis, in spite of their well known courage, were broken, and reeled against the Beles behind them, these in their turn were thrown against the Zizis and other Fingo tribes lying to the south of them, and a general debacle was the result.   Part of the Hlubis crossed the Drakensberg, into Basutoland, but the remnant along with their kindred, the Beles, the Zizis, and Tolos, fled southwards.   Many, however, of the principal chiefs who survived, together with such followers as they could collect, joined and became absorbed in other more fortunate tribes in Natal.   Those who came south were under the leadership of minor chiefs.   The survivors, destitute, famine-striken, and helpless, entered Hintsa's country. This was towards the close of Tshaka's reign. They were welcomed, given grants of land, and like many other broken tribes among the Gcalekas were placed under their own chiefs, an indication of their semi-independent condition.

Who then were responsible for the mischievous statement that the Fingoes were slaves? It is almost idle to attempt to answer that question. It might be possible to reach some finding, were the private correspondence of Sir Benjamin D'Urban available. There was a considerable number of Europeans resident in Gcalekaland, missionaries, traders and others, but none have left convincing evidence of the existence of slavery. Apart from the question of the authorship of the term "slavery" as applied to the condition of the Fingoes in Gcalekaland, the fact emerges that at least one missionary was on unfriendly terms with Hintsa. There was little love lost between the two, and each regarded the other with disfavour. Such a condition of affairs was most unfortunate at the period in question. There is a strong presumption that therein may be found the root of the mischief.

Theal admits that while individuals among the Fingoes were "often subject to oppressive treatment," yet "they are not slaves." Nevertheless, the falsehood continues to be fostered.

The term "emancipation" applied to the exodus of the Fingoes from Gcalekaland assists in its propagation.

That individuals among them were "often subject to oppressive treatment" is most probable, but so also were individuals among the Gcalekas themselves subject to like treatment. Among a people nurtured on superstition and a belief in witchcraft, many deplorable instances of cruelty and oppression occurred, but the perpetrators took no account whatever of a supposed wizard's tribe, nor was an individual discriminated against because of his poverty and helplessness, rather was it the man of substance who most often was the victim.

The community spirit is sometimes moved to its very foundations by events affecting the community adversely or favourably. Nations have been swayed by an intense fervour and passion owing to events touching their independence or their religion. An intense fervour marked the passing of the edict for the emancipation of slaves in all the possessions of the British Empire. The evils of slavery having become clear to the people of England, to all sensitive minds the liberation of slaves became the absorbing topic. Not only was England moved intensely, but so also were many of her citizens in the colonies. Though in South Africa the decree for the total emancipation of slaves was not carried out fully until 1838, many were carried away by the prevailing ardour, and apt to allow their feelings to over-ride their balanced judgment.

A peculiarity of this question of Fingo slavery is that the Fingoes themselves (I refer to those who knew by personal experience) do not speak of their life in Hintsa's country as slavery, and they should know. To take the case of one family in my immediate neighbourhood at the present time. The head of it affirms that there was nothing in the nature of slavery. Moreover, though a Hlubi, his grandfather was appointed chief over a section of Hlubis by Hintsa.

These Hlubis remained in Hintsa's country and did not follow the "emancipated" Fingoes when they left for Peddie. The heads of this family, called Poswa, still hold the position of chiefs or headmen which was conferred on the family by Hintsa. Why, then, did they not follow their countrymen and escape from the bonds of slavery, if slavery there was.

Hintsa is accused of trafficking in slaves, and the Fingoes as living under the heavy bonds of slavery. Even supposing that Hintsa was a man of reprehensible character, as some maintain, yet it cannot be denied that he possessed the sentiments of humanity common to others, holding high his chieftainship in such a manner as to retain the respect and affection of his subjects.

What conditions predicate Slavery?

A slave is an individual who is not a free agent: he is one who has lost his freedom, whose actions are controlled by another. This certainly was not the case with the Fingoes in Hintsa's country. They were free to go where they chose; seek work outside the bounds of Gcalekaland, if it suited them to do so.

A slave, again, is one who, having lost his freedom, is bought and sold for the material profit of his owner. There is no record of such trafficking in human cattle, as the term would imply, in Hintsa's country.

A slave has no property which he can claim as his own, nor can he claim even life itself, or the right to plead on his own behalf. On the other hand, his reward is to be at the mercy of his owner's brutality. The Fingoes had no experience of such conditions; on the contrary, when they arrived, a broken and helpless people, among the Gcalekas, Hintsa received them with kindness, and granted them lands upon which to live, with freedom to observe the customs of their tribe. Besides this, he settled them close to the Great Place, in order the more effectually to protect them. The Ama-Zizi tribe were apportioned land at the Ceru; the Amabele, at Ezolo, a small tributary of the Tsomo River near Nqamakwe; the Ama-Hlubi were stationed near the springs of the Teko River; others at the Zinqayi near Ibeka. In this manner were they received by Hintsa. And besides they were granted freedom to control their own domestic relations under their Chief. They were also given constitutional freedom. The poor and unfortunate among them were at liberty to find service for themselves, and those who chose were permitted to seek a living among the Xosas. And while there were those who did so, they were not deprived of individual liberty, for the law protected them, there being none who were debarred from the right of representing their grievances.

A Native writer, S. M. Mqayi, in his valuable treatise on *The case of twins (Ityala Lama Wele)*, gives a description of the methods and customs observed by the Courts of the Gcalekas with regard to any Fingo who was ill-treated in Hintsa's country. Of course, in the matter of witchcraft in which both Fingoes and Gcalekas believed, they were " smelt out " just the same as other people: not more so. But, whereas slaves possess no property (for one who has no rights, and no control over his own life, but is under the control, and is the property of his owner, can call nothing his own), the Fingoes under Hintsa came with nothing, but left with wealth. When we remember that they entered Hintsa's country in object poverty, and when we contrast that with the fact that, on the day of their so-called "Emancipation" they numbered 2,000 men besides women and children, and that they left Gcalekaland with 22,000 cattle (that is, an average of 11 head for every Fingo male), we can see that their stay in Hintsa's country was materially prosperous. If the accumulation of wealth is slavery then they were slaves indeed. The Scots have a saying that " facts are chiels that winna ling." Do the facts here given tally with the known condition of slaves? The Fingoes arrived in Hintsa's country about 1828 and were "emancipated" by Sir Benjamin D'Urban in 1835. Therefore, the number of years they spent under Hintsa was only seven, and yet, as we have seen, during these few years, although on arrival they had not even a fowl to their name, they became large cattle owners. They came to Hintsa as paupers, and left as rich men. There were some among them who received honours from Hintsa. These facts are easily ascertained; not through Xosa evidence alone, but they are admitted by the Fingoes themselves. *What class of slavery then is this?* Nor did all the Fingoes leave Hintsa's country at the " emancipation," for there were remnants who refused to accept land in Peddie. The Aba-Shwawu, one of the tribes of Fingoes, then under their Chief Deyi, were driven from the Xobo by Tshaka. They arrived in the van at

Hintsa's place. This tribe refused to go out, or to follow those who received grants of land at Peddie, because *they had not experienced slavery*. They remained with the Gcalekas until the disturbances in their own country subsided, and returned to Natal when it was first settled by the whites. The Aba-Shwawu remained with Hintsa for eight years longer, and after that Chief's death returned to Natal about the year 1843.

What then was the manner of this slavery which saw the Ama-Shwawu unwilling to admit its restraints? If slavery was the condition of life in Gcalekaland, how comes it that they refused to leave, when they were not forced to stay?

Sir Benjamin D'Urban.

In December 1834 the Sixth Kafir War began. In January 1835, Sir Benjamin D'Urban arrived in South Africa as Governor of Cape Colony. He had left England with praiseworthy resolutions to see that justice was done to Colonists and Xosas alike. These resolutions, however, can hardly be said to have lasted many days after his landing in the country. Whether this was due to the dominating personality of Sir Harry Smith, with whom he was closely associated from the very beginning of his administration, or whether the circumstances attending the war, already in progress for a month, had their effect in confirming his future policy, cannot be clearly determined; but it is very apparent that Colonial sentiment early won him over from his resolutions of impartiality to the conclusion that it was his supreme duty to further the interests of the Colonists at the expense of the

Native tribes. His conduct in this respect roused lovers of justice among his own people to criticise adversely his administrative acts.

Naturally, the Colonists and those immediately affected by the unrest in the country, desired above all else security. With them, the question of who was, or who was not, responsible for the unsettled state of the country was a minor matter. It was, however, the duty of the Governor to enquire into the origin of the troubles and to deal with the matter primarily as a statesman, and not as a soldier. In short, to hold the balance fairly between the conflicting elements.

The most pronounced colonial estimate of Sir Benjamin D'Urban places him in the front rank of South African governors. On what particular achievements is this based? It is impossible to dogmatize, but probably it is based on four things. In the first place, the Governor threw himself whole-heartedly into interpreting the aspirations of the Colonists, by putting them into effect. In this connection he prosecuted with vigour the war which he found in active progress on his arrival in the country. In the second place, he extended the colonial boundary by which an immense tract of country, that between the Fish River and the Kei, was added to the Colony. In the third, he carried the war into Gcalekaland, and benefited the Colony through the suppression of the power of Hintsa, the supreme head of all Xosa tribes. In the fourth place, the estimate is probably based on the "Emancipation" of the Fingoes, which was a valuable measure in support of the economic life of the Colony, since it brought to it a large number of useful labourers.

In touching on these matters, we would notice that the 6th Kafir War was the outcome of the sequestration of a piece of country in occupation by the Xosas from 1750 to 1820. The object of this measure was to make it neutral territory, and thus if possible to keep Colonists and Native tribes from constant feuds. From the Xosa view point, D'Urban scarcely if ever regarded their interests. One of the Governor's first acts in connection with his administration was to send messages to the Xosa chiefs expressing his intention to meet them, with a view to arranging a settlement of difficulties which were the cause of the unrest and hostilities between them and the Colonists. On the receipt of these messages, and in the hope that something tangible would be arranged to the satisfaction of all parties, the Xosas refrained from active hostilities. For two months the chiefs awaited the fulfilment of the Governor's promise, but he failed to meet them. Hostilities then broke out again. The failure to implement an engagement on so important a matter was culpable on the part of the Governor. It was, however, but the prelude to further acts indicative of a want of judgment. He failed to accurately gauge, not only the effect of his decisions on those upon whom they were imposed, but also their probable rebound against himself. Sir Benjamin D'Urban is in no way responsible for the cause which lead to the 6th Kafir War. Lord Charles Somerset, with the very best intentions for the peace of the country, concluded an agreement with Gaika whereby a piece of country, taken from the Xosas for the purpose, was to be regarded as a buffer country separating the Colonists from the Xosas, into which neither was to trespass. In 1820, a slice of territory, lying between the Fish and the Keiskama Rivers, was taken by the Governor from the chief Gaika, as a *quid pro quo* for assistance given him by the Colonial Government against the would-be usurper, Ndlambe, in 1818. This country was declared to be neutral territory, and neither Colonists or Xosas were to occupy it. The fact, however, is that this neutrality was respected by neither party, the frontier farmers crossing the Fish River, and occupying parts of the neutral strip as seemed good to them, and the Xosas doing the same. There were, consequently, frequent collisions between the two races. These became more and more accentuated, until in 1834 they culminated in the 6th Kafir War, erroneously called " Hintsa's War."

This practically compulsory cession of territory by the Xosa chief was scathingly denounced by the Foreign Secretary of the Imperial Government, Lord Glenelg. Sir Charles Somerset was perfectly right in treating Gaika as paramount chief of the Gaikas ; the securing of the chief's signature under compulsion is, however, another matter. Theoretically, Hintsa was Paramount Chief of all the Xosas, but the Rarabes, of whom the Gaikas are the principal section, had declared their independence by breaking away from Gcaleka, Hintsa's grandfather, and settling in a new country. In actual fact the Gcaleka chief had no jurisdiction over the Gaikas. By courtesy, matters affecting Xosa customs might occasionally be referred to the chief of the older branch, especially when a question of precedent was involved, but that did not prevent the Right-Hand House from following its own line of conduct, irrespectively of what that precedent might be, should it choose to do so. Laws promulgated by the court of the Gaikas were not subject to interference by the Gcaleka chief. The latter's authority in such matters was in reality a cipher.

The position is paralleled by that of the Pondos at the present time. The older or premier branch is that of Eastern Pondoland (i-Qauka); the Right-Hand House is that of Western Pondoland (i-Nyanda). But the latter has declared itself, and is *de facto,* independent of the former, and no interference in the internal affairs of the Western branch by the Eastern would be tolerated. Theoretically, the chief of the Eastern branch is Paramount of all Pondos ; actually, his authority is confined to his own section, Eastern Pondoland. With the Gcalekas and Gaikas the position was similar, Hintsa had no authority over the Gaikas.

In connection with the agreement between Sir Charles Somerset and the Gaikas, and its effects, it is interesting to note that the Xosas were not always responsible for the outrages on the peace of the border.

Cowper Rose, an officer of Engineers who participated in the fighting in the disputed territory, the Zuurveld, that is the territory proclaimed as neutral, writes thus in his book, *Four years in South Africa* (p. 64), published in 1829. " Many acts of aggression and duplicity had taught them (the Xosas) that there was no hope but in resistance, and they carried it on by deeds of ferocity,

only to be surpassed by those of their oppressors."
Then again, the same writer (p. 75, *ibid.*) says in
reference to the neutral territory—" It is not
strange that savages should be unable to see the
justice of all this : that they should be troublesome
neighbours to the settlers in a country of which
they had been dispossessed. They were so : such
instances were exaggerated, and a commando (an
inroad of military and boers) was the frequent
consequence. The crimes were individual, but the
punishment was general ; the duty of the commandos was to destroy, to burn the habitations,
and to seize the cattle : and they did their duty."

The clans involved in this war were the Ama-
Ndlambe under the chief u-Mhlala ; a section of
the Ama-Ngqika (Gaika) under the petty chief
Tyali ; the Ama-Jingqi under the famous Maqoma ;
the Imi-Dange under Botomane ; the imi-Dushane under Siyolo ; the Ama-Mbalu under Nqeno
(English, Eno.) These, with the exception of the
clans under Maqoma, Tyali, and Mhala, were not
Rarabe or Gaika clans, but of the older Xosa stock.
Theal, the historian, states that there were also
" many Gcalekas and Gqunukwebes ;" but such
Gcalekas were free-lances, or adventurers, as no
mention is made of a Gcaleka chief being their
leader. Ultimately, these clans were beaten back
and held in the Amatole mountains by Col. Richard
England with a strong force, and thus Sir
Benjamin D'Urban was free to proceed with a
force under Sir Harry Smith to subdue Hintsa,
who, however, had not armed, having proclaimed
himself neutral.

With regard to this war which began at the Fish
River, the Governor recognized that in order to

reduce the power of the Xosas as a tribe, the authority of Hintsa, the Hereditary Sovereign of all the Xosas, must be broken. In order, therefore, to connect Hintsa, who had declared his neutrality, with the war of the Ama-Rarabe, D'Urban, metaphorically, applied the burning brand of war to the Gcalekas. Hintsa refused to touch it.

The Governor accused Hintsa of harbouring those of the enemy who sought shelter with him, and further, that while he professed neutrality his own people were assisting the Rarabes; also, that he was permitting their plundered stock to be hidden in his country (these cattle are termed by the Xosas *otshinyonga*, "branded flanks"). This he did because he knew that Hintsa was the Paramount Chief and was assumed to exercise authority over all the Xosas by right of heredity, but the Governor was unable to raise that issue, since Lord Charles Somerset had already decided this matter in favour of Gaika, with whom he had concluded a treaty affecting all the Xosas, in 1820, in which Gaika was formally recognized as principal chief. He refrained therefore from raising this point, but brought against him the charges mentioned above.

The Xosas affirm that the first communication sent by the Governor to the Chief was a command to hand over the enemy who had hidden in his country, and that Hintsa replied in the following terms, " If your children were being punished by me, and ran to you, their father, and I followed them up, and said to you: Hand over your children, so that I may again chastise them, would you be willing ? " That was the end of that part of the negotiations. On the other hand, Colonial history tells us that a young officer, named Van Wyk, was sent to Hintsa to say that he was to restore the "branded catttle" which had entered Gcalekaland, and that he must cease from assisting the Ama-Rarabe, on pain of being involved in hostilities with the Colonists. To this threat Hintsa vouchsafed no reply. The second step on D'Urban's part was to send out messengers to Fadana who was Regent for Mtirara, Chief of the Tembus, to warn him not to attack the Europeans. A similar message was sent to Faku, Chief of the Pondos. Though deferring to the message, these Chiefs also saw the possibility of seizing the Gcaleka cattle when Hintsa was fighting with the Europeans. The Basutos also prepared to act in concert with them. These preliminaries concluded, Sir Benjamin D'Urban left part of his army in charge of Colonel England at the Amatole Forests, as already described, to hold in check the Ama-Rarabe, while he himself advanced and crossed the Butterworth River to attack Hintsa if necessary. On the 15th of April of that year D'Urban's army crossed the Kei River. He was met at the ford by Buru, a Councillor of the Chief, who came to enquire why this army was entering Hintsa's country, the country of a neutral. The messenger was told that nothing would happen to Hintsa if he would only comply with the conditions set forth by Van Wyk. Hintsa's reply was required to these conditions within five days. The army of the Governor then moved on slowly and encamped at Butterworth on the 17th of April, there being now only three days remaining, in which to comply with the Governor's ultimatum. When these days had expired without result, the Chief was allowed

N

a further extension of two days, but nothing came of it, and D'Urban proclaimed war.

Thereupon the general of the forces, Sir Harry Smith, entered Gcalekaland with his army and captured 15,000 cattle. The Tembus also attacked the Gcalekas and raided 4,000 cattle. Similarly the Basutos also captured a number of cattle. Thus Hintsa was threatened from all sides. The Tembus sounded the war cry in the rear of the Gcalekas; the Basutos also did so; while the European troops opposed them in front. The warriors of the Gcaleka, not having sharpened their assegais for war, could make no resistance and were surrounded. In these circumstances, there was nothing else for Hintsa to do but to offer himself as a hostage. Having presented himself as a hostage, he should not have been held a prisoner under military restraint, until the compensation demanded from him in cattle was paid. This was fixed at twenty-five thousand head and five hundred horses, a similar number was to be paid at the end of the year, in all 50,000 head of cattle.

Hintsa's younger brother, Buru, and Hintsa's eldest son, Kreli, along with Buru's son, Mapasa, surrendered to the Europeans as hostages together with the Chief. These chiefs therefore should have been under the protection of the military authorities, and yet, though they were in no sense prisoners of war, the Governor, on the occasion of the " Emancipation " of the Fingoes, threatened the Chief by saying that if the Fingoes were interfered with by the Gcalekas, he would hang Hintsa and all those of his retinue who were in the European camp. The interference was entirely

owing to the seizure of Gcaleka cattle when the
Fingoes were coming out from among them. And
notwithstanding the fact that the Governor had
taken no precaution to prevent such happenings
as the raiding of Gcaleka cattle by the Fingoes,
he addressed one who was not a *bona fide* prisoner
but a hostage, and who was informed when he
arrived in camp that no harm would be done to
him, in threatening terms. D'Urban muddled
this business badly.

He placed the responsibility for the disturbances
on the Gcalekas who were only, and naturally,
resisting the seizure of their cattle. Nevertheless,
in fear of his life Hintsa issued an order to his
people to let the Fingoes alone and not to interfere with them. So the Gcalekas refrained from
resistance and looked on while their cattle were
being driven away.

Theal, referring to this, remarks, " the attack
upon the Fingoes, however, was not an act of
wantonness, for the Xosas had been sorely pro-
voked. As soon as the Fingoes were assured of
British protection and of removal to a new country,
they commenced to seize the cattle to take with
them, and what followed (the resistance of the Gcalekas) was the natural result of such conduct."
And again Theal remarks.—" The acceptance of the
Fingoes and their protection gave them encouragement in removing to plunder the Gcalekas of their
best herds." As has already been said, this conduct on the part of the Fingoes, their ingratitude
to their benefactors, is the root cause of the existing hatred between Xosa and Fingo. The Govern-
or's failure to take ordinary precautions against
this wanton conduct was culpable in the extreme,

The compensation cattle demanded by the Europeans were not delivered. Hintsa hearing that the European army was about to return across the Kei to the Colony, and fearing that he would accompany it as a prisoner, requested that a posse of soldiers might be allowed to accompany him to search and see if there might not be any cattle obtainable, and meanwhile his son Kreli together with Mapasa, Buru's son, would remain in camp. His request was complied with, and Sir Harry Smith was dispatched with five hundred men to accompany Hintsa. They descended the ridge above the Nqabara River. It is not quite clear what induced Hintsa to endeavour to give his captors the slip. The explanation usually given, that he merely wanted to escape to save his own skin, is not convincing, for he was quite aware that the Gcalekas had no means of carrying on war, and besides he knew that he had left Kreli, his son, and Buru's son in the hands of the Governor and by escaping he would be placing them in jeopardy of their lives. What really happened? The party who could best answer this is gone, viz.: Hintsa. But Buru left on record that the threats of the Governor had alarmed him, and, in consequence, Hintsa meditated escape. As they descended the ridge of the Nqabara, near the Mbangcolo, Hintsa who was close to Smith suddenly spurred his horse and dashed away. Smith and the crowd followed in pursuit. Owing to the speed of Smith's horse he came up to and alongside of Hintsa and attempted to shoot him, but his revolver missed fire so seizing the Chief by the kaross he pulled him off his horse. The Chief at once rose, threw an assegai at Smith, which missed him, and bolted down the incline, where he entered a small clump of bush close to the Nqaba-ra stream. Here he was shot. A man by the name of George Southey first wounded Hintsa as he ran down the incline, and afterwards shot him again and thus killed him. The body of the Chief after many days was taken away by members of his family, and was buried under the hill Mbongo, near the Mbangcolo. The corpse was not complete, for the head had been mutilated by certain members of Sir Harry Smith's party.

Buru, who accompanied the Chief to reason with him, turned back at the Tywaka and returned to the camp. He knew that Hintsa was going to make an effort to escape, as he feared the Governor would carry out his threat. Buru turned back because he had failed to dissuade his Chief from this step.

This version is based on Theal's story. The statement, however, that Hintsa voluntarily came to offer himself at the British camp as a hostage for the fulfillment of Sir Benjamin D'Urban's demands is not accepted by others, who state the facts as follows: Hintsa came to parley with Sir Harry Smith. During that parley, word reached Smith that the Fingoes and Gcalekas were fighting, and thereupon Hintsa was made a prisoner by Smith. Therefore, Hintsa never was a voluntary hostage, and was unjustly arrested while parleying with Smith. This version, affecting as it does, Smith's conduct, carries us back in thought to his shameful treatment of Maqoma at Port Elizabeth, and to his treatment of Adam Kok in his own house at Philippolis in 1848.

Sir Harry Smith may be excused much on the grounds of his being a soldier, but he should have remembered that he was a British soldier, and a member of that nation which has justly been termed " a nation of gentlemen." If this view, held by many, of the arrest of Hintsa is the true one, it seems to be a distinct violation of the Law of Nations, and Sir Benjamin D'Urban should not have allowed it. That he allowed it, illustrates the contrast in character between these two men : Smith, brusque and dominating, D'Urban weak and lacking in personality.

Whichever of these versions affecting Hintsa's presence in the British camp is the true one—the conduct ascribed to the Governor, in the first, in threatening Hintsa, and the unjustifiable arrest of the Chief, in the second, it matters little—both were a travesty of justice and fair dealing.

The conduct of Sir Benjamin D'Urban was severely criticized in England. Lord Glenelg, the Foreign Secretary, examined into the whole of the circumstances, and condemned the Governor. In his criticism of Sir Benjamin D'Urban's conduct, he took occasion to refer to the agreement between Lord Charles Somerset and Gaika. The substance of his criticism was on these lines : " He, Somerset, began by investing Gaika with an authority which was not his, and punished him and his tribe because he was unable to enforce it, an authority by which we stood to profit at his expense. We held him responsible for his own misdeeds, as well as for those of our enemies, who were also enemies of his (the Ama-Ndlambe), and punished him and his people by depriving them of their territory because of Ndlambe's acts of revenge, and after an attack which was made on Gaika, our ally. Our ally, Gaika, was forced into an agreement with us, although he had not the power to make any agreement according to the law of the Ama-Xosa nation, and we continued to carry on under that agreement, and turned the other Chiefs of Kafirland out of their territory, although they had not been consulted in connection with that agreement."

After having suppressed the power of the Gcalekas, the Governor established a new frontier line between the Colonial and the Xosa territory. The line up to that time stopped at the Keiskama River. The new boundary was now fixed by the Governor at the Great Kei River. But public feeling in England was highly incensed at the conduct of Sir Benjamin D'Urban. Lord Glenelg opposed this arrangement with all his might ; the line was restored to the former boundary at the Keiskama ; and the territory between the Keiskama and Fish Rivers, which had been forfeited under Lord Charles Somerset's regime in 1820, after the battle of Amalinde, was left as it was, but Europeans were prohibited from occupying it, and it was thrown open for settlement by the Xosas. The Imperial Government being dissatisfied with the policy of Sir Benjamin D'Urban, he was retired from the service of the Government, and returned to England. Twelve years passed and the War of the Axe occured. Sir Harry Smith, D'Urban's lieutenant, was then appointed Governor of South Africa, and he proceeded to extend the boundary from the Fish River to the Kei, in this way restoring the boundary to the position in which D'Urban had decided to fix it.

We here give Lord Glenelg's main despatch on these events.

Lord Glenelg's Dispatch of 26th Dec., 1835, to Sir Benjamin D'Urban.

" In the conduct which was pursued towards the Kaffir nation by the Colonists and the public authorities of the colony through a long series of years, the Kaffirs had an ample justification of the war into which they rushed with such fatal imprudence at the close of the last war. . . . Urged to revenge and desparation by the systematie injustice of which they had been the victims, I am compelled to embrace, however reluctantly, the conclusion that they had a perfect right to hazard the experiment, however hopeless, of extorting by force that redress which they could not expect otherwise to obtain. . . . The claim of sovereignty over the new province bounded by the Keiskama and the Kei must be renounced. It rests upon a conquest resulting from a war in which as far as I am at present enabled to judge, the original justice is on the side of the conquered, not of the victorious party."

Shortly after the issue of this dispatch Sir Benjamin D'Urban was superseded as Governor, and Captain Andries Stockenstrom was appointed Lieutenant-Governor, pending the appointment of a Governor to the vacancy.

A final word may be added in reference to Sir Benjamin D'Urban's dismissal. His actions, coming under the searchlight of British ideas of justice, did not commend themselves to the Home authorities. There is at the heart of British life, indivi-

dual and public, what has been justly termed the
moral core, and the *collective sense* based upon it,
whereby acts of injustice perpetrated against an
individual or a section of the community are tested
under this code and judgment is meted out in
accordance with its character.   No one dare flout
British public opinion with impunity.   Sir Benjamin D'Urban came into conflict with it, and he
had to go.

Lord Glenelg's policy has come under the lash
of Colonial historians, but the Foreign Secretary's
reputation remains unsullied, as in him is reflected
the spirit of enlightened British administration.
There are several very important factors to be
taken into account in all estimates of men charged
with carrying out British policy, especially in her
Dependencies or Dominions.   The principal of
these is the avowed policy of securing for the original inhabitants justice and fair treatment.   This
has been characteristic of British policy in its very
best aspect.   Public men like Glenelg, on account
of their detachment from local fears and prejudices, likes and dislikes, were in a better position to judge between the conflicting interests of
the various elements in occupation of the country
than those resident in it.   Such men, moreover,
were influenced by the high moral atmosphere, of
which they themselves formed a part, of the
Mother country—a moral atmosphere distinctly
superior to that of any of her colonies.   In young
countries where public opinion exercises less
restraint,   and where self-preservation and self-
interest tend to assume first place, the primitive
instincts of men, even civilized men, are apt to

assert themselves and be in the ascendant, colouring all opinions, actions and policy.

When, therefore, these primitive instincts are checked and disapproved of, men like Lord Glenelg are scathingly denounced for running counter to them. A sample of the criticisms levelled at this Foreign Secretary is that he was "a man of the best intensions but sadly ignorant of the habits and character of barbarians." He cannot, however, be charged with being "sadly ignorant of the habits and character" of civilized men.

CHAPTER XV

A Friend of the Bantu

Fair criticism requires a calm attitude of mind which will enable one, in spite of irritating circum-stances, to discriminate justly, so that conditions, incidents and people may be placed in their proper perspective. The mind which indiscriminately brackets circumstances which differ, and treats them as if of the same measure, weight and importance, proves that the foundation on which it acts is a false one, and its findings must of necessity be false also. A nation like the Xosas, brave and self-respecting, does not, it is true, submit mildly to the yoke of a foreign government, more especially when foreign rule brings with it oppression and inequality of treatment between man and man. Consequently, as there are always many harsh and impatient spirits among the Bantu as amongst other races, whose minds are so constituted that they cannot or will not weigh matters calmly, the benefits and blessings which accompany a foreign yoke are not always appre-ciated as they deserve to be. The work of the European missionaries whose desire is to raise and enlighten those who sit in gross " darkness and the shadow of death " has not had the deep con-sideration it deserves from some of the Bantu people, nor yet has it been adequately appreciated for its importance. Instead, the missionaries are placed by the thoughtless on the same level with those inimical to the Natives, merely because they are of one colour with those in political authority, and the gulf that really separates them is undiscerned. The same thing applies to those who are not missionaries, but who have distinguished themselves by their sympathy and good feeling in efforts to ameliorate the conditions of the Native races, and their name in legion. Criticism is useful, and lends weight to those who exercise it with judgment, but the friends of the Natives do not deserve to be subjected to hostile criticism, and classed with those adverse to the interests of the Natives simply because they are of one colour. There is not the slightest comparison between the two, which would justify the use of the words of a certain Xosa with a glib tongue, who, bracketing all Whites under one category, remarked that " the covetousness of the whites extends even to red ochre, although they don't paint themselves with it," the meaning being that an indigenous substance is sold to the people of the country for gain, by strangers, though they do not use it themselves—the hall-mark of greed and oppression.

In the days of Bantu adversity, under the Government of Sir Benjamin D'Urban and Sir Harry Smith, when the Bantu had no power in themselves to represent their cause to the Government of England, there arose a missionary of the Presbyterians, the Rev. John Philip, D.D., who endeavoured to champion the cause of the Xosas, and incurred the hatred of many of his own countrymen for that reason. He was a man who thought little of his own life, his aim and purpose being to do good, and to oppose every appearance of oppression especially of those who were powerless of themselves to throw off the burdens imposed

on them by others. He put his whole soul into
the work of protecting the Native races, neither
excusing nor attempting to mollify the enemies of
the truth, and because he did not approve of the
policy of Sir Benjamin D'Urban, he even crossed
the sea to England, taking with him Jan Tshatshu,
Chief of the Ama-Ntinde, to plead their cause.
He travelled all over his home-land in the interest
of his object, and fearlessly explained his reasons
for opposing the Governor of the Cape.   He even
went before a Parliamentary Committee expressing
his mind, and stating his grievances with regard
to the administration of Native Affairs by the
Governor. He succeeded in converting the feeling
of the Committee to the cause of the Xosas, as
also that of Lord Glenelg in the House of Lords,
who was by no means satisfied with the official
communications of his representatives at the Cape
after the manner of Sir Benjamin D'Urban.   The
fruits of this missionary advocacy may be seen in
the Dispatches of Lord Glenelg, and the recall of
Sir Benjamin D'Urban from South Africa. During
the Governorship of Sir George Napier, Dr. Philip
wielded great influence in this country. About
1846, during the War of the Axe, he retired from
the work of the ministry, and went to reside at
Hankey, where he lost his wife shortly after his
arrival there.   His services to the cause of truth
and justice deserve more impartial and faithful
treatment than they have received at the hands of
Colonirl historians. This they may yet secure.*

* Editor's Note : Professor W. M. Macmillan *The Cape Colour
Question*: Faber and Gwyer, 1927, goes a long way towards meeting
this demand.

The Missionaries.

The history of South Africa abounds with the names of white missionaries, who are distinguished for their work's sake—men who sacrificed the fortunes and pleasures of the world, in order to devote their lives to the work of enlightening those who sat in gross darkness. The London Missionary Society, which sent out the Rev. Dr. Philip, had earlier sent out the Rev. Dr. Vanderkemp (Xosa, *Nyengana*) and many others whose names are a household word among the Xosas. Although the foundation of this Society was laid in England, its messengers were mainly Scotch, as for example the Rev. John Brownlee, the father of the Hon. Charles Brownlee, C.M.G. (Xosa, *Napakade*), who was a missionary with the Ama-Ntinde ; the Rev. Henry Calderwood of Fort Beaufort ; the Rev. Robert Moffat of Kuruman in Bechuanaland ; Dr. David Livingstone, also of that country who was not content to preach the Gospel of God's peace, but was also a pioneer in endeavouring to abolish the cancer of slavery from the heart of Africa; and the Rev. Frederick Kayser (Xosa, *Ugqadushe*) at the junction of the Debe and Keiskama Rivers in Chief Botoman's country of the Imi-Dange.

Another Society, the Glasgow Missionary Society, likewise sent out a number of Missionaries, among them the Revs. W. R. Thompson, John Bennie, William Govan, the founder of the Lovedale Institution, James Laing, missionary of Middledrift, the Rev. William Chalmers of Tyumie; the Rev. John Ross, of Mgqakwebe in the Hleke country ; the Rev. Robert Niven of Igqwibira, and others.

There were also other Societies who established mission stations among the Gaikas, like the United Presbyterian Church and Free Church, which go by the name, in this country, of the Church of Rarabe, distinguished by the names of the Rev. Bryce Ross; the Rev. Richard Ross; the Rev. John Chalmers; the Rev. Dr. Stewart, and including the first Native Missionary of the Ama-Rarabe, the Rev. Tiyo Soga. The Wesleyan Society has also names of distinguished men :—the Rev. W. Shrewsbury who established the township of Butterworth; the Rev. William Shaw of the Chief Pato's country (the Amagqunukwebe); the Rev. W. B. Boyce in Pondoland; the Rev. Peter Hargreaves (Xosa, *u-Hagile*); Rev. H. H. Dugmore; the Rev. J. C. Warner; the Rev. J. C. Lennard; the Rev. J. Morris and many others. The Anglican Church has given such men as Bishops Furse, Carey, Talbot, Fuller, and a host of devoted servants, and it is to the credit of this Society that, especially in these days, its Ministers have come out fearlessly to uphold the principle that righteousness and justice must be maintained by the Courts of the land, in all matters arising between Whites and Blacks, without respect of persons.

The Independent Congregationalists and the Moravians and Lutherans have in common with other religious orders done magnificent work in implanting religious knowledge among the Bantu tribes of South Africa. The British nation, as we have already said, the noblest race under the sun, has stood for centuries where stood the Jews of old time, in spreading widely throughout the universe, Knowledge, Truth and Righteousness under the New Dispensation. This nation carries with it the Cross of Our Lord Jesus Christ, holding it aloft wheresoever it goes, bringing the light of eternal life and immortality to those races which sit in darkness.

It is a nation venerated because of Righteousness, that " Righteousness which exalteth a nation." Thus it has sent its sons and daughters to the diverse races of the earth, so that they also might share in the priceless inheritance which is offered to all mankind. And while it is true that the Government of this people has not been free from serious blemishes, which seem at times to cast a shadow over the Word of God, bringing it into derision, yet it must be remembered that of all the things good and bad which this race has brought with it, there is nothing that can exceed in importance the free gift which it brought to the tribes of the Ama-Xosa, that is, the hope of life everlasting in the Kingdom of the Almighty.

Righteous legislation may indeed be abrogated in favour of oppressive acts, or *vice versa*, but this blessing can never alter, and cannot be destroyed. The Native races may forgo all other benefits, but the Word of God once accepted by them—Never! For, they now understand that through its influence they can rise to higher heights of living, and to a nobler nationhood. It may be possible to underestimate the blessings brought by the missionaries, but it would be impossible to estimate them too highly. All their work and sacrifice, so faithfully performed and the adversities they have borne on behalf of the propagation of the Truth, redound to their honour, because they have laboured on behalf of races and tribes who were powerless to seize and inherit those everlasting riches for themselves.   Although the charge given to the Ministers on ordination was to preach the Word of Life, they realized, on taking up the work, that it was necessary also to interest themselves in education, so as to open the minds and understanding.   Their outlook in this direction gradually expanded.   To-day, owing to increase of knowledge, there are new standards available which were not known before.   Schools have been erected throughout the whole of the Native Territories, including Institutions for Higher Education.   We need only mention a few, the most notable of which is Lovedale between the Tyumie and Gaga rivers, belonging to the Presbyterian denomination.   It was founded by the Rev. William Govan, in 1841.   There is also the Blythswood Institution at Nqamakwe which was founded by the exertions of the Rev. Richard Ross, of Toleni, and Captain Matthew Blyth, Magistrate of the Transkei, at Ntlambe.   The Wesleyan Institution of Healdtown is in the very front rank of such schools.   Wesleyan Schools are very numerous. Starting among the Xosas, this denomination penetrated into Pondoland and right on to the border of Natal.

The foundations of that enlightenment which has come to the Bantu have been laid not by the Government, but by the exertions of European Missionaries who are the real helpers of the Native People.

The Rev. Henry Calderwood (U-Kondile).

Among those missionaries who had the confidence of the Government was Mr. Calderwood,

o

He was invited to participate in the administration, and was appointed Magistrate. Before this appointment he was Minister of Berklands, close to Fort Beaufort. He was a man of experience among the Natives and sympathised with them. At the close of the War of the Axe he was chosen to resettle the Gaikas, the Imi-Dange and the Ama-Ntinde tribes, and was instructed to receive all who surrendered, together with their weapons. He was stationed at the Tyumie Drift which divides Lovedale from the hill on which the Stewart Memorial is erected. He was given an assistant, Charles Brownlee *(Napakade)* who had a good reputation. The Hottentots of the Ncwenxa greatly tried Calderwood, especially when they rebelled and joined forces with the Chief Sandile, who was at war with the Government in 1846. He also rendered praiseworthy services in his efforts to settle the quarrel between the Boers who sought to deprive Mapassa, son of Bawana, Chief of the emigrant Tembus, who lived in the Queenstown District, of the tribal lands. He urged the Government to discountenance immediately the action of the Boers, otherwise the Government would be discredited by those tribes who lived on the Border, if the Boers were permitted to attack the Tembus. His advice was accepted, the seeds of another war were destroyed, and the Tembus were restored to their country which was being confiscated by the Boers.

During all his tenure of office as Magistrate, he was a true friend of the Natives, and, although an officer of the Government, exercised his powers with sympathetic discretion and an evident desire to lighten the burdens of the people. He was earnest in endeavours to lay down a form of administration which would suit the Xosas, and help them to became useful neighbours, being also careful to protect their rights as a deserving people. It was very necessary in those days that a person in his position should be endowed with foresight, wisdom and sympathy, in order to carry through his objects.   In this connection, Professor F. H. Brookes, in his *History of Native Policy in South Africa*, p. 87, says with reference to Mr. Calderwood (I paraphrase his remarks) :—In the Division of Victoria East, which is bounded by the Keiskama and Fish Rivers, and other small tributary streams of the Ncwenxa and Tyumie Rivers, it was suggested that this Territory should be occupied by a large number of Fingoes who assisted the Government in the War of the Axe.   This important work was placed in the hands of the Rev. Henry Calderwood who was appointed Magistrate of that Division.   The carrying out of the scheme largely depended on Calderwood although its success was due also to the interest of Sir Harry Smith who gave his support to it.   It was not merely successful in itself, but formed a precedent for many other similar changes of the same character both in the older Colony of the Cape and the Native Territories of the Transkei.   And because there were just such men, who held right views and had a reputation among the Xosas, the yoke of these subjects was made easier than it would have been under military rule.

The Hon. Charles Brownlee, C.M.G.

" Tshalisi " or " Napakade," as he was called by the Xosas, was a son of the Rev John Brownlee, missionary of the Ama-Ntinde tribe. In the troubles of 1834, the beginnings of the War which was later described as Hintsa's War, the Missionary was forced to abandon his home, and fled to Wesleyville near Peddie, close to the old kraal site of Makanda (or Nxele) who lived at the headwaters of the Tyolomnqa (Chalumna). After the war he returned to the Ama-Ntinde and resumed his work of preaching the Gospel, until the War of the Axe, the adversities of which, for the second time, compelled him to leave home. After the war he again returned. The Mission Station of Brownlee (Xosa, *Burneli*) was founded by him at King William's Town. His son, Charles, in the War of the Axe was appointed clerk to Mr. Calderwood, the Magistrate of Tyumie, and his younger brother, James, was assistant clerk under him. In the following year, 1847, he was appointed clerk to Colonel Maclean, at Fort Cox, close to Keiskama Hoek near Sandile's kraal. In the war of Mlanjeni (1852), he was wounded by an assagei in the thigh and during the future course of the war was compelled to remain at King William's Town. While he was in that condition, certain cattle were seized by the Gaikas. It was his duty to follow up the raiders and capture the cattle, but because of his wound his brother was sent in pursuit. He was killed in the attempt. At this time the Chief Sandile had been deposed from the Chieftainship by Sir Harry Smith, and Charles Brownlee was appointed to act for the Chief during 1850. Sutu, Sandile's mother was also appointed to act for a section of the tribe known as Ama-Mbombo. This appointment placed Charles Brownlee in an invidious position, for it aroused Sandile's resentment towards him, so much so that this son of Gaika ordered that Brownlee be killed and his head to be brought to him. That order was fraught with disastrous results, for on the day his brother James went out to recapture the cattle he met his death. The Xosas cut his head off, thinking it was that of Charles. When it was placed before Sandile, who was well acquainted with Charles, he saw at once that it was not his. In spite of this unfortunate affair regarding his brother's treatment, Brownlee entertained no malice against Sandile, but, instead, he did all he could, on all occasions, to speak for the Chief of the Gaikas to the European authorities.

About this period, Colonel L. Mackinnon, Chief Magistrate of Kaffraria, instructed Brownlee to call a meeting of all the chiefs, to consider the unsatisfactory state of Native Affairs, which were regarded with anxiety by the Whites, who suspected that another war was being hatched. The chiefs were invited to assemble at Keiskama Hoek. Sandile came with Maqoma. Mackinnon found that there was a suspicion among the Xosas that the Government had decided to have all the Chiefs arrested, believing that Colonel Somerset's army, which was on the Border, was only awaiting the word to attack the Xosas.

Brownlee did all in his power to dispel the suspicion, warning those who were present not to listen to the prophet Mlanjeni, who was the originator of these false rumours, for he was misleading the people, and by listening to him they would suffer the same evil consequences which they had suffered under Nxele. To which Sandile replied: "Yes, these rumours about Somerset's intention

214 THE SOUTH-EASTERN BANTU

214 THE SOUTH-EASTERN BANTU

do exist, as also that the Chiefs are to be arrested,
and, therefore, if they had been invited to assemble at King William's Town, or Lovedale, and
not at Keiskama Hoek, not one of the Chiefs would
have put in an appearance for fear of arrest."
And he related an experience of the War of the
Axe, when a trap was laid for him by the whites,
who summoned him to the camp to arrange terms
of peace, giving him a guarantee of safe conduct,
whereas Bisi (Colonel Bisset) when Sandile did go
immediately arrested him, and took to him
Grahamstown.   Therefore, he said, the word of
the white man is no longer trusted.   The reason for
the attendance of the Chiefs here to-day is because
they know, and have confidence in, Brownlee,
believing that he could not deal treacherously with
the Xosa Chiefs.

They also regarded him as one of themselves,
as he was acting for Sandile during his deposition
from Chieftainship.   It must be remembered that
Brownlee was not only Magistrate, but also chief
of the Xosas, and was granted Councillors (Xosa,
Amapakati), among others Tyala, who were in the
front rank, so that they should be governed according to their own customs, and avoid anything
which might lead the Gaikas to disaster.   It is not
clear what motive impelled Governer Smith to
place Sutu, Gaika's wife, in charge of the Ama-
Mbombo, and Brownlee in charge of Chief Sandile.   Perhaps the Governor did not wish to alarm
the Gaikas who might conclude that the Chieftainship was to be · abolished.   Therefore, he
brought forward Sutu to reassure them seeing that
none of the Gaika chiefs had been chosen.

Brownlee greatly esteemed the position of Chief imposed on him, not because of the honour conferred, but because he admired and honoured the nation of Rarabe. He felt like one of them and comported himself as such. And while all the Europeans believed that Sandile was scheming for war, Brownlee was engaged in pacifying the mind of the Governor who was leaning towards the alarmists. At the end of the war of Mlanjeni, the Gaikas were removed from the neighbourhood of the Amatole Forests, and placed on a tributary of the Kubusi River (1853), Sandile having now been restored to the Chieftainship by the exertions of Brownlee.

Brownlee accompanied the Gaikas and spent four years there, and built for himself a new home which he named " Tembani," in 1857. The Cattle Killing occured while he was at Tembani, and he exerted every effort to counteract that tragedy and to prevent its spreading to the whole of the Gaikas. He appealed, and exhorted and warned day after day, and month after month, trying to prevent Sandile from participating in it. The name of " Napakade" was given him by the Gaikas at this time, for when they related to him the miracles which were to happen, such as the resurrection of the dead chiefs and people, who it was alleged had been seen crowding in a deep pool of water in the Gxara Stream, he was wont to retort : " Napakade " (never), and this name adhered to him ever after. The name of " Tshalisi " (Charles) was co-existent with that of " Napakade," and we find both forms in use to the present day.

For a brief period after Nongqause (the Cattle-Killing), so named after the Witchdoctress), when the country was pacified, he was appointed Magistrate at Somerset East, where he remained for four years. He was then transferred to King William's Town where he was Magistrate for one year, when he was asked to take the position of Commissioner of Native Affairs by the Government at Cape Town. He held that position for five years, when he was transferred by Sir Bartle Frere to Kokstad in 1880 as Magistrate of Mount Currie district. He was getting on in years, with a long official record of service behind him, in which he endeavoured always to prevent the Gaikas from breaking up as a nation. At length he laid down the reins of office and went into retirement at King William's Town in 1890.

Professor Brookes's remarks, in his *History of Native Policy in South Africa* (p. 107), concerning "Napakade," may be paraphrased. "He who above all others is worthy of praise for introducing a method for the administration of the Natives across the Kei (Transkei System of Native Policy) is Charles Brownlee. We know without doubt that the system did not just spring up of itself, but the foundation was laid from the first with foresight and decision. Under the system devised by Brownlee the Natives of the Transkei are more advanced and progressive (except the Native Tribes of Natal perhaps), and they are the most contented in the whole of South Africa in these days." The Scriptures say, "A good man leaveth an inheritance to his children's children," and the truth of this is realised in the children of Napakade who have all been sympathetically inclined toward the Native races, not by words only but in deeds.

We have a recent example of practical sympathy toward the Gcalekas by one of the members of that family, W. T. Brownlee (Xosa, *Busobengwe*), second son of Napakade, who was Chief Magistrate of the Transkeian Territories latterly, and held the Xosa Chieftainship in great regard. Among other notable efforts he championed the cause of the Gcaleka chief, when attempts to degrade this rank were made by Chiefs of other tribes in 1925. It was on the memorable occasion of the visit of the Prince of Wales to Umtata, where he met the Chiefs of the Native races, and presented them with friendly tokens in the shape of greatly prized walking-sticks. While others like the Chiefs of the Tembus, Pondos, and Fingoes received them, the Gcaleka Chief was overlooked. The whole Xosa nation was chagrined at this neglect of the status of the Gcaleka Chief, "Ngangomhlaba," who represents a great race, and is of more importance in hereditary rank and station than the others. At this juncture Napakade's son, after the manner of his forebears, exerted every effort to get the authorities to rectify the omission, and remove the affront to the Gcalekas. In this he was supported by Rev. B. J. Ross, son of the late Rev. Richard Ross, who is Minister at Toleni in Chief Lusipo's area. The result of their representations was eminently satisfactory for they succeeded in removing the unintended insult.

It was arranged that the Chief should meet the Prince at De Aar where he was received very cordially by the Prince, who presented him in gracefully worded terms with a walking-stick, and the slight was removed from the Gcalekas.

It is by such deeds that the friends of the Natives are discerned, because they work not for themselves but for others, their whole natures rebelling against all departure from just dealings. Such friends are the real champions of the principles of justice, trusted by their own people, a credit to the teachings of Christianity, and they represent not one race or nation only, for their fellowship with human suffering is founded upon Him to whom all the Nations of the Earth belong.

Matthew Blyth.

Captain Matthew Blyth was Magistrate at Ntlambe. He was not satisfied with deciding cases only, but endeavoured to raise the tribes under his jurisdiction. He was a companion of the Rev. Richard Ross, Minister of Toleni among the Fingoes, and they decided to erect a school after the manner of Lovedale. They consulted with Dr. Stewart, Principal of Lovedale. Stewart (Xosa, *Somgxada*) was at first doubtful, but they gave him no time for hesitation. Blyth and Ross roused the Fingoes, and got them to raise funds to prove the truth of their interest.

It was a particularly difficult undertaking, as the Fingoes were divided on the scheme. But Captain Blyth shouldered the burden unhesitatingly, exhorting, driving, explaining, until £1,450 was contributed, and Somgxada (Stewart) was asked to come to the Transkei, and the money placed in his hands. Stewart was thus compelled to take steps to continue the work already begun, and he contributed to the money already subscribed another £1,500, which he received from friends in Scotland. The work was then begun, and the school at Nqamakwe was opened in 1877, and called "Blythswood" after the originator who got the Fingoes to venture on the scheme.   The building cost £7,000.

No other Magistrate has equalled Captain Blyth in energy and perseverance in the work of raising the Fingoes.   Professor Brookes, *History of Native Policy* (p. 112), says of him, "He was the first perhaps of all the Chief Magistrates of the Transkei and the most perfect of the class."

It would be impossible to describe all the deeds he performed which brought forth this eulogium, as they are not sufficiently realized, but their fruits are in evidence.   Captain Blyth has no Memorial Stone, but, as Professor Brookes has remarked of him, the best memorial stone is the success and progress of his people (the Fingoes).

Sandile—1820-1878.

The heir of Gaika, Sandile (English Sandille), was born when his brother of the Right-Hand House, Maqoma (English Makomo), was already in his prime, for at the battle of Amalinde the Gaikas were commanded by him as a young man who had recently attained manhood, whereas Sandile was born after that battle.   During Hintsa's war (1834-5), Sandile was a little boy under the care of his mother Sutu.   Sandile attained manhood in 1840, the year that was followed by the comet (Umgca) 1841, in which year he also took over the reins of government. This chief did not take after his forebears.   His father was a spirited man, and Maqoma his brother was a fiery character, and yet withal having an active brain, cautious, calculating, and among the bravest of the brave. Sandile was a weakling, pliable, and without a settled or reliable mind. He would make an agreement and come to a decision to-day, but on the morrow he would hesitate and then deny all knowledge of it. Such a disposition made him distrusted by everybody. For example, consider the incident of Ngcayecibi. He was willing to join forces with Kreli, but before he could persuade himself to leave home, Kiva left Gcalekaland to fetch him, and aware of his character, Kiva forced the war on the Gaikas by attacking the Whites at the Kabusi, thus involving Sandile in spite of his hesitation. It was the same at the battle of Kentani: Sandile never attacked. When he saw the Chief Mapassa's force (the Tsonyana) just above him—Mapassa was an ally of the Colonial forces—he stopped, and instead of attacking hesitated and refrained altogether to the end. Although he might not be described as a man of courage yet he died in this war like other brave men.

After the battle of Kentani, he recrossed to his own side of the Kei River and entered the fastnesses of the Isi-Denge Forests with his followers. Here he met his death in 1878. Nor did he die in battle, but in a skirmish between a party o fFingoes, under Captain Lonsdale, and the Gaikas. The Europeans were not even aware of the Chief's presence there. The facts were ascertained from a Xosa, named Guba, who was captured. On the fatal day Sandile was with Dukwana, son of Ntsikana, of the Ama-Cira clan. Dukwana had gone out from the mission station at Emgwali (of the Gaikas) to espouse the cause of his Chief. He had the reputation of being expert with the rifle. He also died with his Chief at the Isi-Denge. Dukwana was in earnest in arming himself, for when the Gaikas were surrounded he did execution with his rifle, killing two Fingoes and wounding four others, before he was dispatched. The rest of the body-guard of the Chief was hard pressed, so much so that there was no time to bury the body. This was hidden in a thicket within the forest and abandoned there. The prisoner Guba, being pressed, said he knew the spot where Sandile was killed, and a small patrol of Colonial troops was sent with him. This patrol after a search found the corpse. An examination of the body disclosed that Sandile was shot with a Snider rifle which carried a soft-nose leaden bullet, which expands on striking, making a horrible gaping wound. The bullet had entered the right side breaking two ribs and destroying the liver. He was recognised by one of his limbs which was withered, besides being well known to others who had gone out on the search for him. The body was taken out of the forest (according to Captain Landrey's Official Report) and was carried wrapped in Guba's blanket to a German homestead whose owner, Schuch, was a resident of the Isi-Denge. There he was buried in the garden on the 6th Juue, 1878. Although by nature Sandile was a weak man, yet he was beloved by his people; and although it was clear to the older councillors that by engaging in this war of Ngcayecibi he was misleading his people, still because of their loyalty to their Sovereign Chief, most of those who attempted to dissuade him also perished with him, fighting a forlorn hope,

The War of the Axe (Sixengxe or Zembe), 1846-7.

In 1844, Lord Stanley, the British Colonial Secretary, wrote to Sir Peregrine Maitland, the Governor of South Africa, impressing upon him the necessity of doing everything in his power to bring about a peaceful settlement between those Xosas and Europeans who inhabited the border territory and to beware of affording an opportunity for war. Sir Peregrine Maitland, in the circumstances, concluded a treaty with the Ama-Rarabe, not forgetting to remind them that he had also made an agreement with the Pondo Chief, Faku, and with Kreli, the Gcaleka Chief, wherefore they should understand that the Governor had friends beyond and at the back of them. The heads of the agreement were briefly as follows:— (1) The Treaty of 1819 was revived which made the Keiskama the boundary between Whites and Blacks. (2) On its part the Government claimed the right to build forts anywhere on its side of the boundary. (3) The Frontier Armed and Mounted Police was to have the right to enter Kafirland when on the spoor of stolen stock, and was to be helped in recovering such stock by the Xosas, who were also required to hand over European transgressors of the law, and to compel Native witnesses to testify against them. (4) Missionaries and Government officials in the Xosa country were to be protected.

The Chiefs Umhala, Siwani, Gasela, and Mqayi went to Peddie in response to a summons, and accepted these terms on their own behalf, afterwards touching the pen. Having done this, they were promised £200 to be divided between themselves.   The Chiefs Pato and Kobe of the Ama-Gqunukwebe also affixed their mark, and were promised £100.   Sandile, and the Chiefs Maqoma, Botoman and Xoxo did likewise.   They, however, were not promised a reward, because they took exception to the constitution of the Court of Appeal.   The Chiefs Nqeno and Stokwe also held the pen, and were promised £50 between them. The Fingo Chiefs Njokweni, Mabandla, Nkwenkwezi, Matomela, Kawulela, Jama, and Mpahla received £100 between them on holding the pen. But the treaty effected nothing, for while the writing was still wet the Xosas were already arming, making ready for eventualities in the unsettled state of the country.   About a year passed after the signing of the agreement, during which nothing happened, although there were signs that all was not well.   There was a settled belief in the minds of the people that war was not far off, and Maqoma, who was at enmity with Sandile, petitioned to be allowed to reside among the Europeans, as he had decided to withdraw himself from whatever might happen.   Mqayi also took the same step, believing that war was imminent. And so it was.   It was brought on by a very insignificant thing—an axe.   A certain fellow, named Tsili, of the Tola Clan, a petty chief of the Imi-Dange, stole a hammer-headed axe common in those days.   Entering a shop at Fort Beaufort, he was attracted by an axe and immediately took it.   He was accused of theft, handcuffed and imprisoned ; whereupon Tola went to the Magistrate and pleaded for the release of Tsili.   The Magistrate refused, but observing the attitude of those around him he grew suspicious.   Preparations were therefore at once made to send Tsili to Grahamstown where there was a European Garrison, more especially as there were signs of a hostile movement among the Xosas. To prevent his escaping, the prisoner was marched along with two Hottentot prisoners, all of whom, with a European soldier, were under arrest. Tsili was manacled to one of the Hottentots. On the march, a party of Tola's men came in sight, and the guard at once fled. As there was no key to unlock the handcuffs, Tola's men severed the arm of the Hottentot who was manacled to Tsili at the wrist, and went off with Tsili. In this affair one of the Imi-Dange was shot by the guard before escaping. This man turned out to be a brother of Tsili, the thief. The Europeans demanded from Sandile that Tsili should be redelivered to them, but this was refused. And thus was brought about the " War of the Axe." The European troops set out on the march and were attacked by the Xosas at Middledrift and European cattle were seized. The owners went in pursuit and recaptured them. Later, the soldiers struck camp at Middledrift and marched to Lovedale. They had a convoy of one hundred wagons loaded with ammunition and various commissariat supplies. The convoy was attacked on the way, the enemy charging the centre teams and dividing the convoy, driving off those in charge, pillaging the rear wagons, and going off with much booty after setting fire to the wagons. Others followed up the front wagons, right up to the Tyumie where there was an European encampment. Here they were driven off and retreated, abandoning the wagons. Flushed by these successes, the Xosas felt themselves strong enough to continue the war. They, therefore, swarmed into the Colony, making for Peddie. But before reaching there, they were met by a detachment of European troops who were sent to intercept them. A battle was fought at the Bika which went against the Xosas, who were dispersed : the soldiers returning to Peddie. In the month of June following, the Xosas reattacked and seized in one of the defiles of the Fish River a military convoy of forty wagons, laden with arms and provisions, which was bound for Peddie.

The Affair at the Gwangwa (Xosa, Mgwangqa).

Siyolo, son of Mdushane, and elder brother of Siwani, an obstinate and impatient man, accompanied Umhlala's forces.   Umhala ("The Wild Cat") was a cautious scion of the House of Ndlambe.   These chiefs with their impis had encamped on the Keiskama River, and in the neighbourhood of the Fish River there was a strong force of military, which they determined to attack.   They disagreed, however, as to crossing the flats separating the two rivers, as an army on foot would be seriously exposed.   Siyolo suggested to Umhala marching at early sunrise.   But the son of Ndlambe objected to crossing the plains in daylight. To this Siyolo observed, "What is there to be afraid of, seeing it is not the first time the Europeans troops have been defeated?"   Upon which Umhala replied, "I am surnamed the Wild-Cat, a creature that travels at night, not in the daytime," and he immediately ordered his command to march that night.   He was fortunate, for he arrived at the Fish River without being observed

P

by the enemy. On the other hand, Siyolo got
into motion at sunrise, accompanying the forces
of the Chief Nqeno of the Ama-Mbalu Clan under
the Chief Stockwe. That same morning Colonel
Somerset's force was on the march, coming up
from Peddie and making for a point between the
Fish and Keiskama Rivers. This force came
suddenly upon Siyolo at the Gwanga, he having
almost reached the Fish River fastnesses. A
desperate encounter ensued which went badly for
Siyolo, but from which he extricated himself.
Shortly afterwards, Siyolo's men were observed
crossing the flats and making for the Gwanga
Stream. The artillery opened upon them with
destructive effect. As they broke, the cavalry
were released and the mounted horsemen thun-
dered down upon them. With their heads bent
to the withers, the horsemen charged right in
amongst them and through their ranks to the
other side. Reforming they cut, slashed, and
sabered the Xosas in a manner which was to be a
never-fogotten episode by those who experienced
it. Of all the encounters which distinguished the
War of the Axe, this affair of the Gwanga was described as the worst. Siyolo was severely wounded
and invalided for a long time by his injuries.
"The Wild-Cat," however, which crept by night
and escaped, must have soliloquised when he
heard this, "Did I not say so? That is the reward of obstinacy." Shortly after this it was
evident that the strength of the Xosas had waned,
their warriors being frequently beaten. The
Governor then took an example from Sir Benjamin D'Urban who invaded the country of Hintsa
after reducing the Ama-Rarabe. Governor

Maitland carried the war to Kreli beyond the Kei, although that chief had declared himself neutral. When they met, both parties entered into an agreement the aim of which was to bring hostilities to a close. But the results were negative. Instead of the country becoming peaceful, there were frequent encounters and skirmishes until the end of that year, when another person arrived on the scene. This was Sir Harry Smith who had displaced Governor Maitland. The latter was blamed for adopting the D'Urban Policy and recalled by the authorities in England. When Smith assumed the Governorship, Lord Glenelg, who had dismissed D'Urban for having, in his opinion, unjustly deprived the Xosas of their territory, and who had restored the boundary to the Keiskama River instead of the Kei to which D'Urban had pushed it forward, was no longer in power. Smith had been a colleague of D'Urban in the War of Hintsa, and he now found an opportunity to carry out the policy of his chief by extending the boundary to the Kei River. All that territory between the Keiskama and the Kei was taken from the Natives and added to the territories of Queen Victoria. Only the country beyond the Kei was left to the Xosas. After the battle of the Gwanga nothing succeeded with the Xosas. They were held up in the Forests of the Amatole and being driven therefrom were scattered broadcast.

The English armies on their return from Gcalekaland invaded the Tembus under the Chief Mapassa, son of Bawana, who had rebelled against the English Government. Their land was temporarily forfeited. The Chief Maqoma had requested the Whites to give him a place to reside on, so as not to be involved in a war which he regarded as inevitable, but he was refused and was thus forced to join in the war. But finding that resistance was hopeless he surrendered. Sandile followed suit and with others gave himself up,. saying he agreed with those who sued for peace. The majority of the Ama-Rarabe also laid down their arms on hearing that their Chief was so inclined, but after the harvest Sandile was anxious to renew hostilities. Whereupon a patrol was sent out to arrest him. When it arrived at Sandile's Kraal at the Keiskama, the Chief was not to be found, for he had withdrawn himself. The patrol thereupon seized a number of cattle and drove them off.

The war cry was sounded behind them; the Xosas with Sandile at their head followed up, and pressing on the patrol forced it to retire on Lovedale. Two soldiers were killed in this affair and four wounded, in view of which Sandile, upon consideration, dispatched twenty head of cattle as a peace offering to the Whites. But the Governor informed him the cattle were not wanted. What was required was that Sandile should surrender himself to the Governor, otherwise the war would proceed. At this period Maqoma's impi was under command of his son, Kona, Maqoma himself, on surrendering, having been granted a place to live at Port Elizabeth, so as to be out of the trouble. A month passed, and Sandile, now exhausted, sent word to the Europeans saying that there was starvation among the Xosas, and that therefore he had determined to surrender himself on condition that he was not to be imprisoned or executed. This condition was granted. Thereupon he surrendered with Anta and several others of his councillors. It would seem that this was the occasion which caused Sandile afterwards to say he would never again trust the word of a white man. The reason was that, after surrendering himself for the Peace Conference, he was arrested by Captain Bisset and removed as a prisoner from Middledrift to Grahamstown. This treatment Sandile resented for the whole of his natural life. After the war, the Gaikas were removed from the neighbourhood of the Amatole Forests and, together with the Chief Sandile, placed on more open country about the Kubusi River. The land from which they were ejected was placed under military control, and later allotted to European settlers for agricultural purposes. A large part of the country occupied by Mapassa's Tembus was also forfeited, and English and Dutch farmers settled thereon. By Sandile's surrender, although the Chief Pato of the Ama-Gqunukwebe was still holding out, the War of the Axe was brought to a close.

The War of Mlanjeni (1850—3).

Only three years passed after the War of the Axe when Mlanjeni's war occurred. It is called after Mlanjeni because the general unsettlement of the Xosas at the time brought his name to the front. Mlanjeni, son of Kala, was a Medicine Man of the Ndlambe tribe, under the Chief Mqayi. The Europeans on the border were in a state of anxiety owing to rumours that the Xosas were intending to rise, and Mlanjeni's name was mentioned as that of a man doctoring the warriors.

The Magistrates hesitated to accuse him for want of definite evidence of his complicity, or any infringement of the law on his part. At length, the Magistrate among the Ndlambes (Colonel John Maclean), knowing that these things were reported to be taking place at Mqayi's kraal where Kala lived, sent out policemen to arrest Mlanjeni and his father Kala. The police arrested Kala, but Mlanjeni was not interfered with as he was sick, and the police contented themselves with merely throwing down poles which had been set up by the doctor at the kraal, as a sign of his profession. Nevertheless, war rumours increased, and at length it was reported that the tribes were frequenting his place. The Magistrates reported the situation to the Governor, and impressed upon him the necessity of visiting the scene of disturbance in person, so as to use his influence to allay the excitement. Thereupon Sir Harry Smith left Cape Town for King William's Town to investigate for himself. The real reason for the unsettlement was the law which sought to prevent the Chiefs from permitting the practice of "smelling-out" persons accused of witch-craft, whereby they would lose one of the most profitable sources of their revenues. It was said that, on account of this law, the Chiefs privily advised their witch-doctors to mislead the people, so as to bring them into opposition to the authorities. That was the conjecture. Mlanjeni himself was regarded as only a tool of the Chiefs for stirring up the trouble. Smith held Sandile responsible for the commotion and ordered the Gaika Chief to meet him. But in spite of repeated messages, the Chief refused to obey this order to discuss the matter. Sandile expressed himself to Brownlee to the following effect (*Blue Book,* 1851, p. 41), " After the War of the Axe I was invited by Colonel Somerset who sent Bisi (Major Bisset) to direct me to head-quarters in order to discuss terms of peace. I was given an assurance of safe conduct, and on the strength of this word I put the halter round my neck, for when I arrived in camp I was made a prisoner by Bisset and sent to Grahamstown to be transported to Robben Island, but the Govern-or interposed saying I must be released. Hence I am afraid to trust myself to Smith." Thus the Chief was unable to comply with the command of the Governor remembering the former danger he had experienced, and that piece of treachery caused Sandile never again to trust the word of a white man. He even made a memorial of it by naming one of his sons, who was born at this time, " Bisi," after Major Bisset. Sir Harry Smith could not get away from the feeling that Sandile was secretly preparing for war, and that Mlanjeni by his prophesies was voicing the mind of the Gaika Chief. He therefore deprived Sandile of his sovereign rights, but left Mlanjeni alone. After the removal of Sandile from the Chieftainship (*Blue Book* 1851, p. 45, Sir Harry Smith to Earl Grey), the Governor appointed Sutu, Gaika's wife, temporarily, to take the place vacated by her son over the Ama-Mbombo, the principal section of the Gaikas. It is not clear why she was placed temporarily over this section only, and not over the whole of the Ama-Rarabe. Perhaps it was because the Governor intended to restore Sandile at some future period, when the trouble had blown over. What is clear is that, although all the Xosa Chiefs were present, and they were numerous, not one of them was chosen. They were not trusted. Instead of electing one from among them, the Governor chose Brownlee to hold that position, temporarily, over the Ama-Rarabe, and he was allotted four Councillors from the Ama-Rarabe to assist him in the administration. From that day Charles Brownlee (*Tshalisi*) was constituted Chief of the Ama-Rarabe. It was also proclaimed that a reward of £500, or 250 head of cattle, would be awarded to whoever delivered Sandile or caused him to be delivered, to the authorities, and another £100, or 100 head of cattle, to whoever handed over the Chief Anta. Nobody claimed these rewards. The Xosas displayed their sense of self-respect and patriotism by ignoring the announcement, no matter what the amount or nature of the reward which sought to influence them to treason against their sovereign head. No Xosa has ever betrayed his Chief to outsiders. The Hottentots of the Gqugesi also rose up against the Government and went over to the Gaikas. Some Native policemen in the service of the Whites also went over to their people, taking their horses and accoutrements with them. The Hottentots were under the command of Hermanus Matross, who had been given a grant of land by Sir Benjamin D'Urban at the Gqugesi. Hermanus armed his own followers, and with other confederates thought himself strong enough to attack a fortified township with a force of about a hundred. A section of the Tembus north of the Amatole Range under the Chief Mapassa, son of Bawana, also rebelled, although they did little injury. The brunt of the war was chiefly fought about the forests of the Amatole and their neighbourhood. It was from there that the Xosa hordes issued to attack the villages of Woburn, Auckland, and Juanesberg, overpowering them and leaving ruin and devastation in their track. From the beginning the Xosa force fiercely engaged the Europeans, but they were fighting a foe who had no thought of retreating, and who beaten today fought again on the morrow. The bravery of the Blacks cannot count in encounters with people like these. The black man enters a war with courage, but this in itself is not sufficient, because he fails to provide commissariat beforehand. An army, it has been said, "marches on its stomach," and the Xosa army had no commissariat. No matter, therefore, how bravely a Xosa warrior may fight on an empty stomach: on the morrow his internal economy will begin to talk, and by the third day it will squirm till it brings him to a standstill. Now, totally disabled, his strength having given out, the glory of the combat palls, the war fever abates, and defeat is soon assured. The war of Mlanjeni was carried on for two years, being characterised by many little battles, and it wore itself out by 1853. Before its conclusion Sir Harry Smith was relieved of his Governorship and was succeeded by Sir George Cathcart (Xosa, Katikati). To bring the war to an end, it was necessary to drive Sandile and his forces out of the forest area of the Amatole Range on to the plains, and this was done by driving them to the country bounded by the Xaxazele Mountain and the Kei, i.e., to the district of the Kubusie River which did not offer the same facilities for concealing their forces when the fight became too hot for them. The country from which the Gaikas were ejected was handed over to the whites for settlemennt, who were granted surveyed allotments or small farms. Beyond the Kei, Governor Cathcart made an agreement with Kreli, whereby the risks of creating disturbances by the Gcalekas would be avoided in the interest of peace. Thus the War of Mlanjeni ended.

CHAPTER XVI

KRELI

The Ama-Gcaleka. The Chief Kreli (1820-1902)

The eldest son of Hintsa, by his wife Nomsa, daughter of Gambushe of the Bomvanas, Kreli (otherwise Sarili), was born about 1820, shortly after the battle of Amalinde. He has already been mentioned as going with his father, Hintsa, to surrender to Governor D'Urban. He remained with his father and his uncle, Buru, in the English camp, until such time as their tribe had delivered the cattle demanded from them—"branded cattle" and indemnity cattle, the latter being demanded on the ground of a report that Hintsa was abbetting the Gaikas in their war against the Whites. At that time Kreli was a youth; some say he was already circumcised.

When the time for Kreli's initiation into manhood had arrived, the Councillors met to discuss the steps to be taken. Hintsa, Kreli's father, had been operated upon by one of the Ama-Ngqosini clan, and he turned out to be a man of fiery temper. This was put down to the discredit of the surgeon. Under the influence of this belief they decided not to risk employing a surgeon of the same clan for Kreli, lest he also should develop a temper, or as the Xosa say, "develop a horn." Mdudumane, the surgeon of the Ama-Ngqosini, who had been engaged for Hintsa no doubt had left his mantle with some other member of his clan. Hence, it was decided that a trial should be made of Ntiyane of the Ama-Kwemnta. Those who remembered this decision when they saw that Kreli realized their hopes of a mild-tempered chief, felt that their decision had been dictated by wisdom. It is strange what a hold these beliefs have on the Bantu. With them there is no such thing as coincidence or accident in such matters. In the case of Kreli's son, Sigcawu, they reverted to the Ama-Ngqosini doctors or surgeons, and Sigcawu "developed a horn." For the circumcision of Gwebinkumbi, the tribe returned to the Ama-Kwemnta, and he was as mild as his grandfather Kreli.

Kreli had a considerable number of wives. His chief wife, and mother of his heir Sigcawu, was Nohute, a daughter of the Tembu chief, Ngubēncuka. His Right-Hand wife was Nondwe, who became the mother of Mcotama. While Sigcawu, according to custom was the son of the wife chosen by the tribe, yet he was much younger than others of his father's sons. Kreli's first-born was Lutshaba. Other sons of Kreli but of minor houses are numerous, of whom the best known are Sonwabo, Mtoto, Dingekaya, Golwa, and Somakwabe.

Kreli first came into notice in 1835, when he was incarcerated in the British camp along with his father, Hintsa, his uncle, Buru, and his cousin, Mapasa, Buru's heir. The hardships and anxieties he underwent during his enforced detention, together with the Governor's threats against his father, followed by his parent's tragic death, had a marked influence in the early maturing of his mind, but they also had the effect of destroying his confidence in Europeans. The death of his father, and the manner of it, was an episode never to be obliterated from his mind.

The effect of these experiences on Kreli was permanent and manifested itself in various ways. The Cattle-Killing Delusion, which miscarried in its object and, instead of emancipating his people, brought them to the verge of national suicide, is said to bear evidence of his influence in shaping that tragedy, notwithstanding that it is popularly attributed to Mhlakaza and Nongqause.

When the news of Hintsa's death reached the Governor, Sir Benjamin D'Urban, he interviewed Kreli, and made this agreement with him :—" In order to effect peace, Kreli must submit to the authority of the Whites, the authority extending to all that territory lying between the Keiskama and Kei Rivers ; otherwise, Kreli must fulfil the conditions imposed on his father and pay the cattle promised by Hintsa." Another condition was that Kreli should agree to accept in the country between the Kei and Bashee Rivers certain tribes of the Ama-Rarabe, viz., the Ama-Jingqi of Maqoma; the Chief Tyali and his tribe ; the Imi-Ngcangatelo; the Ama-Mbalu ; the Chief Botoman and his section ; the Chief Umhala with the Ama-Ndlambe ; and the Imi-Dushane of Siyolo. He was also to see to it that they did not recross back into the territory from which they were to be expelled. Kreli was not to revenge himself on his neighbours, the Tembus, because of their attack on him.

Kreli, of course, in the circumstances was compelled to accept these terms. Thereupon he was released. Some portions of this agreement became a dead letter. The proposal concerning the Ama-Rarabe was not carried out. Buru was not immediately released, and it looked as if he had been forgotten, but after two months he was also permitted to depart. Lord Glenelg objected to the transference of the Ama-Rarabe, and he also restored the boundary to the Keiskama. As for the indemnity cattle, they were never paid in full, because the Gcaleka cattle were attacked by sickness and the Chief could not fulfil the agreement. Three thousand cattle was all that could be furnished, and as an alternative Kreli was ordered to hand over to the Government a strip of country running up from the Kei to the Butterworth River, including the village of Butterworth and the lands adjacent thereto; also a strip of country running up to Clarkebury on the Umgwali River in Tembuland, and a road in the direction of the Bashee Drift. All these were to take the place of the unpaid indemnity in cattle. But the decision of Lord Glenelg caused these alternative agreements to become ineffective as the country was restored to the Gaikas, and there was therefore no need for the Ama-Rarabe to go to Gcalekaland. And as a result of the Glenelg decision Kreli was released from all indemnities and every other burden placed upon the shoulders of Hintsa. These decisions of Lord Glenelg were confirmed and put into effect by the Acting Administrator, Sir Andries Stockenstrom, who was sent by the British Government to see that they were carried out. In his callow days it became a habit of Kreli's to make agreements of this nature. In 1844, during Sir Peregrine Maitland's Governorship, another little agreement of the same kind was arranged with Kreli. It was to the effect that he (Kreli) should protect the Missionaries and other Europeans in his country, and likewise travellers passing through his territory to other parts beyond Gcalekaland. Furthermore, he was to hand over all transgressors against the laws of the Colony who sought refuge, or a means of escape, by secreting themselves in Gcalekaland. He was also to abide in peace with neighbouring tribes and to respect the authority of the Magistrates who would be stationed in the country. In return, in the event of his good conduct, Kreli was to be awarded a grant of £50 a year. To these conditions the chief assented by "holding the pen" (making his mark) before two Magistrates, Shepstone and William Fynn. The Governor, before making these arrangements with Kreli, had already concluded similar agreements with the Chiefs of the Ama-Rarabe.

Among the Xosa Chiefs from Palo to Rarabe, notable for their humanity, their oratory and courage, none could approach to Kreli, son of Hintsa. He entered upon the sovereignty at a time of special difficulty in relation to his country and people, and when it was already apparent that they were under the authority of strangers, that is of Europeans. He recognized that, if he did not exert himself, the Xosas would be submerged altogether. Under his rule Kreli did all he possibly could, according to his judgment, to keep the tribes of Palo united and intact. As a humane and peacefully inclined man, a man of character, weighty in council, respected and beloved by his people, Kreli had no rival. Even to-day, the old men who frequented the Royal Kraal, or attended Court as judges and courtiers at the Great Place, weep tears of sorrow at the mention of his name. He won the hearts of everybody because as Sovereign Chief he was condescending to the common people, and addressed in respectful terms and in a friendly manner those of inferior status. The Europeans likewise, in spite of his being often at cross-purposes with them, honoured and respected him. It would be hard to find any European who was acquainted with him to speak disparagingly of him. Instead, all praised and respected him for his own sake. He had no rival in this respect among the other chiefs. Having finished his work of protecting his people, and having been granted length of days, he died in 1902 at the Sholora on the Bashee River, at the age of 82 years, leaving the whole tribe in such mourning, as to remind us of the lament of King David over Abner, which might be repeated of Kreli :—" Know ye not that to-day a Prince and a mighty man has fallen in Israel."

The First Offensive (Um-ngqingo) against the Tembus, 1854

Kreli was residing at the Hohita and the Gcalekas were at peace, little dreaming that their cattle would be slaughtered, for Nongqause had not yet appeared on the scene. No important event had arisen to disturb the relations between Kreli and the Tembus, except that there were bickerings between the Tembus and members of the chief's bodyguard (the Quaka) which was commanded by Runeyi, son of Ganya, and grandson of Mpulu, of the Ama-Ngwevu clan. The Tembus had crossed the border and occupied a portion of Kreli's territory, and the Gcaleka army was therefore mobilised. It was arranged into two divisions, the Qauka under Runeyi, and the Ntshinga under Kwaza, son of Ngqila. The Qauka was first to take the offensive, driving the Tembus across to their own side of the Roda River. Kreli with his division, the Ntshinga, crossed the Roda, but upstream of the Tembus. Renuyi and the Qauka crossed at certain drifts of the Bashee below the Tembus at some distance from Kreli. The impi of the Tembi Chief, Ngubengcuka, was surprised by Kreli's division, while engaged in disputing the passage of the drifts lower down by the Qauka division. The Tembus were driven back by Runeyi and retreated in disorder towards their homes in the direction of Imvani. Here they found themselves surrounded with others of their tribesmen by Kreli and the whole Gcaleka army. And the assegai worked havoc among them, individual Tembus being chased by the Gcalekas in the general *sauve qui peut.* They were scattered in all directions like a covey of young partridges. The story of how they were cornered and trapped in this first offensive has been handed down as a tale to future generations by the Tembus.

The Cattle-Killing (Nongqause). 1856.

Kreli never forgot the shooting of his father, Hintsa. And he remembered that while he was still mourning his departed sire, Governor D'Urban forced him into an agreement which removed the boundary line from the Keiskama to the Kei. Although Kreli was quite aware that such an arrangement would be oppressive to his people as favouring the Whites, still he had no option but to agree while in the hands of an unsympathatic Governor and that Governor's army. He, therefore, consented under *force majeure*, observing also that the House of Rarabe was under a new

Q

administration. All these misfortunes embittered him and the iron entered his soul. He sought for a plan to discomfit the Europeans and to drive them back into the sea from whence they had come. He fancied that the Xosas could be brought to fight with one heart and, by concerted action, to precipitate themselves against the Europeans in one desperate effort to free themselves. But his plan was fated to destroy the nation. There was the tribal doctor, Mlakaza, at the Gxara, a small stream which enters the Kei near its mouth. Let him work his arts. It was customary for the Bantu chiefs to shake the people up by visions purporting to come from the gods. It was not Kreli's fault that he was under the compulsion of these beliefs. They were those of his own people. It is hard for one who has been moulded in this spirit of faith in witchcraft, to extricate his mind from such beliefs. It is the misfortune of those who have been brought up amid such surroundings. Mhlakaza, a scion of the House of Gcaleka (whose family name "Izi-Tenjini" is derived from the tribal totem an ox called by that name), lived under the Chief Mnzabele, and his kraal was on the Gxara Stream, Kentani division. He had a niece named Nongqause, who was a graduate in the school of the mystical arts, and it was said that the impressions which she, as a medium, received from the spirits were transmitted by her to her uncle, Mhlakaza, who promulgated them to the tribes. Moreover, like Nxele and Mlanjeni, who in their day translated the desires of their Chief, Mhlakaza, so the Gcalekas said, was interpreting the mind of Kreli. Two ploughing seasons had passed after the war of

Mlanjeni, when in the third year a marvellous rumour got abroad. The pith of the messages of Nongqause and Mhlakaza may be put in words extracted from a book by M. W. Waters, with reference to Nongqause, and although the words have been placed in the mouth of Nongqause by the writer, they may be taken as a realistic interpretation of what was intended by the original. Nongqause, speaking in her trance, said, "The spirits of our ancestors are speaking. I, Hintsa, speak. I, also, Gaika; and I, Maqoma, among others whose names are not clearly recorded to the ear. But they are among the ancients of Xosa and warriors of old time. Listen! they are speaking. Their words announce their sorrow. We have seen the oppression of our people by the Whites. We can no longer keep silence. We shall come to save the nation from destruction. The spirit translates me to another country: a land of death. I see a multitude of dead cattle and the heavens are crowded with vultures: the grain pits are empty: the land is obscured by the chaff driven by the wind. My soul is vexed with this country of death. It calls me. It summons me to the third heaven, to a land of resurrection. Listen! Listen! They say that when the winter has passed, spring succeeds; when death has passed, the resurrection comes. I see the land of the Xosas a great land. The kraals are full of cattle. The cows with sucking calves are lowing, and the fields are ripe to harvest. I see multitude on multitude, the armies of the Ama-Xosa, great armies. I can distinguish that race among them. There is nothing old."

This is an example of the methods and incidents which led to the destruction of the Xosa tribe. These happenings came at a time when the people were under great tribulation, for during the years 1855-6, before the Cattle-Killing, the pest of lung-sickness had broken out among their herds and reduced the people to the verge of starvation. Mhlakaza's neice in deceptive phrases was saying in effect, "The departed chiefs who died long ago will again arise with their followers, and come back to earth with their herds of cattle which will suffer no more from disease. And after the resurrection the white man will disappear never to return to this country. But in order to facilitate their departure, the tribesmen must agree to observe certain definite conditions, the most important of which are, that all the cattle must be slaughtered; the grain pits completely emptied; and the food scattered, so that the land shall be clouded with the dust of the chaff driven by the wind." These are some of the leading points, although there were other announcements which were broad-casted by Nongqause.

This tragedy began among the Gcalekas, but messengers from the Great Place spread the prophecies throughout Gaikaland.

At the Gxara there is a pool of water close to the sea, near Mhlakaza's kraal, and when the sea is raging and the tide rising, the waters of the pool are disturbed by the incoming tide. On both banks of the Gxara Stream at its mouth, there are wild banana shrubs. Among these Nongqause was wont to sit, seeing visions in the pool. When the news of these happenings spread, the Xosa tribe was filled with anxiety. Certain of the

Chiefs, to satisfy themselves, sent people to look
into this strange matter. These returned with
various accounts. Some were deceptive, saying,
" Yes, we arrived at the Gxara and looked into
the pool with our own eyes. What we saw there
were the faces of our ancestors troubling the
waters as if they would come out, but they are unable to do so, because the people are not united
in fulfilling the conditions desired by their ancestors." Others came back home, saying, " We
should flee with our cattle for there is nothing in
it. We saw nothing to justify all these
rumours, except that the waters in the pool are
disturbed by the incoming tide. We saw no heads
of people in the water, only the shadows of the
banana leaves waving to and fro in the wind, and
mirrored in the pool." Thus the nation was
divided among believers and unbelievers, those
who were willing and those who were unwilling to
slaughter. The believers were called the Ama-
Tamba, the unbelievers the Ama-Gogotya. Sandile himself, because of the exertions of Charles
Brownlee, refused to slaughter with his people,
although there were some believers among the
Gaikas. The majority of the Gcalekas were
believers, for the individuals who objected had no
power to go against the beliefs of their chiefs.
The only House among the Gcalekas which refused
to slaughter was that of the Ama-Mbede under
the Chief Sigidi. Among the Ndlambes individual
kraals slaughtered. The believers cut the throats
of their cattle wholesale, and emptying their pits
scattered the grain to the wind. The real object
of the originators of this thing, it is said, was to
drive the impis to fight desperately in despair of

any food at home, having "burnt their boats behind them." The word went out to the tribe broadly, that on a certain date the sun would rise blood-red—first sign of the resurrection of the dead —then the land would fill with people and cattle and the grain pits would be full to overflowing with food. When the day arrived, the believers had already fulfilled the conditions by killing all their cattle, and scattering the grain, leaving nothing of mealies or kafir-corn. Everybody had risen early looking to the east for the sunrise, the believers most anxious of all. The sun rose while they gazed. The sun revolved in its orbit as usual. At midday they began to doubt, but when it was going down the full truth stared them in their faces. The sun went down over a thoroughly disheartened and wailing people. Hunger now became acute. The people were discomfited, and no voice was any longer lifted in favour of war. Instead, many of them scattered into the Cape Colony and took service with the Whites in order to ward off starvation. It was computed that, between those who died at their kraals, and those who died wandering about the country, twenty-five thousand people perished. The mind cannot by any effort convey a picture of the distress which befel the people of those days, and the depth of a tragedy whereby a living tribe wilfully destroyed itself.

Nongqause.

Although it is said that Nongqause was a daughter of Mhlakaza, the truth is that she was a daughter of Mhlantla, younger brother of Mhlakaza, both

of them sons of Ham, a member of the Ama-
Mfene clan. Mhlantla died and left a son, named
Maxiti, and his younger sister, Nongqause. These
children were brought up by Mhlakaza. Nongqause was arrested by the Europeans at the main
drift of the Bashee about the time of the debacle,
and was given a place to reside on at King
William's Town, where she remained till the day
of her death. This took place about the beginning
of the plague of Rinderpest in 1897.

The Second Offensive (Um-Ngqingo) against the Tembus, 1858.

Shortly after the event of the Cattle-Killing
(Nongqause), and during the tenure of the
Regency of the Tembus by Joyi, on behalf of the
Heir Apparent, Mtirara, the Gcalekas again surrounded the Tembus. Kreli left the Hohita
during the debacle of Nongqause and went to the
Bolotwa. There a petty chief of the Tembus,
named Mqanqeni, saw a troop of horses which
belonged to the Gcalekas and yielded to the temptation to steal them. When the Chief Joyi who
was acting for Mtirara heard this, he remarked,
"What right has Mqanqeni who is not the paramount chief to presume to seize these horses for
himself?" So he also set out to commandeer
Kreli's horses for himself. Whereupon the Gcalekas surrounded him at the Umgwali River, near
Clarkebury in Tembuland. They captured Joyi
and held him prisoner for a time, until Kreli
released him and he returned home. This affair is
described as the Second Offensive against the
Tembus.

The Affair of Umtsheko, 1860.

In this same year Joyi, acting for the Chief Mtirara, went to war with Gqirana, a chief of the Pondomise Tribe at the Qweqwe. A section of the Gcalekas were living at the Mgazana among the Bomvanas, Kreli having taken refuge there after Nongqause. When the combatants were engaged, the lower Tembus, living between the Darabe and the sea, having left their homes unprotected to go and join in the fray, had left their cattle also unguarded. The Gcalekas who were still suffering from the results of the debacle of Nongqause, observing this, went out with Kreli and commandeered them. Hence these cattle are described as the cattle of the Umtsheko, because they were taken in the absence of their owners.

Nongxokozelo, 1875.

The origin of the war between Kreli and Ngangelizwe, Sovereign Chief of the Tembus, arose through an incident which happened in 1870. Nomkafulo, a daughter of Kreli and mother of Dalindyebo, the late Tembu Chief who was married to Ngangelizwe, was brutally thrashed by her husband. She had a leg broken by him, and seizing an opportunity she dragged herself to the kraal of Menziwa, a chief of the Fingoes near the Bashee. Menziwa's people were a section of those Fingoes who had found a retreat in Tembuland and lived at the Tyalara. Nomkafulo, whose marriage name was Novili, was taken over to Sigidi's place. He was the Chief of the Ama-Mbede at the Cizela. From there the princess was taken over to Qora, her father's home. Kreli thereupon reported to the Resident at the Ntlambe, William Fynn, saying: "What reason has Ngangelizwe for thus brutally treating my daughter, the crown of our household?" Upon which Ngangelizwe was dealt with by the Europeans and fined eighty head of cattle, so the Gcalekas say; although the English documents say the fine was forty head. And so that matter ended, but Novili remained at her fathers's home, not returning to Tembuland. She did eventually return, however, after the war of Ngcayecibi. It happened in this way. The Chief Ngangelizwe was invited by the Europeans to assist them and the Fingoes in the war of Ngcayecibi. He consented, seeking an opportunity to revenge himself on the Gcalekas who had injured and otherwise humiliated him in the war of Nongxokozelo. After the battle of Ibeka the Gcalekas were gathered together at the Mqotwane. Ngangelizwe met the Europeans beyond the Shixini River, where he divided up his army into four parts, viz., the Ntshatshongo division, the Mgotwana, the Mqakazana, and the Sihlahleni. Ngangelizwe marched his army to Idutywa (Ngxakaxa) where he had been invited to assemble, but encamped en route after Shixini. This was the time when the Ama-Velelo were defeated by the Whites at the Mqotwane. It was during these incidents that Novili was found by the Tembus and taken to her home in Tembuland. But before the return of Novili the war of Ngxokozelo had taken place. This woman was a daughter of Sombali of the Mpinga clan. The Gcalekas made no war with the Tembus over Novili's case, for Kreli was pacified by the Europeans who counselled him to abide by their decision. He did so,

but with bad grace. In her flight from Ngangelizwe, Novili had left behind her maidservant, Nongxokozelo, in the hands of the brute Ngangelizwe.

On a certain occasion, the Chief, in a violent
temper as was his wont, stabbed the maid to death.
This being reported to Kreli, he sent word to
Ngangelizwe to produce his child, the maid Nongxokozelo.   This, of course, was not possible in
the circumstances.   Whereupon Kreli again referred the matter in question to the Whites,
requesting at the same time that an opportunity
be given him to chastise Ngangelizwe. Rumour
says he was privily permitted on condition that
he should not cross the upper reaches of the
Bashee, which were already granted to European
settlers as a result of the Cattle-Killing. Kreli mo-
bolised his army in the valley of the Nkondwane, at
the Ncihana beyond the Bashee, Elliotdale
district.   From thence in no particular order his
forces crossed the Xuba River and stopped at the
great marsh close to it.   Next morning they
marched to the Tubeni in Bomvanaland, but
before taking the main road which passes Miller
Mission, the Quaka wing, under the command of
Dalasile, son of Gxaba, diverged and made for
Xora. It was in haste to get to grips with the
enemy before the general orders were issued.
But Kreli ordered it to return which it did. The
army travelled up the ridge and when approaching the marshes below the Mbizana hill, the
heavens began to thunder, but again clearing
disclosed Ngangelizwe sitting on the hill of Mbizana. He was recognised by the Gcalekas who
moved forward to attack, but the Chief fled with
a small party who accompanied him to the Buwa

stream. In the morning when the march was
resumed, they sighted the Tembu impi at the
Isitebe where Ngangelizwe had assembled his host.
Whereupon Kreli divided his forces, the Qauka
taking the centre and making for the Xongora
River, under Runeyi. There was an armed force
of Tembus on a ridge facing the Bashee River.
Kreli dispatched the Ntshinga division under Tyila
and the Tsonyana division under Kiva, who for
the first time was given a command on that day,
to attack the Tembu army, and waited results.
The Commander of all the divisions of the Qauka,
from whom the other Chiefs took their orders, was
Runeyi. In issuing his orders, Kreli was supported by Kwaza who commanded the Ntshinga
Division. Kreli in person attacked at the Buwa
stream, and drove the enemy up the Bashee.
The Qauka attacked others of the enemy forces
which were reinforced by the Ama-Qwati tribe.
The forces opposed to Kreli were directly under
command of the Paramount, Ngangelizwe, in
person, together with the Chiefs Menziwa and
Mnqanqeni. Kreli had drawn some warriors from
the Qauka, so as to reinforce the chief Ngubo's
command.

Menziwa, father of Mbande, was a Fingo who
found refuge in Tembuland and was granted lands
at the Tyalara, higher up the Bashee. His presence here in support of Ngangelizwe was doubtless due to reminiscences of the incident of Novili
when he helped her escape to the Ama-Mbede.
He had sworn to her that he would never fight
against Kreli owing to the brutal treatment she
had received from Ngangelizwe. For that reason
he was driven away by Ngangelizwe and took

refuge at Idutywa. But he was taken back by
the Military Authorities to Tembuland and re-
placed on the lands he had vacated. To-day,
doubtless, fearing a repetition of his treatment by
Ngangelizwe he decided to help that Chief. Menziwa's forces took up a position on the ridge overlooking the Tyalara and Buwa Stream on both
sides. The division under Ngubo, son of Malashe,
was ordered by Kreli to attack Menziwa whose
impi went round by the Ntsilana Stream, and
occupied the Ntsilana ridge. But Ngubo was held
up by the Fingoes who held the ridge. Kreli
himself with the Ama-Velelo and Ama-Banqo divisions was engaged with the Tembus at the Mtentu
stream. The sound of the Fingo guns betokened
heavy fighting in that direction, and Kreli dispatched one of his wings to go to Ngubo's assistance. This force got behind the Fingoes coming
up by the Tyalara road. Thus they were surrounded. Pressing the attack and gaining the
ridge, Ngubo's men drove Menziwa's Fingoes into
the arms of the Gcalekas in the rear. That was
the end of it. The Fingoes immediately broke
and ran, going up the Bashee, hiding in the
thickets or wherever cover could be found, and
were thus prevented from rejoining Ngangelizwe
altogether. Menziwa's forces were badly cut up,
although not without having inflicted severe losses
among the Gcalekas. The Tembu army made a
stand at Buwa where it was signally defeated.
Some days elapsed before the junction of the two
main divisions of Kreli's army—the Ntshinga and
Qauka. When the Tembus were driven from the
Buwa Novili's house was burnt down with others.
During the time her house was burning Novili

was at the Qora, her father's home.   The Gcaleka
army pushed on over the Buwa and bivouacked
for the night at Menziwa's homestead at the
Bashee.   From there, in the morning, it went
over the Forest Ridges of the Ngqura and seized
Tembu horses hidden there; it then formed camp
at the Quluqu.   Here the army rested for four
days, then Kreli sent out to see where the Qauka
division was and recalled it to the Quluqu, it
having had no fighting worth recording.   The
army again marched to the junction of the Xuka
river with the Bashee, and while here was visited
by the Missionary, Peter Hargreaves.   He came to
implore Kreli to stay his hand.   Kreli, just before
Hargreaves's arrival, had detailed a force to go
and seize the Tembu cattle which were congre-
gated about the forests of the Ama-Qwati country.
He had ordered them to make ready to march
saying; "I will lead you to where the Tembu
cattle are."   At this stage Hargreaves arrived
saying;   "Please your Excellency, those cattle are
mixed up with the European cattle and I would
be sorry for you to be involved with them, as
when you seize the cattle you will not be able to
distinguish those of the Europeans from those of
the enemy."   A discussion then arose, and Kreli,
always a gentlemen and ready to listen to a
request, even when he held the army of his enemy
in the hollow of his hand, withdrew his army.
The Bomvanas in this affair had a division of their
own assisting Kreli.   Their army was given the
duty of protecting the rear of the Gcaleka army.
They crossed the Xora and took up a position at
the Manzamnyama, in the Mqanduli District, in
order to overawe   the Tembu   clans of the Ama-

Nqanda, the Ama-Nqabe and the Ama-Tshomane in case they should threaten trouble. The Bomvanas were, therefore, outside the fighting zone, for these Tembus did not move, but their part was fulfilled according to the orders of Kreli.

The War of Ngcaycibi, 1877.

The following narrative of the incidents leading up to the War of Ngcaycibi was given by a Gcaleka Councillor engaged in it. It differs materially from the usually accepted version, and is given here merely as one version, not necessarily accepted by the writer. The common version will be given also.

In the year 1865, there was a rearrangement of the tribes of the Gcalekas and Fingoes on new lines. The Gcalekas were squeezed to the seaboard, the new boundary being from Butterworth and the Kei on the west to the Bashee on the east. The Fingoes were moved from Peddie to the territory between the Upper Kei and Butterworth, the number of the Fingoes brought into juxtaposition to the Gcalekas being about 40,000. The Gcalekas exceeded that number slightly. While they were engaged in the war of Nongxokozelo, the Fingoes were snarling at the Gcalekas, and hoping that the Government would release them to attack them. Thus a persistent spirit of antagonism existed although they were still at peace. The Fingoes said, "Although the Gcalekas have defeated Ngangelizwe, they could not defeat us." They looked for trouble and endeavoured to provoke hostilities, and the Gcalekas on their part were in no good humour, remembering their treat-

ment when the Fingoes seized their cattle on
leaving Hintsa's country, in 1835, to live under
the protection of the Whites. In 1877 war broke out.
A certain Fingo, Ngcayecibi by name, lived near
the Ndotshanga, and one day asked for a loan of
pots from Chief Mapassa's people (the Tsonyana)
for the coming-of-age feast (Intonjana) of his
daughter. Mapasa was the great son of Buru.
The pots were lent, and a section of Mapassa's
people (the Tsonyana) went to the feast, or beer-
party (Umgidi). They were, however, not invited
to partake of the beer. Next morning, they
attended again but the same thing occurred—they
were denied beer. Whereupon they demanded
their pots, saying, " Why did you refuse us beer
yesterday and again to-day when you are using
our pots ? " Upon this they were attacked by the
assemblage of Fingoes with kerries. The Chief at
the head of the Tsonyana on that day was Mxoli,
of a lesser house of Buru, although Kiva, son of
Xoseni, of the Right Hand House of Buru was
also present. They drew off and returned home
to arm, one of their number, a Gcaleka, having
been fatally injured. They then attacked Ngcayecibi's kraal and the fight was joined. Mapassa's
party returned from Ndotshanga in the evening.
Kreli, for his part was unconscious of any disturbance to the peace of the country.

The more common, and generally accepted,
versions of the genesis of this war is to the effect
that a Fingo, named Ngcayecibi, whose dwelling
was on the west side of the Butterworth River,
had at his place on a certain occasion a beer
party. As is customary at most Native festive
gatherings, no individual invitations are issued,

all and sundry being invited to be present by general usage. At this beer party, a number of young men, two of them being personally known to the writer, viz., Twana and Nkunzana, members of the Tsonyana clan of Gcalekas, were present, along with a petty Chief of the clan, named Mxoli, son of Mbune and half brother of the fire-brand, Kiva, son of Xoseni, who was the central figure of the war. Drinking went on during the day and to all appearances towards evening the beer was finished, but before leaving the Tsonyana men asked to be supplied further from the *Mfihlo* (beer put aside or secreted for family use). This was refused, and, further demands being made and met with similar refusals, high words were spoken, which led to a scrimmage in the hut, in which one of the Tsonyana was hurt. These then returned home to the Tutura where Mapassa, their principal Chief, lived. During the following few days a body of men from the Tsonyana armed and made for Ngcayecibi's kraal, in order to wipe out the supposed insult. This body crossed over the Butterworth river (Gcuwa) and swept off a considerable number of cattle, and the war cry was sounded on both sides. Kreli knew nothing of this at the time, but later became involved, as it became a tribal rather than a faction affair. Mapassa, the principal Chief of the Tsonyana, when he had compromized his Chief, Kreli, turned round and as a renegade joined the Colonial forces and was prepared to fight against his own Superior Chief. In the subsequent fighting the Tsonyana clan split up, Kiva and Mxoli joining the Gcalekas, while Mapassa joined the Colonists. Just before the outbreak of the war, West Fynn, Magistrate

at Ntlambe, had retired and been succeeded by
Colonel Eustace (Hashebi). Colonel Eustace,
when the commotions began, summoned Kreli to
the Ntlambe. He replied, " O Hashebi, I am
afraid. Stay where you are, have no anxiety, I
shall come to your relief myself." Meantime,
the cattle seized by the Tsonyana were being
restored, though only a certain number, but not
all, were recovered by Kreli. The war became
more imminent. Chief Mapassa withdrew and
went to reside among the Europeans, but a small
number of the Tsonyana under Kiva and Mxoli
remained. The Governor, Sir Bartle Frere, who
was at King William's Town, was informed of the
commotion, but he was unwilling to believe those
who said that war was threatening. Colonel
Eustace, in going to the Ntlambe, was sent by
the Governor to Kreli to inform that chief that
the Fingoes were Government subjects and that,
therefore, if they were interfered with the Europeans would assist them. The Frontier Armed and
Mounted Police were pushed forward and camped
at Ibeka on a rising ground, to close the main
road to Idutywa. They were in command of
Inspector Chalmers. A party of police left the
Ibeka for Idutywa, and shortly after passing the
Impuluse it was summoned to the Gwadana by
Ayliff, who was in charge of an armed body of
Fingoes there. When Chalmers arrived with the
F.A.M.P., hostilities had already begun. It would
seem that Ayliff was to blame for setting the
spark to the timber. He had gone to overlook the
armies of Kreli, who had summoned them to a
council on the flats below Gwadana Hill. Ayliff
approached with his Fingoes the spot where Kreli

R

was addressing his people, informing them that for his part he deprecated war and did not intend to fight. But the Tsonyana who were the cause of original disturbance were divided into two sections. Some of these followed their chief, Mapassa, and silently drew away when they saw the Gcalekas becoming deeply involved, Mapassa declaring that he was neutral. But afterwards he sided with the Whites, although the trouble originated with his clan, the Tsonyana. That circumstance brought Mapassa into disfavour with Captain Blyth, Magistrate at Ntlambe, after the war was over. Blyth scorned a man whose actions amounted to a betrayed of his Chief. So Mapassa was regarded with contempt until the day of his death.

The Battle of Gwadana.

As already related, Kreli was announcing to his army that he was not at war with the Government with whom he was still discussing the situation. The followers of Kiva and Mxoli were not present, but as they were proceeding to the conference they suddenly came face to face with Ayliff's Fingoes. Kiva immediately attacked and the war cry was sounded on all sides. Without awaiting Kreli's orders, the hosts broke away out of control and attacked the Fingoes. There was no commander or word of command in this affair. The cannon opened fire under Chalmers who supported Ayliff. Ten shots were fired when the gun broke down, although it counted for little with the forces of the Ama-Palo (Xosas) who went straight for the guns. An attempt was made to withdraw the injured cannon. The Fingoes, seeing this, mistook it for a retreat, as the Gcalekas were already among them stabbing with the assegai, and their demoralization was complete. They scattered and ran, causing further disorder by getting among the Mounted Police. There was now neither word of command nor any observance of order, everybody striving for himself, and each seeking to be first to reach his home. On the side of the Europeans Ayliff precipitated the war. On the side of the Gcalekas, Kiva did likewise, taking it upon himself to attack without waiting for orders, and while his Chief, Kreli, was still discussing with the Government. The Gcalekas captured the two cannons, but abandoned them as useless. They were later recovered by their owners. The Police and Fingoes were like a covey of startled quail on that day at Gwadana. When the events of the day were reported to Kreli, he summoned his impis to the Qora and addressed them, saying, "What do you mean by going to war when I am still discussing the situation?" The impis replied, "We were attacked and not given a chance." Kreli's question was addressed principally to the Qauka division which went off with Kiva without orders. It was this division only, together with the Tsonyana, which fought at Gwadana. The Ama-Velelo division went in pursuit of the retreating Fingoes and following them to the Butterworth River were hemmed in by the European and Fingo forces. They were under the command of Dalasile, son of Gxaba, of the Right Hand of Gcaleka. They were surrounded all night. Here on the Gcaleka side fell Tsobosini, son of Sokanyile, of of the Ama-Ntande clan, the songster (Imbongi) of the Chief Velelo. After a time the beleagured

impi found an opportunity to extricate itself by
breaking through the cordon at night, and arrived
at Kwaza's kraal at the Qora on the following
morning.

The Battle of Ibeka.

The Gcalekas were elated at their triumph
of yesterday. The Tsonyana force, under Kiva,
made for the Ibeka by way of the Mcuncu. It
was reinforced by Kreli's division of the Ntsinga
and certain elements of the Qauka. They went
up the ridge and over the hill on which Ibeka
stands. The Gcalekas at once attacked the en-
trenched camp. Several times they were driven
back, and they could not penetrate the defences.
Many distinguished men were killed there, and
they wavered. While they hesitated, the Fingoes
were ordered forth with the Police. The Gcalekas
could not withstand the onslaught and retreated.
Next morning, they again attacked but made no
impression, being driven back by the fire of
musketery while still at a distance. In resuming
the attack they had been tempted by the Fingoes
who sallied out anxious to repeat the successes of
yesterday. On this day Kreli's kraal at the Qora
was burnt, the Europeans and Fingoes swarming
on the hill of Ntabelang above the Qora River.
Kreli who remained in his kraal was dragged out
by the Gcalekas who remonstrated with him. He
exclaimed, "I wish to be arrested right here, so
that I may have an opportunity to express myself." The Gcalekas answered, "Where is your
father Hintsa who was blamed for Gaika's cattle?
Your father also was not at war, he died for just
this reason in the camp of the Whites, in whom

he confided." With these words the Gcalekas drew him away. He went down the Qora River towards its extreme end at the estuary near the sea; but separated himself from his army. There was never a day when he took command of the army. While these events were happening his son, Sigcawu, was absent. The truth of Kreli's promise to Colonel Eustace now became apparent. He revealed his trustworthiness by saying to his son, "Go, Sigcawu, to Hashebi and take him away from the Nthlambe, for I told him not to be anxious as I would provide an escort for him. Go and place him in the hands of his own people." Three companies of the Ntshinga division were ordered to accompany Sigcawu as an escort, and crossed the Butterworth River with Hashebi, also the Cegcuana River, and arrived with him at the Toleni Store on the Kei Heights. The Fingoes stood aside and looked on. Sigcawu returned having placed Colonel Eustace at the trading station at Toleni.* Two messengers were dispatched from the Fingo army to meet Sigcawu and say, "The order is for you to proceed on your way seeing that you have escorted the Magistrate no harm will be done to you." Sigcawu returned to the Qora and in the morning the European and Fingo forces swarmed on Ntabezulu.

From the Ntabezulu the European forces divided, a part of their command going down the Mkonkoto Stream to its junction with the Qora in pursuit of a Gcaleka impi. The Rosho division

---

*There seems to be a discrepancy here. Some hold that Eustace was accompanied by Sigcawu only as far as *Butterworth Camp*. The question is, "Was the European camp already established at Butterworth when Eustace was handed over?"

had not answered Kreli's summons when he assembled the forces at the Qora; following the example of the Tsonyana which also did not attend. The Rosho were under Mtirara, son of Tyabo, a scion of one of the chiefs' houses. This division (the Isi-Rosho) encountered the Europeans and suffered severely. The Gcalekas could not hold their ground from that day on to. the battle of Kentani. The Europeans marched freely over the whole country while Kreli was in hiding in the forest of the Ludwesa. There the enemy went to capture him, but he circumvented them and took refuge in the Cwebe Forest in Bomvanaland. On his track the European forces arrived there, and a desperate encounter took place, with hand-to-hand fighting in the bush. Again the Chief escaped. On emerging from the forest, the enemy forces came suddenly upon Kreli's temporary huts at the far end and edge of the bush. These they set on fire and the Chief's tiger karosses and all the paraphernalia of his body-guard were destroyed. Henceforth Kreli was engaged in evading the forces in pursuit of him. Meanwhile, Kiva had been dispatched to Sandile to seek the help of the Gcalekas.

At the Lusizi.

The affair of the Mkonkonto and that of the Lusizi could hardly be described as a battle. The European troops were marching freely throuh the whole of Kreli's country beating up the Forests. They would surprise small parties of people, who were scattered by showers of bullets fired by the Fingoes and mounted men, and these were described as battles. And so it was on the day of the Lusizi fight. After the battle of the Ibeka there was no united force existing in Gcalekaland, for the warriors were divided up into small units to avoid the pursuing enemy. At the Lusizi the troops were moving down leisurely towards the coast hoping to encounter Kreli's impi: instead they came upon a small company of that Chief's household troops. The Gcalekas made feint of surrounding the enemy forces, but after exchanging shots were worsted and scattered. It was then reported to the Whites that a small party had disappeared into a cave in a streamlet of the Lusizi. A body of Fingoes was sent out under the brothers Goss, William and Michael, brave men and fearless. The cave was in a depression at the head of a donga, so that the approach was up stream between the banks. On arrival a party of Fingoes entered between the walls and coming abreast of the cave were immediately fired on by the Xosas, and all were killed. William Goss now entered with three Fingoes and the four met their death there. Upon this Michael Goss went in with two Fingoes and he and one of his men was killed, the third retreating. It was now apparent that death stared those who entered the narrow defile in the face, for as soon as they showed themselves they were shot down. It, therefore, became necessary to try another plan. A Fingo was ordered to creep alongside, and to wait at the top of the face of the cave till someone put his head out and to stab him with an assegai. Another Fingo within the banks in line with the cave presented a stick with a hat on it, and as a Xosa came out to shoot he was immediately stabbed in the nape of the neck by the waiting Fingo. Thereupon the Fingoes swarmed into the cave and killed seven men of the Gcalekas.

The Battle of Kentani.

It did not appear that the Gcalekas had any more fight in them, but there was still some vitality left. The more intrepid spirits were not intimidated by what had happened, although the fighting divisions had been scattered over the land, seeking shelter in forests and being hunted like antelopes. There was Kiva, the son of Xoseni, for example, setting out from the Mnyameni with a detachment of the Tsonyana and a sprinkling of other units, crossing the Kei, and making for Sandile, Chief of the Gaikas at the Kubusie. Promptly, on arrival, he thrust a burning brand into the traders' shops and the settlers' homesteads, and the Gaikas immediately started into life. The Chief Matanzima with a small party came up against a patrol of the Police, somewhere about Draaibosch and at once engaged. The Police were reinforced by a party of soldiers and made a stand, but could not maintain it. They were gradually forced back, both policemen and soldiers, by a force under Chief Makinana, and in the end broke and fled. It is not certain, but it is affirmed, that Kiva was present in person at this engagement. But it is known that on his mission to Sandile he encountered the Europeans. This compromised Sandile, who henceforth, was regarded as a participant in the war. He came out with Kiva, going down the Kei, and crossed over at its junction with the Mnyameni stream. They met Kreli at the lower end of the Qora.

The news was communicated by Kreli to his scattered forces, which concentrated on him at Qora. Having reorganised the scattered elements of his army, he ordered it to march on Kentani and attack the European camp there. To Sandile he remarked, " I have been taken unawares and involved in a matter of which I was in ignorance. I had no thought of war, so attend you to the arrangement of the forces. I have no proposal to make." Thus Sandile was in control of the plan of action at Kentani. Before the attack was made, Sandile was coming up with Kiva from the direction of the Kei, and reached the neighbourhood of Kentani. Coming in sight of the camp Sandile halted, so did Kiva. Meantime the bulk of the Gcaleka army was coming up the main road from the sea. On that day, and for the first time, Kreli accompanied them in person. But the army nevertheless was commanded by Dalasile, son of Gxaba, chief of the Ama-Velelo. Ngxito doctored the army. The Tsonyana of Mapassa came up from the direction of the Kei and were seen to take up a position above Sandile's forces. Sandile at once sent a message to Kreli saying, " We will not attack as here is the Tsonyana stalking us." Sandile was placed in difficulties by Mapassa's force which threatened his flank, and Kiva therefore refrained also from attacking, but watched Mapassa. By this time Dalasile had attacked and fought, and was being driven back and pursued by a detachment of the European army. Another force turned upon Sandile and Kiva. The Gcalekas say that on that day the Gaikas were given no opportunity to attack, although the European account alleges that they did attack. Dalasile's army was scattered by the Whites and fled back by the way it came. Then Ngxito, the war-doctor, came up to them on the flats above Ncengane and re-organized them. It is said by some of the Gcalekas who were present, that by dint of doctoring they were able to force the Europeans back to Kentani. In the circumstances, Kreli crossed the Bashee and sought shelter with Gwadiso, Chief of the Konjwayos in Pondoland, whereupon a message was sent to the Pondo Chief, Nqwiliso, at the Ruze, saying, "Here is Kreli." Nqwiliso therefore set out with some Europeans who came by way of Umtata for the purpose of surrounding him in the forest. When Kreli saw that he was cornered, he came out in broad daylight, into full view, but as he was accompanied by a strong force he was not interfered with. But Ngubo, one of Kreli's officers, was captured by Nqwiliso at the Nomadolo, and also his two younger brothers and three sons, and all were sent as prisoners to Cape Town. As for Kreli, when he saw no hope of refuge in Pondoland, he turned back and recrossed the Umtata River and secluded himself in Bomvanaland. When he arrived there, the Chief of the Bomvanas, Langa, eldest son of Moni, said his bodyguard should be dispersed if Kreli was successfully to hide himself, and he should not be accompanied by any people. So Kreli left Langa's neighbourhood and went to the Mgazana. He disappeared at the Sholora in broken country contiguous to the Mgazana, and this is where he died after several years had passed. Here he remained; not, however, by any authority of the Whites. Time passed and Major

Elliot at Umtata became uneasy, and he sought out Kreli in the interest of peace. He went down and met the Chief between the Mnyama and Xuba rivers. The Major was accompanied by the Magistrate Morris (Ndumiso), T. Merriman (Menemene), Henry Wild and another. The Major addressed Kreli saying, "I have come to take you out of the bush, Kreli. This a peaceful mission, Chief, and you are permitted to go openly among the Europeans. There is no case against you." And he was given a letter of guarantee to that effect. Sometime after this, Kreli was summoned to Umtata, where a great meeting was held, to announce to all and sundry that, "the Chief has come out of the bush. Henceforth he may live in peace."

CHAPTER XVII.

The Abe-Nguni (Aba-Ngoni of Nyasa).

The Genealogy of their Chiefs.

```
(Lunyanda.
(     |
(Magangati.
(     |————————————|
( (I) Mlotshwa, (2) Mafu.
(     |
(Mbekwane.
(     |————————————|————————|
( (I) Zwangendaba, (2) Ntabeni, (3) Mgayi.
(     |————————————————————|        ————————————|—|
( (I) Mbela (Mombela), (2) Mpezeni (first-born, not heir),
(     |
( (3) Mtwalo, (4) Mpelemba, (5) Marawu (Sons of Zwangendaba).
```

The Abe-Nguni of Nyasa migrated from Natal at the time of the disturbances of Tshaka. They had travelled southward from up-country as had the Ama-Xosa, but they turned again and, re-tracing their steps, went north. I have given them a place in this book because I believe they are one in origin with the Xosas. Their name Abe-Nguni also decides me. As of old the name represents the tribe, and the tribe originates from some Chief whose name it bears. It was not by accident that the Xosas were described as Abe-Nguni. The appellation is derived from an ancient chief of the tribe called Mnguni. With regard to this point, Mr. Fuze in his book, entitled *The Black Races*, says of the Ama-Xosa, " The major portion of the tribe of the Chief Mnguni went westward toward the setting sun . . . . .It is this same Mnguni who was father of Xosa, who, it would seem, was the great son of Mnguni. This tribe (Ama-Xosa) has been long separated from their relatives whom they left behind (p. 78). The point raised by this son of Zulu, we have referred to before. Its repetition is meant to draw attention especially to the latter part of Mr. Fuze's statement. He says in brief: "The Xosas in removing from the North (from the Dedesi) left behind them a remnant of their own people, the Abe-Nguni in Natal." Now, we find that the people who responded to that name are the Abe-Nguni of Zwangendaba, and moreover the tribe was known by that name in Natal prior to their migration northward. Evidence to this effect is found in the statements of Ntombazi, mother of Zwide. In order to understand the point it ought to be borne in mind that Zwangendaba, Chief of the Abe-Nguni, had gone with his people to live under the protection of Zwide, the Chief of the Ama-Ndwandwe tribe. The Ama-Ndwandwe were at constant war with Tshaka, often defeating him by the help of the Abe-Nguni. There came a day when the Ama-Ndwandwe were also defeated by Tshaka, whereupon Zwide withdrew with Zwangendaba to the country now described as Wakkerstrom. There a quarrel arose between Zwide and Zwangendaba which was decided by the assegai. Zwide was defeated and made a prisoner by Zwangendaba, but after a time the latter relented, mindful of their former relations, when they fought their numerous battles together, and he released Zwide sending him home with provisions in the shape of sleek cattle. But it would seem this act of kindness did not pacify Zwide. The scandal of his defeat embittered him, and he vowed vengeance on Zwangendaba. The missionary of the Abe-Nguni in Nyasaland, Doctor Elmslie,

says in his book on the history of these people :—
Zwangendaba, who was one of the chief captains
of Zwide, although living under Zwide, was not
subject to his authority altogether.   After his
quarrel with Zwide, that Chief marshalled his
forces seeking to revenge himself on Zwangendaba.   When Zwide's impi was assembled at the
Royal Kraal preparatory to marching out against
Zwangendaba, Ntombazi, wife of Langa and
Zwide's mother, appeared and endeavoured to
discountenance the war, saying to her son "My
child, would you destroy the *Abe-Nguni?* Did
they not release you and send you home with
many sleek cattle ? "   But Zwide was not to be
appeased.   Upon which, Ntombazi adopted a
singular course in order to remove this thought
from her son's mind.   In full view of the assembled host she disrobed herself and stood before
them   completely   naked.   This most unusual
action startled and disconcerted the warriors who,
filled with traditional superstition, regarded it as an
omen of impending disaster ; they were unmanned
and disheartened and refused to fight.   Now,
for my present argument, the important point is
this:— Ntombazi described the people of Zwangendaba as the *Abe-Nguni*.   That was at that
time quite a familiar name, nor was it casually
adopted, nor yet was it given to them by other
tribes like the Tongas who only heard their name
in their flight northward from Tshaka.   There are
those who say : This name of Abe-Nguni originated
with Tongas when Sotshangana (Manukuza) arrived among them, fleeing from Tshaka.   But
Manukuza was a son of Gasa of Zwide's tribe, the
Ama-Ndwande.   In seeking a new country he

proceeded along the seaboard and settled in the territory beyond the Limpopo River which is now described as the country of Gasa (Gasaland). Gasa was a younger brother of Zwide. Others again say: The tribe of Manukuza got their name from the Tongas who called them Abe-Nguni because, as they said, the name implied that they were thieves or bandits. My reply is that Manukuza was one of the Ndwandwe tribe, which was only politically related to the tribe of Zwangendaba. Manukuza's tribe are not Abe-Nguni. True, in former days they were neighbours, assisting each other in their wars, but differing in tribal origin. It is reasonable to infer, therefore, that because of the familiarity of the name it also came to include the people of Manukuza. To the Tongas the name Abe-Nguni may be familiarly connected with thieving, but other tribes do not use it in that sense. Here the tribal title is taken from a person who originated the tribe namely Mnguni. And while on the subject of Manukuza, I may just place before the reader the line of the Ama-Ndwandwe before passing on to the story of Zwangendaba :—

Nxumalo
Ndwandwe
Langa

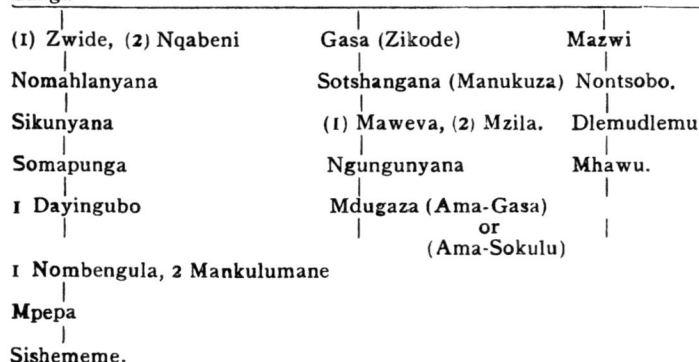

(1) Zwide, (2) Nqabeni	Gasa (Zikode)	Mazwi
Nomahlanyana	Sotshangana (Manukuza)	Nontsobo.
Sikunyana	(1) Maweva, (2) Mzila.	Dlemudlemu
Somapunga	Ngungunyana	Mhawu.
1 Dayingubo	Mdugaza (Ama-Gasa) or (Ama-Sokulu)	
1 Nombengula, 2 Mankulumane		
Mpepa		
Sishememe.		

We left Zwangendaba on unfriendly terms with
Zwide, and it appeared to this son of Mbekwane
that in the circumstances his present abode would
not, to use a Xosa expression, "rear him any
calves." In other words, he determined to leave
Zwide and look for a new country in which to
settle. At that time, these chiefs and their peoples
were settled in the Wakkerstrom district, just
north of Natal, where they had proved a hard nut
for Tshaka to crack. Departing thence, Zwangendaba took the road to Mzilikazi's country, with
whom he was on friendly terms, and who had
preceded him in his flight to the country now
known as the Transvaal and settled there. Zwangendaba migrated about the 1829. That was
the year following Tshaka's death. He followed
the coast line at a distance, then went further into
the interior looking toward the setting sun.
Arrived at Mzilikazi's place they lived on friendly
terms, but only for a time. Therefore, Zwangendaba trekked, this time turning towards the sea
in search of his friends Manukaza and Mhlabawadabuka, sons of Gasa, youngest son of Langa,
son of Ndwandwe. He cleared a road with the
assegai, sweeping, his enemies before him, and
none could stay him in his course. He arrived
there with his following enlarged by accessions
from other tribes he had defeated in his course.
However, he did not stay long with Manukuza,
for trouble arose between Manukuza and his
younger brother, Mhlabawadabuka, and the latter
was driven away. The latter with his following
then joined Zwangendaba. Now, people who
have been accustomed to rule by the assegai and
to live independently, do not easily accommodate

themselves to the rule of others, which becomes irksome to them. So they separated from Manukuza. Zwangendaba while his "feet were still wet" (with travelling) parted from Manukuza together with Manukuza's younger brother, Mhlabawadabuka, making for the North. Smaller parties broke off from them on the way up ; some settled at the Sabi, others at the Zambesi. In the year 1835, Zwangendaba crossed the Zambesi near the township of Zombo, built on the shores of the Zambesi by the Portuguese. He forced his way until he crossed the Tshambezi, a river which precipitates itself into Lake Bangweyolo, and skirting the shores of Tanganyika entered the country of the Ama-Fipa. The Abe-Nguni of Zwangendaba having reached this country settled there, and took possession of the land for themselves. But this tribe was still to break into two sections. Zwangendaba, whose language was outspoken and who, besides being a man of power, was loved and respected by his people, at length lost his vitality, being well on in years when he arrived among the Fipa, and he died there. He left several sons, who are not traceable except the eldest, Mtwalo, and his younger brother, Mombela. The sections which broke away from the Abe-Nguni after Zwangendaba's arrival there, were numerous. The most notable were the Ama-Tuta, Ama-Viti, Ama-Lavi and the Ama-Hehe. These tribes exercised authority over all the country north of the Zambesi and right up to Tanganyika. There were few tribes which dared to fight with them. In order to understand the strength of these tribes, we must remember that the Ama-Sayi (Masai), a tribe of Hamitic origin

S

responsible for the migration of Bantu tribes from their country at the Tana, and was powerful enough to settle among other tribes of the Bantu, is described by Mr. Last as follows:— " The Masai are reported to be the most powerful of the races of Central Africa, but should they ever meet the Ama-Hehe in a life and death struggle there would be wonders and surprises and a reshuffling of tribes, for it is not the first time the Masai have been beaten by the Ama-Hehe." This tribe settled below the Ruaha, a branch of the Rufigi (A. H. Keane, *Africa*, Vol. II., p. 512.) The Ama-Hehe (Wa-Hehe) tribe in September 1891 routed a large force of Germans. It is a very savage tribe, and is a terror to any of the surrounding tribes. And so it was with the Abe-Nguni, they have the capacity to live. They also know how to die like men. Let us now follow the sections which went out from the Abe-Nguni of Zwange-ndaba, and set up tribes of their own. We have already seen that Zwangendaba died in the land of the Ama-Fipa, also termed the Ama-Sukuma. After his death, internal disputes over the succession arose and frequent battles followed. Mgayi, a younger brother of Zwangendaba, broke away with other followers, and went forth till he came to the neighbourhood of the great lake, the Victoria Nyanza. The country did not suit him, so he returned to the place where his elder brother died—the territory of the Ama-Sukuma.

There Mgayi died, and as successor Mpezeni, eldest son by birth of Zwangendaba, was appointed chief. But he was not the heir although the first-born. Mpezeni did not satisfy the Abe-Nguni by his administration and they deposed

him, substituting Mbela (Mombela) who became
Zwangendaba's heir in his place. So Mpezeni
removed with his following, and created his own
tribe which is known by the name of the Abe-
Tuta or Wa-Tuta. Now, there was a certain
chief of the Kalanga, by name Mungwala, who
was promoted by Zwangendaba on the way up,
and placed in charge of a section which had remained behind below the Zambesi. Another
name for Mungwala was Mpapa-Maseko. After
Zwangendaba had gone forward, this Chief followed him and, crossing the Zambesi, fought his way
through the tribes in his path. He reached the
Nyasa and going up eastward he settled down
and built along the shore of the lake. To-day his
descendants are known as the Ngwangwala, or
Ama-Viti. Another section of the Abe-Nguni
went off under an Induna of Zwangendaba's,
named Zulu-Gama, joined Mungwala and became
incorporated with the Ama-Viti. On the death
of Mungwala, Ngomane, his son, succeeded him ;
but the people of Zulu-Gama rebelled against
him, and being defeated by them he also took the
road. He set his face towards the low country,
crossing a river named the Shire, and settled
there. These people are described as the Ama-
Zitu or Aba-Nguni of Ngomane. As for Mpezeni
aforementioned and his brothers, Mtwalo, Mpe-
lemba, and Marawu, they were at incessant strife
for the succession. On their dissensions becoming
unbearable, an influential induna arose, named
Siwelewele, son of Ndlovu, who fathering the
younger members of Zwangendaba's family and
other important indunas, set out with a large
following to occupy a new country. These people
are now called the Central Aba-Nguni.

The Story of Zwangendaba's Doctors.

Dr. Donald Fraser, in his book already mentioned, relates how Zwangendaba set himself in opposition to the methods of his witch-doctors.   That Chief became suspicious of the frequent " smelling-out " of the most influential men of his tribe.   The methods of these witch-doctors looked as if they were prompted by malice.   So, on a certain night when all were sound asleep, Zwangendaba took the blood of a goat which was slaughtered, and stealthily creeping into an empty hut, sprinkled the walls and floor with blood, returning to lie down in his own hut.   In the morning, Zwangendaba was seen to enter the hut with an easy, indifferent gait, only to retreat suddenly, staggering and shouting aloud: " Hear is blood on the walls, and on the floor.   Who has committed this murderous action ? "   Whereupon the elder statesmen were summoned to a conference and all the doctors were shown this surprising thing.   They were commanded to reveal the culprit.   Accordingly, putting their heads together and going through their formal incantations, they pointed out the murderer.   Upon which the Chief arose and explained to the assembly that the spilt blood was a deception of his own, for he, Zwangendaba, desired to ascertain the truth about the methods of these doctors, because many lives had been destroyed on their account. Moreover, he saw it was clear that all those unfortunate victims who died through the findings of the doctors, were innocent of the crimes attributed to them.   Wherefore, he commanded that all these doctors should be executed and not one allowed to live.   And this was done according

to the word of the Chief. Now, to complete the
story of the tribe of the Aba-Nguni, it may just
be said that although the various tribes are all
described as Zulus, Ama-Viti, etc., there is one
thing that will not submerge, and that is the name
Bu-Nguni. All those tribes are included in this
name, describing themselves as such, and are so
described by other tribes. That designation, therefore, will not die. This is not surprising, for the
distinguishing name of a Chief and his tribe, and
a name that binds all clans, even though these
should by natural increase become tribes, will not
easily die, because it is the one thing that binds
together. Therefore, my belief is, as I have already said, that the Aba-Nguni of Zwangendaba
are related to the Xosa. The only thing that
might raise a doubt in the minds of some is, that
the relationship link in the line between the Aba-
Nguni and the Ama-Xosa is not clear. The
difficulty is that nobody has yet appeared to help
trace the line of Zwangendaba back to a connecting point with Mnguni. It goes no further back
than Mlotshwa's father, who was Zwangendaba's
grandfather and was contemporary with Gcaleka,
among the Xosas, that is about 1730, although
doubtless their separation had occurred generations
before this. Mgangati, father of Mlotshwa, lived
in the time of Palo, and Lonyanda, Mlotshwa's
father, about the time of Tshiwo, that is, approximately 1700. In case there should be difficulty
in the minds of some, because of the existence
among the Hlubis of a clan called Aba-Nguni,
it should be pointed out that this clan is of
another stock. The ancestor of these last was
Nguni, and not Mnguni from whom the Xosas are
descended. This Nguni is of Lala origin, and

was the son of Flatelilanga, one the early ancestors of the Imi-Huhu (now Hlubi). Nguni was the father of Vilwana, father of Makatini, who had two sons, Mbanguba of the Great House and Kesa of another House. As Nguni's heir was Mzimkulu, it would appear that the clan which carried on Nguni's name, through Vilwana, is a branch line, either an " Ixiba " or that of a younger son. To complete the chapter relating to the Aba-Nguni of Zwangendaba, it will be enough to describe briefly the entrance of the Word of God among that tribe. After which we shall take up the story of the line of the Aba-Mbo.

The Establishment of Christianity among the Angoni.

In 1874, Dr. Stewart of Lovedale (Somgxada) visited Scotland. The same year the body of Dr. Livingstone, who had done remarkable work in encouraging progress among the Native races of Central Africa, was taken for burial to Westminster Abbey in England. Dr. Stewart was present at the burial, and returned to Scotland inspired with the idea that there should be a Memorial erected to Livingtone in Africa, the character of which should be of a religious nature in the form of a church for the worship of God among the Angoni. This thought he proceeded to elaborate before the General Assembly of the Church of Scotland. The outcome of this suggestion was the founding of the Livingstone Mission on Lake Nyasa, in the country of the Angoni, as a memorial of a man who loved the African race with all his heart. In 1876, Dr. Stewart visited Nyasa to outline the work required in connection with the

Memorial. Several Europeans and four of the Lovedale College staff accompanied him, to assist in laying the fonndations of the work. Among the members of the staff were Shadrack Mngunana, and William Koyi. Koyi was specially distinguished for the work he did there, which is still praised to this day. In the midst of this work he died, witnessing by his life his love for God and the Salvation which is by Jesus Christ. His body rests among his own people in Nyasaland. Great things have been accomplished in that distant land in bringing the light of life to those tribes of the Bantu inhabiting it. The preaching of the Gospel at the beginning was in the language of the Ngoni, but because the great majority of the people belong to the Tumbuka tribe with whom the Ngoni intermarried, their language was adopted by the Ngoni chiefs and people, and has become the general language of the people. It was therefore decided to translate the Bible into Tumbuka, and the preaching of the Word is now through that language. Dr. Livingstone was born at Blantyre, a small town in Scotland. Below Lake Nyasa, to-day, there stands a magnificent Church surrounded by schools and a dense population, and this town has been named "Blantyre" after the native town of Livingstone.

AMA-XOSA CLANS.

The following list does not exhaust the number of clans, but represents the majority, including all the more important ones. The clans are classified in three divisions, namely, clans formed before the formation of the two great modern divisions of the Xosa tribe, the Gcaleka and Ngqika (Gaika), and clans belonging to each of the latter.

1. Xosa clans existing from Xosa down to Palo's time:—Ama-Cira, Jwara, Tshawe, Kwemnta, Togu, Kwayi, Imi-Dange, Ama-Ntinde, Hleke, Gwali, Mbalu, Abe-Nguni.

2. Gcaleka Clans:—Imi-Tshayelo, Ama-Velelo, Mbede, I-Tsonyana, and the Royal clan, Ama-Tshawe.

3. Rarabe and Gaika Clans. Imi-Wangu, Dushane, Ngcangatelo, Ama-Ndlambe, Ntsusa, Gwelane, Jingqi, Qwambi, Nqabe, Ntakende, etc.

Clans of Hottentot Origin. Ama-Gqunukwebe, Sukwini, Nqarwane.

Various Clans.

The central core of all important tribes is that portion which has asserted and maintained its independence. Around this core collect fragments of broken tribes seeking protection and security. Individuals of these broken tribes, through outstanding merit, may attain to the position of councillors; but the tribe to which they originally belong never becomes incorporated into the actual body of the protective tribe, as they have no hereditary claims, so that we might say of them, as was said of aliens who had joined the Hebrews in old times, that "they are not all Israel who are of Israel." Though they take part in all that concerns their protectors, yet they remain apart, retaining the name of the tribe from which they sprang. Fragments of even the distant Basuto tribes broken up by internecine fighting, as far back as 1680, are to be found among the Ama-Xosa. Others of Lala and Aba-Mbo origin, driven out by the Tshaka convulsions of 1812-28, have found a home here also. The great body of the common people is composed of such elements, and for all practical purposes they are part of the Xosa tribe. Besides these extraneous additions, there are a few clans whose origin is doubtful, and others whose origin seems undoubtedly Xosa but which have, nevertheless, lost trace of their point of contact with the parent tribe. These consequently fall within the area of commoners. By those who make a study of Social Anthropology, it will be noticed, that within the narrow limits of the Xosa tribe, there occurs here and there a hiatus, an empty gap, which should be filled by certain clans. Taking, for instance, the period covered by the reigns of Xosa and subsequent Chiefs down to that of Togu, one cannot fail to see that there must have been clans extant which meanwhile have sunk out of sight. Xosa is represented by his principal son, Malanagana, alone. Malangana is represented by his principal son, Nkosiyamntu, alone. Ngcwangu and his son, Sikomo, are each represented by the heir alone, whereas we should expect, under the institution of polygamy, that each chief had other sons besides the heir. Where then are the clans represented by these sons ? It is one of the unsolved mysteries with which we are faced, but its solution may be found partly among the Natal tribes, and partly among tribes of Aba-Mbo stock. During times of tribal upheaval and stress whole clans have taken themselves away from the parent tribe, and joined themselves to strangers. We have an example of this in the Togu clan, which is represented in the home tribe (Ama-Xosa) by single individuals, and as a clan unit among the Pondomise.

Within the Xosa tribe, there are a number of clans that cannot be placed accurately, from their failure to trace out their genealogy, such as the Ama-Nkabane, Ama-Bamba, Ama-Nqabe, Ama-Sukwini, Ama-Nqarwane (the latter two, however, mainly of Hottentot origin), and others. Here we propose to mention a few clans which form part of the Xosa tribe. Some of these are probably of Xosa stock, and others of alien origin.

Ama-Kwemnta (Xosa).

The great battle between Tshawe and his elder brothers, Cira and Jwara, had far-reaching consequences, especially in the complete exclusion of the royal line of Cira from rule, and the usurpation of that rule by the Ama-Tshawe. Before the battle, Bonga, the heir of Cira, refused for some reason to take part in it, and the fighting proceeded without him and his following. On suffering defeat, Cira was so incensed at the conduct of his principal son, to whose defection he ascribed the defeat of the Ama-Cira, that he disinherited Bonga and said, "At a time of great danger to my house you have chosen to stand aside (Uku-Kwemuka or Uku-Kwebuka), and in consequeuce I am deprived of the chieftainship. You and yours have no further part or lot with us. From this day you are no longer Ama-Cira, your name henceforth shall be Ama-Kwemnta ("the Evaders"). The name, Ama-Kwemnta, has from that day stuck like a burr to Bonga's descendants. The members of the Cira clan have fallen to the position of commoners. The Ama-Cira and Ama-Kwemnta do not intermarry, an indication of their close blood relationship. The genealogy of the Ama-Kwemnta is as follows :—

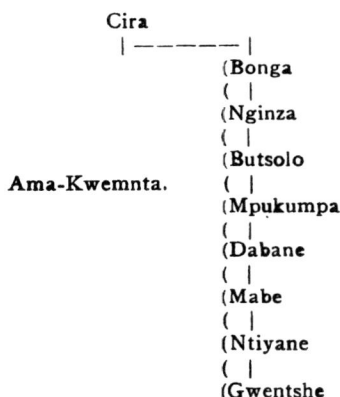

```
                    Cira
                    | ————— |
                            (Bonga
                            (  |
                            (Nginza
                            (  |
                            (Butsolo
    Ama-Kwemnta.          ( |
                            (Mpukumpa
                            ( |
                            (Dabane
                            ( |
                            (Mabe
                            ( |
                            (Ntiyane
                            ( |
                            (Gwentshe
```

The clan name, Cira, has come down to us through some other son of the chief, probably a son of a Right Hand or Minor House. There are a number of small sub-clans of the Ama-Cira, such as the Ama-Xandeshe and the Ama-Mbaba-lana, but they are of little account.

Ama-Qwambi (Xosa).

This clan claims to be of Xosa origin. The Ama-Qwambi say that they belong to one of the Minor (Qadi) Houses of Nkosiyamntu, father of Cira, Jwara and Tshawe. Qwambi is declared to have been Nkosiyamntu's principal son of this Minor House; that is to say, he is the progenitor of the clan, and the members of it have no doubt of their Xosa origin. In these days they are

mostly to be found among the Gaikas (Ngqikas).
To account for this circumstance, they state that
when Rarabe crossed the Kei with his father Palo,
the Ama-Qwambi threw in their lot with Rarabe
rather than with Gcaleka, Palo's heir. They are,
in fact, neither Ama-Ngqika nor Ama-Gcaleka,
but Ama-Xosa, for they came into being before
either of the former two sections, and while the
tribe was known only by the name of Xosa. This
clan has been assigned a particular duty among
the Ama-Xosa. When the son of an important
chief is to be circumcised, the surgical operation
has first to be performed on a Qwambi boy. The
question is naturally asked, " Why is it that the
Ama-Qwambi, who by birth are chiefs, being descendants of one of Nkosiyamntu's sons, are called
upon to act in this subordinate capacity to a
chief's son ? " They answer, that their position
as chiefs was from the very beginning one of
little consequence, for even among the Minor
Houses they were far down in the scale of
importance. They, therefore, were practically in
the position of commoners, and that is why the
duty was imposed upon them. In far distant days
this custom may have had some religious significance, but, if so, there is little that partakes of a
religious character to be observed to-day. The
genealogy of this clan is as follows :—

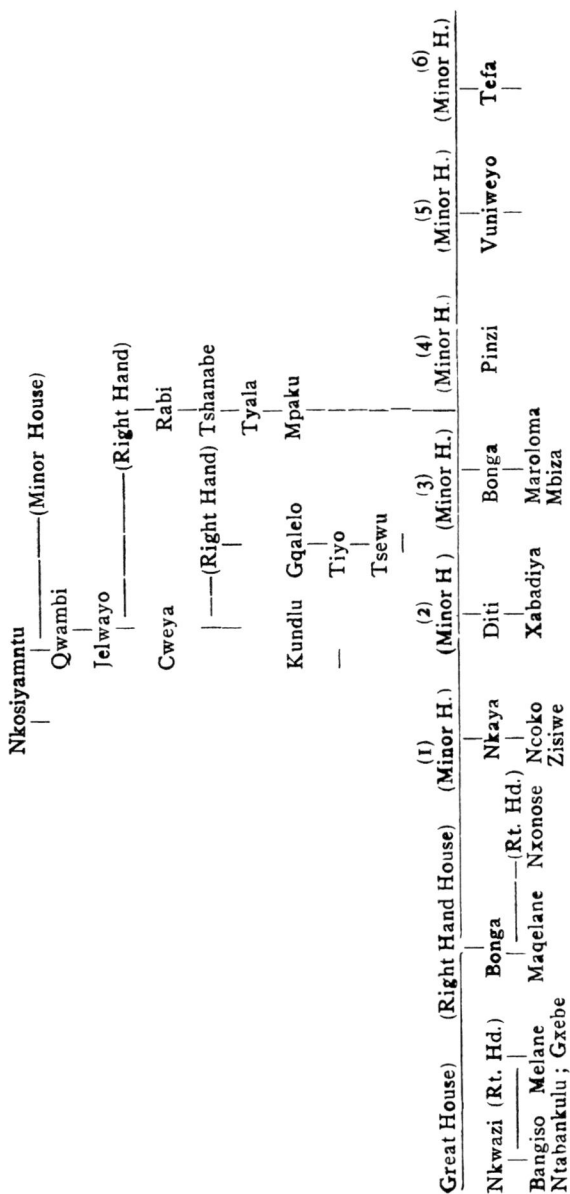

Nkosiyamntu

Qwambi — (Minor House)

Jelwayo — (Right Hand)

Cweya   Rabi

   — (Right Hand) Tshanabe

     Tyala

Kundlu   Gqalelo   Mpaku

   Tiyo

   Tsewu

Great House	(Right Hand House)	(1) (Minor H.)	(2) (Minor H.)	(3) (Minor H.)	(4) (Minor H.)	(5) (Minor H.)	(6) (Minor H.)
Nkwazi (Rt. Hd.)	Bonga	Nkaya	Diti	Bonga	Pinzi	Vuniweyo	Tefa
	—(Rt. Hd.)	Ncoko	Xabadiya	Maroloma			
Bangiso Melane Nxonose Gxebe	Maqelane	Zisiwe		Mbiza			
Ntabankulu;							

Ama-Nqabe (Xosa).

This tribe is fairly large. It occupies a portion of the Mqanduli District in the Transkei. For long, there has been doubt on the question to what tribe they originally belonged. For over two centuries they have been living in their present situation, which is accounted part of Tembuland. From this circumstance it was thought that they were of Tembu stock. On a visit to the Nqabe Great Place, in 1925, to make enquiries into into the matter, I elicited from the chief, Mrazuli, together with some of his principal councillors, that they are an offshoot of the Ama-Xosa, but that when Palo moved towards the Bashee, he left the Ama-Nqabe in charge of the grave of his father, Tshiwo, at the Ngcwanguba, a little further east of their present position. The Tembus, they state, moved into Tembuland when the Ama-Nqabe were already in possession of their part of the country. They further assert, that they had never observed the custom of a tributary tribe, that of slaughtering cattle as a sign of submission to the Tembus. When left behind by the migrating Xosas, they were but a small clan, and they believed that they were one of Sikomo's Minor Houses. The fact that they were left in charge of the grave of a principal chief of the Xosas is a fairly strong indication of their Xosa origin, as so important duty would never be assigned to strangers, or to clans of alien origin. From this tribe (Ama-Nqabe) issued the Ama-Gcina clan, also in Tembuland, and of some consequence as a clan. From the Ama-Nqabe also came the clan of the Ama-Ninwayo, likewise in Tembuland.

The genealogy of this tribe is set forth in one of the general tables.

Ama-Kwayi (Xosa).

Reference has been made to this clan in a former chapter. The term *uku-kwaywa* means to nullify or make void the regal status of a tribe, by a marriage between blood relations. Such a marriage is contrary to the spirit and inclination, as well as custom and law, of the Bantu race. Tribes closely related by blood do not intermarry. When, therefore, custom and law are set aside and relations marry, they are regarded as guilty of incest. The family of the female usually suffers most by this breach of established custom. More especially is this the case when the family is of royal blood. The punishment is deprivation of rank, the family being reduced to commoners. There is divergence of opinion among the Xosas about the identity of the chief who committed this offence. Some hold that it was Ngconde, while others believe that it was Tshiwo. There seems little reason for difficulty here. The chief Togu had as his heir Ngconde, and Ziko was his son of the Minor House. It was this Ziko's daughter who was married irregulary. It is unlikely to have been Ngconde who married her, for he was Ziko's half-brother; hence both would be of about the same age, and by the time she reached womanhood, he would be well on in life. Moreover, Ngconde is said to have died young. The probability is, therefore, that it was Tshiwo, Ngconde's heir, who married Ziko's daughter,* as both would be of the same age. The Ama-Kwayi were among the first of the Xosa

---

* Later information is that this woman was Noqazo, last wife of Tshiwo.

tribes to settle near the Fish River. This was due to their joining Gwali, the wouldbe usurper of Palo's throne. When Gwali fled from punishment, he was accompanied by the Ama-Ntinde, Ama-Kwayi, and Ama-Gqunukwebe. Neither Ngconde nor Tshiwo, his son, crossed the Bashee; on the contrary, both lived and died east of the river, and up to their day no migration further southward took place. Hence it follows, that the lowering of the status of Ziko's clan, the Ama-Kwayi, took place near the Mtata river, and prior to its settling on the Fish River. This clan is one of the oldest of the Xosa clans. The first we know of, in point of time from Xosa, is the Ama-Cira, the next the Ama-Jwara, then the Ama-Kwemnta, next the Ama-Tshawe, and fifth the Ama-Kwayi. Following these in order of birth came the Ama-Gwali, the Ama-Mbalu, the Imi-Dange, the Ama-Ntinde, the Ama-Hleke, then the splitting up of the Xosa tribe into its two great branches, the Ama-Gcaleka and the Ama-Nqika or Rarabe.

Ama-Mbede (Xosa).

This clan is one of Chief Gcaleka's Minor Houses, attached to the Great House. The head of this clan, a son of Gcaleka, was Nqoko. He had two sons by different wives, one was Kalashe and the other Mguntu. Kalashe's eldest son and heir was Mbalo. Nqoko was regent of the Ama-Xosa when Hintsa was a minor, and it was due to Nqoko's advice that the Gcalekas in 1818 joined the Ama-Ndlambe against the Ama-Ngqika in the battle of Amalinde. Previous to the year of the battle Nqoko had lead the Gcalekas against the Ngqikas to punish the latter for interfering with the herds in charge of Gcaleka feed kraals, which had been placed in Ndlambe's country near the Keiskama River, many miles from Gcalekaland. In the fighting which ensued Nqoko and his warriors were driven back into Gcalekaland, and severely handled. This rankled in the old warrior's breast, and when Ndlambe sought to crush Ngqika, old Nqoko assisted Ndlambe with the Gcaleka army. During the time of Mguntu, Nqoko's son, a despute arose as to who was Nqoko's heir. Mguntu claimed precedence on the score of his mother being a Tembu, whereas Kalashe's mother belonged to the home clan of the Ama-Bamba. It had been customary among the Xosas to expect that the heir to the chieftainship would be the son of a mother who belonged to some tribe other than the Ama-Xosa.

The case was brought before Kreli (Sarili) for decision. For a whole day evidence was given, and at nightfall Kreli issued the command that the litigants should rest, and the case would be decided in the morning.

Mguntu arose during the night and accompanied by two of his followers who were armed with sticks, went over and entered Kalashe's hut. The latter was immediately attacked along with those who were with him, and so severely handled that he fled. Next morning Kalashe returned expecting the case to go on, but Kreli said to him,—" Where are you going ? You have already settled the case against yourself, in that you fled last night and left the chieftainship with Mguntu." That settled the question of precedence for the

T

time being. Mbalo, the son of the unfortunate
Kalashe, some time after this was put to death
by Kreli as a wizard. He was a man of outstanding ability as an orator and councillor, and so
incurred the jealousy of his co-councillors who
represented him to the chief as a wizard.

Mguntu, who had, as above related, succeeded
to the chieftainship, had as his heir Sigidi. The
latter had two sons, Matumbu and Dinizulu,
between whom as between their grandfathers,
arose a question of precedence. The case, which
was considered of some importance, was tried in
the court-house at Idutywa. Sigcawu, the heir
to the Paramount Chief Kreli, gave his support to
Dinizulu, on the plea that Kreli had publicly proclaimed Dinizulu as heir to Sigidi. On the other
hand, Dalindyebo, Paramount Chief of the Tembus, supported the claim of Matumbu on the
strength of the fact that the mother of Matumbu
was the daughter of a Tembu chief and had, therefore, a higher status than the mother of Dinizulu.
Judgment was given in favour of Matumbu as heir
to his father Sigidi ; but as a solatium to Dinizulu
in having Kreli's decision in his favour reversed,
he was granted Sigidi's cattle. Thus were matters
of precedence continually causing litigation among
the sons of mothers married under the custom of
polygamy.

The Ama-Mbede clan is of considerable size and
importance within the Xosa tribe.

Ama-Banqo or Ntshilibe (Basuto).

Various clans of origin alien to that of the Ama-
Xosa have through circumstances of different

kinds been compelled to break away from their own mother tribe, and become tributary to the Ama-Xosa. We give a couple of examples.

The names Banqo and Ntshilibe by which this clan is known are entirely modern. The clan is of Basuto origin, and is a small section of the Ba-Kwena or, as expressed by the Ama-Xosa, Ama-Ngwenya ("the people of the crocodile.") The Ba-Kwena came down from the north somewhere, and entered what is now known as Basutoland shortly after the beginning of the 18th century.

A Portuguese, Dos Santos (Theal, *Ethnography* p. 186), reached the Zambesi about 1700 and found the Ba-Kwena already established there. Amongst other statements which he makes, Dos Santos refers to a lake, situated under the Luputa mountains near to the Zambesi, and Lufumba (probably the Ndendelashe) by the inhabitants of these parts. This lake he reports to be teeming with fish, hippopotami and large crocodiles. In accordance with the Basuto custom of using the names of animals as distinctive tribal titles, this tribe took the name of the crocodile (i-Kwena) as its tribal designation. Shortly after the beginning of the 18th Century, down to about 1770 when numbers of Basuto tribes migrated into the country west of the Drakensberg, the Ba-Kwena settled on the Upper Caledon. It was a tribe of considerable importance, and from it sprang others of not much less consequence. I believe that the Ba-Mangwato, Ba-Ngwaketse, Ba-Hurutse and the Ba-Tlokwa are offsprings of the Ba-Kwena.

At the period when possession was being taken of the land internecine warfare was the order of the day.

A section of the Ba-Kwena to save itself struck across the Drakensberg to the eastern side, and settled among the Pondos. Here they sub-divided into two parts, one under Mvelashe and another under Badlula. This division was, however, a latter development. The leader who brought them over into Pondoland was Ndiza (Tiya). Mvelashe and Badlula were grandsons of his. The Ama-Ngwenya (Ba-Kwena) remained in Pondoland until the reign of Kawuta, when a new movement took place. Mvelashe and his younger brother Banqo with their people and possessions set out for Gcalekaland, to become tributary under Kawuta. Badlula remained behind in Pondoland, at the Mnenu and Mtonga. In later times this section met with disaster and fled from Pondoland into Bomvanaland and joined a Pondo clan under Bomvana rule, called the Ama-Rasi. They were so poor and broken when they arrived that the Ama-Rasi gave them 15 heifers as a nucleus whereon to build up their future prosperity. On that account they are generally called Ama-Tokazi (" the people of the heifers ") but their original name is still retained by themselves.

The party under Mvelashe and Banqo had with them members of the Ama-Mvulane (Basuto) and Ama-Ngqusini (Basuto) clans. They moved inland passing through Tembuland in the neighbourhood of the Xwili hills. Here, their cattle proved too strong a temptation to the Tembus, a party of whom attacked the Ama-Ngwenya, but were driven off and their chief killed. It is not very clear who the chief was, but he was probably not an important one, though some declare that it was Ndaba, the Principal Chief of the Tembus. The Ama-Ngwenya then pressed forward and crossed the Bashee near the points spanned by the railway and road bridges of to-day. They then camped, as it was getting dusk. Behind them a Tembu force was collected, which followed the trail of the Ama-Ngwenya as far as the Bashee river, where it observed the Ama-Ngwenya camp-fires on the opposite side. Evidently the Tembus were not keen, for they contented themselves by shouting across the river asking whose camp-fires those were. The Ama-Ngwenya withheld their true name and shouted in reply, " We are Ama-Ntshilibe." As the Tembus were on the trail of the Ama-Ngwenya, and not of the Ama-Ntshilibe, they turned back and went home. This is said to have been the occasion of the first use and application of the term Ama-Ntshilibe to the Ama-Ngwenya, and it has been retained till the present day.

The Ama-Ngwenya at length reached Kawuta's headquarters, and were favourably received. Mvelashe's importance as chief was gradually eclipsed by that of his younger brother Banqo, and the latter came to be recognised as the real chief of the clan. The clan then took the name of Ama-Banqo, but still the nickname, Ama-Ntshilibe, continues in equal use with that of Banqo. The genealogy of the Ama-Banqo is as follows :—

```
Ndiza (Tiya)
    |
Mgabi
    |—————————————|
1. Mvelashe        2. Mbanqo
    |                  |
Ngetu              Fubu
    |                  |
Ludidi                 |
                                              (Rt. Hand.)
                   ————————————————— ——— |
                   1. Jezile,    2. Piyose
                                              Matshitshi
                   (No issue)    (No issue)
```

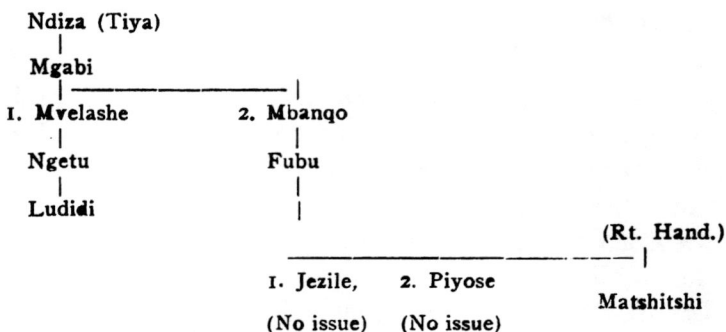

Ama-Ngqosini (Basuto).

This tribe, though now absorbed by the Ama-
Xosa, was originally of Basuto origin.   Sometime
about 1770, internecine warfare broke out as it
was continually doing among the Basuto tribes,
beyond the Drakensberg, of those days.   The
Aba-Kwena clans particularly, if the Bantu tradition is to be trusted, were constantly at war with
each other, as well as with other neighbouring
tribes.   We find sections of the Ba-Kwena absorbed into the body of the Xosa tribe, such as the
Ama-Banqo, and others.   The Ama-Ngqosini believe themselves to be originally of the Ba-Kwena
stock.   Ngqosini had two sons, Ndoko and Gaba,
the former being the ruling chief at the death of
his father.   Ndoko died, leaving as his heir a
child, Ngqili, and as he was a minor, Gaba was
appointed regent.   Ngqili died young before
attaining to the chieftainship, but leaving a son
to inherit his rights.   This child was Mjobi.   Gaba
continued as regent during the minority of Mjobi,
and became so accustomed to the honours of a
ruler that when Mjobi attained manhood and
requested Gaba to hand over the sceptre of autho-

rity to him, the latter declined, saying that, though an old man, he was quite capable of ruling the tribe. This refusal meant war. Fighting took place between the adherents of Gaba and Mjobi in which the former was routed. Gaba fled across the Drakensberg and entered Xosaland during Palo's reign, and became attached to the Xosa tribe. At that time the Ama-Xosa had but recently crossed the Bashee river, now their eastern border. Both the sons of Palo, Gcaleka and Rarabe, were ruling their respective sections of the Xosa tribe. Mjobi at a later period, that is, some years after Gaba joined the Ama-Xosa, also crossed the Drakensberg with his following and entered Tembuland, then nominally under the Chief Ndaba, but his authority was really delegated to his son, Ngubencuka, then a young man.

The Ama-Ngqosini sought to pass through Tembuland to the country further east, which was in great part uninhabited except by Bushmen. It happened that, at the time of the advent of the Ama-Nqosini, the greater part of the manhood of the Aba-Tembu was at Cacadu and Darabe, attending a great feast (*umsito*). Ngubengcuka was with them. Ndaba, however, remained at home, and refused passage to Mjobi and his Ama-Ngqosini, and also to the Aba-Kwena (Bango) and Ama-Vundle, who all travelled together seeking new homes. These tribes were combined under the one name, Aba-Kwena or Ama-Ngwe-nya. Fighting took place and these tribes forced their way through the Tembus. It is said that in this battle a Tembu chief was killed (see section on Ama-Baqo). The Ama-Ngqosini and their companion tribes moved on to the Bashee and, having crossed to the western bank, formed a camp. Meanwhile, news had been conveyed to Cacadu, intimating what had taken place, and that a chief of the Tembus had been killed. The Tembus immediately sent an impi in pursuit, but failed to come into conflict with the Ama-Ngqosini, Banqo and Vundle. It may be here noted that the Ama-Vundle included the Ama-Mvulane, a younger branch of the former. Mjobi having crossed the Bashee, pressed on eastward or perhaps more correctly south-eastward, till he reached the neighbourhood of the Fish River. From the Kei to the Fish River the country was without Bantu inhabitants, with the exception of the Ama-Gwali, Ama-Mbalu, Ama-Ntinde, and Ama-Gqunukwebe, Xosa clans then living close up to the Fish River, having fled thither to escape punishment for an attempt to overthrow the Chief Palo. Having reached this point Mjobi settled down with his tribe, the Ama-Ngqosini. This tribe, though small in number, hunted over the whole of the country between the Fish River and the Kei, regarding the latter as their western boundary. Though separated from the Ama-Xosa by the River Kei, the Ama-Ngqosini were constantly coming into conflict with them, apparently under Gcaleka, and tradition says the former were able to hold their own effectively. Gcaleka being unable to subdue Mjobi, sent for help to Gambushe, Chief of the Ama-Tshezi or Bomvanas, then living at the Mgazi in Pondoland. Gambushe, who added the profession of witch-doctor to that of chief, did not send his warriors to the help of Gcaleka, but instead sent "medicine" with in-

structions how it was to be used in order to overcome the Ama-Ngqosini.   These instructions were
carried out at a time when the majority the Ama-
Ngqosini were on a hunting expedition (*i-Pulo*) at
the Manyubi forest in what is now the Kentani
district.   Mjobi, with the old men and others who
could not attend the hunt, remained at home.
Besides the "medicine" in whose efficiency he
implicitly believed, Gcaleka enlisted the help of
Bushmen, then living along the banks of the Kei,
and sent his army against Mjobi's headquarters
near the Fish River.   In the fighting which ensued Mjobi was pierced by a poisoned Bushman
arrow and died.   The Xosa army then retraced
its steps in order to attack the Ama-Ngqosini at
Manyubi, who formed the greater part of the
tribe.   These were surrounded by the Ama-Xosa,
but by desperate fighting some of the Ama-Ngqosini broke through the encircling Xosas, but instead of turning south-east and making for home,
they proceeded north-east in an endeavour to
reach Pondoland.   This they succeeded in doing,
and attached themselves, those that were left of
them, to Gambushe, whose "medicine charms"
were held to be mainly responsible for their overthrow.   Numbers, however, with their wives and
families submitted to the inevitable and attached
themselves to the Ama-Xosa, thus becoming
incorporated with the Ama-Xosa tribe.

Mjobi's heir was Ngxangana.   He also had two
sons, Ngqanga and Fulali, who belonged to a
house designated "ixazi" ("an old rag.")   This
term is unusual, and its actual significance somewhat obscure.   It was probably a house of little
account, as the name is evidently a term of con-

tempt. The head of the house, Ngqanga, became a witch-doctor. In connection with the initiatory rites for this profession, a pool in a river plays an important part. The novitiate enters such a pool and disappears for many days finally emerging a full-fledged doctor. The pool in which Ngqanga was initiated into the mysteries of his profession is called Cihoshe. It is in the Fish River, close to the sea. Near this pool was a ford which no woman dared to cross without first asking permission from Cihoshe. When any woman tried to cross through the river at the point without observing the ritual, she was immediately held fast by the waters. It was necessary, therefore, that any person noticing the unfortunate position of the woman should propitiate Cihoshe, the God of the pool, by making the following acknowledgement and prayer :— "Mercy, Oh Chief, this woman has offended, she is so-and-so's wife, let her go, I pray you!" The prayer was invariably answered favourably, and the sinner was liberated. This legend still holds the imagination and belief of many in bondage. When Ngqanga died, his mantle fell on Bomela, a relative, but of the Ama-Nywabe clan, said to be a branch of the Ama-Ngqosini.

Aba-Mbo.

Aba-Mbo Tribes.
1 Aba-Mbo.
2 Ama-Mpondo,
3 Ama-Mpondomise.
4 Ama-Xesibe.
5 Ama-Qwati.
6 Imi-Tetwa
7 Ama-Ngwana
8 Ama-Bomvana.
9 Ama-Bomvana.
10 Ama-Swazi.
11 Ama-Tshezi.
12 Ama-Tshomane.

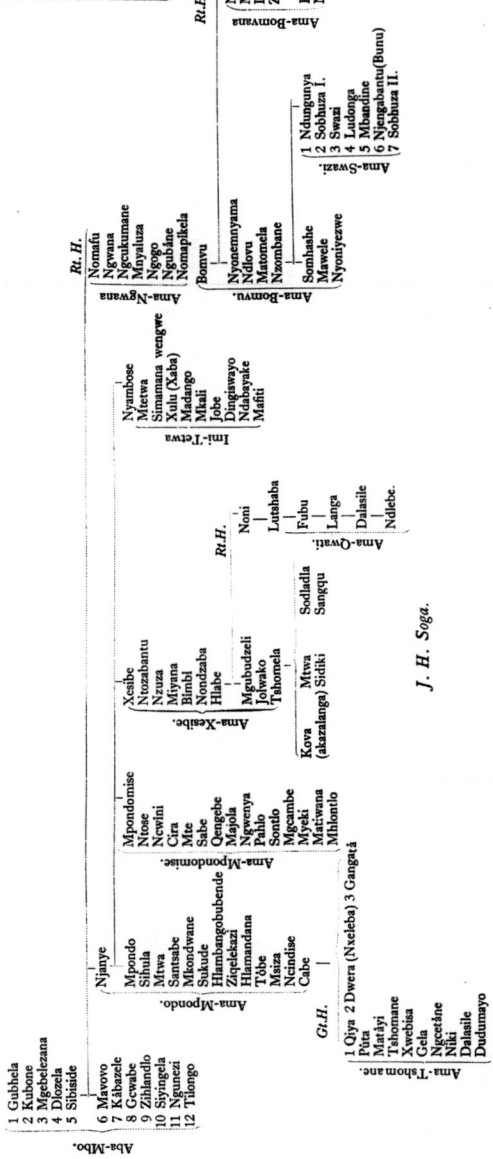

Aba-Mbo.
1 Gubhela
2 Kubone
3 Mgebelezana
4 Dlozela
5 Sibiside
6 Mavovo
7 Kábazele
8 Gcwabe
9 Zihlandlo
10 Siyingela
11 Ngunzi
12 Tilongo

Ama-Mpondo.
Njanye
Mpondo
Sihula
Mtwa
Santsabe
Mkondwane
Sukude
Hlambangobubende
Ziqelekazi
Hlamandana
Tobe
Msiza
Ncindise
Cabe

Ama-Tshom anc. (Gt.H.)
1 Qiya 2 Dwera (Nxeleba) 3 Gangata
Pota
Matayi
Tshomane
Xwebisa
Gela
Ngcetine
Niki
Dalasile
Dudumayo

Ama-Mpondomise.
Mpondomise
Ntose
Ncwini
Cira
Mte
Sabe
Qengebe
Majola
Ngwenya
Pahlo
Sento
Mgcambe
Myeki
Matiwana
Mhlontlo

Ama-Xesibe.
Xesibe
Ntozabantu
Nzuza
Miyana
Bimbi
Nondzaba
Hlabe
Mgubudzeli
Jolwako
Tshomela
Kova Mtwa
(akazalanga) Siditi
Sodladla
Sangqu

Ama-Qwati. (Rt.H.)
Noni
Lutshaba
Fubu
Langa
Dalasile
Ndlebe.

Imi-'Tetwa
Nyambose
Mtetwa
Simamana wengwe
Xulu (Xaba)
Madango
Mkali
Jobe
Dingiswayo
Ndabayake
Mafiti

Ama-Ngwana (Rt. H.)
Nomfu
Ngwana
Ngcukumane
Mnyaluza
Ngogo
Ngubane
Nomaphikela

Ama-Bomvu.
Bomvu
Nyonemnyama
Ndlovu
Matomela
Nzombane

Ama-Swazi.
Somhashe
Mawele
Nyoniyewe
1 Ndungunya
2 Sobhuza I.
3 Swazi
4 Ludonga
5 Mbandine
6 Njengabantu(Bunu)
7 Sobhuza II.

Ama-Bomvana (Rt.H.)
Njilo
Mgweda
Dubandlela
Zwethsha
Kiti
Nkumba

Ama-Tshezi
Tshezi
Tyingana

J. H. Soga.

The material originally positioned here is too large for reproduction in this reissue. A PDF can be downloaded from the web address given on page iv of this book, by clicking on 'Resources Available'.

CHAPTER XVIII.

THE ABA-MBO.

We will now consider the second stream of those Bantu occupying the country between the Drakensberg and the Indian Ocean. As has been already indicated the three streams, on this side of the continent, of the Bantu race are the Abe-Nguni, the Aba-Mbo, and the Ama-Lala. We divide them thus, as we find them already flowing in different sections. The time of the original formation of each is lost in the misty past. We have attempted, however, to place in order the genealogy of the Aba-Mbo, and to place the various families in their order of precedence. In the chapter devoted to the Ama-Zimba and Aba-Mbo we endeavoured to trace their migration from the north, until the latter's arrival in Natal, in 1620. In this genealogy are indicated the principal families or tribes included under the name Aba-Mbo, at least as far as these are apparent and known. It may be repeated here, though already stated, that there are some tribes calling themselves Aba-Mbo, and believing themselves to be such, which are not really so. This we find to be the case principally among Ama-Lala tribes, which were overwhelmed and submerged by the Aba-Mbo, subsequent to the latter's advent into Natal. Any claim to belong to a particular section of the Bantu must show a genealogical point of contact between those who make a claim of this nature and the house of supposed origin. The first chief of the Aba-Mbo in time, according to tradition, was

Gubela (Gubhela). His principal son was Kuboni, and Kuboni's son was Mgebelezana, whose son was Dlozela, whose heir was Sibiside. To Sibiside three sons were born, Mavovo of the Great House, Njanya and Nomafu representing two lesser houses. Njanya's first-born were twins, Mpondomise and Mpondo, the respective progenitors of the tribes who bear their names. A younger son of Njanya was Xesibe, and, according to some, Nyambose, father of Mtetwa, from whom the Imi-Tetwa tribe derives its name—the tribe of the great Dingiswayo, under whom Tshaka served. Nomafu's principal son was Ngwana, the progenitor of the Ama-Ngwana tribe, the terrible *Mfecane* or " freebooters," who destroyed the Hlubi tribe, and themselves were completely broken at Mbolompo near Umtata, in 1828, by a combined British, Gcaleka and Tembu force. The last in the direct line of the Ama-Ngwana was Bomvu. Bomvu's Great Son was Nyonemnyama who discarded the name of Ama-Ngwane and adopted as the tribal name that of Bomvu, his father, so that it became the Ama-Bomvu. Bomvu's son of the Minor House was Mpalampala, whose section of the tribe is called the Mpalampala Bomvu *(Ama-Bomvu-ka-Mpalampala.)* The Right Hand Son of Bomvu was Njilo whose section were and are called the " lesser Bomvus " or Bomvanas.

Bomvu's great-great-grandson of the principal line was Nzombane. The latter's right hand son was Mdungunya, father of Sobuza I, and grandfather of Swazi ; after whom the Swazi tribe is named. The Swazis, therefore are derived from the Ama-Bomvu. This Swazi tribe, although great and powerful, is of recent origin. It is the

Ama-Mpondo.

Sibiside
Njanya
Mpondo
Sihula
Mtwa
Santsabe
Mcondwane
Sukude
Hlamangobuicinde
Zigcekazi
Hlamandana
Tobe
Msiza
Ncindise
Cabe
Qiya 2. Dwera (Nxeletoa)
Putu
Matayi
Tshiommane
Xweisisa (Sango)
Gela
Ngcetane
Niki
Dalasile
Didumayo

M.H. — Qwane
Rt.H. — Pika
Ama-Ntusi

Caza
Sobatsha, 2. Ncamazele — Kentane
Ngwelane — Fundakubi
Munwana
Zondwayo

M.H. (Pika line):
Gavu
Mbangwa
Nongcongolo
Nompandana
Nomandi

M.H. — Qwane
Ama-Rasi:
Ukuwana
Rasi
Ciya
Yokwe
Yezeni
Mbamba
Menco
Gungubele

M.H. — Ngcaugule
Ama-Dingata:
Gcuta
Dingata
Shoba
Nyohela
Makotwana
Mlikwa
Gquba
Zake
Mzondi
Nyukani

Rt.H. — Ginsqi
Same
Nonjaca
Matiwana
Rili
Mgcotyelwa

M.H. — Kwalo
Rt.H. — Ntlane
Nemjana
Valela

M.H. — Gqwaru
Gqwaru
Njilo

M.H. — Qadi
Ama-Qadi:
Tshizi
Mishange
Mugonyama
Maiwa
Pali
Sangzongxo
Mbongwana
Siwema
Siqukwane

Konjwayo 2.
Ama-Konjwayo:
Kiwo
Ngcekula
Nsikinyane
Makunda
Nogcname
Gwadiso
Godloza
Ntenteni

3. Gangata
Bala — twins
Citwayo
Ndayeni
Tahle
Nyavuza
Ngqungqushe

Paku
2. Cingo
3. Mngewenqi
Ndamase — 2. Mbangazita — 3. Stata

Rt.H. — Mtengwane
Mbolo
Xaba

M.H. — Kanya
Somdizela

Dikiso
Jivaza

Rt.H. — Nyangiwe
Rt.H. — Madolo
Makesonke

Mqikela
Sigcawu
Nguwiliso
Mhlanga
Bokleni
Poto
Dumezweni

Marelane
Mandlonke
Toli

Lft.H. — Palo
Mgoqi
Felanto

Rt.H. — Dalasile
(i-Xibu) — Jekwa

M.H. — Momoza
Hobo
Rt.H. — Wawa

Nganda
Mlata
Nqonyama
Malohle

──── = Royal line.
━━━━ = Reigning line.
∿∿∿∿ = Right-hand line.

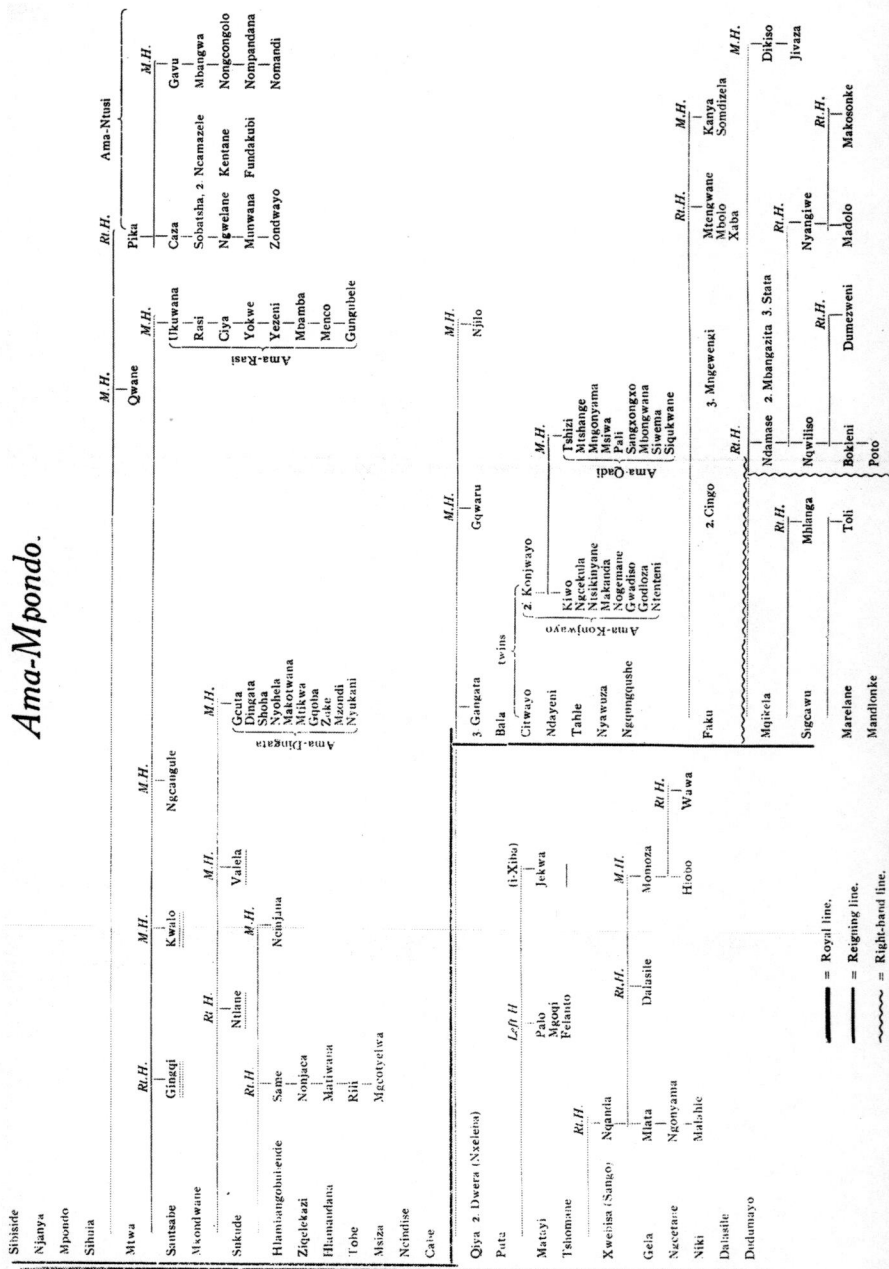

The material originally positioned here is too large for reproduction in this reissue. A PDF can be downloaded from the web address given on page iv of this book, by clicking on 'Resources Available'.

last to emerge in the line of those tribes mentioned here. The Swazis left their native country in Natal in 1843, to form an independent tribe of their own in the North, in what is now described as Swaziland. Briefly, the first branch to be developed from the Aba-Mbo were the Ama-Ngwana, who were followed by the Mpondomise, Pondos, Xesibes, Imi-Tetwa, Ama-Bomvu, and Ama-Bomvana and lastly the Swazis. And these tribes produced others, as witness the Ama-Tshomane who are Pondos of the royal line and from whom issued the Ama-Nqanda. Similarly from the Pondos originated the Ama-Dwera, Ama-Gangata, Ama-Konjwayo, and other tribes of lesser importance. The Ama-Cwera and the Ama-Mpinge are also Aba-Mbo for they issue from the chief Mpondomise.

The Pondos (Aba-Mbo.)

This is an important branch of the Aba-Mbo. Mpondo and Mpondomise, as has been said, were twins of Njanya. The elder is said to be Mpondomise. It is not clear whether they preceded the Aba-Mbo in entering Natal, or whether they came with a mixed crowd of their own tribal relatives in 1620. What is known is that the Pondos were first heard of about the Dedesi (F. Brownlee's *Historical Records*, p.111) where they were neighbours to the Pondomise and Xosas and the Ama-Lala tribes, viz., the Ama-Zizi, Ama-Bele, Ama-Hlubi, and the Ama-Tolo. Tradition says that the Pondos were the first among other tribes to leave the Debesi, going towards the sea and settling beyond the Umzimvubu, and the Mpondomise followed, settling above the Pondos close to the sea near Mtamvuna. After sixty years had elapsed, from the time when the Aba-Mbo arrived in Natal, the Pondos in 1686 were reported to have settled down at the place already mentioned. In 1686, survivors of the wreck of the Stavenisse, which came to grief on the coast beyond the St. John's River, related that they traversed the country of the Pondomise and the Pondos in their efforts to reach Cape Fown. And this narrative shows that these tribes together with the Tembus, Hottentots, and Xosas were all in line bordering on the sea. The boundaries of the Pondo country were more clearly defined in 1827. At that time they lived between the Mzi-mvubu (St. John's) and Mngazi, pent up there out of fear of Tshaka and Dingaan, although they still claimed all the country above this to the border of the Mtamvuna.

The Chief of the Pondos whose is most famous is Faku, eldest son of Ngqungqushe, because his regime corresponded with the arrival of the Europeans in Natal and at the Cape, who preserve records in writing of Faku.

But before Faku's time great events had happened in Pondoland. We might mention one only :— The overthrow of the Great House, the chieftainship being usurped by a young son, as frequently happens still. This happened in the time of Qiya, eldest son of Cabe, who was sovereign of all the Pondos. Cabe begat Qiya, Dwera, and the youngest Gangata. On a certain day, while hunting, Qiya quarrelled with Gangata who had killed a blue-buck. This little antelope is famed for overturning dynasties. Briefly, the trouble over the blue-buck led to fighting in which Qiya's party was beaten, and with him Dwera who went to his assistance. He then crossed the Umtata River and settled on the west side. The first wife of Qiya refused to go to a new country and turned back on the road. Cabe, therefore, recommended her to Gangata as a wife, and she bore him a son called Bala or Baliso. Thus the Chieftainship passed from the Great House, which today is known as the Ama-Tshomane, to the House of Gangata in which the chieftainship now rests. Bala's issue by his chief wife was Citwayo and Konjwayo, the chieftainship falling to Citwayo, the elder. Konjwayo is the progenitor of the Ama-Konjwayo, a tribe which is ruled today by Ntenteni, son of Godloza, son of Gwadiso, whose father was Nogemane. The heir of the Right Hand House of Gangata was Gqwaru. In the line of Gangata the Great House is called the Qaukeni of Mqikela. The head of the Right Hand House was Nyandeni. Today the Chief of the Qauka is still a child named Mandlonke, son of Marelane. The chief of the Nyandeni is Poto, son of Bokleni, a young man who is dealing in a commonsense way with tribal matters generally.

The Chief Ngqungqushe—about 1820.

Ngqungqushe, father of Faku, was a son of Nyauza, son of Tahle, son of Ndayeni, head of the House of Gangata who overthrew Qiya, the heir to the chieftainship of the Pondos. Further than that he was killed by the Bomvanas, there is nothing of importance recorded of Ngqungqushe. His death was brought about over a matter concerning Ngezana of the Tshezi tribe, in fact a Bomvana. It happened in this manner. The eldest son of Jalamba, son of Tshezi, whose name was Mbili, had one son, named Ngezana (I am not here concerned with Mbelu whom he begot outside of legal order). Ngezana lost his father while still a child, and was brought up by his uncle Gambushe, younger brother to Mbili.

When he came to manhood, Ngezana was given the oversight of his father's followers, but the majority of them, having been used to Gambushe's rule, evinced no desire to support their Chief. Whereupon Ngezana angrily demanded them from Gambushe. They growled at each other and then appealed to arms, when Ngezana was defeated. Sometime after this another dispute arose between them on account of a person called Beme, of the clan Jola. We are unable to deal freely with the story of Beme for it originated from an immoral custom, called the *upundlo*. But I may just remark that Gambushe brought a case against Beme for committing this rank offence at Gambushe's own kraal. Whereupon Beme put himself under the protection of Ngezana. The political sky was darkened and a battle ensued in which Ngezana was again defeated. Ngezana's wife was a daughter of Ngqungqushe, and after his defeat Ngezana appealed to Ngqungqushe for aid. The latter out of friendship agreed, and also because Gambushe was a thorn in the flesh to the other Pondo chiefs. Joining forces, the impis of Ngqungqushe and Ngezana marched on Gambushe's kraal. The Tshezi chief being unprepared to meet the attack, drew off his forces from his kraal, leaving the family behind. When he felt himself ready Gambushe returned and drove back the confederate army from the threshold of his kraal. An unfortunate episode then happened, for when the enemy was being driven from the Royal Kraal, Mayaba, wife of Gambushe, was assegaied in the arm. Whereupon Gambushe became terribly wroth and, with eye flashing lightning, forced the fighting and defeated the Pondo army between the Mtalala and Dangwana. The assegai was plied on both sides and terrible havoc wrought, but Gambushe was not to be denied. The armies of Ngqungqushe and Ngezana were scattered and pursued by the Ama-Tshezi to the point in the rear where the Great Chief, Ngqungqushe, was resting with his bodyguard, and he was "Sent to join his ancestors." This affair caused lasting bitterness between Faku and the Bomvanas whereby Gambushe was eventually forced into exile by the Pondos. The grave of Ngqungqushe is at the Dangwana, on the spot where he died.

Faku (1780-1867).

The eldest son of Ngqungqushe succeeded his father after his death. There are those who say that a majority of the tribe refused to come under Faku's authority. These latter went away and joined themselves to Sinama, a chief of the Xesibes. But Sinama drove them away sending them back to Faku, because the Xesibes are related to the Pondos, both tribes emanating from Njanya. Sinama married a daughter of Nyawuza, Faku's grandfather. At this period the terrible Tshaka was scattering the tribes of Natal. There were

U

few, if any, who could stand against him—at any
rate, none after the defeat of the Ama-Ndwandwe
of Zwide, who was powerful enough to try conclusions with Tshaka. Therefore, Tshaka looked
round for enemies to the more distant tribes, and
espied the Pondos whom he attacked. He made
frequent raids upon them in search of cattle for
the support of his army. The fear of these constant attacks caused Faku to secrete himself, and
he found a favourable retreat in the fastnesses of
the Mngazi heights. By this time, the people
were reduced to a state of poverty by the frequent
raids. Besides the victims of Tshaka's forays,
the Pondos were joined by refugees from many
broken tribes who were scattered by the eruptions
of those days. Sonyangwe, son of Kalimeshe,
chief of the Bacas, fled to the Mzimkulu and settled there. His son of the Right Hand, Ncapayi,
passed on to Pondoland, and was a great burden
to Faku, by frequently attacking the Pondos.
His gratitude for all that Faku had done for him
took the form of frequent armed raids. So also
were the Xesibes continually disturbing the peace,
especially Jojo, son of Mjoli, of the Right Hand
House of Xesibe. These things kept the country
in a constant ferment, unsettling Faku's country
and people. After Hintsa's war, as that debacle
is called, in fact in the following year, 1836, Sir
Benjamin D'Urban, Governor of the Cape, sent a
message to Faku saying peace should reign between the Pondos, Xosas, and Tembus, as if he
was not aware that he was the cause of the Pondos attacking the Xosas from behind in that war.
When things were more settled, he said, "Let the

Pondos lay aside their assegais." And again, " Faku should permit the missionaries to pass " who were escaping from the unsettled state of the country. Of course, Faku willingly agreed to these points. After the Tshaka terror had ceased, through his murder, there began to be more stable conditions in Pondoland. So Faku issued out of his fastnesses at the Mngazi and crossed the Mzimvubu, settling at the Mzintlava and claiming all the country between that river and Umtata. But before long he was placed in a dangerous position, for the Boers who had just arrived in Natal were a cause of anxiety to the tribes abutting on them, and they sent out a commando to fight Ncapayi in 1840, and were joined by Fodo, a chief of the Ntlangwini tribe, who was an ally of the Boers, with his impi. Ncapayi's Bacas were, therefore, defeated, and the Boers seized immense booty, justifying themselves by the plea that the Bacas had crossed the boundary and helped themselves to the Boer cattle. Faku soon perceived that these people would not be in want of a pretext for war against him. So he asked to be taken under the protection of the English. They replied by sending up Captain Smith ("Ndimiti," according to the Pondos) with a small force to prevent the Boers if they should attempt to fight Faku. Smith fixed his camp at the Mngazi, but the decision to put Faku under British protection was not completed then. It was not until 1895 that this was accomplished, during the time when Cecil Rhodes was Prime Minister of the Cape. The Pondos were now no longer anxious to come in under the Government as there was nothing distressing them, but Rhodes expressed his dissatisfaction

with the constant friction among the Pondos themselves, especially that between the Chiefs Sigcawu
and Mhlangaso, and he threatened war. That no
fighting took place was due to the diplomacy of
Major Elliot ("u-Meja,") who was Chief Magistrate
at Umtata, and who opposed the forcing of war
upon the Pondos which Rhodes apparently desired
with all his heart. The Pondos on that day were,
therefore, saved from white men by a white man.
The disposition of Faku was peaceable and tract-
able, always willing to live in friendly relations
with all people in his country. He was not opposed to the Bacas when they remained at peace,
for he remembered that they had come to him as
refugees, although they were always bringing
down trouble on themselves, which he desired to
avoid. He desired peace also with the Xesibes,
and they themselves were responsible for any
retaliation on his part, because they refused to
keep quiet. But although he was a peaceable
man, and well esteemed by everybody, he was
sometimes forced to arm and fight. It was so
when his father Ngqungqushe was killed by the
Bomvanas. He was forced to arm in order to
punish Gambushe, who after the Ngqungqushe
affair was compelled to leave Pondoland and
settle in the country between the Umtata and
Bashee. On two separate occasions Faku led his
army against the Bomvanas. In the first offensive, Faku crossed the Umtata River and attacked the forces of Gambushe, but he was only able
to come within sight of the Xora River estuary,
when he was driven back by the Ama-Tshezi. On
another occasion he again attacked the Bomvanas,

this time being reinforced by the Bacas, the Izi-Lilangwe and Imi-Zizi (not Ama-Zizi). He divided his army into two parts, the Pondos taking the same route they had done before. The Bacas moved higher up, both divisions making for the great place of the Ama-Tshezi or Bomvana at the Gusi. It soon became apparent that this time the Bomvanas would be overpowered. They, therefore, began by driving away their stock and families to the Bashee so that they might shelter with the Gcalekas beyond. When their families had crossed the Bashee and the cattle were being driven over, the Bacas came up, and capturing a portion of the cattle drove them away, as they were afraid of bringing the Gcalekas down on themselves. The Pondo army was engaged in picking up the remnants of the scattered cattle, but they also made for home when they heard that the Bomvanas had gone across to the Gcalekas. But that very night the Bomvana impi stealthily followed on the track of the Pondos, and fell upon them at the Mpame forest while they halted to feast on the captured stock at night. Taken by surprise, the revelries were soon over, as also the courage for fighting, and the assegai worked its will. Faku's army was driven back and made tracks for home. But on account of the anxiety of the Bomvanas, in regard to their families, their army did not press the pursuit but turned and made for Gcalekaland. There they remained for nearly thirty years with the Gcalekas, being in fear of Faku, until the cattle killing time, when they returned to their own country.

The Agreement of 1844.

The year 1844 saw the agreement concluded between the Governor, Sir Peregrine Maitland and Faku. The principal heads were these: The claim of Faku to the overlordship of all the country lying between the Umtata and Umzimkulu and between the Drakensberg and the sea was recognised by the Government; also that Faku would be protected against any subject of the Government setting up a claim to the land. Faku on his side, agreed to live in friendly relations with the Cape Colony, and to prevent his people from oppressing or illtreating British subjects passing through his territory. He agreed also to put forth every effort to arrest criminals hiding in his country and hand them over to the authorities. Again, he promised to restore stolen stock when the spoor was traced into Pondoland; to protect missionaries and traders resident in his country, and also the post which passed through his country to Natal. He would also avoid with all his might the making of any war with other tribes living within certain demarcated limits in his country, and to assist the Colony with his whole army when Government required their services. The Government in return promised to show its friendliness by paying Faku, during the whole time he observed this agreement, money or stock equivalent to the amount of £75 a year. The missionary with Faku, the Rev. Thomas Jenkins, explained to the Chief the purport of the different heads separately. When Faku had heard them he signified his approval and accepted them. Whereupon Faku and Ndamase touched the pen, with four Council-

lors.   All this took place in the presence of
Shepstone, Fynn, and the Missionary Jenkins.
This agreement reveals an understanding between
the Government and the Pondos, and does not
mean that Faku had placed his country under the
British Government.   Nevertheless a magistrate
was sent, Henry Fynn, but after a time the office
of Magistrate among the Pondos was abolished.
Up to his death Faku observed the agreement.
This chief of the Pondos stands alone among the
other Pondo chiefs for personal weight, wisdom,
and understanding.   If the evidences of greatness
could be stated Faku would be placed in the
category of chiefs like Kreli, Rarabe and Palo
among the Ama-Xosa, Mshweshwe among the
Basuto, and Dalindyebo among the Tembus.
Faku died in 1867 at a great age.   He was about
87 years old.

Nqeto of the Ama-Qwabe (1829).

When Faku had just come to the chieftainship,
the Pondos were visited by a man who was fleeing
from the wrath of Dingana who murdered his
brother, Tshaka, and this stranger created a
commotion in Pondoland.   He was Nqeto, son of
Kondlo, of the Qwabe tribe, and of the Great
House of Malandela of which Tshaka was of the
Right-Hand House.   Although Nqeto was not a
Pondo, we will make a few observations about him,
for he had something to do with Faku's country.
In Tshaka's time, Pakatwayo, Nqeto's elder
brother, represented the Great House of Malandela,
the Qwabe.   There was neither agreement nor
cordiality between him and Tshaka.   For his part,

Tshaka cared nothing for ties of relationship. It was a simple thing for him to kill without compunction everybody who showed the slightest claim to the chieftainship of the tribe. He did not hesitate to slay his relatives or to treat them cruelly when they fell into his hands. Under these circumstances he attacked the Ama-Qwabe, who were defeated and Pakatwayo their chief was killed. The latter's younger brother, Vubuku-lwayo, then succeeded to the chieftainship of the Ama-Qwabe. He leaned toward Zwide, the noted chief of the Ama-Ndwandwe and enemy of Tshaka. Another section of the Ama-Qwabe under Nqeto, younger brother of Vubukulwayo, sided with Tshaka. Soon afterwards Tshaka was killed by Dingana. Although an evil character, Tshaka did not equal Dingana, the greatest savage among savages. Nqeto was not satisfied to live under Dingana's rule, and he removed with his people making for the South. This was about 1828. Dingana pursued him with his impi when he heard that Nqeto had fled, but did not overtake him. Nqeto gathered together under him on the march certain motley remnants of tribes which had been scattered by Tshaka. They crossed the Umzimkulu and Mzimvubu, going in the direction of Umtata. Nqeto was seeking to put a broad strip of country between himself and Dingana. He passed above the Pondos, and came into conflict with the Pondomise and was compelled to fall back. When he could not gain a place to rest his followers, he forced himself into Pondoland. Here he held out for a time, settled down and built near the Mzimvubu. We do not know what

occurred between Nqeto and the people of Morely
(Wilo Mission) which was newly erected, but he
destroyed this mission of Shepstone's in 1829.
After this affair, and in the same year, Nqeto
massacred a small party of Europeans, on their
way to Natal, making for Dingana's kraal, in
charge of Lieutenant Farewell who was on familiar
terms with the potentate. Dingana was seeking
to revenge himself on Nqeto. He was in the
habit of sending spies and detectives into
Pondoland to gain information by which to get at
Nqeto. Farewell hearing Nqeto was close to
where he had encamped determined to see him.
It may be remembered, considering the tragedy
which occurred on this visit, that Nqeto was being
waylaid, watched and hunted by Dingana's spies
seeking his life, and they were ever on his track.
Nqeto was a fugitive, and a desperado determined to preserve his life. Now, what was Farewell's object in going there, for one of Dingana's
spies accompanied him and was furnished on his
way to Nqeto with a greatcoat to conceal his
identity? But Nqeto was not deceived, for he
recognized him. It was natural, therefore, for
Nqeto to think that this conduct of Farewell's proclaimed him to be a spy of Dingana's, and equally
to be anxious to secure his destruction. However,
he allowed the party to return to camp, but swore
to wipe them out. That same night the camp
was surrounded and every living soul within it
was murdered, Farewell among the rest. To say
that Nqeto was enticed by the desire of plunder
is not convincing. What is evident, and more
reasonable, is that the Chief was fighting for his

life, with his back to the wall. Faku on his part could not bring himself to rest with such a savage as this neighbour. Thus these chiefs were continually at feud, till at length Nqeto was overpowered by Faku. Feeling himself unable longer to hold out in Pondoland, Nqeto returned to Natal. Dingana hearing that his half-brother Nqeto had returned, hastened to lay a trap for him. And in this way Nqeto of the Ama-Qwabe met his end.

Mqikela.

Faku's great son and heir, Mqikela, while still a young man gave evidence, by his conduct, that he was not amenable to discipline or parental control. Freedom to act as he chose and to follow his own inclinations was the guiding principle of his life. He held the views and opinions of his father and the councillors of the tribe in supreme contempt. He would listen to no advice from Faku, until the latter had perforce to leave his son to his own devices.

Having attained to the chieftainship on the death of Faku, he began to cause annoyance to the Government at the Cape, by acting in a high-handed manner in connection with the agreement made by Faku and Ndamase and the Government, whereby these two chiefs were to receive certain sums from the Government in lieu of the dues exacted from ships touching at St. John's harbour. In consequence of Mqikela's conduct, the financial support which he was receiving from the Government was withdrawn.

One of the first acts of this turbulent chief, shortly after he assumed the chieftainship of the

Pondos, was to force on a war with the Bacas. The Pondos were not in sympathy with this wanton act of aggression on the part of their headstrong chief, as there was no cause of quarrel between the two tribes, but as Mqikela was determined to signalize his entry into manhood and control of the tribe by an attack on the Bacas, his people were forced, in the end, to give in and let him have his way. This inconsiderate adventure turned out a complete fiasco, and is known as the battle of Notinta, so called after one of the commanders of the Pondo army.

Mqikela marshalled his forces, but before setting out the *tola* or war-doctor advised against the enterprise. However, he was over-ruled and the Pondo army advanced towards its destination.

Diko, uncle to Makaula, was Regent of the Bacas during the minority of his nephew.

The Pondo army advanced in three divisions. The Vungeni division was on the right; that of the Great Place, the Qauka, held the centre under the chief and leader Notinta ; a third division was on the left. Bacaland roughly was the name given to the district bounded on the West by the Tina River, and on the East by the Mvenyane east of the Kenira River, and South to North from about the Osborn mission to the Mganu hills. All these points were within the Mount Frere area.

The Baca Great Place was between the Kenira and Mvenyane rivers at place called Lutateni. As the Pondos came on, the Bacas fell back on the Mganu hills, sending off in advance their families and cattle. When these were made as secure as possible, the Baca warriors stopped at the foot of the hills and turned to face the enemy. The right division of the Pondo army came into conflict with the left of the Bacas, but was put to flight. Meanwhile the Pondo centre had reached Lutateni and was resting before advancing to the attack, when superstition stepped in and won the battle for the Bacas.

While Notintwa was resting his men, a calf—some say a black one, others say a white one—which had been disturbed in its sleep by the noise of the army, raced for home which was in the hands of the Pondos, bellowing as it went. The Pondos took fright at what to them was a most unusual occurrence : they immediately put it down to supernatural influence. The war-doctor also realised that his prognostications were coming true, for he shouted, " All is lost, that is Ncapayi's spirit come to the help of his children." The Pondo warriors, in consequence, became disorgan - ised, and Makaula, the Bacas' young chief, and son of Ncapayi, saw his advantage and took it. He gave the Bacas the order to charge. They launched themselves with such irresistible force against the Pondos that the latter broke and fled, following the ridge up which earlier in the day they had advanced on Lutateni. The whole three divisions of Mqikela's army were now in flight, making for home, but before them lay the river Kenira. They reached the ford Nopoyi on the Kenira, with the Bacas working havoc among them with the assegai. The congestion at the drift was so great that the Pondos could do little to defend themselves. The slaughter that followed was very great, so that the memory of this disaster is still kept fresh in the minds of the Pondos. Mqikela's great adventure turned out to his own disadvantage and the disgust of his people. Instead of signalizing his entry into manhood, as he desired, by "washing his spears in the blood of his enemies," it was his enemies who "washed their spears " in the blood of his unfortunate subjects.

Mqikela's rule, which lasted about twenty years until his death in 1888, was not otherwise distinguished by any event of great importance. He maintained his reputation for indifference to the opinions of others, and was captious and cruel.

In 1878, the district of Mount Currie, in which the town of Kokstad lies, and which about the year 1860 had been granted to the Griquas under Adam Kok in place of land on which they had been settled in Griqualand West, was alienated through a rebellion on the part of the Griquas against the Government. Mqikela more than connived at the attitude of the Griquas. He allowed them to enter into his territory, and make their preparations for war in Pondoland. He even supported them with a force of Pondos, under the sub-chief Josiah Stata, more widely known as Josiah Jenkins, because as a youth he had been brought up in the family of the Rev. Jenkins, a missionary among the Pondos.

On account of this conduct and of his disregard of the treaty arranged in 1844 between Sir Peregrive Maitland, Governor of Cape Colony, and Faku, father of Mqikela and Paramount chief of the Pondos, the Government withdrew its recognition of Mqikela as Paramount Chief of Pondoland. Further, the position of Nqwiliso, great son of Ndamase, Faku's right-hand son, as an independent chief was confirmed, thus curtailing Mqikela's power. Faku himself, disgusted with the insubordination of his heir Mqikela had urged Ndamase, his favourite son, to cross the St. John's river and occupy the country westward of it, as he would then be practically independent of Mqikela. This Ndamase and his followers did. and the subsequent action of the Government was a recognition and confimation of Ndamase's independent position. From that time to the present Pondoland has been subdivided into two divisions, called the Qauka, or Eastern Pondoland. and the Nyanda, or Western Pondoland. The former is ruled by the descendants of Mqikela. and the latter by those of Ndamase.

Ndamase

Ndamase was the eldest son of Faku, and chief of the Right Hand House. He early proved himself to be a man of courage and resource. Consequently he was, while still a young man, chosen to be commander-in-chief of his father's warriors. Most of the battles fought during Faku's long reign where under Ndamase's leadership, and perhaps no other Pondo chief did so much to consolidate the tribe. During Faku's reign. the Pondo tribe was subject to many disturbances from without as well as within. Nqeto, the chief of Ama-Qwabe, and a relative of Tshaka, when driven out of Zululand by Dingaan (Dingana), tried to take possession of a portion of Pondoland whereupon to settle. Ngozi, chief of the Tembu tribe from the Qudeni district of Natal, when driven out like

Nqeto, came into Pondoland and sought to take forcible possession of a part of the country, only to be defeated and killed. The Bacas and Xesibes, as well as other broken tribes were constantly trying conclusions with the Pondos by force of arms. In most of these engagements Ndamase was commander-in-chief of the Pondo warriors, and successfully maintained the prestige of his countrymen.

Apart from these matters there is little to record about him. His was a much finer character in every way than that of Faku's heir, Mqikela; he was wiser in counsel, braver in action, more manly in bearing and of a more humane disposition.

The reason why there is so little to record about Ndamase is that Faku's reign was an unusually long one, and though Ndamase had actual control of the Western section of Pondoland for some time before his father's death, yet he was nevertheless his father's subordinate. He lived only a few years after Faku's death. He died nine years after Faku, in 1876. He was succeeded in the chieftainship by his son, Nqwiliso.

Nqwiliso.

The disparity between the ages of Faku's two sons, Mqikela, the heir, and Ndamase, of the Right-Hand House, is evidenced by the fact that Mqikela was about the same age as Nqwiliso, Ndamase's heir.

On his accession to power, Nqwiliso made it clear that, while recognising Mqikela's house as the Great House of the Pondos, yet he intended

to follow in Ndamase's footsteps and owe allegiance
to no one, and maintain his position as an independent chief. That meant that he would suffer
no interference from Mqikela. In this declaration
he was supported by the Government.

In 1869, the Governor, Sir Philip Wodehouse,
desired to secure the mouth of the St. John's
River for the Cape Colony. Ndamase, who was
then ruler of Western Pondoland, refused to
accede to this. When, however, Nqwiliso became
chief the subject was again mooted. This time
the Government proposal was agreed to, on the
strength of a promise made to Nqwiliso to recognise his claim to the paramountcy of Western
Pondoland. This was in 1878. For a distance of
nine miles inland from the mouth of the St. John's
River a narrow bit of land on the western bank
was purchased by the Government for £1000
pounds from Nqwiliso.

In 1880, occurred a signal act of treachery on
the part of Mhlontlo, chief of the Pondomise, a
tribe closely related to the Pondos, viz., the brutal
murder of Mr. Hamilton Hope, Mhlontlo's magistrate. This incident is referred to more fully in
the section on the Pondomise. Suffice it to say
here that, in the above year, there was considerable unrest in which a number of tribes were
involved.

The cause of the unrest was the passing of the
Natives Disarmament Act, as well as the methods
attending its enforcement. The Basutos, or at
least sections of them, became alarmed and
decided to resist. In East Griqualand, Makwayi's
Basutos, who had crossed over the Drakensberg

and were occupying part of the district of Matatiele, were the first to rise. The repercussion of
this rising was felt among the Pondomise and
other tribes. It is said that the Native tribes
throughout the Cape Colony were never so near
combining against their white rulers as they were
on this occasion. Several tribes followed Makwayi's example, among them the Ama-Qwati in
Tembuland, and the Ama-Mpondomise. The Pondomise tribe is split up into two main divisions ;
one occupying the country west of the Tsitsa River
to the Tsolo hills, under the chief Mditshwa.

The Chief Magistrate of the Transkeian Territories, Major Elliot, received information through
Native sources, that Mditshwa's Pondomise had
surrounded the magistracy at Tsolo, at that time
on the east bank of the Inxu River, where a
number of Europeans had sought refuge with the
local magistrate, A. R. Welsh, Esq. He immediately sent to Nqwiliso to ask his assistance in
effecting their liberation. Nqiliso represented to
the magistrate, in reply, that the besieged Europeans would not trust him; therefore he would
only consent to do as asked, provided some Europeans accompanied his force. This being agreed
to (see article on Pondomise), Nqwiliso placed a
force of Pondos under the leadership of his son,
Bokleni and his own brother, Qumbelo, and sent
it forward to Tsolo, where in due time it arrived
and succeeded, without a battle, in liberating the
besieged from the stone jail at Tsolo and bringing
them in safety to Umtata.

For this act of loyalty, Nqwiliso was publicly
thanked by Major Elliot on behalf of the Govern-

v

322 THE SOUTH-EASTERN BANTU

ment. As Nqiliso's intervention had a good deal
to do with thwarting and rendering abortive
Mditshwa's efforts at rebellion, it should be noted
that his action on that occasion was a supreme
test of his good faith and loyalty to the Government while at the same time it must have been
a heart-breaking thing for him to do. Why?
Because he was a blood-relative of the chiefs of
the Pondomise, and he was thus virtually fighting,
or prepared to fight, against his brothers. Pondo
and Pondomise, the pregenitors of their respective
tribes, were twin brothers, and sons of Njanya.
According to Pondo ideas of rank and position,
Mhlontlo was held to belong to Mqikela's house,
Eastern Pondoland, and Mditshwa to Nqwiliso's
house, Western Pondoland. Nqwiliso, then, was
arming and marching against one of his own house,
in a quarrel which was none of his.

Nqwiliso's authority, as chief of Western Pondoland, was a source of envy to some of the other
Pondo chiefs, and notably to Gwadiso, chief of
the Ama-Konjwayo.

Here, again, we have an example of the custom
of *isi-zi* being the occasion of strife and of rival
claims to chieftainship (see Chap. IV, Isi-zi and
Konjwayo).

The Ama-Konjwayo are a tribe closely related
to Nqwiliso's house. Their chief until recently
(1927) was Gwadiso. These two chiefs were of
close descent. A former Pondo chief of the ruling
house, by name Bala, had twin sons, Citwayo and
Konjwaya, the former being an elder twin. From
these two, therefore, we have the continuation of
the ruling line in Citwayo's descendants and the
creation of the Konjwayo tribe. But the origin

of these two houses from twins was the source of constant jealousy and friction between them.

Konjwayo's great son was Kiwo, the latter's great son was Ngcekula, and Ngcekula's son was Ntsikiyane. Ntsikiyane's son was Makanda, and his son was Nogemane, the father of Gwadiso. This line of important chiefs, whose tribe became a prominent one, was ever ready to claim that Konjwayo and not Citwayo was really the elder twin. The old source of quarrels, the *isizi*, was again to be the cause of calling in question Nqwiliso's superiority. To the *isizi* custom was added another cause of strife, e.g., tribal boundaries.

It happened that Gwadiso's uncle Mcunukelwa died, and the former refused to send, in accordance with custom, the *isizi* cattle to Nqwiliso. Instead, he kept them as his own perquisite, and this led to an open quarrel. Added to this was a question of boundaries. A certain man, Mbombo, had his kraal at Old Bunting on the boundary between the two tribes. A day arrived when Mbombo's daughter was to be married to a son of Sitelo, another of Gwadiso's uncles. The young woman, however, refused to be married to him. This so incensed Gwadiso that he seized all Mbombo's cattle. Nqwiliso, who regarded these proceedings as flouting his authority, began to arm his warriors.

He formed them into three divisions. The left division proceeded towards Gwadiso's Great Place at Mpoza, the centre passed though the Qokama forest making for Ntibane; the third division kept close to the Umtata River, its destination being Ndungunyeni. The aim of this arrangement was to prevent the Konjwayos from crossing the

Umtata River, and thus placing themselves outside of Pondoland. The Konjwayos must be kept within the Pondo boundaries and the final issue decided there, without the interference of other tribes.

The Konjwayos did not wait to be attacked but advanced on Nqwiliso's army. Nqwiliso's right drove the Konjwayos' left before it and forced it on to the Mdumbi River mouth, where it scattered.

The Konjwayo main force covering Gwadiso's Great Place was overwhelmed and driven in the opposite direction, being pursued to the Umtata River, where it crossed over and entered the territory of Dudumayo, chief of the Tshomanes. Gwadiso himself fled into Eastern Pondoland. Nqwiliso's forces then withdrew and went home. But meanwhile Gwadiso had slipped back and was reforming his warriors, and while doing so he sent a message of defiance to Nqwiliso, saying, "Nqwiliso will have to burn Mandayi's hut, before I will acknowledge defeat."

Mandayi was Gwadiso's chief wife at Mpoza. The challenge was accepted and Nqwiliso's forces came on in the formation adopted in the earlier conflict. The opposing armies met at Mpoza and a fierce battle ensued. Many were killed and wounded on both sides, among the killed being a chief, Mdunyelwa, a grandson of the great Faku. Another chief, Libode, after whom the village of Libode is called, was desperately wounded. For a second time Gwadiso's forces were driven to the sea coast and were broken up. Mandayi's hut was burnt to the ground. Gwadiso had now to acknowledge defeat.

Tyabule.

The following incident shows how easily wars occur among the Bantu tribes. All matters adversely touching precedence and authority, especially of a ruling chief, are as often as not settled by the test of battle. The boundaries demarcating the land separating one chief from another provided a polific source of trouble. The case of Tyabule, however, came short of actual fighting.

In the Ngqeleni district of Pondoland, at a place called Mabeje, a certain Tyabule had built his kraal. It so happened that he had chosen a spot exactly on the boundary separating Nqwiliso from Gwadiso.

This was but one of his kraals, for he was a rich man, with many cattle, procured mostly by theft. He was a noted thief. On a certain day two cream-coloured horses arrived at Tyabule's kraal at Mabeje. The heir of Nqwiliso, Bokleni, was told about them and he became anxious to secure them for himself. Knowing that they had been stolen, he planned to get them by ordering that, as stolen property, they were to be taken to him. The horses were thus taken to Bokleni, and he appropriated them.

Gwadiso, on the other side of the border, heard of this, and immediately confiscated all Tyabule's cattle that he could secure, both at Mabeje and at Tyabule's other kraals. The latter, however, had many cattle lent out to friends of his own to milk, called *inqoma*. These he now collected and was still a rich man according to Native ideas. Nqwiliso intervened here by sending to Gwadiso and asking why he had confiscated Tyabule's cattle. The Konjwayo chief replied "Tyabule is one of my people, not yours." Instead of attacking Gwadiso, Nqwiliso sent a small force to Tyabule's, fearing resistance from the latter's many sons and friends, his object also being to confiscate the cattle which had been collected. When the owner remonstrated with the chief, Nqwiliso said, "You are one of those individuals who make strife between chiefs, you build your huts on the boundary and neither one chief nor the other knows whom you serve." Though war was avoided by this expedient, it was always possible as boundary disputes were frequent. These boundaries were usually fixed by the paramount chief between his sons as soon as they were appointed to rule over sections of the tribe.

Nqwiliso, by reason of his loyalty to the Government and his readiness to carry out its requirements, was a trusted chief, one who had the confidence of the Government, especially on account of his faithfulness during the rebellion of Mditshwa and Mhlontlo, at the time of the enforcement of the Disarmament Act.

Sigcawu.

Sigcawu followed his father, Mqikela, as ruler of Pondoland, on the latter's death in 1888.

Mqikela's chief wife had no issue and, in accordance with custom, a male child from one of the Minor Houses, whose mother had died, was taken and placed in the Great House to be trained there as the heir. This child was Sigcawu.

Sigcawu was like his father, Mqikela, in this respect that action came more readily to him than talking. He was of good physique and fearless.

On his assuming the chieftainship of the Pondos, he met with opposition from his uncle, Mdlangazi. Pondoland was rent in twain, and fighting took place between their respective forces. Mdlangazi (also known as Josiah Jenkins) was ultimately forced across the Natal border, unsettling the tribes on the east bank of Umzimkulu River.

This trouble was settled through the instrumentality of the Chief Magistrate, Colonel Stanford, then stationed at Kokstad. Josiah Jenkins was for a time banished from Pondoland, and settled near the town of Kokstad in Griqualand East. He returned later from exile and settled at Mbizana.

One consequence of this trouble was that the Natal Government sent a protest to the Cape Government, requesting the latter to put an end to this state of affairs. These constant faction fights, taken together with stock thefts which the Pondos carried on among the neighbouring tribes, and the general state of irresponsibility on the part of the Pondos to law and order, induced the Cape Government to take action. In 1895, Cecil Rhodes, who was then in power, collected a force of 4,000 men, formed partly of various white detachments, partly of Native tribes prepared to assist the Government. With these he made a demonstration against the Pondos, entering their territory and threatening war. The Chief Magistrate of the Transkeian Territories, Major Elliot, however, saw no just reason for forcing war on the Pondos, as all that was desired could be obtained without war, especially as the Pondos had not armed themselves and assumed an aggressive attitude. Major Elliot's intervention was the means of preserving peace.

As a result of negotiations between representatives of the Cape Government and the Pondo chiefs, the Pondos agreed to become tributary to, or come under the protection of the Cape Government.

Dalgetty.

What the actual facts of the case are it is impossible to say, since the records pertaining to it are not available to the writer; but the Pondos state that, on a certain day in 1895, the chief Sigcawu went to confer with the magistrate at Flagstaff and, in accordance with Pondo custom, was accompanied by a large armed retinue. On reaching their destination, in order to *cel'amehlo* (" to ask eyes,") that is, to make an impression, they circled round Flagstaff several times, the while the court-praiser (*imbongi*) was shouting the praises of his chief. The Pondos assert that Colonel Dalgetty, of the Cape Mounted Rifles, who was near, was displeased, thinking that the movement was a demonstration to surround Flagstaff. Representations were made to the Government and a force was sent to take Sigcawu a prisoner, but divining the purpose of this menace, the chief secretly went off to Kokstad and offered himself as a hostage for the Pondos. The Rev. P. Hargreaves, the missionary at Emfundisweni, accompanied the chief. Sigcawu was tried for rebellion before Chief Justice De Villiers, in Cape Town, and judgment was given against him. The importance of the case to the Pondos may be realized by the fact that they engaged the services of Attorney Jones of Kokstad to defend their chief; his remuneration to be 1,000 head of cattle.

On the conclusion of the trial an appeal to the Privy Council was lodged. The judgment of the Colonial Supreme Court was reversed by the Privy Council, and an order made to release Sigcawu and allow him to return home. The Rev. Peter Hargreaves was a true friend to the Pondos, indeed to the Bantu in general, while at the same time he was faithful to his own race. He holds a great place in the hearts of the Pondos, and his name will not be readily forgotten.

The Ama-Tshomane.

In following up the genealogy of the Pondos, we should trace to its conclusion, or as it at present stands, the royal line. This line is no longer the ruling line, having been overthrown by a younger branch. This took place approximately about 1677, or two hundred and fifty years ago, that is, allowing twenty-five years to represent a generation. From the present chief, Dudumayo, to the time of Qiya when this overthrow took place, is ten generations.

There were three brothers, sons of the royal and ruling chief Cabe, named respectively Qiya, Dwera and Gangata, the first named being heir, and the last named a younger son with no particular prospects of reaching the chieftainship by legitimate means. As so often happens, however, under the conditions of life inseparable from a polygamous tribe, an ambitious younger son seeks to usurp his elder brother's place by an appeal to the assegai. A pretext, however childish, is sufficient to cause a conflagration. The beautiful little blue-buck has more than once been, if not the real *casus belli*, at least the pretext for war, and as such was destined

indirectly to cause the downfall of the legitimate
heir to the chieftainship of the Pondos, and to
raise up in his stead one who had no real claim
to the position. A tribal hunt had been organised,
and was attended by the various chiefs. Cabe's
third son, Gangata, succeeded in killing a blue-
buck, and in accordance with the custom pertaining to supreme chiefs, the heir to the chieftainship, Qiya, claimed a portion (usually a leg) as his
perquisite. This Gangata refused and, in doing
so, practically " threw down the gauntlet " to the
heir.

On the return home of the hunters, the sections
of the tribe represented by Qiya, supported by
Dwera, on the one hand, and Gangata on the
other, prepared for an armed conflict. The battle
which ensued was fiercely contested by both sides
until Cabe, the Chief, threw in a force to assist
Gangata. This latter force turned the scale in
favour of the younger brother. Qiya, incensed at
his father's conduct, collected his family and
adherents, and crossed over the Umtata River to
the west bank, where the tribe has been settled
ever since. This tribe is known at the present day as
the Ama-Tshomane, having adopted the name of a
great-grandson of Qiya's as the tribal designation.

About fifty years after this event, there occurred
on the coast of Pondoland, the wreck of some
unknown vessel. The Pondos state that the actual
place was near the Lwambazo. From this wreck,
tradition says, three men and a little girl were
washed ashore alive. The girl, whom the Natives
named Gquma (roar), from the circumstance of
her issuing from the roaring waves, was adopted
into one of the chief's families. When she grew

up she was married, some say by Xwebisa, Tshomane's heir, others say by Sango.* Dudumayo,
present chief of the Ama-Tshomane, gave the
writer the name of Xwebisa, from whom he is
directly descended, as that of the husband of
Gquma. Of the three men (Europeans), one was
taken off by a ship which approached the shore,
but the other two, to whom the Pondos gave the
names of Jekwa and Hatu remained and lived
among the Pondos, taking to themselves wives,
and were the progenitors of the Abe-Lungu tribe
whose present residence is with the Bomvanas of
Bomvanaland. Gquma became, on the accession
of her husband to the chieftainship of the Ama-
Tshomane, the chief's principal wife.

Her issue were three sons and a daughter. The
principal son and heir by her to the chieftainship
of the Ama-Tshomane was Gela ; the second son
was Mlawu and the third Mdepa ; the daughter
was called Bess or Bessie.

Bessie was married to Mjikwa, the son of Wose.
The latter was son of Nkumba, the principal chief
of the Ama-Nkumba. The Ama-Nkumba are the
Great House of the Ama-Tshezi, or Right-hand
house of the Bomvanas. (See Table of Bomvanas).

The descendants of the three sons of Gquma
are as follows :—

(1)	Gela	(2)	Mlawu	(3)	Mdepa (Depa)
	Ngcetana		Makasi		Majibana
	Niki		Menese		Ntleki
	Dalasile		Ntabankulu		Matanzima
	Dudumayo		Sidumo.		

The name of Mdepa, or according to Europeans
Depa, is to be met with in history. Being a son,

* Xwebisa and Sango may be the same individual—a family name
and a royal title.

even a third son of a principal chief of the Tsho-manes, he held the position of a chief, though a minor one, in the tribe. The district controlled by him was that within which Old Bunting now stands, and stretched across the Umtata River to include the Wilo.

He had repeatedly asked that a missionary should be sent to him, which request was ultimately granted by the Wesleyan Denomination sending William Shepstone in 1829. The mission station, Wilo, was however, shortly after it was established, destroyed by Nqeto, a relative of the notorious Tshaka, and chief of the Ama-Qwabe, the main branch of the Ama-Zulu tribe. Driven out by Dingana from Zululand, Nqeto came south and entered Pondoland in 1829. Meeting with opposition from Faku, the Pondo chief, he decided to occupy a portion of the land by force. In the fighting which ensued the mission station of Wilo was destroyed by Nqeto. This was the man who was responsible also for the deaths of Lieutenant Farewell and his party of Europeans as they passed through Pondoland on their way to see Dingana, Tshaka's successor. Nqeto was in the end killed by Dingana and his tribe broken up.

At this time Mdepa would be about 80 years of age. According to popular estimates, he must have been born somewhere about 1750.

If his mother Gquma was, as is just possible, a survivor from the *Bennebrock* wrecked on the coast of Pondoland in 1713, she would be about 40 years or a little over when her son, Mdepa, was born.

Van Reenen places the date of the wreck from which these survivors were saved about 1730 or

40. If this be so, we cannot give the ship's name, as we have seen no record of the destruction of a vessel on the Pondoland coast during those years.

Pondo Clans.

From Sihula are derived the Ama-Ntusi and Imi-Qwane.

From Mtwa are derived the Ama-Gingqi, Ama-Kwalo, Ama-Ngcangule, and Imi-Twa.

From Mkondwane we have the Ama-Ntlane, Ama-Valelo, Ama-Gcuta.

From Sukude we have Ama-Same and Ama-Ncinjana.

From Cabe we have Ama-Cabe, Qiya, Dwera, Gangata, Njilo, Gqwaru, Tshomane and Nyanda.

From Gangata we have Ama-Bala, Imi-Capati.

From Bala we have Ama-Citwayo, Konjwayo, Jola, Nyati, Ngcoya.

From Citwayo we have Ama-Ndayini.

From Ndayini we have Ama-Tahle and Biba. (See Table of Ama-Mampondo).

CHAPTER XIX.

AMA-MPONDOMISE (ABA-MBO)

According to the accepted tradition among the tribes immediately concerned, Pondomise and Pondo were twin sons of Njanya, the son of Sibi-side. The claim is made by the descendants of the former that he was the elder twin brother, and while many Pondos agree that this was so, many others are prepared to dispute the statement.

The Lion's Skin

When a dispute arises, the Pondomise usually ask the question, " Where did you Pondos hide the Lion's Skin? " The allusion is to a custom indicating superiority of rank on the one hand and inferiority on the other.

It was decreed by law and custom among Bantu tribes that the principal chief of the tribe had a first claim to certain animals killed in the hunting field. In the case of a lion, he claimed the skin, head and claws as his special property. The story goes that on a certain occasion Pondo, who was (the Pondomise state) the younger twin, killed a lion, and that Pondomise made a claim for the skin, but met with refusal from Pondo; that war threatened between the rival factions; and Pondo, fearing to put the matter of his own claim to be the elder twin to the test by battle, elected to separate from Pondomise and settle elsewhere with his followers; since when both tribes have lived a separate existence. The point

Ama-Mpondomise.

J. H. Soga.

The material originally positioned here is too large for reproduction in this reissue. A PDF can be downloaded from the web address given on page iv of this book, by clicking on 'Resources Available'.

of the story is that Pondomise was exercising the right of the superior chief when he made his claim, and that the truth of the story which is a matter of general acknowledgment proves the Pondomise to be Njanya's royal house.   Apart from other branches of the Aba-Mbo who settled in Natal from 1620 (E. A. Walker, *Historical Atlas of S.A.*, p. 6), the first place at which we hear that the Pondomise resided is at the Dedesi (F. Brownlee, *Historical Records*, p. 116), a stream believed to be one of the rivulets under the Drakensberg, forming the sources of the Umzimvubu, "which is near to where Langalibalele crossed the Drakensberg," when pursued by the Natal Government forces.   The writer, in 1926, made a journey to the upper reaches of the Umzimvubu with a view to securing corroborative evidence of the existence of the Debesi, but without success.   This, however, is not to be wondered at, since from the early years at least of the seventeenth century until about 1860, that is, a little over two hundred years, the country within which the Dedesi would be, was uninhabited, and was until lately known as No-Man's-Land. It has now been reoccupied by new tribes, such as the Ntlangwini, Basuto, and others, as well as by European farmers.   Consequently as there were no inhabitants at the time of reoccupation to perpetuate the old names of the locality, new ones have been subsituted.   Tradition informs us that a number of tribes took possession of the country bordering on the Drakensberg.   First among these to arrive were the Ama-Xosa, then followed Ama-Mpondo and Pondomise.   All three tribes in quick succession, after approximately a residence

of twenty-five years or so, moved away eastward
and settled along the coast, the Xosas on the
west bank of the Umzimvubu (St. John's River),
the Pondos on the east bank, and the Pondomise
north-east of them again. From here the authentic history of these tribes begins.

As an instance of the untrustworthiness in certain particulars of some of those men who are
recognised as tribal authorities on the genealogy
of the tribes, we would mention the name of Mabasa, late regent of Mditshwa's Pondomise (F.
Brownlee, *Historical Records*, p. 116) who gives
the Pondomise genealogy as follows :—

> *Sikomo*
> Njanya
> *Malangana*
> Ntose
> Ncwini
> etc. etc.

and mentions (ibid., p. 119) that from the three
first the Pondomise and Ama-Xosa were considered of one race and origin.

In the broad sense, but not that intended by
Mabasa, the Xosas and Pondomise are of one race
and origin, namely the Bantu race. The inclusion,
however, of undoubted Xosa chiefs in his genealogy makes it clear that he means that they were
closely related. In reply it must be stated, (a)
that the Pondomise are Aba-Mbo, and the Ama-
Xosa are Abe-Nguni—two separate and distinct
branches of the Bantu race with no known point
of genealogical contact; (b) that the names of
Sikomo and Malangana, both real Xosa chiefs,
have been inserted into the Pondomise genealogy
without sufficient reason.

In this connection two points of importance have to be noted.

(1) In the Xosa genealogy, Sikomo was the grandson of Tshawe and was principal son and heir of Ngcwangu. He was father of Togu who was alive in 1686. Malangana was Xosa's heir and grandfather to Tshawe. Between Malangana and Sikomo elapsed a period of four generations, at least one hundred years, whereas Mabasa makes the period two generations and *inverts the order* of these names, making Sikomo grandfather to Malangana, whereas according to Xosa genealogy Sikomo was the son of Malangana's great-grandson.

(2) Pondomise and Pondo were twin sons of Njanye, and therefore the genealogy of these two tribes should be the same. The Pondos do not include either Sikomo or Malangana in their genealogy.

The only reason which can be suggested for the inclusion of these two Xosa chiefs' names in the Pondomise genealogy by Mabasa, is that from long and close association with the Ama-Xosa the names of chiefs of the latter have through the passage of time been mixed up by Pondomise genealogists with their own. Tradition in this particular as in others has failed to be accurate.

Pondomise's Great Son was Ntose, whose Great Son and heir was Ncwini. Ncwini had a younger brother, Dombo, by the same mother. The great majority of Pondomise clans derive their origin from these two chiefs. Ncwini's Great Son and heir was Dosini, but he had an older son, Bukwana, by his first wife. According to a generally accepted rule among Bantu tribes, the son of the first wife

w

of a chief has no claim to the chieftainship. By a later wife, a Bushwoman, Ncwini had a son, Cira, who became his father's favourite, and displaced the rightful heir, Dosini, from the chieftainship. It is from this Cira that the main line of the Pondomise comes. The notorious Mhlontlo, who murdered Mr. Hope in 1880, is the eleventh chief in the direct line of descent from Cira. The sixth in the line from Cira was Pahlo, whose son of the minor House was Mgabisa. The great-grandson of this chief was Mditshwa who shut up a number of Europeans along with the magistrate, Mr. Welsh, in the prison at Tsolo, shortly after the murder by his (Mditshwa's) nephew, Mhlontlo, of the Qumbu magistrate, Hope. This section of the tribe, not being the royal line, has adopted the name of u-Zalaba.

A curious instance may here be given of one way, at least, of supplying a successor to a deceased chief who leaves no male issue in the principal house. Chief Pahlo of the main line had no sons in his Great House. He had, however, daughters of whom the eldest was Mamani. The Right-Hand Son of Pahlo was Sontlo, and Mgabisa was of the Minor House (*iqadi*), but as a result of what follows Sontlo became principal chief, and Mgabisa also got promoted and became chief of the Right-Hand House.

It happened in this way. Nyauza, the Great Chief of the Pondo tribe, who was quite familiar with the conditions affecting the Pondomise succession, had a daughter, Ntsibaba, whom he sent to be wife to Mamani, chieftainess of the Pondomise tribe. Nyawuza was perfectly aware that Mamani was a woman, and probably correctly gauged the course of events, and that these would be to the advantage of his daughter. When Ntsibaba arrived at the Pondomise headquarters, with a retinue befitting a Great Chief's daughter, Mamani made her welcome, as it would have been a serious insult to send the daughter of an important chief back to her father. Mamani met the difficult position in which she was placed by sending for her half-brother of the Right-Hand House, Sontlo. She publicly adopted him as her son and appointed him also as her successor, on condition that Sontlo would marry Ntsibaba. To all this Sontlo agreed, and in time became the Principal Chief of the Pondomise. Thus by a little matrimonial diplomacy was secured the continuance of the succession of the Principal House of the Pondomise.

Mgabisa was as a result of Sontlo's advancement appointed to the vacant Right-Hand House. The son of Mgabisa was Velelo, Diko being Velelo's son, and the notorious Mditshwa, or " Gqirana " as he is sometimes called, was Diko's son. The present chief Lutshoto is grandson to Mditshwa, his father being Mtshazi. Lutshoto comes of a turbulent line of chiefs, and though deprived by the Government of his full status as a chief retains the loyalty of the Pondomise. He has, however, caused some anxiety at the present time by allowing himself to be the medium through which the Bolsheviks and their agent, Wellington Butelezi, or " Dr. Wellington " as he calls himself, have caused considerable unrest among the Pondomise and the neighbouring tribes. This movement is partly a commentary on the severe strain to which the loyalty of the Bantu tribes has been put by recent legislation passed or proposed by the Government, such as the Native Land Act (1913); the Bill amending this Act (1927); the Union Native Council Bill (1927); and the Representation of Natives in Parliament Bill 1927. The aim of all these measures is to fix and definitely settle the policy of the Union with regard to the position of the Bantu within its borders. Apart from these measures, the Bantu have laboured under what they believe to be discrimination against them in the Courts of Justice; added to which is the general attitude of the European to the Bantu. The widespread feeling of uncertainty and irritation produced by these and other causes finds its repercussion in isolated and abortive efforts on the part of sections of the Bantu to restore the balance.

With a people whose folk-lore and fireside tales partake largely of the mysterious and the irrational, and who have grown up under the baneful influence of witchcraft, it becomes an easy matter to pass from the rational to the absurd. Hence many fall an easy prey to the machinations of foolish agitators like "Dr. Wellington." They have been beguiled by promises of the arrival of armies of Negro Americans who, as the result of the peace terms following the recent great European war, have been ordered to emancipate the Bantu from British control. Men representing themselves as agents of "Dr. Wellington" have been surreptitiously passing from tribe to tribe, and collecting money from their dupes, on the strength of their representations that this is to form the sinews of war should emancipation be refused. Fortunately, three factors have been at work to nullify any serious evil arising from this agitation :—

(1) The wise and patient attitude of the magistrates of the Native Territories who, after forbidding "Dr. Wellington" to enter the Territories, maintained an attitude of quiet alertness, and refused to be alarmed and so cause an exaggerated estimate of the unrest.

(2) Time, whose passage was to prove how hollow were the specious promises made, as they failed to materialise.

(3) The commonsense of the great majority of the Bantu, who refused to have anything to do with the movement.

In Pondomiseland where the people as well as their Chief, Lutshoto, had a grievance against the Government, in that it would not grant Lutshoto recognition with the full status of Principal Chief, the agents of "Dr. Wellington," or rather parasites feeding upon the credulity of their countrymen, found willing ears. Much damage was done even among members of various denominations by drawing them within the orbit of the movement, so that through the withdrawal of the children from Government-aided schools the cause of education suffered a blow which it will take years to repair. The peculiarity most evident in connection with this alleged Bolshevik agitation was that, in the main, the scheme was propagated, and had its greatest success among the red-blanket, or heathen, Natives.

Somewhere about 1650 or 1660 the Pondomise, who had followed the example of the Ama-Xosa and Ama-Mpondo and moved from the Dedesi to the sea-coast, settled alongside, but east of, the

Pondos. For a time we hear nothing about them until after the occupation of Natal by Europeans. There was a subsequent movement inland by this tribe, and at present we find it between the Tina and the Tsitsa River.

There are two vain divisions of the tribe. That under Mhlontlo's successors extends from the Qanqu, a small tributary of the Tina, on the east, to the eastern bank of the Tsitsa River on the west. The other branch, known as Mditshwa's Pondomise, occupies a considerable portion of the Tsolo district, west of the Tsitsa River.

There are no very important wars to record in which the Pondomise have been engaged, as the greater part of their battles were fought in the course of raids on their neighbours' cattle. These neighbouring tribes were the Pondos, Bacas, Xesibes, and Tembus. We would just mention two of these minor affairs, first the war between the Pondomise and the Bacas when the latter were fleeing before Tshaka; and Hope's War, as it is called.

War between Pondomise and Bacas.

In the former war, Mditshwa's section of Pondomise were under their chief Velelo, and that of Mhlontlo was under Myeki.

The Bacas were under Madikane. When these, in their flight from Tshaka, say about 1825, reached Bencuti (Shawbury) they settled down for a time. The Pondomise, their neighbours, had been weakened by internal feuds and, taking advantage of this, Madikane attacked them. For three days they fought with each other until ultimately the Pondomise were compelled to give ground.   They were driven across the Tsitsa in confusion.   Under these conditions the Pondomise sought for assistance from the Tembu Chief, Ngubengcuka, who agreed to help them.   A Tembu impi set out for the scene of operations and crossed the Tsitsa at the Ntshaba Drift.   Here the Tembus were met by the broken Pondomise, who had reorganised their forces, and together they attacked the Bacas.   The Tembu force overcame the Bacas opposed to it, but the Pondomise were driven in by the Bacas facing them, an action recalling the battle of Sheriff Muir.   The Bacas pressed their advantage, and clearing the Pondomise out of the way, invaded Tembuland.   Ngubengcuka's Tembus were recalled to face the invasion, but at the Gqutyini were severely beaten and lost many warriors.   Thus the Bacas overcame both the Pondomise and the Tembus.   Two months later the Pondomise, whose position had become precarious, sought the help of the Ama-Gcina, who are a section of the Ama-Nqabe, and they also applied to the Gcalekas (F. Brownlee, *Historical Records*, p. 113).   In this new engagement the Bacas were surrounded and suffered heavily.   Their families were taken prisoner, their cattle confiscated, and those of the Bacas who succeeded in effecting their escape sought the protection of Faku, chief of the Pondos.   It was in this engagement that the Great Chief of the Bacas, Madikane, and chiefs of lesser note, Matomela and Mqukubeni, were killed.   These events took place about 1835.

Hope's War.

The war erroneously called Hope's War, was really the war caused by the Disarmament Act of the Government, whereby the Bantu tribes were to be deprived of their guns. Hope's murder was merely an incident in the resistance offered by some tribes to the enforcement of the Act.

Some years previous to this, in 1872, a Commission had been appointed by the Governor, to enquire into the causes of unrest among those tribes that had been driven out of Natal by the Tshaka disturbances and had settled in the portion of country then called No-Man's-Land, and now East Griqualand, that is, the territory between the Mzimkulu and the Mtata Rivers. The majority of the tribes that had sought refuge here, were weary with the constant raids and fighting and were anxious to be taken under the protection of the Cape Government. The following chiefs gave in their applications;—Makaula, son of Ncapayi, chief of the Bacas; Mhlontlo, chief of the Pondomise; Ludidi and Zibi, chiefs of the Hlubis; and Lebenya, a minor Basuto chief. Mditshwa, however, chief of the western section of the Pondomise, did not see his way to ask the Government's protection. As a measure arising out of the Nongxokozelo affair, in which Kreli, the great Gcaleka chief, engaged in a punitive expedition against Ngangelizwe of the Tembus, the Government decided to appoint a magistrate to preside over the tribes between the Mzimkulu and Mtata rivers. For this post Mr. J. M. Orpen was selected and stationed at Tsolo in Pondomise Territory in 1873. Mditshwa, whether he saw in this a subtle menace on the part of Government or not, expressed a wish to come under the wing of Government. His fear of the Pondos who were ever ready to make raids into his country may have been the cause which inspired Mditshwa to take this step. Some of these tribes, which under stress of raids by their neighbours, had sought Government protection, no sooner felt the danger removed than they began to look askance at the Government and its laws for regulating their conduct.

The enforcement of the Disarmament Act, recently passed, determined the most bitter of the tribes to take action.

Trouble first broke out among the Basutos in 1880. Their compatriots on the eastern side of the Drakensberg made overtures to the Pondos and the tribes in No-man's-land to join them in resistance to the Act. To counteract this movement on the part of Basutos, Mr. H. Hope, magistrate of Qumbu in the territory of Mhlontlo's section of Pondomise, sought to win over Mhlontlo to the side of the Government. With this object in view a meeting was arranged between Mr. Hope and Mhlontlo, to take place at Sulenkama, on the main road between Qumbu and Mount Fletcher. This spot was within a short distance of Mhlontlo's Great Place. If up to this time there had been any doubts as to the attitude of the Pondomise, those doubts were to be rudely dispelled by an act of ferocity that startled the whole country. In October 1880, according to arrangement, Mr. Hope, along with three young Europeans, Henman, Warren and Davis, the latter a clerk in the magistrate's office at Qumbu, arrived at Sulenkama. The Europeans met Mhlontlo and a large body of armed Pondomise, ostensibly prepared to march against the Basutos. The war-song *(um-guyo)* was sung by the whole body of warriors. Braves *(ama-qaji)* sprang forward and gave exhibitions of their prowess. Meanwhile the Europeans had been surrounded, and at a given signal the warriors threw themselves upon them. In a moment three of them were transfixed with assegais, lifted up into the air, and then dropped to the ground, covered with innumerable wounds. So died Messrs. Hope, Warren and Henman. Davis owed his salvation to the fact that his father, Rev. W. J. Davis, had been a missionary among the Pondomise and was respected by the tribe.

Guns and ammunition which Mr. Hope had brought to arm the Pondomise against the Basutos, were immediately seized and taken possession of by the Pondomise, who then set out to help the Basutos. These Basutos were an overflow into Griqualand East from Basutoland proper, and thus lived on the eastern face of the Drakensberg mountains.

Mhlontlo's objective was the Mount Fletcher District where he hoped to join the Basutos; but on the march thither he turned aside to Maclear on his left, where he attacked a small party of Europeans and Lehana's Botlokwa, who were under the charge of Mr. J. R. Thomson, the magistrate. Desperate efforts were made by the Pondomise to capture the place, but as desperately and determinedly did Mr. Thomson and his handful of loyalists successfully resist, until help came from the Kokstad direction. This was a force of Ntlangwini from the Mzimkulu, a river that forms the boundary between Natal and Cape Colony. I believe this force was under Mr. Donald Strachan. The Basutos, on their part, sent reinforcements to

Mhlontlo, and a number of Tembus also assisted him. However, even with this help the Pondomise were unable to conquer. A small force of volunteers from Dordrecht made forced marches to the assistance of Mr. Thomson. By their help he and his party were extricated and the Pondomise defeated. Mhlontlo, perceiving that the " game was up," fled into Basutoland and was in hiding there for some years. He was ultimately pardoned by a later Cape Government, but was not allowed to resume his office as chief of the Pondomise. He died shortly after his liberation. In both of these engagements, namely that under Mditshwa at Tsolo, and that under Mhlontlo at Sulenkama, individual Natives gave signal assistance to the Europeans. At Qanqu near the Tina River, the head-quarters, or Great Place, of Mhlontlo, was an Anglican Mission under a Native clergyman, Stephen Bangela. He was a spectator of the massacre of Mr. Hope and his companions. His first thought was to put the Europeans on their guard. Being fortunate in seizing a horse near by, he jumped on its back with nothing to guide it but the rope with which it had been knee-haltered, and set off at full speed to inform the magistrate of Tsolo of what had happened. Mr. Welsh passed him on to Major Elliot at Umtata, where again he told his story. Mr. Welsh, immediately on receiving this information, sent such notice as he could to European neighbours, barricaded himself and such friends as were able to join him in the jail building, and made preparations for resistance, as he foresaw that Mditshwa would follow Mhlontlo's lead. Having been apprised of the recent events, Mditshwa immediately surrounded the Tsolo jail with a body of warriors. Then he suggested to the Europeans that they should put themselves under his protection, promising to accompany them to Umtata and to see them safely out of danger. A local teacher, however, Philip Lokwe, managed to convey word to them not to trust Mditshwa's word as he intended treachery.

Major Elliot received word of this happening also, and seeing the necessity of sending help to the beleagured in Tsolo, though unable himself to spare any men from the protection of Umtata, sent to Nqwiliso, the Pondo chief of Western Pondoland, asking for a force of Pondos to relieve Tsolo. Nqwiliso agreed provided some Europeans accompanied his force, as he held, and probably correctly, that the Europeans in Tsolo would doubt his *bona fides*. This was agreed to. The Rev. James Morris, Wesleyan Missionary at Buntingville in Pondoland, offered to accompany this force. As it passed Umtata on its way to Tsolo, half a dozen more Europeans volunteered to join it. This force of Pondo warriors was placed by Nqwiliso partly under charge of his son and heir, Bokleni—a somewhat turbulent character—and partly under Qumbelo, a younger brother of Nqwiliso—a more stable character. Tsolo was reached without opposition, the beleagured were released and led by Nqwiliso's Pondos to the safe shelter of Umtata.

The scene of Mr. Hope's murder is marked by a monument to his memory and that of his unfortunate companions.

Mditshwa was shortly afterwards taken prisoner and was kept in confinement for three years.

Ama-Xesibe.

J. H. Soga.

To face section on Ama-Xesibe Chap. XIX, page 349.

The material originally positioned here is too large for reproduction in this reissue. A PDF can be downloaded from the web address given on page iv of this book, by clicking on 'Resources Available'.

Ama-Xesibe (Aba-Mbo).

Njanya, the father of the twins, Pondomise and Pondo, was also the father of Xesibe. The latter is said to be *imfusi* by his countrymen, that is, the first child born after twins. He was probably by the same mother as the twins. There are two important divisions of the Ama-Xesibe, namely the Great House and the Right-Hand House. The heir of Xesibe of the Great House was Ntoza-bantu, and that of the Right-Hand was Mganu.

The fourth in descent from Ntozabantu was Nondzaba who not only continued the succession, but was the originator of a clan which has identi-fied itself with much of the fighting in Tembuland since the time of Ngubengcuka, viz., the Ama-Qwati. They represent Nondzaba's Right-Hand House. They were for a time resident in Pondo-land when the Principal House, or main section, of the Xesibes were compelled by the Tshaka disturbances to seek refuge with the Pondos. During Ngubengcuka's reign in Tembuland, the Ama-Qwati left Pondoland and sought to take forcible possession of a part of Tembuland. They were resisted and driven northward by the Tem-bus. They then made for Basutoland where they remained for a short time, but the Basutos event-ually compelled them to leave the country. They then returned back to Tembuland and entered it as suppliants on this occasion. They were given the district in which they at present reside by Ngubengcuka.

The ancient residence of the Xesibe tribe was about the sources of the Mpanza. Though a fairly powerful tribe at the time, the Xesibes fled from Tshaka and allied themselves to Maraule, chief of the Ama-Fuze, or Ama-Funze, in the neighbourhood of the present Greytown. Believing that matters had settled down, they returned to their old site at the Mpanza, but they stood in the way of Ngozi, chief of the Aba-Tembu, who was in flight from the terrible Tshaka. Ngozi attacked them as they refused to give him a free passage. Overwhelmed by the Tembus, the Xesibes returned to the Mvoti and again joined Maraule. When Maraule was later attacked and overcome by Tshaka, he sought refuge in the country about the Ntlozane Mountain. It became necessary then for the Xesibes to separate from the Ama-Funze. In several scattered parties they moved south to Pondoland. It was natural for them to make for Pondoland in their day of trouble, as the progenitors of the Pondo and the Xesibe tribes, namely Pondo and Xesibe were brothers. The several sections of the Xesibes came together here, that is, between the Mtamvuna and Msikaba rivers. Some fragments of the tribe remained in Natal under petty chiefs. One of these, Soqotsha, was chief over the Xesibes at the Ndaleni. These occurrences took place about 1820.

Their close blood-relationship to the Pondos did not prevent the Xesibes from occasionally turning their assegais against them. In one of these fights, in which the Xesibes were assisted by the Bacas, themselves fugitives from Tshaka, the Pondos, led by Mbangazita, commander of Faku's forces, were hopelessly beaten. Such a condition of affairs could not be tolerated by the Pondo Chief, Faku. He, therefore, approached the Governor, Sir Peregrine Maitland, with a view to securing recognition of his control over all the country between the Mzimkulu and Mzimvumbu rivers. This having been agreed to, Pondoland came to include the country between the Mtamvuna and Mtsikaba rivers, that is, the district occupied by force by the Xesibes for about twenty-five years.

The section of the Xesibes which figured most prominently in these disturbances was that of the Left-Hand House under the chief Jojo, son of Mjoli and grandson of Sinama, who headed the tribe in their removal from Natal to Pondoland.

The Great House, though also in Pondoland, was less in evidence. The Right-Hand House of Mkwekwe was totally eclipsed by the Left-Hand House, and scarcely appears as a separate entity in the tribal history of those days.

The Principal House of the Xesibes, that is Mgubudzeli's, moved through Pondoland and sought refuge among the Tembus. This section settled down under Mtwa in what is now the Mqanduli district, and it is amongst them that the Mqanduli magistracy is situated. The Left-Hand House under Jojo, after various vicissitudes, approached Sir H. Barkly, the Governor, with a view to being taken under the Cape Government.

This request was acceded to, and they came under the authority of the Colonial Government in 1874. Jojo's Xesibes are settled in the Mount Ayliff district of Griqualand East. This portion of the tribe is at present ruled by Makaweni, a grandson of Jojo, and son of Mfundisi. Chief Sodladla's Xesibes, who are a minor section of the Great House, are located in the Mount Frere district of Griqualand East.

Ama-Ngwana (Aba-Mbo).

Tradition informs us that Sibiside, father of Njanya, from whom are derived the Pondomise and Pondos, had a son by another wife. This son was Nomafu. The heir of Nomafu was Ngwana from whom the tribe takes its name. This tribe is either simultaneous in time of formation with the Pondos and Pondomise, or earlier by one generation. The eighth in descent from Nomafu was Bomvu, from whom we have the Ama-Bomvu. The heir to Bomvu was Nyonemnyama ("Black Bird.") This chief and his successors carried on the line of the Principal House. The half-brother of Nyonemnyama, and principal son of Bomvu in the Right-Hand House was Njilo, the progenitor of the Ama-Bomvana.

The fourth in descent from Bomvu in the line of the Great House was Nzombane, whose Great Son and heir was Somhashe. Another son of Nzombane, was Ndungunya, father of Sobuza and grandfather of Swazi.

Thus we have the following tribes descended from Nomafu:—(1) Ama-Ngwana; (2) Ama-Bomvu; (3) Ama-Bomvana; (4) Ama-Swazi. (See Genealogical Table II.) The name of the Ama-Ngwana came into prominence through the warlike chief of that tribe, Matiwana. He was a man of extreme courage and force of character. It is difficult to determine the designation of the house to which he belonged, whether Right-Hand or Minor. Matiwana was son to Masumpa, who was the son of Luhlongwana. The latter, it would appear, was one of the sons of Ngwana and probably was younger brother to Ngcukumane. Matiwana was a contemporary of Tshaka's,

and it was through Tshaka that he was finally,
after several desperate battles, compelled to cross
over the Drakensberg and settle on the Caledon,
a branch of the Orange River. This Matiwana
was also the immediate cause of the destruction
of the Ama-Hlubi tribe, and incidentally of that
of the Beles, Zizis, and other tribes now known as
Fingoes.

Owing to his courage, strategy, and ability as
commander of the Ama-Ngwana warriors, Matiwana's name was one to conjure with. Tshaka
not excepted, he was probably the finest
leader of Bantu warriors of his day. The difference between him and Tshaka lay in the fact that
his resources in men were limited, while those of
Tshaka were unlimited. The latter's regiments
were spread over Zululand in a number of garrisons,
each garrison being the headquarters of a formidable force. Each force was composed of conquered
tribes incorporated into his fighting machine.
When one of these forces was beaten in battle, as
was not infrequently the case, he had others in
readiness to be called up, and thus he dealt with
Matiwana and the Ama-Ngwana, bringing force
after force of fresh troops against the wearied
troops of his enemy.

Matiwana was driven out of Natal on at least
two occasions. On both he crossed the Drakens-·
berg to the western side. On the first, entering
Basutoland, he came into collision with Sikonyela,
chief of the Ba-Tlokwa. In the fighting which
followed the Ba-Tlokwas were driven in upon
Mshweshwe's Basutos.

Sikonyela is the chief concerning whom the
compact was made by Dingana and Piet Retief

x

in 1838, whereby the latter was required by Dingana to secure 300 head of cattle from Sikonyela as a preliminary to consideration of the question of a cession of territory to the Boers by the Zulus. The cattle having been secured and restored to Dingana, there followed the infamous massacre of the Boers. The Ba-Tlokwa, Sikonyela's tribe, were subsequently known as the Mantatees, who became famous as freebooters.

Then for a time the Ama-Ngwana settled down on the banks of the Caledon. As formidable neighbours they were greatly feared both by the Basutos and the Ba-Tlokwa, who left the Ama-Ngwana in peace.

Subsequently, having returned to Natal, in the hope of re-occupying his old country, Matiwana fought the Ama-Hlubi, his nearest neighbours, broke them up and drove Mpangazita into Basutoland, where he himself eventually landed. The battles between the Ama-Ngwana and Ama-Hlubi are more fully mentioned in the chapter devoted to the Ama-Hlubi, and are consequently merely mentioned here in passing.

Later Matiwana returned a third time to collect from former allies of his, some cattle which had been left on his previous departure for Basutoland. These allies were the Ama-Nyamvu under chief Mcoseli, and the Ama-Njilo under Noqomfela. He found that these chiefs had appropriated the cattle, and had emptied his grain pits, making use of the contents for their own support. Matiwana immediately attacked both tribes and destroyed them, and both Mcoseli and Noqomfela fell in the battle. Matiwana, however, did not remain here but returned to Basutoland, fearing continued attacks from Tshaka. Indeed, the latter followed him up into Basutoland, sending in an army under his *nduna* (" captain "), Dlaka. This army drove Matiwana further into Basutoland, and he was granted permission by Mshweshwe to settle near Mafeteng. Both Hlubis and Ama-Ngwana continued to be neighbours and to fight with each other, until the Hlubis were finally beaten and dispersed on the banks of the Caledon and their chief Mpangazita killed.

In 1828, owing to the unsettled state of the country, and still apprehensive, even at that distance, of attacks from the Zulus, the Ama-Ngwana under Matiwana crossed the Orange River somewhat higher up than Aliwal North. They then made for Tembuland by way of Esikobeni, past the Xonxa and Xalanga, crossed the Kiwa River and travelled up along the headwaters of the Bashee River and reached the Mbolompo, having driven the Tembus before them So great was the fear which the Ama-Ngwana instilled into the minds of the surrounding tribes, that Ngubencuka, head of the Tembus, solicited the help of the Cape Government against them. He also sought the assistance of Hintsa, chief of the Ama-Xosa. Both acceded to the call for help. The Governor sent Colonel Somerset and a force of a thousand soldiers. It is said that Hintsa sent a formidable force estimated at 18,000 to Ngubencuka's assistance. This force would probably comprise the whole of the fighting strength of the Gcalekas.

The Ama-Ngwana at this juncture became known as the Mfecane (" freebooters "). They feared nothing in human form, within reason, and awaited in confidence the hosts approaching against them. They had complete trust in themselves, but now found themselves face to face with something unknown to them which seemed at the time supernatural. They were familiar with war, were accustomed to famine and hardship. But on this day they were to meet with what they had never met with before—the destructive power of artillery and the deadly effect of small arms. Horses, too, are said to have been seen by them for the first time, and to have caused amazement among them. But the truth of this latter story is open to doubt.

The troops under Somerset opened the engagement with artillery. The Ama-Ngwana attempted to come to close quarters with their stabbing assegais, but they could do nothing. Long before they could approach within charging distance they were cut down, falling by an unseen hand, at long distance. A sound as of thunder they heard, smoke they saw, but did not know what killed them. Their women urged them on saying, *Bajokeni, noko balwa ngezulu*—" Keep at them even though they fight you with lightning," but it was no use. The Ama-Ngwana broke before the storm of shot and shell. Neither the Gcalekas nor the Tembus took any part in the actual fighting. They were lookers on, and only went forward to collect the booty, and to dispatch the wounded.

Matiwana collected the remnants of his force and harangued the warriors. His address was to the effect that the Ama-Ngwana feared no human foe, and that it was no disgrace to be conquered by supernatural forces. Some elected to seek shelter with the Tembus, other went into Pondoland and were allowed to settle in the neighbourhood of the Mngazi River.

One party decided to return to Basutoland and join Mshweshwe. In regard to this party, it is stated that when they had reached the summit of the Drakensberg Mountains a blizzard overtook them, and the driving snow and intense cold prevented further movement. The men then formed an outer ring, placed their women and children in the centre, and sought to protect them from the elements by holding their shields over them. Of the whole party only one or two survived. The Ama-Ngwana perished as they sat with their shields protecting their families. The authenticity of this story is proved by a Native well known to the writer, who was the grandson of a little girl who survived, and alone travelled forward seeking some habitation for refuge, until she met a Basuto hunter who took her to his home. This episode is made the subject of a story, "The White Hecatomb," by W. C. Scully. Matiwana with a few followers returned to Zululand, intending to surrender himself to Tshaka, but the latter was already dead, and his brother, a more bloodthirsty individual, if it be possible, than himself ruled in his stead.

Matiwana presented himself to Dingana, saying, *Nditole mntaka-Senzangakona ndidiniwe* "Son of Senzangakona, I am tired, pick me up." Dingana professed to receive him in friendship and accepted his submission, but ere long he had him killed. The place of Matiwana's execution is still called *Kwa-Matiwana* "Matiwana's place." So died a man of supreme courage and resource.

Ama-Swazi (Aba-Mbo).

From the Ama-Ngwana with whom we have just been dealing, there issued another tribe of considerable importance, the Ama-Bomvu, which tribe derived its name from Bomvu, a Ngwana chief. Four generations from Bomvu we have his descendant, Nzombane, whose Great Son was Somhashe. He had, however, another son, Ndu-ngunya, the progenitor of the Ama-Swazi. Ndu-ngunya's son and heir was Sobuza I., and the latters's heir was Swazi from whom the Ama-Swazi take their name.

It may be mentioned that in the genealogy of the Ama-Mpondo, one of their earliest chiefs was Luswazi, and it is sometimes asserted by the Pondos that the Ama-Swazi are derived from him. There is nothing in support of this statement beyond the mere assertion, which is purely an assumption based on the similarity of the names of Swazi and Luswazi. No genealogy is quoted in support of that view.

On the other hand, the Swazi genealogy is represented by only seven generations. If we allow 25 years to a generation and calculate back from the present ruler, Sobuza II, to Ndungunya, the first of the Swazi chiefs, we get 1775 as the starting point of the Ama-Swazi tribe. Ndungunya's heir was Sobuza I. Swazi was Sobuza I's heir. Swazi's son was Ludonga, and his son was Mba-ndine. The son of the latter was Bunu or Nje-ngabantu, whose son is the present Sobuza II.

The Ama-Swazi tribe is the last or most recent tribe of the Aba-Mbo stock, for even the Bomva-nas are an earlier offshoot from the Ama-Bomvu.

The fact that the Swazi tribe is of considerable size and importance at the present time, is apt to suggest for it an ancient origin. We must remember, however, that it only came into prominent notice in 1843, when, under the chief Swazi, it moved away north to its present position, to escape the seething cauldron of unrest—the aftermath of the devastations of Tshaka and Dingana, and the fear that Mpande (Panda) would emulate his brothers. The numbers of the Swazi tribe were greatly augmented by the adhesion of broken tribes seeking refuge and security, even at the expense of losing their identity in that of the tribe offering them protection.

Unlike the majority of other tribes which sought new homes at a distance from Natal and in doing so moved southwards, Swazi led his tribe northwards. In his progress he crossed the Maputa and finally settled to the west of the Tonga tribe, and south-west of Lourenco Marques.

The existence of ancient gold mines in Swaziland stimulated the cupidity of Europeans. As a consequence of trouble arising between the Transvaal and the Swazis under Mbandine, the latter expressed a desire to be under the Imperial Government. By a convention which regulated this matter in 1890, the Swazi's were given a measure of independence especially in regard to tribe life, but reservations were made in regard to Europeans living in Swaziland. These were to be outside of the authority of the Swazi chief. The country has, therefore, become a Protectorate of the Imperial Government.

CHAPTER XX

AMA-BOMVANA (ABA-MBO)

The Ama-Bomvana are also of the Aba-Mbo stock. They are descended ultimately from No-mafu, the first of the Ama-Ngwana tribe, but more directly from Bomvu who, though a chief of the Ama-Ngwana, gave rise to the Ama-Bomvu tribe, which, therefore, is an offshoot of the Ama-Ngwana.

Bomvu's Great Son, who carried on the Bomvu dynasty, was, Nyonemnyama. The Right-Hand Son of Bomvu was Njilo. This son was the progenitor of the Bomvanas (literally, "the little Bomvus.") Though from a different branch of the Aba-Mbo, yet they are near relatives of the Pondos, Pondomise, Xesibes and other tribes descended from Njanya. As has already been indicated, Njanya and Nomafu were both sons of Sibiside, but of separate houses. The near relatives of the Bomvanas are the Swazis, Bomvus and Ama-Ngwana.

Our earliest historical knowledge of the localty of the Bomvana tribe places it in the country about the Mkomanzi (Mkomaas) river, and mid-way between where Scottsburg and Richmond now stand. Some Bomvanas, however, state that their original home was on the Mngeni (Umgeni) river, just north-east of Durban.

Approximately about 1650, an incident hap-pened which caused part of the Bomvana tribe to leave Natal and settle in Pondoland. The *isizi* custom was responsible for this. One of Njilo's

Ama-Bombana.

Bomvu 1575
1. Njilo 1600
2. Mgwedu 1625
3. Dabandlela 1650
4. Zwetsha 1675

5. Kiti 1700
6. Nkomba 1725
7. Wese 1750
8. Mjikwa 1775
9. Gqwabile 1800
10. Vasani 1825
11. Sizanguzane 1850–1922

Gt. H.

Ama-Bomvana = Ama-Nkumba.

Tshizi 1705

Rt. H. (Umi-Ganu *)
Msila, etc.
Rt. H.
Gt. H.
Rt. H.

1. Tyingana   M. H.
   Kanya   Rolashe
   Mbelu   Buba
   Mtshu   Mandi
   Makunzi   Tyityimba
   Pali   Maraxa
   Tyelinzima

Ama-T-shezi

2. Matsholo
   Xutsha
   Reeza
   Zondwayo
   Sidiya

Ama-X-utsha

3. Jalimba
1. Mbili

Ngexana
Rt. H.
Mbelu

Ama-Ngezana:
Mpola
Sizibo
Nzimankulu

Ama-Ngezana:
(Nongcobo
Magexa
Ndesi
Welese

Ama-Mbulu:
Gayiya
Tense
Nxani
Ndima
Stefanisi

2. Gambushe—about 1745–1836
1. Ntabenge
1. Moni

(Ama-Wezashe)
3. Pahlolo
Dikana

2. Somdzaba 3. Matyojivu

1. Nkintshana (Jongilanga
   Sandile   (Mrazuli
   Ntabenzila

1. Ndayi   2. Nzutu
   Sakapase   Marxam
   Soluhemvu Pakamile
   M. H.   M. H.
   Mhlana   Ntabenkulu

(Ama-Nqojiya)
4. Nqojiya
Xhoshti
Rt. H.
Maxawu Mveki
Nteni   Njobe   Mdehliwa
        Gosiwe M. H.
               Makwange

(Ama-Tshezi)—Rt.H. of Bomvanas.

(Umishekololi)

4. Tembu
Mjadu
Rt. H.
Faku   Menemene
Ngwaliso Mhlonlo
Rt. H.
Tyeleko   Lashhjeruqe
Dalindyebo
Pangiwonga
Ntabenzila

2. Lanxa

1. Ngonyama
   Gwebindlala
   Ngabezulu

Rt. H.
Sirabu
Ngqwangele

2. Tyali
Zwetake   Sirabu
          Dalihango

2. Zwelibanzi
   Fudumele

*Ami-Ganu the Rt. Hd. House of Dihandlela. See Table P. 375

To Ama Chav. XX.

Umlibo webukosi lo qobo = Royal line.
" " obutsahryo = Reigning line.
" " base Kanene = Right Hand line.

J. H. Soga

The material originally positioned here is too large for reproduction in this reissue. A PDF can be downloaded from the web address given on page iv of this book, by clicking on 'Resources Available'.

wives died. She was probably living with her grandson, Dibandlela. On the death of this wife Njilo demanded the *isizi* cattle from Dibandlela. The latter probably thought that the *isizi* should be his, as the deceased chieftainess was under his protection. Consequently, he refused to deliver up the cattle. Njilo sought to enforce his demand, and war threatened. Dibandlela decided to flee and seek a new home. Collecting all his followers with their families and cattle, he set out for the south, directing his course to Pondoland. Fearing pursuit from Njilo's forces at a certain spot on his journey Dibandlela determined to make a sacrifice to the spirits of his ancestors and secure their protection. A trench was dug across the course which his pursuers would probably take, and the tribal doctors with their incantations and mystic medicines rendered it impervious to Njilo's forces.

This incident is still related as one of the prominent events of their flight by the Bomvanas, and the spot thus doctored is spoken of as *Umse-le ka-Dibandlela* ("Dibandlela's trench.") These events took place about a century and a half before the time of Tshaka. Evidently, there was a later migration of a section of the tribe which had remained in Natal. This was during the Tshaka disturbances, when it is told that, in their determination to escape to Pondoland, they over-ran one of Tshaka's strongholds, called *Kangela-mankengane* ("Watch the rascals.") This stronghold, or perhaps more correctly military depot, was placed on the border of the Ama-Tuli country, whom it was intended to over-awe. The spot is now known as Congella.

As these Bomvana's passed this military station, they "lifted" some of the cattle belonging to the station, among which was one of Tshaka's dancing oxen. Reaching Pondoland, they joined their relatives who had been resident among the Pondos for several generations.

The Bomvanas remained in Pondoland until the early years of the nineteenth century, when they were compelled by circumstances to get out of the country.

BOMVANALAND.

Its occupation by the Bomvanas.

The territory now included under the name Bomvanaland was in occupation of the **Ama-Xosa** from, at least, the time of their Great Chief, Togu, (1686), till the time of his great-grandson, Palo, (1702-1775). The Ama-Xosa in Tshiwo's time, that is in the time of Palo's father, and previous to 1700, took possession of the vacant country between the Umtata and Bashee Rivers.

At a later period, during Palo's reign, they resumed their migratory movement, and took possession of the country between the Bashee and Kei Rivers, leaving a country which had been their home for about fifty years, and in which was the grave of one of their Great Chiefs, Tshiwo, who lies buried at Ngcwanguba. The grave of Ngconde, father of Tshiwo, is said to be at the Cumgce (Buntingville) in Pondoland, and that of his father, Togu, is stated to be at Qokama, in the Ngqeleni district of Pondoland. The locality of chiefs' graves gives us an indication of the movements of a tribe. Beyond those just mentioned, only one

other Xosa chief's grave is indicated, that of Sikomo, father of Togu, circa 1650.   It is stated to
be at a place called Ntumbankulu, somewhere
about the Umzimkulu.

In his early manhood Palo is said to have lived
west of the Umtata River, and it was during his
reign that the wreck of the *Bennebroek* occurred,
on the 16th February, 1713, on the coast of Pondoland, some considerable distance to the eastward.

For a further period of about sixty years, after
Palo moved south-westward and settled beyond
the Bashee and between that river and the Kei,
the country between the Umtata and Bashee
rivers remained vacant—a No-man's-land.   This
is the territory now known as Bomvanaland.   Palo
moved into the Cis-Bashee approximately about
1740, and the re-occupation of this land took place
about the end of the first decade of the 19th
century, that is during the later years of Kawuta's
reign.   The new occupants were the Bomvanas,
an Aba-Mbo tribe, and related to the Pondos
though of a different house.   A genealogical table
of this tribe has been compiled to accompany this
chapter.   A table of the Imi-Ganu, the Right Hand
House of Dibandlela, Great Chief in his day of the
Bomvanas, is also supplied.

We will now narrate the incidents leading up to
the occupation of No-man's-land.   Though thus
named, on account of its evacuation by the Ama-
Xosa, the latter still maintained a claim to it,
which none were prepared to dispute.

When the Chief Mbili,* eldest son of Jalamba
died, his son Ngezana, a mere child, was placed
under the care of his uncle, Gambushe.   During

---

* See genealogical table.

the minority of Ngezana, his uncle had alienated
and retained the hearts of many of Ngezana's
adherents, so that when the latter came of age and
assumed his office as chief of his father's people,
he found that many were lost to him, having
transferred their allegiance to Gambushe, and
that his authority was to a great extent under-
mined and usurped by Gambushe. This, naturally, became a *casus belli*. After some abortive
negotiations between the two chiefs, a state of
war was declared. Ngezana lost no time in arming his adherents and attacking Gambushe. In
the fighting which ensued Ngezana lost heavily,
and his army was finally put to flight.

Ngezana now sought the active assistance of
his father-in-law, Ngqungqushe, the Principal
Chief of the Ama-Mpondo. This was readily
given. The combined impis of these two chiefs
attacked Gambushe's Great Place. The attack
was repulsed, but among the wounded was discovered Mayaba, Gambushe's wife. This infu-
riated the chief, who, following up his retreating
enemies, came up with them at the Dangwana.
Ngqungqushe's headquarters were at some distance behind his main forces. The attack by
Gambushe's men was pressed with such vigour
that the army of Ngqungushe and Ngezana was
completely overthrown, and in the furious pursuit
the headquarters of old Ngqungqushe were over-
run, and this great chief killed.

The death of so important a chief, whose person was held as sacred by his tribe, was the cause,
not only of bitter feeling against Gambushe, but
also, later on, of a war of reprisal against him.
Gambushe seems to have been a man of strong

character, beloved by his own followers for his
courage and open-handedness, but he was also a
source of great trouble to the more important
chiefs of the Ama-Mpondo. Shortly after the
events narrated above, the chief of the Ama-Xosa,
Hintsa, while still a very young man, managed
to involve Gambushe in hostilities with his neighbours the Aba-Tembu, during the minority of the
latter's chief, Ngubencuka. It would appear that
when Ndlambe attacked Hintsa for espousing the
cause of Ngqika (who had been guilty of a serious
offence against Ndlambe, and thus caused the
war of 1818), Hintsa sent his cattle over to the
Tembus to secure protection for them during the
fighting. Hintsa, at the conclusion of the fighting
and preparatory to settling with his father, Kawuta, in the neighbourhood of what is now the
town of Butterworth, sent over to the Tembus
for his cattle. The Tembus refused to give them
up. Hintsa then appealed to Gambushe whose
daughter he had married—the mother, subsequently, of the Great Chief, Sarili (in English,
Kreli), to intercede on his behalf with the Tembus. Gambushe immediately took the matter up
and, along with two of Hintsa's representatives,
sent two of his own men. These men proceeded
to Ngubencuka's kraal, where they declared their
message. The Tembus refused again to restore
Hintsa's cattle and attacked the messengers,
wounding Gambushe's chief envoy, Mhana. The
war-cry was immediately sounded and the warriors of Hintsa and Gambushe crossed the Bashee
and Umtata Rivers respectively and entered
Tembuland.

Ngayiya and Ngaleka, minor chiefs under Ngubengcuka, were in occupation of the south-eastern
boundary of Tembuland, and upon them fell the
attack of the invading forces. Their warriors were
unable to stem the assault and retired leaving all
their cattle in the hands of the Ama-Xosa and a
section of the Ama-Bomvu and the Ama-Tshezi.
This caused a state of war to exist between the
Tembus and Tshezis.

About this time also, Gambushe was attacked
by Faku in revenge for the death of his father,
Ngqungqushe. Taking advantage of this state of
affairs, Ngayiya and Ngaleka seized the opportunity to attack Gambushe and retrieve the cattle
lately taken from them. At length, Gambushe
realising that his life was in jeopardy, as he had
enemies on either side of him, viz., the Aba-
Tembu beyond the Umtata and the Ama-Mpondo,
decided in his old age to get out of Pondoland and
seek a safer haven for himself and people. Facing
him on the western side of the Umtata River was
the considerable territory vacated by the Ama-
Xosa during Palo's time, and still a No-man's-
land. He decided to negotiate with Hintsa in an
effort to secure the right of occupancy. The
Paramount Chief of the Ama-Tshomane, a branch
of the Ama-Mpondo, at this time was Ngcetane.
As the superior of Gambushe, the latter confiden-
tially intimated to him his hopes, and asking, in
the event of Hintsa's answer being favourable,
that he might have the chief's countenance and
help in his undertaking. Ngcentane, on the
grounds of relationship, agreed to assist as far as
possible, when the time came, the accomplish-
ment of Gambushe's severance from the Ama-

Mpondo, and his placing himself under the protection of Hintsa.

We would narrate here the steps taken on behalf of Gambushe which led to the occupation of No-man's-land—the vacant territory between the Umtata and Bashee Rivers, evacuated many years before, but still recognised as being under the authority of the Ama-Xosa. For, though the main body of Hintsa's people had crossed over into what are now the Willowvale and Kentani districts, isolated families of the Ama-Xosa still, here and there, had their kraals in the Trans-Bashee.

One of Gambushe's people, a man named Nogaya, of the Abe-Lungu clan, was a trader in bluebuck skins and *mtomboti* necklaces. He traded as far as Hintsa's kraal, near Nqabara (now Willowvale district), traversing on his way thither the unoccupied country. On his return he gave a glowing account to Gambushe of the vacant country through which he had travelled, stating among other things that animal life was plentiful and that at the Mnenga he saw a herd of elephants, and also came across an eland that had been killed by some animal. Gambushe was so highly interested in the description of this piece of country, that he asked Nogaya on his next trip to endeavour to see the Gcaleka chief, and enquire whether Gambushe would be allowed to occupy No-man's-land. He was also to intimate to Hintsa that the cause of his desiring to leave Pondoland was the fact that "smelling out" and inter-tribal fighting were rendering life unbearable, or as he expressed it, *ngu-tshingi-liyatsha apa* ("everything is ablaze here.")

Hintsa at first treated the matter as a joke, as he did not believe that a Pondo clan would break away from a tribe which was reckoned to be so closely knit together and exceedingly clannish. Nogaya, however, on his return home gave a favourable account of his conversation with the Gcaleka chief, and he asked Gambushe to grant him a certain number of men to accompany him back to Hintsa as an authorised representative of Gambushe's to present this request officially before Hintsa. Gambushe then called together the section of the Tshezis which was under him, told them of Nogaya's report, and asked them for their opinion on it. The Tshezis were unfavourable to this project as they did not trust Hintsa. Nogaya then asked that two men should be allowed to go with him, not as officially representing the chief, but to accompany him in the capacity of his own friends. Two men were selected to accompany Nogaya, namely Rubulana of the Imi-Rabe clan, and Mzangela of the Ama-Qam clan. On their arriving at the kraal of Hintsa and presenting their request to him, he called together his relatives and principal councillors and laid the matter before them. After deliberation with these people, Hintsa called Nogaya and the other two men and said, addressing Nogaya, *"Mfo u ase-Belungwini kutiwa lusapo lwam masibone nga-mehlo lento uyitetayo singayiva nge ndlebe zodwa."* ("Man of the Be-Lungu clan, my family says we must see with our eyes this thing you speak of, and not hear it only with the ears.") Nogaya immediately gave thanks to Hintsa, accepting these words as an indication of willingness to

hand over No-man's-land to Gambushe.   Next
morning Nogaya with his two friends left for
home.   On the way he said to them, "I understand the chief's meaning; it is that we have to
buy the land with cattle;" or, as he expressed it,
Sibeke inkomo ngapambili ("put cattle in front.")
Instead of going direct to Gambushe, Nogaya went
home to his own family, had a meeting with them,
and finally informed them that he was going to
take his great *badi* (red and white speckled ox)
to Gambushe, so that the latter would have no
doubt about the *bona fides* of his messenger.   The
chief was favourably impressed with the facts as
presented by Nogaya; so also were the members
of the chief's family.   In connection with this
transaction even the names of those who contributed to the purchase price of, or thank-offering
for, the land are recorded.   Mangxa, Somndzaba,
and Filekade, the younger sons of Gambushe,
followed Nogaya's example, each giving an ox
towards purchasing the land.   Nozingwa of the
Ama-Kawula clan also gave an ox; so also did
Matyunjwa, an inferior son of Gambushe's who had
been installed as head of the kraal of his grandfather, Jalamba.   Gambushe himself contributed
four oxen, thus making a total of 10 head of
cattle.   These were driven through No-man's-land
and across the Bashee to the chief Hintsa.   The
usual formalities were gone through at the Great
Place.   An ox was killed on behalf of Nogaya
and Gambushe's other messengers, thus sealing the
compact.   This transaction was a private venture
of Gambushe's, the Bomvanas as a whole not
being admitted into his confidence.

In securing from Hintsa this land, which had been won by the spears of the Xosas, Gambushe was not only entitled to right of possession, but in a certain measure became a vassal of Hintsa. Nogaya, Rubulana and Mzangela with a few others remained at Hintsa's kraal, but sent back to Gambushe the young men who assisted in driving the purchase cattle, under the leadership of Beka-meva, a young chief, son of Ntshunqe, with the intimation that, in accordance with instructions from Hintsa, the clan should be assembled by Gambushe and come across the Umtata River and occupy No-man's-land.

Hintsa soon afterwards gave orders to Nogaya to return home and if he found Gambushe had not yet collected his people, he was to urge him to do so, within a couple of days, promising that he himself would collect, and give orders to a body of fighting men to cross over into No-man's-land, in order to see that Gambushe was not molested by either the Pondos or Ndaba's Tem-bus.* This Hintsa did, sending over three impis; the first went as far as the Matanjana stream on the Ngcwanguba flats ; another impi was stationed at Tafa-!e-hashe ; a third was placed at the Futye stream near where the village of Elliotdale now stands. Gambushe and his people then crossed the Umtata River at the Luvulo drift. The crossing was effected under the protection of Ngcetane, chief of the Ama-Tshomane, who sent an impi as far as the Ntshilini near the Luvulo drift, to cover Gambushe's passage across the Umtata.

Note. * Ndaba's name was in use as chief of the Aba-Tembu, Ngube-ncuka being a minor.

When once he was over, he came under the protection of Hintsa's forces.   As the entry of Gambushe was unopposed, Hintsa gradually withdrew his impis.   That stationed at Futye first withdrew by way of the Ncihana and crossed the Bashee going home : the other two impis fell back to the Gusi.   Here a couple of oxen were slaughtered as a thank-offering to the Xosas or Gcalekas.   On the Gcalekas' return home, Gambushe allocated sites for the various families which had come over with him.   Being now somewhat advanced in years, he did not build a kraal of his own, but elected to live with his Principal Son, Ntshunqe, whom he had placed at the Ntlonyane near an old Native site which is now called Manganyela. Ntshunqe's Great Son, Moni, was placed at the Gusi, while Magadule the Right-Hand Son of Ntshunqe was placed at the Nkwalini.   The formal occupation of the land was now complete.

The Bomvanas have now in little over a hundred years become a considerable tribe, numbering over 30,000 souls.   Gambushe, however, was not to be allowed to rest in peace.   Faku, in revenge for the death of his father, Ngqungqushe, broke into Bomvanaland with a considerable force, determined to destroy Gambushe.   This force crossed the Umtata River and came south as far as Qana bush on the Xora River, but was unable to force its way as far as the Gusi, for Gambushe's men had armed themselves and came to meet them. Faku, therefore, retreated, realising that the force opposed to him was too strong for him.   Ntshunqe, Gambushe's son, led his men across the Xora River and, passing round above Faku's impi, intercepted it at the Mzilatya where fighting took place. Faku was over-powered and his force driven home. The Pondo chiefs then called in the help of the Bacas, a Natal tribe which had become tributary to the Pondos, and occupied the northern edge of Pondoland. In answer to this request the Bacas came to the help of the Pondos. They passed through the Mtshekelo and Ngqatyana, captured Moni's Chief Kraal at the Gusi, and forced their way right down to the Elomkosi drift on the Bashee. Here they came into contact with those Bomvanas who had been detached to drive the cattle across the Bashee into Gcalekaland. The Bacas succeeded in capturing some of the cattle, but dared not face an attack on the Gcalekas. They therefore contented themselves with the stock which they had secured and returned home with them. Meanwhile, the Pondos crossed the Umtata at the Luvulo drift, acting independently of the Bacas.

This impi was met by the whole of Gambushe's fighting force at the Mncwasa river, overwhelmed, and driven back through the Nzulwini river, next through the Emapuzi river, and finally the remnants of the Pondo force were driven through the Luvulo drift, the same which they had crossed with confidence earlier in the day, back into Pondoland again.

Since the early years of the nineteenth century, therefore, Bomvanaland has been the home of the Bomvanas.

The ultimate effect of these repeated attacks by Faku on the Bomvanas was to drive them into Gcalekaland beyond the Bashee. They crossed the Bashee river, therefore, about the year 1820,

possibly a little later. The Bomvanas remained
with the Gcalekas for about thirty years, when
they returned and re-occupied the territory granted to them by Hintsa. The reason for this step
was the suicidal policy of the Xosa tribes, known
in history as the "Cattle Killing Delusion."
When the prophecies of Nongqause were being
made public, Ntshunqe, at that time Principal
Chief of the Bomvanas, sent Mpahla, an illegiti-
mate son of his, to the Gxara stream, the scene
of the alleged miracles and the neighbourhood of
Nongqause's kraal, with instructions to look into
the matter and return to report.

On his arrival at the Gxara, Mpahla studied the
situation carefully, and did not allow his common-
sense to be over-ridden by superstition. He then
returned and gave in his report. He said "I
stood on the edge of the pool on the Gxara, and
looked into the water to see the forms of those
who were to rise and deliver us, as I was bidden.
What I saw were the shadows of the leaves of the
wild banana trees which overhung the pool, but
no forms of men. These shadows moved, but the
motion was due to the tide making wavelets—
that was all. This talk is all nonsense." Ntshunqe
decided to get out of Gcalekaland, as he dared not
remain and refuse to listen to Mhlakaza, the Great
Chief's witch-doctor, or to believe in the visions
of Nongqause, the witch-doctor's niece. Thus the
Ama-Tshezi section of the Bomvanas, under their
chief Ntshunqe, returned to the country bought
from Hintsa, and from which they had been expelled by Faku. The Great House of the Bomvanas, the Ama-Nkumba, however, elected to remain

in Gcalekaland, joined in the slaughter of cattle and impoverished itself.

The Imi-Ganu.

This clan is a section of the Bomvana tribe. It is the Right-Hand House of Dibandlela, Great Chief of the Bomvanas, and third in descent from the original founder of the tribe, Njilo.

It is an older house than the Ama-Tshezi, or Right-Hand House of Zwetsha, Dibandlela's Great Son and heir. The clan takes its name from Mamganu, a woman, and a member of a clan whose origin is derived from Mganu, chief of the Right-Hand House of Xesibe. She married a descendant of Msila, Right-Hand Son of Dibandlela, a man called Mncupu, and commended herself so much to the house into which she married that the whole clan took its name from her. It is somewhat unusual for a clan to take the name of a woman as the tribal or clan designation, but there are several notable instances of the kind, e.g., the Ama-Qiya of the Tembus, and the Ama-Hlubi of the Imi-Huhu.

The Imi-Ganu is not so large and powerful a clan as the Ama-Tshezi, though a generation older. Its present situation is in the Tafa-le-hashe section of Bomvanaland.

Genealogical table of the Imi-Ganu.

Imi-Ganu

Bomvu
Njilo
Mgweda
Dibandlela ——————— (Rt. Hd.)

Zwetsha (Rt. Hd.)

Kiti Tshezi

ect. etc.

Msila
Sigcala
Ntshintshise
Mgwadla

1. Mncupu (m. Mamganu) (Rt. Hd.) (M. Ho.)   2. Lutimbela

Mbambaza   Nditya   Lukanda   Konzapi
Ngcetane   Mahlumba   2. Mpangwe   Mali
Ndevu   Gadu   Ntshobi   Matandela   Makinana
Fundakubi   Sidimba   Mbali   Binyela   Gela
   Honono   Tshemese   Ndesi
   Mgqamba
   Sicengu

376 THE SOUTH-EASTERN BANTU

The Abe-Lungu Clan.

From time to time, there has been a good deal
of controversy as to the origin of the Abe-Lungu
clan of Bomvanaland.   Some ascribe its origin
to survivors of the *Grosvenor*, which was wrecked
on the coast of Pondoland in 1782.   But, the
known facts are all against this theory of the clan's
origin.   There are facts, historical and traditional,
which indicate the formation of a clan of European
origin among the Natives of Pondoland prior to
the wreck of the Grosvenor.

I.   Historically, we gather from Theal's Vol-
umes I and II, that Europeans and others of various
nationalities had, as the result of being shipwrecked, found a home in Pondoland as far back
as 1622, when the wreck of the *San Jano Baptista*
took place east of the Kei River.   Then, in the
year 1647, two other vessels were wrecked somewhere in the same neighbourhood, the *Nossa
Senhora da Atalaya* and the *Sacramenio*.

One, at least, of the survivors of these ships was
found by the crew of the *Stavenisse*, forty years
later in 1687, living in Pondoland.   The *Stavenisse*
herself was wrecked on the same Coast in the year
1687, and it is recorded that, of the survivors of
the latter vessel, nine persons were " supposed to
be living among the Natives."

In 1685, two years before the *Stavenisse* came
to grief, the wreck of the *Good Hope* (Dutch) took
place ; and during the same year as the *Stavenisse*
the *Bona Ventura* was wrecked in the bay of
Natal, 1687.   In 1688, the *Centaurus*, built from
the last two mentioned wrecks, was intended to
take survivors of the *Good Hope, Bona Ventura*

and *Stavenisse* to safety ; but when the *Centaurus* set sail, five persons preferred to remain. Then in 1713, the *Bennebroek* was wrecked on the Coast of Pondoland. There were 57 European survivors and 20 Malabar slaves. A year later, 1714, a *decked boat*, while waiting for the *Clapham Galley* from India, entered a river, (name unknown), and found seven survivors of the *Bennebroek*, four of whom she took to the Cape, whilst the other three " presumably remained with the Natives." All these wrecks took place before that of the *Grosvenor*, some as much as 160 years previously, and others at various periods up to the time of the *Bennebroek*, the last historically recorded wreck, a period of about 70 years before the *Grosvenor*. In all this, one fact stands out clearly, namely, that many recorded wrecks (and possibly some unrecorded ones) took place on the Pondoland Coast, from the opening years of the Seventeenth Century on, and that some survivors from these, either compelled by circumstances which they were powerless to alter or as a matter of preference, settled among the Natives and accommodated their lives to the new conditions in which they lived.

II. Then there is supplementary information supplied by the two expeditions under Hermanus Hubner in 1736 and van Reenen in 1790, from which we gather the existence of alien communities among the Natives of Pondoland. The former in the course of his travels penetrated as far north-eastward as Pondoland, where he met a party of three Europeans, whom he names Miller, Clerk and Billyert, with numerous wives and

children.   These had been shipwrecked "many
years before."   About fifty years later, Van
Reenen's expedition found in Pondoland, on a
branch of the Umngazi river, three aged white
females, survivors of some shipwreck which was
supposed to have occurred in 1730 or 1740.   One
of these women was called *Bessie*, but "none of
them could speak any known European language."
At this place there were at that time about 400
persons of mixed race, and the assertion is made
that the three old women were of the same party as
Miller, Clerk, and Billyert, mentioned by Hubner.
Two points contained in the above records which
call for some attention are, first, Van Reenen's
dates, 1730-40, and secondly the person called
Bessie.   It is evident that both Hubner and Van
Reenen are referring to the same persons, but as
against Van Reenen's imaginary dates, 1730-40,
the earlier explorer, Hubner, says in 1736 these
people were shipwrecked "many years before."
Surely if they had been wrecked in 1730 Hubner
would have been more definite as to the date; and
if they were wrecked in 1740, he could not have
made any reference to them as this date was later
than the date of his expedition.   It is fairly
clear, therefore, that this colony of mixed race
existed some time before 1730.

The *Bennebroek*, wrecked in 1713, comes nearer
in point of time to the actual formation of the
Abe-Lungu clan, than any other recorded wreck.
At the same time, it is possible that some unrecorded wreck, other than the *Bennebroek*, may have
been the actual vessel.

History and tradition meet in the person of
"Bessie."   Van Reenen met this aged person in

1790. Native tradition makes mention of a white female bearing the same name "Bessie," and further adds that she was the daughter of Gquma (a name given to a European girl who came ashore from a wreck), who had been taken to wife by Xwebisa, son of Tshomane, Paramount Chief of Pondoland. Native tradition fills in some of the necessary details.

III. The Native traditional account of the Abe-Lungu clan compiled from the best available Native sources, is to the following effect : During the reign of Matayi, Paramount Chief of Pondoland and father of Tshomane, the Ama-Nanga clan, under their chief Cimbi, was resident in the neighbourhood of the Lwambazo river, where one of the shipwrecks occurred. The Lwambazo is some miles N.E. of the Umzimvubu, or St. John's River. On a certain occasion, Cimbi sent word to Matayi, informing the Paramount Chief that he had with him several white people, survivors who had come ashore from a wreck. They were four in number, three males and one female child. These the Natives named, respectively, Bati, Jekwa, Hatu and Gquma. According to Native ideas, as they came from the same "house," (viz. the ship), they were necessarily all relatives one of another. This need not, however, be accepted seriously. The two first named were supposed to be brothers, and the young girl Gquma was supposed to be the daughter of Bati. In course of time, Gquma was given in marriage to Xwebisa, or Sango, Principal Son of Tshomane of the Ama-Tshomane clan. Xwebisa was, therefore, grandson of the Paramount Chief, and in his own turn became later Paramount Chief of Pondoland.

The dowry paid to Jekwa or Bati for Gquma is said to have been 300 head of cattle. Some time after this, a vessel arrived off the mouth of the Lwambazo River and Bati decided to leave in her. This may have been the consort of the *Clapham Galley*. Bati made over his property to Jekwa.

To Xwebisa and Gquma were born three sons and one daughter. The eldest son, Gela, ultimately became Paramount Chief of Pondoland ; the second son was Mlawu, the third Mdepa, and the fourth child was a daughter, Bessie (vide Van Reenen's Expedition, 1785-90). The genealogy of this family may be given here, and is as follows :--

Table I.

Xwebisa or Sango (m. Gquma)

Gt. House

(1). *Gela* (became Paramount Chief)	(2). *Mlawu*	(3) *Mdepa*	(4) *Bessie* (m. Mjikwa)
Ngcetane ,,	Makasi	Majibana	Gqubile
Niki ,,	Menese	Ntleki	Vusani
Dalasile ,,	Ntabankulu	Matanzima	Sizunguzane
Dudumayo ,,	Sidumo		(died 1922)

Gquma died at Mgazi about 1770. Her daughter Bessie married Mjikwa, son of Wose, Chief of the Ama-Nkumba clan, and at the same time, Principal Son of the Great House of Zwetsha.

This is the premier clan of the Ama-Bomvana. Xwebisa and Gquma's family, though claiming foreign blood in their veins, still retains, by virtue of descent through the male line, their original clan name of Ama-Tshomane, derived from Tshomane, the father of Xwebisa. The present chief of this clan is Dudumayo, great-great-grandson of Gela, the eldest of Gquma's family. Bessie, mentioned by van Reenen 1790, the daughter and fourth child of Xwebisa and Gquma, married Mjikwa, son of Wose, chief of the Ama-Nkumba clan. Her descendants are represented today, or, at least, until recently, by Sizunguzane, chief of Zwetsha's Great House, the Ama-Nkumba, and lineal head of the Ama-Bomvu. (See genealogical table of Bomvanas).

The actual progenitors of the Abe-Lungu clan were the two men already mentioned, Jekwa and Hatu.

Jekwa, the reputed younger brother of Bati, lived at the kraal of Puta (*ixiba*), the grandfather of Thomane. He married several Native wives. The genealogy of the Abe-Lungu clan is as follows :—

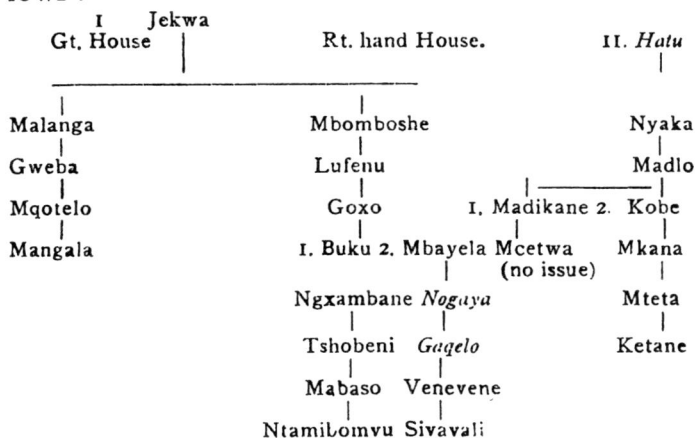

```
        I    Jekwa
     Gt. House  |            Rt. hand House.              II. Hatu
                |                                             |

        |                     |                           
     Malanga              Mbomboshe                       Nyaka
        |                     |                             |
     Gweba                 Lufenu                         Madlo
        |                     |              |—————————————|
     Mqotelo               Goxo          I. Madikane  2. Kobe
        |                     |              |             |
     Mangala          I. Buku  2. Mbayela  Mcetwa      Mkana
                                   |        (no issue)     |
                          Ngxambane Nogaya                Mteta
                               |        |                  |
                           Tshobeni  Gaqelo             Ketane
                               |        |
                            Mabaso   Venevene
                               |        |
                          Ntamibomvu Sivavali
                                ——  ,,  ——
```

Note I.
Nogaya was the messenger of Gambushe to Hintsa concerning the occupation of Bomvanaland.

Note 2.
Gaqelo, son of Nogaya, was one of the sources of information concerning the transfer of No-man's-land to Gambushe.

The Abe-Lungu clan being descended from sources alien to the people among whom their lot in life was cast, maintained their separate identity, and were on that account likely, sooner or later, to come into conflict with their neighbours, notwithstanding the fact of inter-marriage with them. This is what actually happened. The Ama-Nanga clan, with whom they had been identified from the beginning, found some occasion for offence, and attacked the Abe-Lungu clan, being jealous, probably, of their growing numbers and strength. The latter were worsted and sought protection from the ruler of the Ama-Tshezi clan. The plan adopted by the Tshezi chief, by way both of protecting them, and minimising their chances of becoming a menace to their neighbours, was to sub-divide the Abe-Lungu clan. One section was place under the care of Badlula, who was chief of the Ama-Ntshilibe, otherwise the Ama-Banqo clan. Another was handed over to Sina, chief of the Ama-Tshutsha, and a third was committed to the care of Ntshele, chief of the Ama-Ntshele clan. These three clans were neighbours of the Abe-Lungu and all lived in the neighbourhood of the scene of the wreck, the Lwambaso river. Tradition indicates this arrangement as having taken place sometime before the occupation of Bomvanaland, and apparently after van Reenen's visit. The Abe-Lungu clan, though one in name, derived its origin, as we have seen, from two sources. It might just be added that, at the time of the wreck of the *Grosvenor* (1782), this clan was already extant, and was one of the Bomvana clans which crossed over from Pondoland about 1810 with Gambushe to occupy the district in which they live today. Between 1782 and 1810, a period of less than 30 years, the formation of a strong and numerous clan from the meagre numbers of the original derelict foreigners would have been impossible. A table tracing the descendants of *Gquma* and Xwebisa has already been given above. The descendants of *Bessie* many be usefully given here also.

Table II.

Ama-Bomvana :
:
: Bomvu
: |
: Njilo
  |
  Mgweda
  |
  Dubandlela
  |
  Zwetsha
  |
  |

Great-House		Rt. hand House	
Kiti		Tshezi	
		(Ama-Tshezi)	
Nkumba (Ama-Nkumba)		etc.	
Wose		etc.	

Mjikwa married Bessie (dr. of Xwebisa or Sango and Gquma)
|
Gqubile
|
Vusani
|
Sizunguzane

Minor offshoots have not been taken into account in this or other tables.

In concluding this section, it might be mentioned that, in opposition to those who profess to see European characteristics of colour and feature markedly distinguishing the Abe-Lungu clan from others, there is nothing either of colour or feature to show that they are in any way different from purely Native clans.

During researches by the present writer, into the history of the Abe-Lungu clan, it was discovered that there is in Pondoland another clan of alien origin, the *Ama-Molo*. We will not speculate as to whether or not Molo may be a corruption for Moor, a common term in those days, applicable not only to Natives of Northern Africa, but to members of coloured races in general. But Lascars were frequently cast ashore in Pondoland. From the wreck of the *Bennebroek* twenty Malabar slaves were saved. It is possible that some of these remained with the Natives after the rest had sought to reach civilisation. Native tradition asserts that the progenitors of this clan were dark men whose hair was straight, long and black. The names of these men, two in number, are given as *Bayi*, son of Molo, and *Mera*. This clan, however, is neither so numerous nor so remarkable as the Abe-Lungu Clan.

Capt. Coxon of the Grosvenor.

The name of Gambushe, though in no sense connected with the story of the unfortunate wreck of the *Grosvenor*, suggests one or two thoughts in connection therewith. As is known, Capt. Coxon and his party of survivors travelled from the scene of the wreck for eight days, when they reached a " very large river." This must undoubtedly have been the St. John's river (u-Mzimvubu) in Pondoland. On the following day, the ninth, they went up the river on the east bank in search of a ford. Unable to find a crossing, the party slept that night on the bank of the river. Apparently, they now realized the hopelessness of proceeding to the Cape on foot, hampered as they must have been with ladies and children not inured to travelling long distances on foot, in an unknown country, inhabited by strange and some-times hostile tribes ; and infested with wild animals.

Perhaps the party began to see their initial mistake in leaving the neighbourhood of the wreck, where they might have collected sufficient mate-rial to construct a boat, with which to endeavour to reach the Cape by sea. The following day, the tenth, the party turned back. From that moment no further news has ever been recorded of this party. The writer has endeavoured to get some information from the Natives, which would throw some light on the fate of Capt. Coxon's party, but could obtain nothing definite. With the country in control of Europeans, the " raw " Native sits tight on anything which he imagines might be brought against him or his tribe, and end in re-prisals for former misdeeds. A fragment of in-formation, however, was given by an old Native of the Abe-Lungu clan, though he was evidently un-willing or possibly unable to enter into details. It was to the effect that a tradition exists concern-ing a party of Europeans who were travelling in Pondoland and, owing to the hostile attitude of some Natives, had built a thornwood fence round their position, as a means of defence. As they had a few guns among them, they enjoyed a measure of security. The Natives then engaged the party in talk, using signs, whilst the guns of the Europeans were resting against the fence. Unperceived, a number of young men got behind the flimsy encircling fence and extracted the guns. Those in front then sprang in and a general massacre followed. All Europeans were killed with the exception of one or two children. This was all that could be got from the reticent old man, who apparently feared that he might involve himself in possible trouble.

The question arises, " To what party of Europeans could this incident refer ? " It could not be Hubner's hunting party, as this was destroyed by the Xosas at Palo's Great Place, and is historically recorded.

It was not Van Reenen's expedition, for it returned in safety from a search for the *Grosvenor* survivors.

No other instance is known of a party of Europeans having been killed in Pondoland during the eighteenth century.

The probability, therefore, is that this incident explains the end of Capt. Coxon's party, which has been shrouded in mystery.

The enquiries of Government expeditions into Pondoland, when searching for survivors of the *Grosvenor*, would naturally close everyone's mouth, under the circumstances.

Coxon unfortunately turned back when within a few miles of help, had he only known it. On the opposite side, that is the western, of the St. John's River, at the Little Mgazi (Mgazana), lived the tribe descended from Europeans, designated by Van Reenen " Bastards." This is the Abe-Lungu clan, and it numbered at that time about 400 members. This clan was under the protection of Gambushe, Chief of the Bomvanas, who had his Great Place at the Mgazi, a few miles nearer to the St. John's River than the Mgazana. Had Capt. Coxon managed to cross and then turned down towards the sea he would most probably have fallen in with this clan, and undoubtedly have received much needed help and protection.

Imi-Tetwa (Aba-Mbo),

The Imi-Tetwa tribe I have included under the heading of Aba-Mbo, though the evidence concerning the Bantu branch to which they belong is somewhat meagre.   It is affirmed by many Zulus of Natal as well as by others, that the Imi-Tetwa are Aba-Mbo.   M. M. Fuze, a Native of the Ama-Ngcobo tribe, in his informative book entitled *Abantu Abamnyama* (Black People), speaking about the movements of tribes says:— ''Another tribe which left long ago is that of the Ama-Mpondo, who on their departure left behind them those of Madango . . . . . . They are not far apart in relationship, notwithstanding that you now see those of Faku, son of Ngqungqushe (Pondos) so far separated from them by reason of Madango's section remaining here (Natal).   They are born of the same father, Pondo being the elder.''   The same father referred to is Njanya, the son of Sibiside (see Aba-Mbo Table).   The Imi-Tetwa house is apparently one of Njanya's Minor houses. Mtetwa's father was Nyambose who would be, therefore, the progenitor of the Imi-Tetwa.

We give here the Table of the principal line of Imi-Tetwa chiefs.

Njanya.
_____ |
Mpondomise. Mpondo. Xesibe. Nyambose
                             |
                          Mtetwa
                             |
                          Simamana
                             |
                          Xulu
                             |
                          Madango
                             |
                          Mkali
                             |
                          Jobe
                             | _____
                     I Tana. 2 Dingiswayo. 3 Mawewe 4 Sha-
                             | ngana, 5 Mondiso
                          Ndabayake
                             |
                          Mafiti
                             |
                        etc., etc.

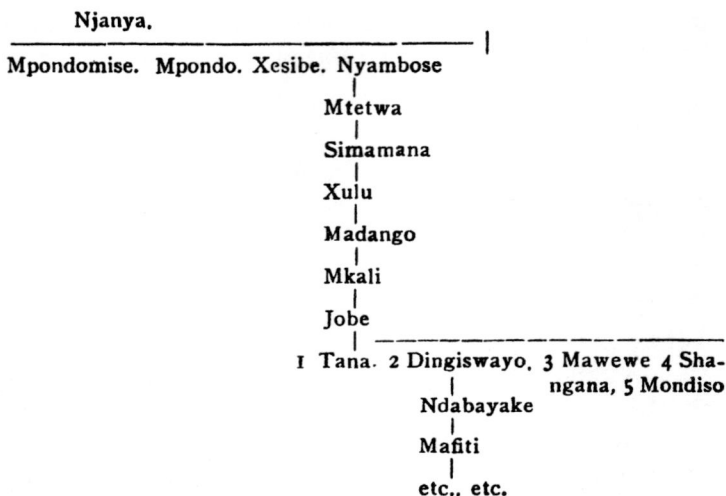

The history of the Imi-Tetwa has, at least from
the time of Dingiswayo on, been fully related in
publications dealing with the times of Tshaka, so
that it is not necessary to do more than give a
general review of the tribe.

The name of Tshaka, chief of the small tribe of
Zulus, has acquired so great a notoriety, that all
other tribes which fought under him are indiscriminately called Zulu. The fact, however, is that
the main fighting strength of Tshaka's forces, at
the beginning of his wars, was composed almost
entirely of the Imi-Tetwa, the Zulu tribes being
insignificant in numbers. At the time of Jobe's
reign, the Zulu tribe was tributary to the Imi-
Tetwa and consequently depended for its existence
on the protection of the more powerful tribe. The
whole of the Zulu tribe was incorporated into the
Imi-Tetwa army by Dingiswayo, son of Jobe, and
tribal distinctions were in a large measure lost;
for the Imi-Tetwa, as has been stated, were Aba-
Mbo while the Zulus were Ama-Lala. This

subordination of tribal distinctions, or the amalgamation of these two tribes of different stock, was ultimately responsible for Tshaka, himself a Zulu assuming the chieftainship of the Imi-Tetwa and Ama-Zulu, whom he combined into one tribal unit and thus forged a powerful aggressive military organization.

During the chieftainship of Jobe the Imi-Tetwa were a powerful tribe, known and feared for their powers in arms by the tribes of Natal, but later, under Jobe's son, Godwana or Dingiswayo, they secured a position of supremacy which, once obtained, was scarcely ever to be wantonly questioned. The only tribes that dared to dispute the supremacy were the Ama-Ngwana under Matiwana and the Ama-Ndwandwe under Zwide. Jobe had a number of wives, with also a considerable number of sons, prior to the declaration being made as to which was the Principal Wife, and which among the sons was to be heir. When Jobe was getting old, he selected Tana as the son who should rule the tribe when he himself was no longer able to do so. There were five sons to the Principal Wife, Tana, Godongwana (Dingiswayo), Mawewe, Shangana, and Mondiso. Part of the tribe desired that Mawewe should be chosen heir. These endeavoured to sow distrust of Tana in the mind of Jobe by stating that filial affection was not a cardinal virtue of either of the two eldest sons, and that they were plotting to assassinate the old chief. Jobe believed the report and was so incensed that he gave orders to the executioners to destroy both sons. He seemed to be specially annoyed with the second son, Godongwana, and his orders were that, whatever happened,

Godongwana was not to be permitted to escape. One night the hut in which these two brothers and a few of their retainers slept was set on fire, and as each of the occupants attempted to escape he was killed. Godongwana, however, succeeded in breaking through and escaping, but with an assegai in his back. He went into hiding, but his sister who heard of his escape and realized that he could not be far off, made search for him and ultimately found his hiding place. She managed to withdraw the assegai and secretly furnished him with medicine and food. Being proscribed, he could not expect any mercy if found, consequently he decided to seek safety in flight. The question arises, " Where did he go ?" There are three theories whose advocates try to answer this question; each theory being based upon Godongwana's introducing military service in his tribe on the lines of European military systems. Some hold that during his exile he wandered to the Cape and there saw British soldiers drilling and learned something of their methods of attack. Others hold that it was a practically impossible feat for a young friendless exile to traverse so great an extent of country, and pass through so large a number of strange tribes, and that he must, therefore, have gone to Delagoa Bay and become familiar with Portuguese methods of warfare. Yet others, again, hold that he probably reached some friendly tribe and remained with it ; that during his stay some European traveller (there were such at that time) was passing through Zululand, from whom Godongwana learned about European warfare. Whichsoever theory is correct, the outstanding fact is that on the death of his father, Jobe, he returned, took possession of the chieftainship of the Imi-Tetwa, introduced the regimental system in his army, and taught it to rely for victory on coming to close quarters with the enemy. Moreover, instead of the old Native method by which each warrior carried a bundle of assegais to be thrown at the opposing force, only one throwing assegai was to be carried, along with a short-stemmed broad-bladed one for hand-to-hand fighting. The throwing assegai was to be used only when within throwing distance of the enemy. The introduction of this new system revolutionized the whole character of the fighting of the Natal tribes. It became more sanguinary and infinitely more effective. Other tribes adopted this new mode of fighting, but never perfected it as did the Imi-Tetwa.

Of the three theories mentioned I am inclined to accept the third as the most probable, for this reason—Godongwana was accompanied home by sufficient followers to enable him to fight for the chieftainship, which was then in the hands of Mawewe. This following would most probably be due to members of the tribe (Imi-Tetwa) in sympathy with Godongwana who, hearing of his retreat, flocked to him in sufficient numbers to make it possible for him to fight his way home to the throne.

His brother Mawewe, who had been elected by the Imi-Tetwa to the chieftainship on the death of Jobe, heard that Godongwana was on his way home with a considerable following, and realizing that his elder brother would make a bid for the chieftainship, sent one of his officers to find out the strength of the opposing force. It is suspected that this officer (*induna*), on meeting Godongwana, secretly arranged to assist the latter. He

returned and made his report. Mawewe mobilised his forces and appointed this same officer
to the chief command. When the two forces came
into sight of each other, this officer divided his
warriors into two divisions. He evidently knew
that among them there were many who were luke-
warm in the cause of Mawewe, for it must be
remembered that the Imi-Tetwa army had absorbed
within itself a number of conquered tribes who
could not be expected to be whole-heartedly faithful
to their conquerors. The *induna* having divided
his forces, placed those whom he knew to be
faithful to Mawewe in the van, he himself headed
the rear division which he could trust to follow his
lead. He had already tampered with their loyalty
to the reigning chief.

The opposing forces met and a fierce battle
began. The van of Mawewe's army was hotly
engaged with Godongwana's warriors, when the
induna with the second division attacked his own
vanguard in the rear. They were thus assailed
on two sides and though fighting desperately had to
give way. Mawewe then fled to a neighbouring
and powerful tribe, the Ama-Qwabe, under their
chief Pakatwayo, and was welcomed by that chief.
This act of Pakatwayo's was the cause of frequent
battles between the Imi-Tetwa and the Ama-
Qwabe. It may be mentioned here that the Ama-
Qwabe were the Principal House of Malandela,
while the Zulus of Senzangakona, father of Tshaka,
were the Right Hand House.

Having taken possession of the chieftainship,
Godongwana was given a new name in accordance
with custom. He was now to be known as Dingiswayo (" the Wanderer ;" literally " caused to

wander"). When firmly settled in his position of
authority he introduced the new system of warfare.
He did away with the carrying of a bundle of
assegais, and the quiver. In place of these each
warrior carried one light-bladed throwing assegai,
and one heavy-bladed thrusting assegai. The
purpose of the innovation was to compel his men
to come to close quarters with an enemy, and make
certain of victory by creating havoc in the enemy's
ranks with the stabbing assegai. Even after the
introduction of these new measures, it was only
after many sanguinary battles that the Imi-Tetwa
overcame the Ama-Qwabe. Pakatwayo, chief of
the latter, was a born soldier and strategist.

It was as a captain in Dingiswayo's army that
Tshaka first came into notice, by his courage and
resource as a commander. It was with the weapon
forged by Dingiswayo that Tshaka created havoc
among the tribes of Natal and brought most of
them into subjection to himself. Dingiswayo was
easily the greatest general of his day in Zululand.
He was, however, distinguished also for treating
a fallen enemy with consideration and mercy. Not
so his successor, Tshaka ; neither consideration
nor mercy were weaknesses to which he was subject. Nor was there much, if any, of the virtue
of gratitude in Tshaka's composition. This is
emphasized by the story, if true, of his betrayal of
his chief and friend, Dingiswayo. War had broken
out, it is said, between Dingiswayo and his powerful
neighbour, Zwide, chief of the Ama-Ndwandwe,
who occupied the country north-east of the lower
Black Umvolosi river, and west of St. Lucia Lake.
Dingiswayo, though well advanced in years, accompanied his warriors, Tshaka being placed in

command of one of the main divisions. Being
aware of the spot from which Dingiswayo intended
to direct the battle, Tshaka sent word to Zwide
informing him of the fact. Zwide then sent out a
party of his men by a circuitous route, and succeeded in capturing Dingiswayo and his staff. The
Imi-Tetwa, when they heard of the fate of their
chief, became disheartened and left the field to the
victorious Ama-Ndwandwe.

Dingiswayo was kept prisoner by Zwide for
three days and was then put to death.

On the death of the chief, the Imi-Tetwa, or at
least a powerful section of them, selected Mondiso,
the youngest of Jobe's sons and brother of Dingiswayo, as chief. Another party, composed mostly
of conquered tribes which had been incorporated
into the Imi-Tetwa army, was against Mondiso.
This internal division within the tribe gave the
unscrupulous Tshaka, who was now commander-
in-chief of the army, an opportunity to force himself
on the Imi-Tetwa as their chief, though himself a
Zulu. Faced by the convincing argument of the
military forces who espoused Tshaka's pretentions, the two parties sank their differences and
accepted Tshaka as chief. Hence the powerful
Imi-Tetwa tribe came under the rule of an alien
chief.

CHAPTER XXI.

AMA-LALA.

In an endeavour to find the meaning of the term Ama-Lala, we have to consider two things that are available to us, for much is hidden from our perception.

(1) The term *lala*, as has been indicated elsewhere, is applied to skilled workers in ore, etc. The great Makalanga tribes were famous in this respect, and the tribes inhabiting Natal in pre-historic times were also reputed to be so skilled.

It is known that, from time to time, large sections of the Makalanga broke away from the parent tribe, and some, at least, of these settled in what is now Natal. The name *Ama-Lala* ("the skilled workers") would most probably be given to these early inhabitants by their neighbours, just as the name Matebele was applied, by Mzilikazi's neighbours, to his tribe on account of its peculiar dialect.

(2) Then we have to consider the term *tekedza*. *Uku-tekedza* (Zulu) or *uku-teketa* (Xosa) means "to lisp like a child," i.e., "child language." There are various forms of the word, but it is not necessary to follow these out. It might just be said that they are mostly from one root, and signify various shades of the same meaning. Now, one of the distinguishing features of the Lala tribes is this dialectic peculiarity, which marks them out from tribes of other branches of the Bantu race.

It might reasonably be said in regard to *tekedza* that it merely defines a peculiarity in enunciation, and that this is not confined to one tribe of the Bantu race, but found among many, and takes various forms.

The Ama-Xosa do not *tekeza* or *teketa*, except in individual cases where it is a defective form of articulating, rather than a peculiarity of dialect. This defect is due, probably, to malformation of the ligaments of the tongue. Such an individual would say, e.g. *u-yuyamiye* for *u-lulamile* (" he is gentle"), the letter "*y*" being substituted wherever an " *l* " occurs.

If the Aba-Mbo *tekedza*, it must be in a very modified form, as it is not much in evidence ; but the great majority of tribes whose origin is derived from the one time great Makalanga tribe, which I take to be the parent of the Ama-Lala tribes, do *tekeza*, but in a variety of forms.

Among some Lala tribes, the substitution of the letter " t " for " z " is the distinguishing dialectic feature. This marks one group.

The Ama-Baca and Ama-Wushe, on the other hand, introduce the sibilant after the letter " t," e.g. *ukutsi* for *ukuti* (" to say"). Besides this, there is transmutation of " u " and " owe " to " wi," e.g. *kwitsi* for *kuti* or *kowetu*. In the latter we have the sibilant " s," also appearing. This form of *tekedza* is called *uku-tsefula*. This marks another group.

The Ama-Hlubi, also of Makalanga origin, substitute the letter " g " for " d," and also occasionally introduce the sibilant as do the Baca. For instance, the Xosa word *nditi* (" I say ") is transformed into *ngiti* or *ngitsi*, and so on. This form is called *uku-ngingiza* (" to stammer ").

Tekedza is, therefore, a peculiarity of enunciation introduced in various forms into various tribal
dialects, and though various in form may combine
the tribes using these different forms into a common group.

There is an interesting fact mentioned by Bryant,
which may have some bearing on the tribal name
and dialect of the Ama-Lala. He tells us that
close to Mount Wedza, in Mashonaland, i.e., in a
country belonging in olden times to the Makalanga,
there is a tribe specially skilled in working metals.
This tribe calls itself *Pa-Marara*, and their country
is called *Tekedza*. These names are not accident-
al, and they are too significant to be lightly set
aside. To deal, first, with the word *Pa-Marara*, it
should be remembered that the form of prefix
to tribal names varies considerably with Central
African tribes, some adopting the prefix *Wa-*,
others *Va-*, *Ba-*, *Ma-*, and so on. In this *Pa-
Marara*, the initial consonant is probably a softened
form of " *B*," *Pa* for *Ba*. Then again, some tribes
use the letter " *r*," while others do not, but use
the letter " *l* " instead.

These two letters are transmutable, and in the case
before us *Pa-Marara* would become *Pa-Malala*.
The only difficulty, here, is what appears to be a
double prefix *Pa* and *Ma* before *Para*—*Pala*. I am
inclined to believe that the true prefix is *Ma-*, and
that the *Pa-* is merely a redundancy, or used together with *Ma-* is just another form of *Ama*. Hence
we would have *Ama-Lala*. This is, however, so
far somewhat speculative.

A question emerges from this, " Is it an accident
or a coincidence that these two words *Ma-Rara*

(*Ma-Lala*), and *Tekedza* should be found connected together, and indicating a tribe of Makalanga origin, and its place of residence, as mentioned by Bryant ?"

Theodore Bent, who was sent out by the Royal Geographical Society of Great Britain, many years ago, to Mashonaland for investigation and research work in connection with the Zimbabwe ruins, states that at some indefinite period a part of the Makalanga tribe broke off and travelled eastward, as he was informed by the Mashona, eventually settling in what is now Natal.

Taking these facts together, it seems not so much a theory as a certainty, that the Ama-Lala of Natal, who use the *tekedza* form of speech, are one and the same people as those mentioned by Bent.

As the people immediately concerned are unable to give an unequivocal answer as to the origin of the name Ama-Lala, we are compelled to make use of such material as comes to hand, and use our own judgment in an endeavour to find a solution. The Ama-Lala are not alone in their inability to determine the significance of their name, for other branches of the Bantu are equally at fault. Some Aba-Mbo tribes, for instance, speak of themselves as Ama-Xosa : some Ama-Lala believe themselves to be Aba-Mbo, so that it is advisable for those engaged in research work not to accept first appearances as final. All evidence must be analysed and tested in the light of known principles, and the circumstances affecting the life of communities, their relationship, origin, laws and customs.

The term Ama-Lala is used in this book particularly for the tribes of undoubted Makalanga origin, such as the Ama-Tonga, Imi-Huhu, Ama-Hlubi, Ama-Bele, Ama-Zizi, Ama-Zengele,

Ama-Kuze, Ama-Kumalo, I-Ntlangwini, and Ama-Ndaba, as well as others of less note. In short, all such tribes as can be correlated and shown to be derived from a common source.

Some tribes of Lala stock cannot be so easily traced, since they may have broken off from the parent Makalanga at a different period from the above-mentioned tribes. For instance, the Ama-Ngcolosi are said to be of Lala stock, and have a number of minor branches, e.g., the Ama-Ngcobo, Nyuswa, Qadi, Wosiyane, etc., but they cannot be brought into correlation with the Imi-Huhu and other tribes, because they are probably from a totally different and widely separated branch of the Makalanga.

It may be repeated here that the Makalanga in the beginning of the 16th Century were the most formidable and widely-spread tribe in East-Central Africa, and we know from various sources that, from time to time, sections broke off and sought new homes, following the line of least resistance, that is south-eastward to Zululand and Natal.

It seems clear that the Ama-Lala occupied the country now called Zululand and Natal before the arrival of other tribes, and certainly before the Aba-Mbo. According to their own traditions, the Aba-Mbo came from the north-east.

In 1552 a Portuguese ship, the *Sao Joao*, was wrecked on the Pondoland coast, apparently somewhere about the Msikaba mouth. The survivors tell of meeting Bantu tribes all along the coast belt. In their efforts to reach Delagoa overland, they passed through these tribes, meeting everywhere with consideration and kindness. They tell us, however, nothing as to the name of these people. We infer, nevertheless, that they were Ama-Lala.

We would touch, here, upon a point which seems to be raised by a remark of Bryant's, if we have understood him correctly. He says, in reference to the Aba-Mbo tribe (*Zulu-English Dictionary*, p. 20), " from its manner of speech at that time, it would seem that, along with *other Lala tribes* of Natal,......it belonged to the *tekeza* group of Bantus." Here the Aba-Mbo are bracketed with the Lalas in a supposed common form of *tekeza* speech. Now, while *tekeza* may fairly be regarded as one of the distinguishing marks of a Bantu group, it may be acquired by a tribe not belonging to that particular group. There are other important matters which go to differentiate one group from another, such as the points by which correlation is determined, etc. A tribe, such as the Aba-Mbo, which overran Natal shortly after its advent, conquered many of the earlier inhabitants of the country (e.g., the less warlike Lalas), and later incorporated whole tribes into its military system, might naturally be expected to impose its speech upon the conquered. But the reverse sometimes occurred. The great majority of Lala tribes were indeed conquered by the Aba-Mbo, but some of the more virile Lala tribes were not conquered, and were as likely to transmit their particular form of speech to certain tribes of Aba-Mbo, as *vice versa*. The point sought to be emphasized here is, that the Aba-Mbo are not of Lala stock, and that this fact transcends a mere similarity in speech (which similarity, moreover, is not admitted), since such similarity may be either acquired or imposed according to circumstances.

The Aba-Mbo brought with them their own form of speech, and I take it that what we call the Zulu language is the original Aba-Mbo language. The Zulus at the time of the Aba-Mbo entry into Natal were an insignificant tribe, and were conquered by and became tributary to the Imi-Tetwa, an Aba-Mbo tribe, under the Chief Dingiswayo. The Zulus, I believe, were of Lala stock, but through incorporation into the Imi-Tetwa army adopted the manner of speech of their conquerors and lost their own.

Certain languages, or shall we say, forms of speech have a virility not possessed by others, and where these latter come into contact with the former the stronger naturally prevails. This may be seen in the virile si-Xosa, an exceedingly pure form, which takes nothing from the surrounding tribes, but gives its speech to them. From Natal to the Cape si-Xosa is spoken, even tribes of Aba-Mbo origin, such as the Pondos, as well as those of Lala origin, e.g., the Hlubis, Zizis, Bacas and others, are gradually, but unmistakably, losing their original mode of speech and adopting si-Xosa.

The *tekeza*, south of Natal, survives only among those tribes that live in proximity to the border, and even among these it is fast dying out.

We give here a number of offshoots from the Makalanga tribe. These do not complete the list of tribes, however, whose origin is Kalanga.

AMA-KALANGA.

Ama-Lala		Mashona	Kololo	Nyayi	Tonga
Hlubi	Zondi	—	—	Tembe	Tshobi
Zizi	Fuze			Loyi	Ntlanga
Bele	Wusho			Nwanati	Kwakwa
Tolo	Baca			Luleke	Tevi
Ntlongwini	Ngcolosi			etc.	Ruwe
Cele	Nyuswa				
Tuli	Qadi				
Nganga	Osiyane				
etc.	etc.				

AA

Ama-Hlubi (*Ama-Lala*).

It will be seen, by reference to Chapter VIII, that the Ama-Hlubi are of Lala or Makalanga origin. The name Hlubi, however, is of comparatively late date. According to the genealogical table of this tribe, there are sixteen names of ruling chiefs, covering approximately a period of 400 years, before the tribal name became Ama-Hlubi. The tribal name was changed on the death of Ncobo, the sixteenth in decent from Ludiwu. Half way between these two names occurs that of Mhuhu. From his time down to that of Ncobo the tribe was called Imi-Huhu. What the tribal name was before that it is impossible to say. The first born of Mhuhu, though not the heir, was Zengele. The house of the Ama-Zengele is designated the *isi-zinde*, a term equivalent to the *i-xiba* of the Xosas, that is, a grandfather's house. The Ama-Zengele represent, as far as we know, the oldest house of the Imi-Huhu. Another son of Mhuhu was Bele, of the Right Hand House, progenitor of the Ama-Bele of the present day. The sixth in decent from Mhuhu, in the direct line, was Dlamini I. It is from his Right-Hand Son, Sibalukulu, that the Ama-Zizi, Ama-Tolo, Ama-Kuze, I-Ntlangwini and other tribes are derived.

We have then the following prominent tribes all related :—the Ama-Hlubi, Zizi, Tolo, Kuze, Ntlangwini, Bele, Zengele and others of less note. The royal salutations of these tribes may differ, but each salutation, it will be found on reference to the genealogical table, is taken from a representative chief.

It may be said here, in parenthesis, that the Zulu salutation is *Ndabezita*. This is the name of a

The material originally positioned here is too large for reproduction in this reissue. A PDF can be downloaded from the web address given on page iv of this book, by clicking on 'Resources Available'.

great Bele chief, and this is strong presumptive evidence of the Zulus being of the same stock as the foregoing tribes.

But to return to the Ama-Hlubi.

One or two tribes that issued from the Imi-Huhu prior to the change of the tribal name to Hlubi may just be mentioned, though by reason of their number, they are of less importance than those already referred to. These are the Ama-Ndlovu and the Ama-Kumalo (Mzilikazi's tribe, the Matebele). The Kumalo issued from Mhuhu's great-grandson Mntungwa ; and the Ama-Ndlovu from Ndlovu, Great Son of Mntungwa.

Correctly classifying the tribes mentioned above the proper designation of the following tribes should be Imi-Huhu, namely Ama-Bele, Ama-Zengele, Ama-Kumalo, Ama-Ndlovu and their branches. These tribes are pre-Hlubi.

The change of the tribal name from Imi-Huhu to Ama-Hlubi took place on the death of Ncobo, the sixteenth in line of descent from Ludiwu. The circumstance will be related presently.

The royal line descended through Ncobo to the present great chief Mtunzi, thus :—Ncobo, Dlomo, Mashiyi, Ntsele, Bungane, Mtimkulu II, Langalibalele, Siyepu, Mtunzi.

The *isi-takazelo* (" royal salutation ") of this house is according to individual choice either *Ntsele* or *Bungane*.

The Right-Hand Son of Mtimkulu I was Radebe. The salutation of all sections of this house is *Radebe*.

The name Hlubi.

Ncobo, the last ruler under the tribal name Imi-Huhu, was a man of depraved character, who carried his excesses to such an extent that the tribe determined to get rid of him.   The person of a chief is held sacred, so that none could be found among his tribesmen to kill him.   The resolution to destroy him was confirmed by his own vile conduct.   All his wives were deliberately put to death by him, when they became pregnant.   The scheme for his destruction was the organization of a hunt, at which the chief was to be present.   He was excessively corpulent and in consequence unable to go far without assistance.   The hunters chose a spot infested with hyenas, and took with them a number of cattle to be slaughtered for the maintenance of the party.   The chief was ignorant of the nature of his surroundings and entered heartily into the preparations.   The cattle were slaughtered close to the lair of the hyenas, in order to whet their blood-thirstiness.   The whole company then spent the greater part of the day in feasting ; but on the approach of night they crept away and made for home, leaving the obese chief and one old servant on the camping ground. Ncobo was never heard of afterwards.   Thus, the Hlubis say, they got rid of an obnoxious ruler.

Radebe, brother of Ncobo, but of the Right-Hand House, then became a claimant for the chieftainship of the house left without male issue, but the adherents of the Great House had other plans. Before his death, Ncobo had placed a feather in the hair of a daughter of Hlubi, a man of the Bele tribe, as a sign of their engagement.   The Imi-Huhu and Bele tribes having developed separately for about two hundred years, each was regarded as far enough apart to set at naught the restrictions imposed by the law of consanguinity.

Hlubi's daughter, notwithstanding that the nuptials had been left incomplete by the death of Ncobo, was installed in the Great House as chieftainess, under the name of Mamhlubi.   The law indicated in Genesis xxxviii, 8, was in operation with most of the Bantu tribes, and in this instance Radebe's son by Mamhlubi was Dlomo.   Dlomo, therefore, became heir to Ncobo and to the chieftainship of the Great House.

It happened, at this time, that Zulu, heir of Radebe, that is, of the Right-Hand House, was about to come of age.   In this connection it was necessary that he should *shwama*, that is, perform certain ablutions with herbs, the ceremony being of a religious nature.   These herbs were in the custody of the Ama-Kasibe, doctors of the tribe, attached to the Great House.   But in fear lest Zulu might, when admitted to manhood, lay claim to the chieftainship of the Great. House, while Dlomo was an infant, the adherents of this House refused the use of the herbs.

The tribe was soon startled by the announcement that Zulu had performed the ceremony, and suspicion immediately fell on the Ama-Kasibe who were charged with surreptitiously handing over the herbs to Zulu.   War threatened between the Great House and the Right-Hand House, in which latter the Ama-Kasibe had sought refuge. In the subsequent fighting Ncobo's partisans were defeated and fled to the mountains, and sent word to Radebe, saying, " We refuse to come under your authority, you were appointed merely as the Regent, we are Mamhlubi's people." Radebe, not wishing to break up the tribe, bowed to the inevitable and recognised Dlomo as the prospective

Paramount Chief of the tribe, but as the Great
House now called itself Mamhlubi, having discarded the name of Ncobo as well as that of Mtimkulu
as the tribal designation, both parties agreed to
unite under the name Hlubi and dispense with the
female prefix " Mam." Thus the name Imi-Huhu
was displaced by that of Ama-Hlubi.

There is a fanciful story told of how the chieftainship originally arose among the Hlubis. It is
to the effect that in early times the people lived
merely as families with no uniting head. The
necessity of altering this becoming apparent in the
time of Dlamini I, it was decided that the various
families should appoint representatives to a meeting when a test would be set the result of which
would determine who was to be chief. To each
aspirant was assigned a tree which, at a given
signal, was to be cut down. The first to succeed
would be declared the chief. The successful
individual was then given the name of *Mtimkulu*
(" great tree ").

The story, however, takes no account of the fact
that long before Mtimkulu's time important tribes
of that stock had already been formed. Five
generations before this, the Ama-Bele and the
Ama-Zangele were in existence ; and between these
and Mtimkulu I other tribes of Imi-Huhu stock,
such as the Ama-Ndlovu and Ama-Ndaba, were
already formed. The story, therefore, though it
commends itself to many a Hlubi, is of the nature
of a fairy tale.

The Native's love of embellishments is responsible for the growth, round about some simple fact
or incident, of these fanciful accretions. This
tendency is assisted by his belief in the supernatural

and miraculous. Hence, we have stories such as the above related in all seriousness. The following story again has a germ of truth in it, whilst attempting a whimsical explanation of the complete submergence of the Principal House of the Ama-Radebe at the time of the great chief Maqubela, and in consequence of the rise into importance of the house of Mvunga, younger brother of Maqubela. Maqubela's house actually disappeared amid the disasters of Tshaka's time. The story relates that the Hlubis were great rain-doctors. Their fame was so great that Mshweshwe, the Basuto chief, and Tshaka, the Zulu chief, in times of drought, sent to the rain-doctors of the Hlubis to ask them to unlock the heavens. On a certain occasion, the family of Maqubela, at the break of day, were surprised to see two men sitting in the court-yard. They were recognised to be emissaries of Tshaka. They were asked where they came from, but returned no answer. To other questions also they maintained absolute silence. Thus they sat until their attitude got on the nerves of Maqubela's family. Meanwhile a messenger was dispatched to Mjoli, the aged father of Maqubela, to inform him of this singular behaviour on the part of these men. Mayaba, the head of one of the minor houses of Radebe, who was present could stand the suspense no longer, and remarking, " It is impossible to sit still with either Tshaka's or Mshweshwe's evil omen before us," killed both men with his assegai. The messenger to Mjoli had not yet returned when this climax was reached. Immediately a cloud arose in the heavens accompanied by the noise of a great wind. The cloud came on rapidly together with a violent hurricane

408 THE SOUTH-EASTERN BANTU

of wind, and struck Maqubela's kraal, sweeping
everything before it, and carrying away Maqubela,
every member of his family, cattle and houses.
The messenger to Mjoli returned to find an empty
void at Maqubela's place. Some time afterwards
members of the family were seen to return singly
but without Maqubela. The cattle also returned,
but it is not stated whether the huts returned or
not. On the seventh day, Maqubela returned.
He was asked, " Chief, are you hungry ?" He
answered, " I am not hungry." " What have you
eaten ?"—" I have eaten nothing." " What has
happened, chief ?"—" I don't know." Following
upon these events, quarrels and fighting took
place between various sections of the Ama-Hlubi.
The Hlubis declare that it was after this evil omen
and its results that the disasters to the Hlubi tribe
occurred. The only explanation which comes to
mind, if we eliminate the picturesque details, is
that Tshaka intended to attack the Hlubis, and
taking advantage of their superstitious fears, had
instructed his emissaries how to conduct themselves
in order to create in the minds of the Hlubis a
presentiment of impending disaster, and thus to
render them an easy prey. Disunion within the
tribe was very apparent after these events, but
whether they had any influence in bringing about
that state of affairs, is a moot question. Since the
time of these occurrences, the house of Zungu, the
principal son of Maqubela, has completely disappeared, and the house of Mvunga, his full brother
is regarded as the Great House of the Ama-Radebe.
The present chief, Mlindazwe, is a great-grandson
of Mvunga. His present residence is at Toleni,
close to the Presbyterian Mission, Cunningham,
the missionary of which is the Rev. B. J. Ross, M.A.

The Wars between the Ama-Hlubi and Ama-Ngwana.

In the second decade of the nineteenth century, the Ama-Hlubi were one of the largest and most powerful tribes in Natal. But by reason of internal jealousies, though the tribe retained a semblance of unity, it had no real cohesion. Mpangazita, head of Bungane's Right-Hand House, was practically independent of his half-brother, Mtimkulu II, Paramount Chief of the Ama-Hlubi. In times of tribal danger, however, they united for mutual protection. The Ama-Hlubi in 1819 occupied the valley of the Buffalo River, as well as of its upper tributaries and their sources, close under the Drakensberg mountains. There is no very definite information of conflicts between this tribe and Tshaka's Zulus, but Tshaka certainly set other tribes against the Hlubis in order to dissipate the strength of so formidable a tribe. At his instigation, it is said, the Ama-Ntyali tribe under the chief Kondlo became embroiled in war with the Ama-Ngwana. Kondlo secured as allies the powerful Imi-Tetwa tribe of the chief Godongwana, under whom Tshaka served as one of the leaders of his army. He secured also the help of the Ama-Vezi. This combination was too strong for Matiwana and his Ama-Ngwane tribe, and he was ultimately defeated though not crushed. At the beginning of hostilities, Matiwana placed the cattle of his tribe in the care of his immediate neighbour, Mtimkulu II, Great Chief of the Ama-Hlubi. When hostilities were over, Matiwana sent for his cattle but Mtimkulu refused to give them up. He considered that the Ama-Ngwana had been rendered so weak as to be incapable of resenting forcibly his misappropriation of their cattle. For a time Matiwana sat still to recover his strength and wait his opportunity, meanwhile nursing his injury, and preparing for reprisals and revenge.

Mpangazita had at this time on his own account been waging war with the Batlokwa (Bahlokwa), a Basuto tribe, resident on the western side of the Drakensberg. From this war he returned victorious, bringing with him large herds of captured cattle. Matiwana noted this and decided that his opportunity had arrived. It was also evident to him that this great addition to the wealth of the Hlubis would be the means of drawing other tribes within the orbit of Hlubi influence. He determined to strike, and strike immediately.

Matiwana made no secret of his intention to attack the Hlubis for their treachery, and they naturally made preparations to meet the Ama-Ngwana. Both the Great and Right-Hand sections of the Hlubis combined to resist Matiwana, under their respective chiefs Mtimkulu and Mpangazita. The Ama-Ngwana attacked with violence, cleft a passage through the enemy and separating the two divisions, turned their attention on Mtimkulu. The Hlubis did their best to stem the attack, but Mtimkulu fell, and the Hlubis' resistance withered away. They broke and fled. Mpangazita with the great portion of his force scaled the Drakensberg and fled into Basutoland where he remained. Matiwana settled down on the territory vacated by the conquered Hlubis. His motive in doing so was mainly a desire to remove himself as far as possible from Tshaka. He would, moreover, be close to the mountains, whither, in the event of his being attacked by Tshaka, he could send his cattle. Matiwana's neighbours in his new home were the Ama-Bele, the Ama-Zizi, and Ama-Tolo. A few Hlubis remained on a part of their territory.

Matiwana's Second War.

Though this war, to be now mentioned, was between Tshaka and Matiwana, that is between the Zulus and the Ama-Ngwana, we make a brief reference to it here, as indirectly it brought the Hlubis under Mpangazita back across the Drakensberg to assist Tshaka by attacking the Ama-Ngwana in the rear ; and because its final result was to compel both the Ama-Ngwana and the Hlubis to become neighbours on the Caledon river, where the latter were finally broken and scattered by the fierce Matiwana. Two years or so after the death of Mtimkulu II, rumours of war agitated the tribes in northern Natal. The source of these rumours was Tshaka. He had now consolidated his position as chief, not only of the Zulus, but also of the more powerful Imi-Tetwa, whose armies he had so often led to victory. Tshaka could not endure to see an independent tribe anywhere within reach of him. He saw, not so far away, the powerful Ama-Ngwana and determined to crush them. It might be said justly of Matiwana that he feared nothing on earth and had his forces been numerically equal to those of Tshaka the latter would not have become the universally feared despot that he ultimately became. But Matiwana's forces were limited, whereas those of his enemy were practically limitless. Tshaka was still a young man, not yet having attained his thirtieth year. This was in 1821. Prior to the battle between these two great warriors, the Ama-Nyamvu tribe resident on the Mgeni, being in dread of Tshaka, moved up under their chiefs Mcoseli and Sivuku and placed themselves under the protection of Matiwana. The Ama-Njilo under chief Noqomfela did likewise. The fight between Tshaka and Matiwana was a desperate affair. Matiwana at length being pushed back against the Ama-Bele, this tribe instead of allowing the Ama-Ngwana through their lines to the Drakensberg, closed up and showed a disposition to fight. Matiwana then exerted all his strength and drove Tshaka's forces a considerable distance back, and the two armies rested preparatory to renewing the conflict.

Suddenly, Matiwana turned round and threw himself against the Ama-Bele. The impact was so violent that the Beles broke and cannoned against their neighbours the Zizis, these in turn staggered against the Tolos, causing confusion and consternation which culminated in a general stampede. The debacle was so great that these tribes lost all semblance of cohesion, and scattered far and wide seeking refuge in disjointed fragments among such other tribes as would give them sanctuary. From that day all trace of the principal chiefs of the Ama-Bele and Ama-Zizi has been completely lost. In time some of the fragments of these tribes under minor chiefs, reached Gcalekaland and found a resting place. They gave themselves the name of Fingoes to indicate their forlorn and miserable state. After a breathing space, Tshaka renewed the conflict with the Ama-Ngwana, driving them steadily back with his reinforcements, and compelled them to take to the Drakensberg. Meanwhile, other things were happening, the Ama-Njilo and Ama-Nyamvu drew back, leaving Matiwana to his own resources. Mpangazita, beyond the Drakensberg in Basutoland, had been informed of what Tshaka contemplated, and was prepared, should opportunity offer, to throw his weight into the scale on Tshaka's side. When he learnt that Matiwana was being driven by Tshaka on to the mountains, he felt that his chance to be revenged on his old enemy had come. He immediately ascended the Drakensberg from the west eager to assist in the destruction of the man who had caused him an enforced exile for two years in Basutoland, and had forcibly taken possession of his old country. He met Matiwana's forces on the mountains, as they retreated before Tshaka, fighting, and attacked them in the rear. By this time, the violence of Tshaka's attack had spent itself and he was withdrawing his warriors. This enabled Matiwana to give his whole attention to Mpangazita. The Ama-Ngwana and Ama-Hlubi went over the top and descended the eastern slopes of the Drakensberg locked in deadly strife. Both armies passed through Basutoland, driving and being driven southwards, until exhaustion compelled both combatants to stop. From that time these two tribes settled down on the Caledon river. It was here, in 1825, that the Hlubi tribe was finally crushed and scattered by Matiwana's Ama-Ngwana. These Hlubis were of the Right-Hand House under Mpangazita, who after the war in which Mtimkulu and the Great House had been destroyed by Matiwana, still maintained their cohesion.

Mtimkulu's Hlubis were in worse case and scattered here and there, the greater portion accepting the protection of Tshaka and becoming tributary to him. These were the Hlubis who assisted Tshaka in the destruction of the powerful Ndwandwe army of the great chief Zwide. With them was Langalibalele, the heir of Mtimkulu.

In 1848, these Hlubis left Zululand and entered Natal, coming under the authority of the Colonial Government. The Government placed Langalibalele close to the Drakensberg, to keep in subjection the Bushmen who were a constant menace. The story of the Hlubis is so interwoven with that of the Ama-Ngwana that we make no excuse for relating matters affecting the latter while dealing with the former. It was stated that the two tribes of the Ama-Nyamvu and Ama-Njilo, previous to the last battle mentioned, had joined Matiwana for protection, but when he became involved in war with Tshaka, both these tribes held aloof, and when Matiwana was driven to the Caledon, they remained and occupied the territory vacated by the Ama-Ngwana. Matiwana heard that they were making use of his grain and cattle which had to be abandoned in his retreat. When hostilities between him and the Hlubis were, for the time being, suspended, he retraced his steps with an army, crossed over the mountains and fell upon the two faithless tribes, inflicting a terrible punishment upon them in which their leading chiefs were killed.

Final battle between Matiwana and Mpangazita.

About the year 1825, disaster overtook the Ama-Hlubi at the hands of their implacable enemies, the Ama-Ngwana. Both tribes resided in the neighbourhood of the Rugwane river (the Cale-)don). Both were still under their respective chiefs, Mpangazita and Matiwana. What the immediate cause of the outbreak of war was, is no longer known, but it needed a spark only to set alight the tinder that was ever at hand. The Ngcayecibi war was started by a beer-drink quarrel, and big things were the result. So it required a little thing only to start a conflict between tribes at deadly enmity. In this conflict the power of the unusually brave Ama-Hlubi was to be broken for ever. The scene of the battle is supposed to be close to where Maseru now stands. The battle was long and desperate. For five days it lasted, both sides attacking with the broad-bladed stabbing assegai, anon withdrawing to reorganize and reform, and again coming to deadly grips. On the last day it became apparent that the Hlubis were in a bad way ; they had lost heavily, but their spirit was undaunted. Noting their condition, Matiwana forced the fighting, and as the end drew near, the special Hlubi regiment, the chief's bodyguard, called the *Amafanankosi* (" those who die with the chief "), drew round him : but the attackers never slackened or wavered, and the Hlubi chief's body-guard was cut to pieces. They fought with their backs to the river, but the Ama-Ngwana were not to be resisted. At last Mpangazita fell, and with his death the Hlubis broke. Such of them as managed to cut a way through their enemies sought refuge with various tribes. One body under Mehlomakulu, the Right-Hand Son of the dead chief, Mpangazita, joined itself as tributary to the Matebele chief, Mzilikazi ; another sought protection under the Basuto chief, Mshweshwe. Others again, as families or individuals, scattered far and wide.

Sidinane.

For much of the material connected with the Hlubi wars, and the story of Mehlomakulu, I am indebted to articles written by W. C. Scully, Esq., in the *The State* of 1909.

Mpangazita's son and heir, Sidinane, together with a number of followers, escaped from the field of battle, but had not gone far before he was surrounded by a foraging party on the warpath, belonging to Mzilikazi's Matabele army. Information of the capture of Sidinane was sent to this chief, and instructions were issued by him to the effect that Sidinane and all his family were to be put to death ; but that the rest of the Hlubis were to be incorporated in his army. Private information of this decision was conveyed to Sidinane, who immediately decided on flight. Taking with him one wife and her infant son, as well as two retainers, he escaped and set out for Gazaland. Arriving there, he was received with marks of friendship by the Gaza chief. After a time, however, he became restless and resolved to throw himself on the mercy of the old enemy of his house, Matiwana, and become subject to him. With this end in view he set out for the Ama-Ngwana headquarters which he reached in safety. A large number of Hlubis, after the death of Mpangazita, had joined themselves to Matiwana. That astute chief realized when Sidinane joined him, that the Hlubis would naturally cleave to their own chief, and that this would make for rebellion. Matiwana was not the man to willingly place himself in jeopardy. He therefore, put Sidinane to death. There is something of mystery surrounding Zibi, the heir of Sidinane, and the place where he was secreted until he reached man's estate.   We find Zibi in 1895 ruling a section of the Hlubis in the Matatiele district of Griqualand East.   His heir was Bushula who represented, until recently at least, that section of the Hlubi tribe known as Mtimkulu's Right-Hand House, the house of Mpangazita.

CHAPTER XXII

The Ama-Lala

Mehlomakulu (Ama-Hlubi)

Mehlomakulu, Right-Hand Son of Mpangazita, after his father's death at the Caledon river, attached himself as a subordinate to Mzilikazi, the Matebele chief, and was placed by him in charge of a small band of warriors, chiefly of those Hlubis who had joined the Matebele after the destruction of their army ; but he was put under Soxokozela, one of Mzilikazi's chief officers. For some time Mzilikazi treated Mehlomakulu with consideration ; but when he realized that this young man was held in great respect by the Hlubis, he began to suspect that ultimately Mehlomakulu would dispute his authority, and decided to rid himself of so dangerous an officer. He, therefore, sent for Soxokozela who resided at some distance from the Great Place. On the latter's arrival, in private conference they decided on the death of Mehlomakulu. A Hlubi, who was present when this decision was made, managed to convey secretly an intimation to the young chief of the measures intended against him. At this news the Hlubis were greatly disheartened, especially as they were too weak openly to defy Mzilikazi. They, therefore, counselled Mehlomakulu to seek safety in flight, as he alone was the object of Mzilikazi's jealousy. This proposal to set his chief adrift did not meet with the approval of Mehlomakulu's uncle, Sigulugulu. When he found that his remonstrances were ineffectual in changing the mind of the Hlubis, he determined to accomplish

his purpose, viz., to compel the Hlubis to defend
their chief by other means ; and so with one or
two kindred spirits he left the meeting and made
his way to Soxokozela's quarters. Without further
parley they killed the induna and all the members
of his family. Having committed this deed of
blood, they returned to Mehlomakulu and his
Hlubis with a *fait accompli*, thus involving all the
Hlubis in a serious offence. Coming into the
presence of the Hlubis and their young chief he
announced, " Soxokozela is no more, we have
killed him together with his family ; look, our assegais are yet red with their blood." The Hlubis
understood that the act had placed them beyond
the possibility of mercy at the hands of Mzilikazi
and that of his Matebele. They immediately
attacked Soxokozela's adherents, killing all who
fell into their hands. They collected all the cattle
and their own women and children and fled with
Mehlomakulu at their head. They made for the
Caledon River of sinister memory, and reached it
on the sixth day, closely followed by one of the
Matebele regiments. This regiment had a considerable element of Hlubis in its composition.
When the opposing sides approached each other,
the Hlubis in the Matebele regiment went over
to their compatriots. This prevented the forces
from engaging immediately. At the break of day,
on the morrow, the Matebele charged, but the
Hlubis had prepared an ambush for them and
though the Matebele tried notwithstanding to
force an issue, they were overpowered. A small
remnant extricated itself, however, and retired.
Mehlomakulu's name, in consequence of his
success, attained a certain fame. Hlubis scattered

among different tribes rallied to his standard, and
it seemed as if the Hlubi tribe would again rise on
the ashes of the past to something like its former
importance. The curse, however, of this tribe
was internal jealousy. Those Hlubis who had
joined Tshaka, and to whom he had granted land
whereon to reside about the resources of the Tugela,
were under the regency of Marwanqa, one of
Bungane's minor sons. Another section of the
tribe was under an induna, who had charge of
Langalibalele, the heir to Mtimkulu, then still
in his childhood.

Mehlomakulu, not wishing to further test the
strength of the Matebele warriors, decided to go
to Natal. He accordingly set out from the Caledon,
but on his reaching Natal found Marwanqa's and
Langalibalele's factions at loggerheads. He attached himself forthwith to Marwanqa's party, and the
strained relations culminated in war. Marwanqa
was worsted. In consequence of Mehlomakulu
having espoused the cause of Marwanqa, which
was really his own cause, there was enmity between
himself and Langalibalele. Mehlomakulu thereupon appealed to the Europeans and was by them
settled in the district of Herschel. Here, for the
remainder of his life he lived, dying an old man.
His descendants are still to be found in that district,
and at Ncome in the district of Mount Frere,
Griqualand East.

Langalibalele (Ama-Hlubi).

Langalibalele was the heir to Mtimkulu II.
This Mtimkulu was the son of Bungane and his
principal wife Ngiwe, daughter of Sobuza I, Chief
of the Ama-Swazi. A younger brother of the heir

and by the same mother was Ludidi. Langalibalele's Great Son was Siyepu, and Siyepu's Great Son, the present Principal Chief of the Hlubis, is Mtunzi. About 1848, Langalibalele left his residence at the source of the Tugela and entered Natal. The reason for this move was that Mpande (Panda,) the successor of Dingana, evinced dislike to Langalibalele, though he did not forcibly interfere with him. Still the conditions of Langalibalele's continued residence at the Tugela under these circumstances were so irksome, that he was forced to depart and secure land for his tribe from the Natal Government. The Government placed him close up to the Drakensberg, in order to overawe the Bushmen who resided thereon, and were a constant menace to the tribes within their reach through their depredations. Cattle and horses were their special prey. Langalibalele soon made the position of the Bushmen untenable and compelled them to evacuate the eastern side of the mountains. They crossed over the Drakensberg and took up their abode on its western face, overlooking Basutoland. Langalibalele's settlement here was in 1849, and he remained for nearly thirty years. In 1872, the discovery of Diamond Fields at Kimberley, and the operations there, caused a large number of Natives to proceed there in search of work. Many Hlubis went and returned with guns, purchased with their wages. This arming of the Hlubis caused anxiety to the Natal Europeans, and the authorities intimated to Langalibalele that all guns were to be registered at the various magistracies. He was further required to put a stop to the importation of fire-arms into his country. Apparently no notice was taken by the chief of these instructions. When, however, he became aware that the Government was making armed preparations, he took fright and endeavoured to cross over into Basutoland. Two Government forces were sent to intercept him, the more important being under command of Sir B. Pine. It does not appear that this force came into touch with the Hlubis. A smaller force, composed of Europeans and Basutos under the command of Colonel Durnford, fell in with the Hlubis at the Xowe, among the escarpments of the Drakensberg. Durnford's force was compelled to retreat, and this afforded Langalibalele an opportunity to enter Basutoland. This did not turn out to be of any advantage, but rather the reverse to Langalibalele for the Cape Government representative in those parts, Griffiths, took him prisoner, together with his induna, Mabuhle, and handed them both over to the Natal authorities. Mabuhle managed, though manacled, to effect his escape and fled for protection to Cetywayo in Zululand.

Langalibalele was tried and received a life sentence. He was sent as a prisoner to the Cape Flats, the place assigned for his imprisonment or exile.

Ludidi (*Ama-Hlubi*).

Ludidi, the younger full brother of Langalibalele, during one of the many warlike disturbances in Natal, came south and entered Tembuland and was granted a piece of land for himself and followers at Ngqungqu, in the district of Mqanduli. While resident there, he got into touch with Adam Kok's Griquas in the Kokstad district, and received a grant of land at the Kenira. As he moved up to take possession, he had to pass through Mditshwa's Pondomise at the Tsitsa. As the Hlubis approached the Tsitsa ford they found their passage barred by the Pondomise. Ludidi purchased from them right of way with four head of cattle. The purchase having been completed, the Pondomise allowed them to pass. As the Pondomise stood aside a young irresponsible Hlubi shouted tauntingly to the Pondomise, " You demanded, and demanded, then ran away." This brought the Pondomise back and both sides engaged in a sharp encounter, but Ludidi's Hlubis were too much for Mditshwa's men, who were badly knocked about. Ludidi, having cleared the Pondomise out of his way, proceeded to the Tina river, passing through Mhlontlo's Pondomise who, however, did not dispute his passage, and he finally reached his destination at Kinira without further mishap. Bad blood had, however, been created by the Pondomise attack at the Tsitsa drift, and Ludidi determined to punish them, adopting a characteristically savage method of doing so. Having sown his crops, Ludidi waited till the harvest, and then invited the Pondomise to help him with gathering in the grain, promising payment in the form of a portion of the harvest. After the harvesting was completed Ludidi invited the Pondomise into the cattle kraal for the purpose of receiving their wages. Without suspecting foul play, they entered, were immediately attacked by the Hlubis, and, unable effectually to defend themselves, lost about forty killed. This savage deed bred a hatred between the two tribes that lasted for many a year. At Ludidi's death, he left two sons by his Great Wife, Madonela and Mtengwane.

Until recently, both these sons were in control of sections of Ludidi's Hlubis, in the Mount Frere district.

Ama-Bele (Ama-Lala).

A reference to the Ama-Hlubi geneological table will show that Bele was Right-Hand son of Mhuhu, the Principal Son being Mhlanga, and the son of the *ixiba* or *isizinde* being Zengele. A calculation of twenty-five years to a generation, twenty generations representing the number from Bele to the present ruler, would assign Bele to a date five hundred years back exactly, roughly to 1430. The Ama-Bele would, therefore, originate about 150 years earlier than their relatives, the Ama-Zizi. The present ruler is Aaron, a grandson of the Mabandla who entered Hintsa's country with a mere remnant of the tribe, and was granted land at Peddie at the " emancipation," by Sir Benjamin D'Urban. If we accept the theory that the Hlubis, originally the Imi-Huhu, are a fragment of the Makalanga and, therefore, are Ama-Lala, then the Ama-Bele who are a branch of the Imi-Huhu are so likewise. It is difficult to say definitely when the Ama-Bele reached Natal, but it was long before historic times. The two main branches of the tribe are the Royal line, and that of the eldest son, though he was neither the heir nor the head of the Right-Hand House. These two branches came into existence with Kuboni, the thirteenth in line of descent from Mhuhu, and his eldest son Dlambulo. The royal salutation of each branch is respectively " Kuboni " and " Dlambulo." The traditional history of the Bele tribe is of the most elusive character. The tribe seems to possess no

Ama-Bele.

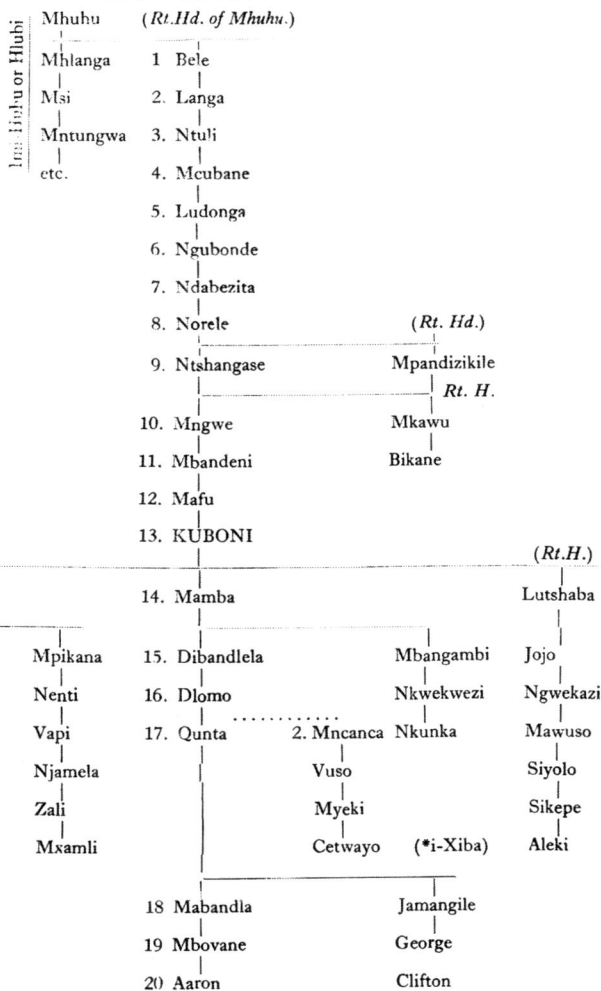

To face section on Ama-Bele. Chapter P.424

J. H. Soga

Note : *I-xiba - Son placed in deceased chief's house, to continue its existence. The deceased chief would, in this case, probably be Qunta, No. 17.

The material originally positioned here is too large for reproduction in this reissue. A PDF can be downloaded from the web address given on page iv of this book, by clicking on 'Resources Available'.

Ama-Zizi. Ama-Tolo. Ama-Kuze.—I-Nilangwini.

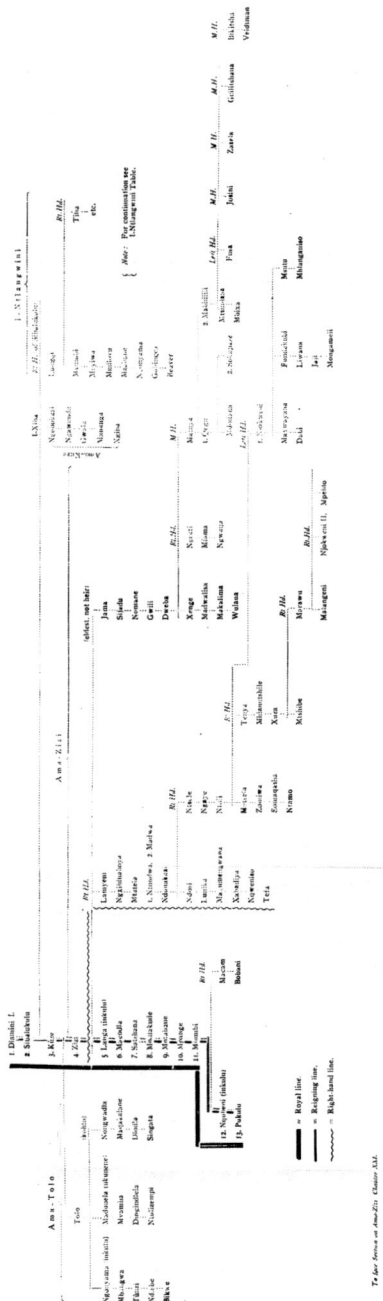

The material originally positioned here is too large for reproduction in this reissue. A PDF can be downloaded from the web address given on page iv of this book, by clicking on 'Resources Available'.

outstanding recorder of tribal tradition. The
genealogy of the tribe suffers in consequence.
Prior to the occupation of Natal by the British,
and much earlier than the time of Tshaka, the Ama-
Bele resided close under the Drakensberg mountains. The territory occupied by them was from
the junction of the Ndaka (Sunday's river) and the
Tugela as far as the Buffalo river, then cutting along
the Biggersberg it dropped down along the Klip
River to its junction with the Tugela, and along
this last to the point of junction with the Sunday's
River. The Ama-Bele were the immediate cause
of the destruction of the tribes living along the foot
of the Drakensberg, by refusing to allow Matiwana
on his retreat before Tshaka to pass through their
country, against which he had been pressed by the
Zulu despot. Reference is made to this in the
section on the Ama-Hlubi. It was to this tribe
that the Xosa chief, Jwara, went on the memorable
occasion of the war between Cira and Tshawe,
which altered the succession from the Great Son
of Nkosiyamntu, Cira, to the son of a Minor House,
Tshawe. The Ama-Jwara are exceedingly numerous within the Bele tribe, though in origin they
are not Ama-Lala, but Abe-Nguni.

Ama-Zizi (Ama-Lala).

The Ama-Zizi are of the same stock as the
Hlubis and Beles, but later in time of origin. If
we refer to the table of the Ama-Hlubi, we will
notice that the name *Dlamini* is the fourteenth in
the line of succession. Dlamini's Right-Hand
son was Sibalukulu. This last is the progenitor
of the Ama-Zizi. Sibalukulu's Great Son was
Kuze. The successor of Kuze was one of two

twins. By his principal wife Kuze had the twins, Tolo and Zizi, sometimes called Tolwana and Zizana. The former is said to have been the elder. When these two came of age and the question of appointing an heir had arisen, the matter was settled in an essentially primitive fashion. On the day of the ceremony connected with the proclamation of the feast of First Fruits (*uku-shwama,*) Kuze, the father of the twins, called them before him ; to each one he gave instructions how to act on this occasion. Addressing Tolo he said, " You are to take this root and chew it ; then take a piece of pumpkin and likewise chew it, then take a bite of this black substance (*um-sizi*), chew, and swallow it." Zizi received the same instructions, but added in addition to these, " you are to dance facing towards the rising sun, then towards the setting sun (east and west)." The last item of this programme was apparently the deciding factor. Zizi was thereupon proclaimed heir to the succession. As related by the Zizis, the whole proceeding seems meaningless and childish, but no doubt it had its reasonable interpretation for those immediately concerned. Whatever may have been the inward meaning of this ceremony, it is clear that Kuze favoured the younger twin and gave him the necessary hint for his success. While the salutation of the Ama-Zizi is *Dlamini* that of the Ama-Tolo, doubtless commemorating this contest is *Dlangamandla* (" eat vigorously "). It is said that Tolo was of a malicious disposition and that this set his father against him. The issue of this ceremonial contest brought on war between the two brothers, in which Zizi was worsted. From that day the two separated finally, each brother

I-Nilangwini.

DLAMINI

SIBALUKULU

Rt.H. Kuze — Zizi — Tobu

Rt.H. Langqi — Zandi

Mvumbi
Meyiwa
Mdiovu

Rt.H. Mabane — N•ele

Ngonyanna — Nomaguga
Gobingca — Mt•o
Kuknlela
Maikofeli

Rt.H. Tiba — Mabandla
Mvumbi

Rt.H. Mengwa
Gasu — Mrweh:
Nombewu — Nongcana
Fodo — Sondananashi
Mdungawe — Sirali

Rt.H. Balemi
Sidoyi

M.H. Bushulu
Thomas
Dumak•ele

Mzongwana — Kalane — Mordecai
2. Vayisi *(no issue)* — Pata
Setusa
2. Mbotweni

M.H. Vapi
Ngqambayi

Delimuzi — Magqeleni
Sohlatala — Gobodo

Rt.H. Nguza — Dulini
Li.H. Bidla — Makoba — Ndolwane
Silwanyana — Mnukwa — Beaver

Rt.H. Hlabati — Mzinibili
Rt.H. Siqoko
Rt.H. Bishop

J. H. Soga.

The material originally positioned here is too large for reproduction in this reissue. A PDF can be downloaded from the web address given on page iv of this book, by clicking on 'Resources Available'.

ruling over his own adherents. In Tshaka's time, coincident with the arrival of Europeans in Natal, the Zizis resided next to the Beles. Their territory started at the Upper Klip river, the boundary proceeding from that point to the sources of the Tugela, then along the foot of the Drakensberg to the Bushman's river. The Ama-Tolo boundary was from the right bank of the Bushman's river to the Drakensberg and the sources of the Mko-manzi. The Ama-Kuze territory stretched from about Estcourt to the Buffalo river. That placed them next above the Ama-Bele. The I-Ntlangwini tribe were neighbours of the Ama-Kuze, and stretched across country in much the same way as the Kuzes, that is from the Bushman's river to the Buffalo. All these tribes were closely related, and though independent of each other, prove their common origin by the use of the same salutation, *Dlamini*. When the Ama-Zizi entered Gcaleka-land on their dispersion from their ancient home under the Drakensberg, the complete collapse of their tribal life was clearly revealed by the fact that the remnants who succeeded in reaching Hintsa's country were under the leadership of Njo-kweni, and his son Msutu, both belonging to the most insignificant of the Minor Houses of the Zizis. The leadership of Njokweni in the days of Zizi travail gave his house a position of importance which it has maintained up to the present.

I-Ntlangwini (Ama-Lala).

There are several tribes that derive their origin from Sibalukulu, the Right-Hand Son of Dlamini. These are the Ama-Kuze, Ama-Tolo, Ama-Zizi and I-Ntlangwini, and are all of considerable importance. The Ntlangwini are the Right-Hand House of Sibalukulu, whose Principal Son in this house was Lungqi, the genealogy of whose descendants has a special table arranged for it in this book ; hence, it is not necessary to overload this section with the names of a large number of chiefs. Historically, we first meet with this tribe in residence between the Bushman's river and the Buffalo. The names with which we are made most familiar at that time (1838), are those of Nombewu and his son, Fodo ; mention is also made of Baleni and his son, Sidoyi. Though these chiefs acquired fame or notoriety, they were no by means the most important by birth. They were rather chiefs of moderate status.

At the time when Ngoza, or Ngozi, Chief of the Tembus settled at the Qudeni Mountains in Natal, was trying to escape from Tshaka, he found his way to the south barred by the Ntlangwini and Kuze tribes. As he came in contact with them, he attacked and swept them out of his way. They were considerably broken in consequence, and many of the Kuzes joined Ngoza. The Ntlangwini, however, when they felt unequal to stopping the Tembus, turned and attacked the Ama-Nqondo and Ama-Nkabane behind them and drove them among the Bacas, among whom many of them are to be found to this day. In the main, however, the Ntlangwini were not broken, but moved out of Ngoza's way, and returned and reoccupied their homes.

Sometime later a confederacy was formed by certain tribes in the upper parts of Natal, which were in constant danger from Tshaka. There was

reason for the confederacy. It was not aimed at
Tshaka, but against those powerful tribes occupying
the country to the south, who disputed the passage
of any fugitive tribes flying from destruction. One
of the most obstinate and dangerous of these tribes
was the powerful Ama-Baca, occupying the territory within which Maritzburg now stands. The
confederacy determined to cut a way through this
tribe. The members of the confederacy were
the Ama-Nyamnywini under chief Mkalipi, a
section of the Beles under Mdingi, the Dunges
under Mboyiya, the Ama-Funze under the great
Maraule, son of Nonyanda, the Ama-Gwenyane
of Nocandambedu, and also two sections of the
Ntlangwini under Nombewu and Baleni, respectively. The confederacy succeeded in its enterprise and
swept the Bacas out of its path. Nombewu, the
more important of the two Ntlangwini chiefs, went
on to the Mzimkulu and settled there. Ncapayi,
a Baca chief, remembering the rough handling his
people had received from the Ntlangwini on the
above occasion, came into conflict with Nombewu,
in which the latter chief was killed. Fodo, Principal Son of Nombewu, then ruled the tribe. It was
he who in 1840 assisted the Natal Boers against
Ncapayi. On Fodo's side this assistance was by
way of revenge for his father's death. Ncapayi
was badly handled by this combination. The
incident induced the Governor of the Cape, Sir
George Napier, at the request of the Pondo chief,
Faku, in whose country Ncapayi was living, to interfere. He sent a certain Captain Smith (Pondo,
Ndimiti) with a small force of soldiers to take
station at the Mgaza, Pondoland, as a check to any
further enterprise of the same kind on the part

of the Boers. It may be as well to state briefly here the alleged cause of the raid by the Boers into Pondoland. The Boers stated that they had lost a number of cattle, and when the spoor was traced it led into the district in Pondoland occupied by Ncapayi's Bacas. They further alleged that they had been invited by the Pondo chief, Faku, to punish Ncapayi. The Boers, then, with the assistance of the Ntlangwini under Fodo, attacked the Bacas, killing, it is stated, thirty men, ten women, and four children. A large number of cattle were seized, as well as sheep and goats. Fodo's impi, it was said, also captured and took away with them a number of women and children. This last action increased the long-standing hatred between the Bacas and Ntlangwini, which originated with the latter tribe joining the confederation which broke the power of the Bacas. This raid caused considerable trouble between the Cape Government and the Natal Boers, for the Government claimed both the Boers and the Bacas as its subjects. To the charge made against Faku that he had invited the Boers, he gave a decided denial. After this affair Fodo was deposed by the Cape Government from his chieftainship. In the section of this book dealing with the Pondos, reference was made to Nqeto, chief of the Ama-Qwabe, who in his flight from his relative, Tshaka, endeavoured forcibly to settle in Pondoland. This was the individual who murdered Lieutenant Farewell and party, and was later driven out of Pondoland and returned to Natal. Baleni, a Minor Chief of the Ntlangwini, a man of sinister reputation, acted as a spy for Dingana after Tshaka's death, and reported to that blood-thirsty monarch

the return of Nqeto. Needless to say, Nqeto did
not long survive this betrayal, being secretly put
to death by Dingana. The son of this Baleni,
named Sidoyi, assumed the chieftainship on his
father's death, but for some misdeed was deprived
of his chieftainship by the Government in 1857,
and Zatshuke was installed in his position. It is
a comment on the desposition of Native chiefs,
that their own tribes do not recognise the deposition and just carry on the tribal affairs as formerly,
only yielding in such matters as directly concern
the relations of the tribe with the Government.
Sidoyi, though deposed, continued in fact to be
the ruler of the tribe, in spite of Zatshuke's appointment. In evidence of this, when Hope's war
broke out in 1880, Sidoyi had to be recognised by
the Europeans as Chief of his section of the tribe.
It happened in this way. During the year just
mentioned, the Basuto chiefs, Lerothodi and
Masupa (Masumpa), were arming to assist the
Pondomise chief, Mhlontlo, in his rebellion against
the Cape Government.* This action affected the
Basutos on the eastern side of the Drakensberg,
in the Matatiele district, and caused them in like
manner to arm, with the intention of assisting
their countrymen. Sidoyi, at this critical time
came forward with his Ntlangwini and acted as a
buffer between the Europeans and Basutos, and
prevented the Basutos from over-running the
Kokstad and Mount Ayliff districts, and consequently materially helped in breaking the back
of the rebellion. As a recognition of his valuable
services, the Government granted him a portion
of land for himself and people in the Kokstad

* Perhaps it would be more correct to say they rose on their own
account in opposition to the Disarmament Act.

district. Sidoyi died shortly after these events, and his son, Mzongwana, became chief of these Ntlangwini. Mzongwana, however, in 1897, joined Le Fleur in the Griqua rebellion. He was in consequence, deposed and a commoner, Sodidi, was appointed regent. Of all the tribes who derived their origin from Sibalukulu the Zizis, Tolos, Kuzes and Ntlangwini, the last were easily first as a fighting tribe, distinguished for its courage and enterprise. The Jabavu family are members of this Ntlangwini tribe.

Ama-Tolo.

The first chief of this tribe was Tolo, the elder twin brother of Zizi. The latter, a favourite of his father Kuze, became heir to the chieftainship of the Ama-Dlamini and Principal Chief of the main line of the Imi-Huhu, now Ama-Hlubi, from whom are derived the Ama-Tolo, Ama-Zizi, Ntlangwini, and other tribes whose royal salutation is *Dlamini*.

The heads of the three main branches of the Ama-Tolo were, respectively, Ngonyama of the Principal House ; Madubela of the Right-Hand House, and Nongwadla, of the Left-Hand House. Tunzi, son of Ngonyama, remained in Natal after the dispersion of his tribe caused by the Tshaka upheavals. Ndlebe, the son of Tunzi, took the remnants of that section of the tribe and settled on the border of Pondoland between the Ncambedlana and the Nkawukazi rivers, in the eastern neighbourhood of the present town of Umtata. The original home of this portion of the Ama-Tolo was along the west side of the Bushman's river and on towards the Drakensberg mountains in Natal.

Witchcraft was responsible for the removal of this section from the Ncambendlana to its present residence at the Ncembu. At this time Ndlebe as well as his heir were dead, and Mloko, grandson of Ndlebe, was a minor. The tribe consequently was under a regency ; the regent being Bikwe, a younger son of Ndlebe, and uncle to the heir, Mloko. A relative of the regent, called Gxididi, was " smelt out " and an accusation of destroying Mloko's house laid against him. Secret notice was given to Gxididi that a party of men had been appointed to put him to death. He immediately left the kraal which was next to the Mhlakulo hill, Gungululu, and sought refuge with two sons of Bungiwe, Mva and Dambuza, at a place called *Isixobo sika-Ngolo* (" Ngolo's rocky ledge ") in the direction of Umtata.

Gxididi having secured the sympathy of this minor branch of the Tolo tribe and of the Pondos, among whom they had settled, shouted the war-cry. The district in consequence began to arm. The Pondos with whom were Gxididi and his Tolo adherents, set out on the war path and advanced towards Bikwe's headquarters. This impi halted on the ridge overlooking the Cwerana, as it came face to face with Bikwe's impi. Gxididi, the cause of all this commotion, fired a shot into the ranks of Bikwe's impi, whereupon the fighting became general. Bikwe's forces were driven back by the combined force of Pondos and Gxididi's Ama-Tolo as far as the Cwerana (Gungululu) drift. This drift is on the main Umtata-Kokstad road. Here Mloko, the boy-heir, was shot in the

CC

leg and fell. The Tolos attempted to make a stand and protect the person of their young chief, but all to no purpose. They were forced back by the Pondos, leaving the chief to the mercy of their enemies. The person of a Bantu chief is held sacred, so that when he was overtaken by his enemies his life was spared, and a horse was given him to ride home on. This, however, he did not do, but succeeded in joining his uncle, Bikwe, and the Tolo army. Meanwhile, another Pondo force under Qumbelo approached the Tolo impi from the rear, or, as they were retreating, on its front, so that it was hemmed in between the two Pondo forces. At this Nqeketo, one of the chiefs serving under Qumbelo, besought the latter not to destroy the Ama-Tolo, but rather to take them under his protection. This was agreed to and Mloko surrendered to Qumbelo. Ndlebe's, or now Mloko's, Tolos immediately forsook their homes and marched inland settling on the Ncembu in the Maclear direction. There they are at the present day.

The Right-Hand House, Madubela's, of the Ama-Tolo under their chief Dingindlela was also broken and dispersed by the Ama-Ngwana under Matiwana. For a time this section came under the protection of the Ntlangwini tribe, the greater portion remaining with Sidoyi's Ntlangwini on the Mkomanzi in south-eastern Natal.

The Left-Hand House, that is Nongwadla's, being dispersed along with the main sections of the tribe, sought refuge with other tribes. The greater portion of the Ama-Tolo became tributary to the Pondos, but many families and individuals entered Gcalekaland, then under Hintsa. Some of the latter left Gcalekaland at the time of what is erroneously called the " emancipation " of the Fingoes and settled at Peddie. The royal saluta-tion of the Ama-Tolo is *Dlangamandla* (" eat with vim or force "). Its derivation is from the exercise imposed by Kuze, the father of Tolo and Zizi, to settle their respective claims to the chieftain-ship, and is mentioned in the section on Zizi.

The Ama-Tolo genealogical table is attached to that of the Ama-Zizi. Only the three principal branches, however, are given. The minor branch-es have not been detailed.

Ama-Baca (*Ama-Lala*).

The Ama-Baca and Ama-Wushe are kindred tribes. The latter, the Ama-Wushe, were the senior house, but were so badly dismembered by Macingwane of the Ama-Cunu that they became absorbed by the lesser tribe, the Ama-Baca. The term Baca is equivalent to the term *Uku-Mfenguza* (" homeless "), by which the Fingoes on their arrival in Gcalekaland indicated their condition, and from which term their name, *Fingoes,* is derived. It is said that the Bacas were so called because they fled from Tshaka and became a homeless people. I think, however, that some previous time and in-cident must be responsible for the name, as prior to the tribe's disaster at the hands of Macingwane, while it was still resident, in Tshaka's time, in the district now known as Pietermaritzburg, the tribe was known by the name *Baca*. There is no chief of that name from whom the tribe is named ; consequently, their name, " homeless, " most probably rests on some foundation of fact. But the question is, " When ?" In Tshaka's time, the Ama-Wushe were a powerful and numerous tribe, one section of which was under the chief Mqinambi, on the Kharkloof river, a tributary of the Mgeni ; another was under the chief Hlepu, son of Ngcwanekazi, and resided about the upper reaches of the Mgeni ; a third was under the chief Nondzaba, and occupied the territory bordering the lower part of the Mgeni. The Bacas were the immediate neighbours of the Ama-Wushe. Both tribes are said to have derived their origin from a chief, Mjoli. The earlier history of these tribes is lost in the misty past. It seems, therefore, appropriate to relate at this stage, the cause of the disruption of these tribes by the Ama-Cunu of Macingwane.

Macingwane.

A brief genealogy of the Ama-Cunu may be here given. The tribe takes its name from
Mcunu, father of
Luboko, father of
Macingwane, father of
Ndima, father of
Lembede.

About the year 1780, the new military system introduced by Dingiswayo chief of the Imi-Tetwa tribe, began to have far-reaching effects, as the surrounding tribes adopted it and reorganised their forces to suit the new system. None, however, was able to reach the state of efficiency to which the Imi-Tetwa had attained. Those tribes nearest in residence to Dingiswayo were the first to feel the effect of the broad-bladed stabbing assegai, and close-quarter fighting. These tribes were gradually conquered and absorbed by him. The

Zulus were one of these, and became tributary to the Imi-Tetwa. A number of tribes were not easily overcome, and maintained their independence until the rise of Tshaka, who reversed the positions of the Imi-Tetwa and Ama-Zulu, and combined them both into an irresistible fighting machine. Tribe after tribe fell before it and became incorporated in the regimental system of the machine. In consequence of this menace to their independence, a number of the more powerful tribes, realising the hopelessness of maintaining a state of war with Tshaka, preferred to get out of his way, and seek new territory for themselves.

The Ama-Cunu tribe under their chief Macingwane was one of these. A custom observed by Tshaka, with the purpose of securing his position as chief, was to destroy all chiefs who fell into his power, and incorporate their people with his own. He feared even that his own children might some day dispute the title of chief with him, and inhumanly put his children to death.

This, strange though it may seem, rather commended itself than otherwise to some of the hereditary chiefs, one of whom was Macingwane. He was a man of a fierce and turbulent nature, haughty and overbearing. Like Tshaka in temperament, he was like Tshaka devoid of the finer elements of character. Family affection was subordinate to expediency. He put to death his two sons, Mayana and Ndabezimbi, lest they should some day try to wrest his chieftainship from him, and usurp his authority. The location of Macingwane's tribe, the Ama-Cunu, was between the Mhlatusi and Tugela rivers. It was, consequently, just to the south of the Tetwa-Zulu tribe. Tshaka could not long tolerate so powerful a neighbour as **Ma-cingwane** so close to him, and made an attack upon him. In the fierce battle which followed Tshaka was badly defeated and retired. But Macingwane realized that his success was only temporary and that, according to his custom, Tshaka had only retreated for a time, and would ere long be back again in irresistible force. Prudence dictated flight as Macingwane's best line of action. He, therefore, decided immediately to evacuate his present position and seek " pastures new." Collecting all his people, cattle and effects, and putting his army in fighting order, with the women and children in the centre, he moved out and proceeded southwards. Between Macingwane and his immediate objective, the Mzimkulu river, were numerous tribes, most of them smaller and less formidable than his own. These were the Ama-Pumulo under Dibandlela ; the Langeni, Mpemvu, Nqondo, and the Ama-Funze of chief Maraule, the Nyamnywini of Mkalipi, the Ama-Sani, Mbedu, Nyamvu, and the Ama-Baca and Ama-Wushe. Such of these tribes as were unable effectively to oppose Macingwane gave him right-of-way through their country, others he swept aside. The Ama-Baca and their relations, the Ama-Wushe, were unable to check Mancigwane's progress, and they were badly shaken in an attempt to oppose him. Macingwane then passed on to Mzimkulu. The troubles of the Bacas were, for the time over, but not for long.

Confederacy of Tribes exposed to attack by Tshaka.

Through the removal of the Ama-Cunu to the Mzimkulu, a number of tribes were uncovered

and exposed to attack by Tshaka. They determined to migrate like the Ama-Cunu, in order to
escape the attentions of their ruthless neighbour.
They realized that their only hope to reach No-
man's-land in the south lay in forcing a passage
through the Ama-Baca who would dispute their
advance.   There was, for them, no alternative but
to come to a trial of strength with the Ama-Baca
and Ama-Wushe. A confederacy was, therefore,
formed. The tribes concerned in forming the
confederacy were a section of the Ama-Bele, the
Ama-Dunge under several chiefs, viz. : Mboyiya,
Ngwana, and Mkani ; the Ama-Funze, the Nyamnywini, and the Ntlangwini under Nombewu.
The first attempt of this combination to force its
way through the hostile Ama-Baca proved unsuccessful. The confederacy then decided on a
second effort, but required an addition to their
number. This was secured through the attach-
ment to their cause of a tribe a considerable
distance away, towards the sea-coast, and inhabiting the country about the lower reaches of the
Umvoti river. This was the Ama-Gwenyane tribe
under the chief Nocandambedu. This second
effort was more successful and these tribes got
through, at the same time completely breaking up
the Ama-Wushe and dismembering the Ama-
Baca. These latter secured a certain amount of
cohesion by collecting the dismembered fragments
under the chief Madikane, son of Kalimeshe,
Great Chief of the Ama-Baca. Madikane now
moved south, also following the line taken by the
Ama-Cunu, and on arrival entered into an alliance
with them. This was at the Cekwane (Dronk
Vlei) a tributary of the Upper Mzimkulu river.

Before long Madikane could not endure Macingwane's over-bearing manner and severed his connection with him. He marched still further south with his people, but encountered the Pondomise of Cape Colony. Fighting took place between the two tribes and Madikane broke through the Pondomise, continued his progress, crossed the Drakensberg, and entered Basutoland. The chief of the Basutos, Mshweshwe, who had been constantly worried by the arrival in his country of tribes flying from Tshaka, refused to allow the Bacas to reside in his country. Madikane then recrossed the Drakensberg and settled between the Rode and Mganu Mountains, Griqualand East, where the Baca tribe is still in residence. The relentless Tshaka sought out the Bacas in their new home. On account of the necessity to provide food for his enormous armies, Tshaka was wont to go far afield in order to secure additions to his commissariat, attacking such tribes as had sufficient cattle to tempt him. This was to him sufficient justification for setting his armies in motion. Spies informed Tshaka of the large number of cattle in possession of the Bacas. He sent a strong force against them, and the battle of Ntsiza was the result. The Ntsiza mountain overlooks the Mzimvubu river and the village of Mount Frere, 18 miles to the west, which, however, in those days was non-existent. A description of this battle is given by W. C. Scully, Esq., at one time magistrate of the Bacas, in the *State* for 1909. The following facts are based on his article. On a certain day, in the beginning of winter, the Bacas learned that one of Tshaka's Zulu impis was on the war path and was approaching Baca territory. Madikane warned his people and prepared for the coming fray. The women and children together with the cattle were sent to the Mganu hills above Ncome and Mandileni. Meanwhile the Baca impi was stationed between the Kenira and Mzimvubu rivers, at the Lutateni. The leaders in supreme command were Madikane and his son Ncapayi, of the Right-Hand House, his Great Son, Sonyangwe, being dead. At length information was given to the chief that the Zulu impi had been seen on the top of the Ntsiza mountain. It had apparently approached from the Kokstad direction, but on the west side of the Ntsiza range, which lies north and south between Kokstad and Rode, and at the latter spot turns due west, where the range takes the name of Nunge. Night fell with Tshaka's impi still on top of the mountain, where it apparently remained in bivouac, intending to attack on the morrow. During the night the wind blew from the east, accompanied by a cold rain. Dark clouds gathered about the Ntsiza, and the wind changed round to the west, whereupon snow began to fall, accompanied by a bitingly cold wind. Morning broke with the eyes of Madikane's warriors searching the position where the Zulu impi had last been seen. Nothing was to be seen, but a white pall of snow, which had fallen over-night, covering the Ntsiza. As the eyes of the onlookers became accustomed to the new aspect of the surroundings, black spots became visible here and there, descending and coming towards them. They were the remnants of Tshaka's impi. There was no need to enquire what had happened, the truth was apparent enough. Tshaka's impi had in great part perished in the snowstorm. The remnants collected together and turned homewards, keeping under the Ntsiza on its eastern side. Madikane was informed of this, and immediately detached Ncapayi with a force to intercept them. Tshaka's warriors could expect little mercy, they themselves never showed any. Ncapayi crossed the Mzimvubu below its junction with the Kenira, and hurried on to Rode after the retreating foe. Coming up with the Zulus, he sprang at them, as a wolf among sheep. The Zulus were broken in two, but continued their retreat close under the mountains ; but the Bacas got ahead of them, and a fierce engagement followed. It was not the fashion of Senzangakona's children to hesitate. They threw themselves upon the Bacas, cut a passage through them, and managed to cross the Mzintlanga river, reduced in numbers, but, from their discipline, to be reckoned with it. The Bacas then returned to their homes. This was the last occasion when a Zulu impi came to attack the Bacas. Madikane was killed later by the Tembus (1836). Reference is made to this fact in the chapter dealing with the Aba-Tembu.

Ncapayi.

Before Madikane died, he had advised Ncapayi to reside in Pondoland under Faku. The reason for this is apparent. Ncapayi had now reached manhood, but was not the heir of Madikane's Great House. It is true that the heir, Sonyangwe, was already dead, but his son was in Natal and in time would claim the chieftainship. Sonyangwe had been killed near Ntabankulu by the Ama-Bele residing there, but Mdutyana, his heir, remained behind in Natal.

Ncapayi saw the wisdom of his father's advice and went to Faku, by whom he was welcomed and received as a tributary chief. We have mentioned in the section dealing with the Pondos, the arrival in Pondoland of the Ama-Qwabe of Nqeto. The arrival coincided with that of Ncapayi. It may be remembered that Nqeto, a relative of Tshaka's who had served in Tshaka's army, being in favour with the tyrant, would not serve under Dingana, in consequence of which the new ruler sought Nqeto's life, thus compelling him to flee. He entered Pondoland and sought to secure for himself a position in the country by violence, but was finally ejected, returned to Natal, and was put to death in accordance with Dingana's instructions. The favourable reception of Ncapayi by Faku, as has been said, coincided with Nqeto's arrival. The Pondo chief, anxious to be rid of so troublesome a neighbour as the Qwabe chief, secured the assistance of Ncapayi in an endeavour to eject him. Faku then attacked Nqeto and drove him towards the Mzimvubu. On a point of land surrounded on three sides by the river Mzimvubu Nqeto made a desperate stand. At this moment Ncapayi attacked Nqeto's forces on their exposed flank and broke down their resistance. Nqeto fled back to Natal, where he was shortly afterwards put to death.

During the same year in which his father, Madikane, was killed (1836), Ncapayi entered Tembuland to avenge his death. The Tembus under Ngubencuka made an ineffectual stand, and the Bacas swept away a large number of cattle, with which they returned home. This booty so affected the cupidity of Faku that he came to an arrangement with Ncapayi in 1838 to make a combined

attack on the Tembus. They entered Tembuland
on three successive occasions, and each time their
raid was attended with complete success. They
practically denuded Tembuland of cattle, and
reduced the people to so abject a state of poverty,
that Colonial Europeans sent them necessaries of
life, and tided them for the time being over their
difficulties.

So greatly did the Tembus fear Ncapayi that
many moved further inland and settled at Xalanga
and Glen Grey. Ncapayi was regarded in the
light of a fearless freebooter. Cupidity was the
force which welded together the Faku-Ncapayi
combination, and it was cupidity which caused its
dissolution. On the return home of the raiders,
the division of the spoil did not commend itself
to either of the leaders, and forthwith both " solicited the services of the assegai," as Natives would
put it, to judge between them. The judgment was
indecisive, and it became difficult to say which of
the two was the more powerful. Seven years later
(1845) the question of supremacy was settled by
the death of Ncapayi. The freebooter collected
a strong force and set it in motion against Nyanda,
that is the Right-Hand section of the Pondos, at
that time under Ndamase, the son of Faku, who was
still in control of the whole nation. Ncapayi
attacked unexpectedly and raided a large number of
cattle, with which he essayed to return home.
Meanwhile the alarm had been raised, Faku assembled a powerful force, came up with the Bacas,
and attacked them on all sides. Ncapayi had made
his last raid. Faku drove the Bacas before him on
to a ridge overlooking the Mzimvubu (St. John's

river). At the extreme end of this ridge is a precipice overhanging the river ; many Bacas were forced over it and crushed before reaching the bottom. Ncapayi was wounded and forced over the rock, falling on to a ledge some distance from the bottom. He was in a helpless condition, both arms broken, besides a severe assegai wound. Here he lay for days, beseeching those who came to look at him to put an end to his misery and kill him : but none dared to kill a chief unless in battle. Faku, to whom reports were constantly made, at last gave orders that Ncapayi be killed. Thus died Madikane's son, a man of fearless nature and courage unsurpassed.

Makaula (1845).

Ncapayi at his death left as his heir Makaula, at that time but a boy, and not fit to rule the tribe. A regent was, therefore, appointed in the person of Diko, uncle to Makaula.

Madikane had looked forward to the heir of the Great House, by name Mdutyana, taking control of the tribe, hence he advised Ncapayi to attach himself to Faku. But Mdutyana continued to reside in Natal, finally dying there without making any claim to the chieftainship of the Cape Colony Bacas. Not until Makaula, of the Right-Hand House, had left Pondoland for Bacaland and had been in supreme control of the tribe for some years, did Mdutyana's son, Nomtsheketshe, leave Natal to claim his inheritance. But he came too late, finding Makaula firmly established ; and the rule passed from his house to the Right-Hand. So it remains to this day.

On the accession of Makaula, conditions were changing, and tribe after tribe, in order to get out of the maelstrom of intertribal war, sought to come under the protection of the white man's government. Makaula, on behalf of his people and himself, made a request to be taken under the protection of the Cape Government. For the consideration of the request, a commission was appointed in 1875 under the chairmanship of C. D. Griffith. The other members of the commission were A. T. Cumming and S. O. Probart, these last being, respectively, magistrate of Kokstad and member of the Colonial Parliament. The first, C. D. Griffith, represented the head of the Government.

Three principal points of the agreement drawn up between the parties concerned, assent to which was required from the Baca chief, may be briefly stated thus :— (1) Every individual to have the right of bringing his case before a magistrate without interference ; (2) A hut tax levy to be instituted ; (3). Government's refusal to permit that anyone should be put to death, or punished, or fined, on account of having been " smelt out " by witch-doctors.

The conditions were agreed to, and the Bacas became Government subjects. From that day the Bacas have enjoyed a peace such as they never had before. Makaula died in 1906, having suffered for years from paralysis. His son, the present ruler, is Mngcisana.

The Baca and Wushe genealogy is as follows :—

Ama-Zulu.

J. H. Soga.

```
                                              Rt.H.
Gumede                                        Ntombela
Malandela                                     Zulu
Nozidiya                                      Nkosinkulu
Qwabe                                         Mageba
Msomi          M H.                           Punga
               Gasa          Ama-ZULU         Ndaba
Singila                                       Jama
Vumane                                        Senzangakona      Rt.H.
Kude, 2, Moyeni                               Tshaka, 2, Dingana   Sojiyiswa
Kondlo         Rt. H.                            3, Mpande         Mapita
               Mafongonyana                      4, Mhlangana      Zibebu
Pakatwayo      Sidumo                                              Konela.
Sopana         Sigcotshana
Njakaba
```

(Eldest) not heir
Mbhedu

Ama-_-QWABE

Note: Numbers 2, 3, 4, indicate brothers
of the name goiog before.

Gt.Ho.	Mjoli	Rt.Ho.		
|	|	|		

<table>
<tr><td rowspan="4">Ama-Wushe</td><td>Nondzaba</td><td rowspan="7">Ama-Baca</td><td>Zulu</td><td></td><td></td></tr>
<tr><td>Godongwana</td><td>Kalimeshe</td><td></td><td></td></tr>
<tr><td>Mkilwa</td><td>Madikane</td><td>Rt Hd.</td><td></td></tr>
<tr><td>Josiah</td><td>Sonyangwe</td><td>Ncapayi</td><td>Rt.Hd.</td></tr>
<tr><td></td><td>Mdutyana</td><td>Makaula</td><td>Diko</td></tr>
<tr><td></td><td>Nomtsheketshe</td><td>Mngcisana</td><td></td></tr>
<tr><td></td><td>Rolobile</td><td></td><td></td></tr>
</table>

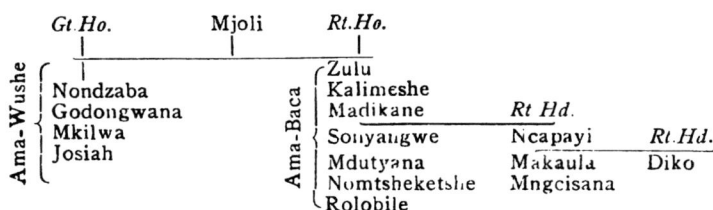

Ama-Zulu (*Ama-Lala*).

The Ama-Zulu are placed, perhaps without complete justification, under the third of the eastern Bantu streams—the Ama-Lala. There are one or two observations which may be made in this connection. As has been indicated in the chapter on the Correlation of Bantu tribes, the royal salutation is one of the most important factors in determining the branch or stream to which a tribe belongs. The Zulu salutation is *Ndabezita*. This name was that of an important Bele chief. If the salutation indeed refers to him, there can be no doubt that the origin of the Zulus is Lala. But, if we refer to the genealogy of the Zulu tribe we will notice that the great-grandfather of Tshaka was " Ndaba," and this name suggests the possiblity or even probability that the praise name of Ndaba might be *Ndabezita*.* If this be the correct source of the Zulu *isi-takazelo*, then the difficulty of assigning the tribe's true place is great. Then, again, we learn from Bryant that the Zulus of Tshaka had an earlier *isi-takazelo*, namely *Lufenu-lwenja*. Now, how did that salutation originate ? Was it from some ancient chief ? Or did it come into use from some frivolous or unchaste circumstance ?

* The Ama-Cunu informed the writer in 1929 that Tshaka, who was a law to himself, appropriated the title *Ndabezita* for himself from the Ama-Cunu, whose royal salutation it was. This, after Tshaka had driven the Cunus out of the country.

If the former, we would point out that only one chief bears a name somewhat similar, *Lufele-Lwenja*, an ancestor of the Imi-Huhu, Hlubi, Bele, Zizi and other tribes. It would be easy to explain the difference of one syllable in the above versions of what may be one and the same name, by supposing the second form to be a modern concession to good taste. Apart from these considerations, the probability is in favour of Lala origin, for the Zulus are not Abe-Nguni nor are they Aba-Mbo. They may, of course, be Basuto, but this is unlikely. One point should not be lost sight of by those interested in following up such questions, viz., that Zulu genealogy begins at a much later date than that of many of the other important tribes. The tribe must, therefore, have come into being long after the others, so that the field of research for the origin of the name is narrowed down considerably. Unless the Zulu tribe is a late independent importation into Natal, its genesis must be sought for within the bounds of the three main streams of Eastern Bantu. Strictly speaking, the Zulu tribe is the Right-Hand House of Malandela. The Great House has a name of its own, namely, Ama-Qwabe. In comparison with the Xosa tribe, the Zulus are considerably later in origin. Using the same method of calculation for both, that is, considering a generation to be 25 years, we find that the time of Xosa would be about 1535, and the time of Malandela, the father of the Zulu tribe, 1575. The Hlubi, again, the oldest in origin according to their genealogical table, date back to the 14th century, and are thus a much older tribe than either of the two former. Malandela's Great Son was Qwabe, and his Right-Hand son was Ntombela, the father of Zulu, after whom the tribe is named. Both the Ama-Qwabe and Ama-Zulu developed independently of each other, and occupied separate territory. The Zulus, who were tributary to the Imi-Tetwa tribe, lived contiguous to the latter, both being between the Black and the White Umvolosi, above their junction. The Ama-Qwabe were below the junction of the two rivers, and were astride the Lower Umvolosi all the way down to the coast, in the neighbourhood of Cape St. Lucia. The term *Zulu* is used to-day in a wide application quite unjustified by actual fact, as it is made to include generally all the tribes in Natal. There were, and still are, tribes numerically superior to the Zulus, and of a totally different origin, which in common parlance are drawn within the sweep of that name. This misuse of the name *Zulu* has become stereotyped, and is not likely to be altered now. This tribe became famous in the beginning of the 19th century through the fame, or notoriety, of its leader, Tshaka, but its glory was really a reflected glory, for the marrow of Tshaka's army were the formidable Imi-Tetwa, Godongwana's tribe, by whom the Zulus were held in subjection, until such time as fortune made Tshaka ruler as well as commander over both.

CHAPTER XXIII

Tshaka

The history of this chief is so well known, having been dealt with most comprehensively by historians, that it would be a work of supererogation to attempt here any lengthy description of the man and his warlike adventures. A few remarks, however, may not be out of place. A genealogical table of Tshaka's tribe has been furnished for this work, but it has been confined entirely to the reigning line of his house. Tshaka was the son of Sanzangakona, the eighth in line of descent from Malandela, the founder of the tribe. At the time of Tshaka's birth, Jama, father of Senzangakona, ruled the Right-Hand House of the founder, his son being still a youth in charge of his father's cattle. Tshaka was born out of wedlock, his mother being a maiden of the Nguga tribe, and a daughter of Mbengi, chief of the Nguga. Her son was born at her own home, but the condition of his birth was always against him, until he became famous. He was consistently treated with contempt by the members of Mbengi's family and looked upon as a pariah. Being by nature a boy of spirit, he resented with his whole soul the attitude of his relatives towards him, but unable to defend himself against a household of enemies, his revolt was internal, and its open manifestation being suppressed, the fires of hate were kindled against his fellow-men. It is related of him that on one occasion, when a mere child, he had been playing with the child-heir to the chief Mbengi. The game was one often engaged in by Native children : the moulding of clay cattle, and pitting them against each other in imaginary fights. Each boy holds in his hand his champion ox and forces it against that of his opponent. The one which has received most damage is declared the loser. On this occasion Tshaka's ox proved the victor. This small matter, however, accentuated the dislike felt by the family towards this semi-outcast. That he dared to get the better of the chief's son was, they held, an unpardonable impertinence, a piece of bad breeding of the most flagrant kind. He became an Ishmaelite ; every man's hand was against him, and his against every man. Tshaka's treatment became so bad that his grandmother took the boy away from her daughter Nandi and went with him to her own people. They belonged to the great and warlike tribe, the Imi-Tetwa, then under the renowned chief, Godongwana. Here Tshaka grew up. In time he was trained, along with the Imi-Tetwa warriors, in the new system of warfare, which was destined to do terrible havoc among the tribes of Zululand and Natal. Tshaka was an apt pupil and distinguished himself by personal courage and military capacity.

The finer qualities of his character, however, were so seared by his treatment as a boy that they remained withered to the end of his life. He delighted in the sufferings of others ; to him they were as blood is to a tiger. It gave him pleasure personally to inflict pain, and mercy was a virtue unknown to him. He was vindictive, ruthless, cruel, his only redeeming quality being courage and a genius for leading men. As a tactician and a strategist he was beyond other leaders of his time,

but he had in greater measure than they the material to practise with in the formidable regiments
of Godongwana's army, which, unlike those of
other tribes, were always mobilized and ready for
war. In spite of all these latter advantages which
he possessed, there were leaders of other tribes
who when the opposing forces were fairly equal,
often beat him. Thus, there was that terrible
fighter, Matiwana of the Ama-Ngwana, and again
Zwide of the Ama-Ndwandwe, but their resources
in men were limited. Tshaka had a number of
depots or headquarters of regiments whose motto
might well have been *Semper paratus*. Of these
the principal were Nobamba, Isi-Rebeni, Bulawayo,
Gibinegu, Mbelebele, Dukuza and Kangelamanke-
ngane, all ready practically at a moment's notice
to take the field. The necessity of keeping these
armies fed was one of the main inducements for
attacking and destroying other tribes. Tshaka
soon made a wilderness of the districts round about
him, hence we find him sending his armies, for
no other purpose than to replenish his commissariat,
to great distances. They went to Basutoland ;
they went north to Swaziland, and south as far as
Pondoland. It would be interesting to record the
famous battles in which Tshaka was engaged but
they are so well known that we pass them over.
Both Bryant and Bird deal with these, and their
books are available to most students. Old Zwide
of the Ama-Ndwandwe often taught Tshaka a
severe lesson, but in the end he went the way of
the rest.

By the time Godongwana, chief of the Imi-
Tetwa, was too far advanced in years to accompany
his armies in person, Tshaka had so distinguished

himself as a successful general that he was entrusted with the supreme command. This was of immense service to him in several ways. By means of this position he was able to usurp the chieftainship of the Zulus, partly by the assistance or connivance of Godongwana. By the death of Godongwana, which took place not long after this, he was also able to take advantage of the quarrels of that chief's sons about the chieftainship of the Imi-Tetwa, to unite the factions within the Tetwa army caused by these quarrels, and have himself proclaimed chief. He thus became chief of the two tribes, the Imi-Tetwa, and his father's tribe, the Ama-Zulu. Having accomplished this he entered on a course of devastation such as had never been known before by the Bantu. By his excesses he depopulated large tracts of country, exterminating certain tribes, while others sought voluntary exile in distant parts, and others joined themselves to him as tributary in order to save themselves. Tshaka's rule lasted for about sixteen years, from 1812 to 1828.

The circumstances leading up to the usurpation of the Zulu chieftainship may be briefly stated. Senzangakona, the father of Tshaka, was reported to be dying. Tshaka then applied for leave of absence to his superior, Godongwana, in order to visit his father. This was granted. It was not, however, from filial devotion that he desired to go home. He had other and more sinister designs in view. Arrived at his father's place, he did not present himself to the old man, but sought out the heir, Nomkwayimba, and killed him. This information being conveyed to the dying chief, the shock was so great that Senzangakona immediately expired. Tshaka followed up this brutal act by killing Mfogazi, the next in order of succession to Nomkwayimba. He had now rendered it dangerous for any aspirant, other than himself, to assert his claims and, having secured the interest of Godongwana, placed himself securely on the throne. Then war followed war with unvarying regularity. Dingiswayo, for whom Tshaka professed great affection, was killed in a war with the Ama-Ndwandwe of Zwide. This tribe had often fought with Tshaka and had frequently beaten him. It was the most powerful of all the tribes that refused to become tributary to the Imi-Tetwa. Tshaka, the unconquerable, had in the death of his chief found a pretext for another trial of strength with his great rival. He spoke disrespectfully of Zwide, of Ntombazi, Zwide's mother, and of Langa, Zwide's father, expecting that his expressions of contempt would be carried to the Ndwandwe chief, and his expectations were realized. Two men of importance in Tshaka's service, Ngqwangube and Nikizwayo, were under sentence of death, and fled to Zwide. These men reported Tshaka's words to the Ndwandwe chief who sent back the following message, " Son of my old friend, why do you revile me so ? Fix your spears in their shafts. I am coming."

Last battle of the Ama-Ndwandwe.

The Ndwandwe army took the field shortly after this warning. Its immediate objective was the headquarters of Tshaka at the Gqori hills, where Tshaka had two depots of troops, namely, Mbelembele and Sirebe. The Ndwandwe warriors were commanded by Noluju, Zwide's general.

When he came in sight of the Gqori, Noluju arranged his warriors in two divisions. One division he sent against the Mbelembele, and the other against the Sirebe. The Zulus were likewise formed up in two division, each defending its own headquarters.

Ngqengelele, son of Vulana was commander-in-chief of Tshaka's forces. As Zwide's warriors came on to the attack, Tshaka surrounded by his body-guard, all bearing black shields, took up a position to view the battle. Fighting against the Mbelembele, Zwide drove in the right wing of Tshaka's force, while at the same time Zwide's right wing was driven back by the Zulus. Exactly the same thing happened at Sirebeni. When Tshaka observed that his army was in danger of being cut to pieces, he grew restive and demanded that his shield, black and white in colour, should be handed to him by his bearer, intending personally to lead his men. The regiments forming his body-guard he divided and sent one body in support of his right wing at Mbelebele which was badly shaken, the other he sent against the left wing of Zwide's warriors who were threatening to break through his right wing at Sirebeni. These arrived just in time to avert disaster and, taking advantage of the check imposed on Zwide's forces, succeeded in carrying out an encircling movement, and thus at both points had the enemy at a great disadvantage. Desperate fighting followed, and for a long time the issue hung in the balance, but in the end, after a sanguinary contest, the Ndwandwes broke through the encircling Zulus, but only to retreat. The victory was so decisive that Zwide with the whole Ndwandwe tribe made preparations to evacuate their old country. This decision they carried out and moved right up to the Wakkenstroom district from the sea-board near St. Lucia lake. Part of Zwide's army was composed of Zwangendaba's Abe-Nguni, who later separated from Zwide and went north. These are the Abe-Nguni or Aba-Ngoni, of Nyasaland, and are, as has been stated at the end of the part of this book dealing with the Ama-Xosa, to be of the same stock as the latter.

Perhaps the wars in which Tshaka engaged as supreme chief of the Imi-Tetwa and Ama-Zulu reveal the best side of the man, or at least do not display conspicuously the evil that was in him. His warriors and their leaders by their excesses help to share any responsibility, and to keep his shortcomings in the background. The savage nature of this inhuman tyrant comes into clearer relief through the details of his private life. In a fit of ungovernable fury over some trivial matter, he stabbed his mother, Nandi, to death, and afterwards made a great show of extreme grief. Mr. Henry Fynn states that the Zulus told him that Nandi died from dysentry. But A. M. Fuze (in *Abantu Abamnyama*) in reference to this says, " Is it likely that the Zulus would open their hearts to a white man on the real facts of a matter of this kind ?" Which, in short, means that Tshaka actually killed his mother with his own hands. There are so many instances of his extreme brutality that it would require a separate volume to record them all. We therefore pass them over and refer to the last, which so exasperated everyone that the natural corollary was the determination to put him to death. The Zulu army had been despatched on an expedition against the Pondos. Though they overpowered the Pondos, the Zulus were yet unable to follow them into the fastnesses of the Mgazi and completely crush them. So, having exacted a promise from them that they would become tributary to Tshaka, the Zulus contented themselves with this and the captured cattle and returned home. In the absence of his army on this expedition, Tshaka professed to have had certain revelations made to him, through the medium of dreams. He summoned the wives of many of the absent warriors before him. He, then, went through the formulae of the witch-doctor, and charged each one with being guilty of a certain offence. Each individual was asked, " Are you guilty ?" When the answer was " No," the unfortunate woman was put to death. Others, hoping to escape the same fate, would reply " Yes," but they also were put to death. Thus he trifled with the lives of human beings, disregarded the sacred ties of human affection. The tiger had tasted blood. It is said that four hundred of the wives of his warriors were done to death by him on this occasion. Having temporarily satiated his lust for blood, he began to think and, in thinking, to fear the effect of his excesses on the army. Consequently on its return, he allowed it no time to rest, but sent it off immediately on another expedition, this time far to the north-east. That the death of Tshaka was being privately canvassed is evident from an incident which took place about this time. It is related that a notorious thief, Gcugcwa, was brought before Tshaka. It should be mentioned that certain forms of theft were punishable by death. This man was of the Ama-Qwabe tribe, that is, the

Principal House of the Zulus, and was therefore a relative to the tyrant, and of some standing by birth. When he appeared before Tshaka, the latter said to him as if in salutation, *Sakubona Gcugcwa* (" I see you, Gcugcwa "). Gcugcwa replied, " Yes, *Ndabezita*, I see you also." A second time Tshaka said, *Sakubona Gcugcwa*. The culprit saw a veiled menace in the salutation, but replied as before. The Qwabe thief was no coward, and feared not death. When Tshaka, therefore, a third time said to him *Sakubona Ccugcwa*, Gcugcwa replied " Yes chief, you see *me* to-day, but others will see *you* to-morrow." " Seize him," said the chief, and Gcugcwa was led to instant execution.

Retribution is a slow traveller, but reaches its destination in the end. The principal conspirators working for the death of Tshaka were his two brothers, Dingana and Mhlangana. They had not, as is sometimes stated, gone out with the army on its expedition to the north-east, but had on some pretext remained at home. They got into touch with Tshaka's immediate personal attendant, Mbopa, son of Sitayi, and succeeded in gaining him over to their interest by promising him a large tract of Zululand, and recognition as chief of that part of the country.

Dazzled by this offer he became a tool in their hands. A sister of Senzangakona, Tshaka's father, named Mkabayi, was still alive. She had seen her two nephews, Nomkayimba and Mfogazi, cruelly put to death and their inheritence seized by Tshaka. She never forgave him and carried an aching heart with her through life. The conspirators knew this and broached the subject to her. She gave them every encouragement and used all her influence and powers of persuasion to detach Mbopa from his allegiance to Tshaka, and with the help of the promises made to him by Dingana and Mhlangana succeeded. Mbopa dissembled before his master till the fatal day arrived. Tshaka was engaged with Faku's representatives who had come to tender the submission of the Pondos as tributary to the Zulu chief, at the same time placing before him the cranes' feathers, and other articles demanded as an indication of their submission. The meeting was in progress within the cattle kraal of the Great Place. Tshaka seemed to be dissatisfied with the tribute, and was remonstrating with the Pondos, when Mbopa entered, followed by Dingana and Mhlangana. Mbopa took advantage of the chief's attention being distracted to plunge his assegai into Tshaka. Dingana and Mhlangana also set upon him, stabbing him repeatedly till he died. The Zulus thus sacrificed one tyrant, but in Dingana they got another and, if possible, a worse one.

Matabele or Ama-Kumalo (Ama-Lala).

The name Matabele is not the true name of this tribe. It was a nickname given to it by the Basuto tribes, when it arrived in Basutoland on its flight from Tshaka. Its original name, or at least the name of the ruling section was, and is, Ama-Kumalo, said to be an offshoot of the I-Ntlangwini tribe. The Matabele tribe first came into prominence under the chieftainship of Mzilikazi, who at one time was a prominent captain in Tshaka's army. Apparently, previous to this he was a captain in Zwide's army, that is, the Ama-Ndwandwe or Nxumalo army. Zwide was the last of the powerful chiefs whom Tshaka overcame. It was due to the breaking up of the Ndwandwes that Mzilikazi transferred his allegiance to Tshaka. He was placed by Tshaka between the Mlalazi and Mhlatuzi rivers, in charge of his military station Bulawayo. The Rhodesian Bulawayo is named after this station. It is said that, on a certain day, Mzilikazi was sent by Tshaka with a strong force to attack a certain tribe. Being unsuccessful in this enterprise, and knowing that Tshaka's custom when any of his armies failed to conquer was to put to death the leaders and such other individuals as he regarded as cowards, Mzilikazi gave up all thought of returning and facing his chief's wrath. He, therefore, went westward, crossed the Drakensberg, and settled in what is now the Transvaal, after having scattered such tribes as were in his path. He adopted the practice of Tshaka with tribes conquered by him, namely, to incorporate them bodily into his army. By this means he increased the number of his fighting men. These were augmented also by members of tribes fleeing from Tshaka's iron hand. In his flight from Tshaka, he followed that great warrior's example, adopted in his warfare with Zwide. Late in Tshaka's reign, Zwide chief of the Ama-Ndwandwe set his army in motion and advanced to attack Tshaka. The latter, realizing that the Ndwandwe army was the equal of his own in courage and numbers, retreated before it, burning and laying waste the country over which he passed, and thus brought disaster upon the Ndwandwes through starvation and exhaustion. When they were in this condition, Tshaka turned on them and inflicted a severe defeat. This policy Mzilikazi followed out, expecting in his flight to be pursued by Tshaka. The whole country passed through by him was thus rendered a wilderness. He settled at Mosega, the headwaters of the Marico river, Potchefstroom district. Shortly after this, Zwangendaba, chief of a section of the Abe-Nguni, who was also a captain in Zwide's army, fled from Tshaka and followed the line taken by Mzilikazi. He ultimately met with the latter, and for a short time they remained together, but trouble arose between them and fighting ensued, as the result of which Zwangendaba was beaten. He then retired northwards devastating the country as he went. The Aba-Nguni of Nyasaland are the descendants of his people.

Mzilikazi, coming into contact with the emigrant Boers, made several attacks upon them, but was not strong enough to overpower them. He then returned to Kapaying (1834).

Previous to this, in 1830, Dingana, now chief of the Zulus, sent an army against Mzilikazi, but in the fighting which took place honours were easy.

Dingana's army again retired into Zululand. Later, through pressure of the Boers under Pot-gieter and Retief, Mzilikazi retired still further north, crossed the Limpopo and settled between the headwaters of the Gwaai and Shangani rivers, and named his great place Bulawayo. The remnants of the once great Makalanga tribe in that neighbour-hood were reduced to servitude, more especially the Ama-Tshona (Mashona or Swina) whom the Ma-tabele compelled to become herds to the Matabele cattle. The Chartered Company, under the aegis of the Imperial Government, was given control of the territory called Rhodesia, and came into conflict

with the Matabele under Mzilikazi's son Nombengula (Lobengula) in 1893. Nombengula was defeated and retiring northward died at the Zambesi
in 1894. The Ntlangwini tribe regard the Kumalos
as their relatives, and if this be correct, they come
under the third group of eastern Bantu, according
my division, namely Ama-Lala.

The genealogy of the Ama-Kumalo (Matabele)
as given here, covers only a few names, these are :

      Kumalo
      Matshobana
      Mzilikazi (Mosilikatsi, Anglice)
      Nombengula (Lobengula, Anglice)

*Manukuza or Sotshangana—Ama-Nxumalo or Ama-
Ndwandwe.*

Gazaland takes its name from Gaza (Zikode),
one of the sons of Langa, and brother of Zwide
of the Ama-Ndwandwe. To which branch of the
Bantu race the Ama-Ndwandwe belong is not yet
clear, but the probability is that they are Ama-Lala
or possibly a branch of the Abe-Nguni. Gaza,
on the break-up of the Ndwandwe army, could
not submit to be ruled by a chief of another than
his own tribe. The story goes that for a time,
at least, he submitted to the authority of Tshaka,
and was created one of his captains. Tshaka was
shortly afterwards killed by his brother Dingana,
who then became chief of the Ama-Zulu. An
expedition against the Portuguese on the Zambesi
and Delagoa was authorised by Dingana. Neither
the cause nor the exact purpose of the expedition
is now known, but Gaza was placed in nominal
command of it, though his son, Sotshangana,
otherwise Manukuza, was actually in command.

The difficulty experienced by Europeans in the spelling of Bantu names gives us various versions of the name Manukuza; thus— Manikus, Manukusi, Manikusa, etc.

The original name of this chief was Sotshangana and it is from him that the Ama-Tshangana (English : *Shangaans*) take their name.

From the setting out of the expedition against the Portuguese, it seems clear that the Ama-Nxumalo had no intention of returning again and placing themselves under the mercy of the Zulu potentate, more especially should the expedition be a failure. Their main object was to look for some new land whereon to settle.

In the latter days of Tshaka's rule and during that of his successor Dingana, such expeditions as that of Mzilikazi and Sotshangana (or Manukuza) had a tendency, whether successful or not, to keep away from Zululand, and form independent kingdoms. One of Tshaka's or Dingaan's pleasantries did not commend itself to his warriors. On the return of any of his armies from war, he had the whole force collected before him and demanded of the leaders to point out to him such men as had proved themselves cowards. These were immediately put to death, and many, innocent of cowardly conduct, died because the officers knew that, should they fail to point out certain individuals and declare that there were no cowards, the despot would have the whole of that army slaughtered. Win or lose, many innocent would have to die to provide amusement for Tshaka.

Mzilikazi's expedition did not actually fail, but he did not return. Manukuza's expedition also did not fail, but he also dared not return.

The Ama-Nxumalo, were, as has already been stated, otherwise called the Ama-Ndwandwe, the last and most formidable tribe to be conquered by Tshaka. The tribe occupied territory west of, and abutting on, Lake St. Lucia. When beaten by Tshaka, the tribe proceeded north and temporarily settled in the Wakkerstroom District. Here those sections which were politically united to the Ndwandwes began to break off. First the Kumalo under Mozilikazi, then the Abe-Nguni under Zwangendaba and now a great part of the Ndwandwes under Gaza, a half-brother of the paramount chief Zwide. The mission on which Gaza was sent provided the tribe with an opportunity of getting away, and keeping away from Zululand. On the northward progress of Gaza's people, they badly handled the Tongas and other tribes in the line of their march between the Limpopo and Zambesi. None of these tribes could offer opposition to Manukuza. Having reached what is now called Gazaland, after the name of the chief of this section of the Ama-Ndwandwe or Ama-Nxumalo, Manukuza settled down for two years. So far, he had not carried out the terms of his commission against the Portuguese, and when he subsequently did attack them it was on his own account. A certain measure of success attended his efforts against the Portuguese, and he maintained the independence of his tribe.

Manukuza fixed his Great Place, Nodwengu, at Tshama-tshama, near the headwaters of the Bosi river. His country was bounded on the east by the Indian Ocean, and on the west by Matebeleland.

Ama-Ndwandwe.

Nxumalo
Ndwandwe
Langa
Zwide, 2. Nqabeni.
Nomahlanjana, 2. Sikunyana, 3. Somapunga, 4. Dayingubo, 5. Nombengula
Mankulumane
6. Mpepa
7. Sishemane.

Ama-Gasa or Ama-Tshangana

Gasa (Zikode)
Sotshangana (Manukuza), 2. Mhlabawadabuka
Maweva (deposed)
Mzila
Guzana (Ngungunya), 2. Mdunyazwe.
Mdugaza.

Ama-Sokulu:
Mazwi
Nontsobo
Dlemudlemu
Mhawu.

To face page 463, Chapter XXIII

The material originally positioned here is too large for reproduction in this reissue. A PDF can be downloaded from the web address given on page iv of this book, by clicking on 'Resources Available'.

Manukuza was famed for his wisdom and courage, and had many of the attributes of leadership possessed by such great warriors as Matiwana of the Ama-Ngwana, and Mzilikazi of the Matabele (Kumalo).

After the death of Manukuza, he was succeeded by his son, Maweva, who was later deposed, a younger brother, Mzila, taking his place. Mzila's sons were Guzana, *alias* Ndungunya, and Mdunyazwe, the former being the heir. The son of Mdungunya, Mdugaza, was born in 1882.

The genealogy of the Ama-Ndwandwe or Nxumalo is here given.

CHAPTER XXIV

Aba-Tembu (? Ama-Lala)

This tribe is here placed among the Ama-Lala. It is doubtful, however, to which branch, if to any, of the three dealt with in this book the Aba-Tembu belong. They have no point of contact with either the Abe-Nguni (Xosas) or Aba-Mbo. The royal salutations of this tribe are *Sitole* and *Mvelase*. The assumption is that these two chiefs may have been brothers,* or Sitole may have been father of Mvelase, since the former's name does not appear in the list of Mvelase's descendants. Neither of these two names, however, nor those of their descendants, have a place in the Abe-Nguni or Aba-Mbo genealogies. The tribe consequently must either be a distinct branch, possibly of Lala stock, or of Basuto origin. If either of these two possibilities is correct, then the Tembus are of Makalanga stock, since both Ama-Lala and Basuto are supposed to be from the same source. If the Tembus are pressed as to the original source from which they came, they never give a satisfactory answer. Some venture the statement that they are of Basuto origin, while others unconvincingly say that they are of Zulu origin. The last assertion is manifestly incorrect, as the Zulu tribe is of comparatively recent origin, whereas the Tembu genealogy reaches much further back than that of the Zulus. The tribe may be classed with the Ama-Lala, since they were first known to be living side by side, in what was later called Zululand, with the original inhabitants of that part of the

---

* Later research shows Sitole to be only a nephew on the female side, therefore, he is not a true Tembu.

Ama-Tembu.

Ama-Tembu genealogical chart.

Rt.Hd. = Right hand house.
Lt.Hd. = Left   "   "
M.H. = Minor house.

━━━━ = Royal line.
──── = Reigning line.

To face Chapter XXIV.

The material originally positioned here is too large for reproduction in this reissue. A PDF can be downloaded from the web address given on page iv of this book, by clicking on 'Resources Available'.

continent, viz. the Ama-Lala tribes. In early times, that is, before the advent of the Aba-Mbo into Natal, 1620, there were several sections of the Aba-Tembu in that country, one section living at the sources of the Ntsele, another about the Qudeni mountains, where it still resides. About the time of the Aba-Mbo occupation of Natal, one section of the Tembus came south, and settled apparently about the Mtamvuna river in Pondoland. This presupposes that the *Stavenisse* was wrecked in that neighbourhood for, according to the survivors from the wreck, the first tribe encountered on their southward journey to the Cape were " Temboes," and next below them the Mapontemousse, and further south again the Maponte, below these the Matimbas and the Gossibes (Xosas). Shortly after the Aba-Mbo irruption into Natal, these tribes, then living close under the Drakensberg moved down to the coast and settled in the order given. The Xosas, who went furthest south and west, were in 1686 on the west bank of the St. John's river, the others east of it.

The Tembus, then, apparently were in the neighbourhood of the Mtamvuna river.

Orthography of foreign names presented difficulties to writers in the early days of which we are writing. We have for instance in the list of tribal names, as set down by the survivors of the *Stavenisse*, spellings which, but for the possession of other facts, would be hard to the decipher. For instance, we find the first and fourth names on the abovementioned list given as " Temboes " and " Matimbas, " respectively. Presumably these two names refer to two sections of the same tribe, the Aba-Tembu. The first of these names has no tribal prefix, and the other has the " *ma* " prefix, whereas, if they actually are the Tembus, the prefix should be " *Ba-*" or " *Aba-*". Yet, recognising these peculiarities my belief is that the two names, as stated, refer to two branches of the same tribe. If tradition is to be depended on, these Tembus must have been the rearguard of the main body, which at that early date had penetrated inland as far as central Tembuland, for we are told that a battle took place at Msana, a tributary of the Bashe river, and about 10 miles above the present Bashee Bridge. This battle was fought in the time of Nxego (1650 approximately) for supremacy. The contestants were the two principal sons of Nxego, Hlanga and Dlomo, and the contest resulted in favour of the latter, i.e., younger son. As a consequence the main divisions of the present-day Tembus, the Ama-Dlomo, otherwise Ama-Hala, are the ruling line, while the Ama-Hlanga, otherwise Ama-Qiya, have been displaced by them.

It is sometimes asserted that the Tembus came south from somewhere far north under the leadership of Hala simultaneously with the Xosas. Certain facts, however, point to an earlier entry of this tribe than the date of Hala's leadership. These facts are :—(1) Hala was not the great chief of the Tembus, but only the head of one section, the Ama-Dlomo ; (2) chronologically, Hala lived approximately about 1650 ; (3) Nxego, Hala's grandfather, lived and died at the Msana, a small river which flows into the Bashee, well in the centre of Tembuland, approximately about 1600. (4) A great battle took place at the Msana between the brothers Hlanga and Dlomo for the chieftain-ship. The latter was the father of Hala.

It is clear, therefore, that Tembuland was occupied by the Tembus at least 50 years, or even more, before Hala's time from about 1600 onwards and possibly earlier.

This is somewhat earlier than the occupation of the country between the St. John's river and the Umtata by the Xosas. It may be remembered that Togu, the great Xosa chief, was east of the Umtata in 1686, as we learn from survivors of the *Stavenisse*. There were, however, some Tembus (see Bird, *Annals of Natal*, p. 41) on the coast of Pondoland much further east than the Xosas. These may have joined up later with those already in Tembuland, or they may have gone north and settled in Natal, where we have the Tembus of the Qudeni Mountains.

The line of movement of a migrating tribe is best followed, failing other means, by locating the graves of the principal tribal chiefs. Tradition, unfortunately, does not carry us back consecutively for any great length of time without a hiatus. This is exemplified in the case of the Tembus. Most of the graves of their chiefs may be traced from the present time back to that of Nxego, that is approximately to 1600. Beyond that nothing is known of the locality of the graves of earlier chiefs. All known graves of Tembu chiefs are located in what is known as Tembuland. Nxego's is at Msana, a tributary of the Bashee river, Hlanga's is at Nkanga in the Willowvale district, for in the 17th century his clan, the Ama-Qiya, occupied part of the country between the Bashee and Kei rivers, particularly the Kentani and Butterworth districts.

In connection with the other main section of the Tembu tribe, the Ama-Dlomo, we have the grave of Tato (1700) at Mkutu, a few miles east of the Bashee; that of his son, Zondwa (1725), at Darabe, Mqanduli District, and that of his son, Ndaba (1756), close to that of Tato at Mtentu. These facts determine the position of the tribe from the beginning of the 17th century as being practically where it is at the present time. Failure to trace earlier graves makes it impossible to dogmatize as to the direction of the line of migration previous to that time.

Hlanga and Dlomo.

The history and traditional tales of the Tembus come into clearer perspective from the time of Nxego. Before that all is hazy and obscure in the extreme. Hlanga and Dlomo were full brothers, belonging to the Royal House. While still in control of the tribe, during the adolescence of his sons, Nxego realized that the hearts of his people leaned towards the younger son, Dlomo, and he made efforts to rectify matters by giving Hlanga, the elder, special training in the methods of governing. This son, however, had little inclination to give himself whole-heartedly to cultivating those qualities which would most commend him to the common people. With all Bantu tribes open-handedness, on the part of a chief, is a *sine qua non*. Readiness to feed the multitude must be an unfailing quality. Courage, also, to lead men to victory in war, and wisdom to guide them in council, mark out the character desired by the tribesmen in a chief. Dlomo had these, or at least the promise of them, in greater measure than the heir. But the training of Hlanga, through his indifference to these desirable qualifications, availed little. His lack of them was a barrier to his assuming the chieftainship after his father's death.

Hlanga was beloved of his father, for he had certain qualities which endeared him to his parent ; and Nxego, noting the growing influence of the younger son, sent Dlomo away from home to the cattle feed kraals, to look after his father's herds, hoping thus to keep him away from direct contact with the tribe until Hlanga's position had been made secure by the voice of the people. But the younger men of the tribe followed Dlomo in ever increasing numbers into what was practically exile. The feed kraals thus in time became a serious menace to the peace of the tribe, if Dlomo elected to make a bid for the chieftainship. Nxego realizing the situation sent for Dlomo to return, but the son refused both to return or to send home the cattle.

This defiance of the supreme authority required to be punished. Nxego, together with the heir, collected an army and set out to punish Dlomo. The rearguard of Nxego's force was the Ama-Ndungwana clan, under their chief Ndungwana who was Nxego's eldest son but not the heir. When the army was on the march, Ndungwana sent secretly to Dlomo, advising him to fight with determination, for when the opposing forces joined battle the Ndungwanas would attack Nxego's forces in the rear and thus assist Dlomo. This act of treachery, when put into execution, turned the result of the battle in favour of Dlomo. This placed him in supreme power, and he immediately usurped the chieftainship. This defeat of Hlanga was the reason for his section of the tribe leaving Tembuland and settling for many years between the Bashee and Kei rivers. He was later asked to return, when there was no further chance of him giving trouble.

Ama-Qiya.

After the usurpation of the chieftainship by Dlomo, Hlanga married Nobeta, a daughter of Qiya, principal chief of the Ama-Tshomane, the superseded royal house of the Pondos. Nobeta was a contrast to her husband in that she had a strong character and outstanding personality, whereas Hlanga had neither. On the day of her marriage she brought with her from home the *ubu-lunga* animal, which from its semi-sacred character could not be appropriated by the husband. Along with it were dowry cattle given to the bride by her parents, called *i-nqakwe*, and a number of others sent to be driven along with these, and lastly an animal for slaughter. This profusion on the part of her parents at once proclaimed Nobeta to be a daughter of a great chief, and, taken together with her personal qualities which were soon in evidence, won the hearts of Hlanga's following. In their praises (*izi-bongo*), they called themselves "*inkomo zom-Qiyazana*" ("the Qiya maiden's cattle"). From this circumstance the name of this section of the Aba-Tembu ever since has been the *Ama-Qiya*, and not as it should be the *Ama-Hlanga*.

From the period in which these events took place, probably the latter half of the 17th century, until the time of Zondwa's son, Ndaba (1750), a man of captious, aggressive nature, there is little of history

or tradition to mark the life of the Tembu tribe.
He was a contemporary of the Xosa chief, Rarabe,
though much younger than the latter, with whom
he frequently came into collision, on which
occasions he invariably showed the white feather.
Yet it was in conflict with Ndaba's Tembus that
Rarabe met with his death. That was in 1770.
Rarabe little thought that his suggestion that Ndaba
should be chosen as the Tembu chief would,
when acted upon, cause him the loss of his heir,
Mlawu, who like himself fell in a skirmish with
Ndaba's Tembus. It is said that Ndaba's father,
Zondwa, pre-deceased his son. Tato the father
of Zondwa was still alive when the question of
appointing an heir to Zondwa arose. Rarabe was
on a visit to Tato, and the subject of the appointment was mooted in his presence, and his opinion
asked about it. The succession had not been
arranged while Zondwa was alive, but there were
three sons eligible for the position of heir. Tato
told Rarabe that, were it not for Ndaba's wildness
he would be in favour of Ndaba. Rarabe is said
to have answered, that that was the very reason
Ndaba should be chosen, as wildness in a chief,
while still a boy, was rather in his favour than
otherwise. Through life Ndaba was flighty and
wild, but did nothing remarkable on behalf of his
people. His grave is at the Mtentu on the east
bank of the Bashee river, and is marked by a clump
of yellow-wood trees.

Ngoza or Ngozi.

Reference might be made here to the elder
branch of the Aba-Tembu, and to Ngozi, sometimes
called Ngoza, chief in Tshaka's days of that branch.

It is averred that this section, which had its residence at the Qudeni in Natal, represents the principal House of the Tembus, and that the Cape Colony Tembus are an early break off from them. The principal names of the chiefs preserved to us are the following, which do not, however, exhaust the list :—

Mvelase
Nyandeni
Mkupukeli
Ngozi
Nodada
Mganu
Ngqamzana.

This branch of the Aba-Tembu was settled, as has been said, at the Qudeni mountains, which are situated at the junction of the Buffalo and Tugela rivers, but on the east side. These Tembus were separated from the Zulus by the great Butelezi tribe, to which the Tembus were attached as tributary. In accordance with his custom, Tshaka sought to incorporate the Butelezi with his own tribe, and in pursuance of that object attacked them. They were overwhelmed and their chief killed. The Tembus realized that they would be the next victims to follow the fate of the Butelezi and feel the weight of Tshaka's hand. Ngozi who was then chief, looked about him for a means of escape. The section of the Ntlangwini under Nomagaga was immediately to the south of him and barred his way in that direction. Ngozi asked for free passage through their country. This was refused. Ngozi then attacked the Ntlangwini and their relatives, the Ama-Kuze, and swept them aside. He then settled down on the territory from

which he had driven the Ama-Kuze. Ngozi
was popular with most of the tribes near him, and
in consequence many individuals from those tribes
joined him. He had, therefore, a formidable
army. The dispossessed Ama-Kuze complained
to Tshaka about their ejectment and asked for his
assistance. Tshaka was always ready to interfere
in the affairs of other tribes, and such a chance was
not to be lost as was now presented to him by the
request of the Ama-Kuze. He attacked Ngozi,
but the unexpected happened and his forces were
badly beaten by the Tembus. It is related that
during the course of the battle, Tshaka took up a
position on one of the spurs of the Qudeni overlooking the battle. Whilst he was observing its
progress there was near him one of Ngozi's officers.
Jobe, but they did not recognize each other.

A messenger came up to Tshaka to inform him
that his army was defeated. At the same time, as
was right, the man made obeisance to his chief
(*ndabezita*). He was unaware that there were
strangers present. Tshaka was furious, probably
on account of the unpleasant news of his defeat,
but also because his identity was revealed by the
salutation. In his fury he had the messenger
instantly put to death. Though Jobe had Tshaka
at his mercy, he was so taken aback that he could
do nothing, and the Zulu chief got away in the confusion of the moment.

Ngozi knew well enough that Tshaka would
draw on some of his other garrisons for fresh
warriors and renew the attack, when it suited him.
He, therefore, decided to move on. When he
entered the territory of the Ama-Dunge who were
in his line of retreat they gave him passage, not

being prepared to resist one who had just administered a defeat on the terrible Tshaka. At the Mpanza, Mjoli's Xesibes dared to refuse passage to Ngozi, and they were so badly handled that they fled for protection to Maraule of the Ama-Funze. Ngozi next attacked the Ama-Ncwabe at the Mnyambuvu, next below the Xesibes. Still he had a long way to go and to pass a number of tribes before he dared to settle with his tribe. At the headwaters of the Mlazi he attacked the Ama-Nkalane, swept them out of his way and came face to face with the Ama-Wushe and the Ama-Baca, but these tribes had recently been severely handled by Macingwane of the Ama-Cunu, and got out of Ngozi's way, as they could not offer opposition to so dangerous a leader of men. Lastly, he drove the Ama-Qondo under their chief Gawu, out of his path, and the road was now comparatively clear.

He moved on towards the country now called Griqualand East, at that time a No-Man's-Land. On his way, Ngozi met Macingwane, chief of the Ama-Cunu, of whom notice has already been taken. Joining forces, these two crossed the Mzimkulu, but both were destined to meet death shortly afterwards, Macingwane at the Ntsikoni, between the Mzimvubu and the Mzintlanga, and Ngozi in Pondoland.

After the death of Mcingwane, Ngozi, trusting to the powerful forces under his control, proceeded onward and entered Pondoland. Faku objected to the presence of so powerful a neighbour and attacked Ngozi. Ngozi fell in the fighting which ensued. His people, with enemies on every hand were scattered here and there, seeking refuge in scattered parties with various tribes. A few went back to Zululand and joined their old enemy Tshaka. These fought both Tshaka's and Dingana's battles, but came out with Mpande when he went over and joined himself to the Europeans.

Unlike most chiefs of those times in Natal, Ngozi was liked by both friend and foe. He was a man of courage unsurpassed.

Ngubencuka.

There is little to relate in connection with Ngubencuka. In historical works he is known as Vusani, but this was his family name, not that of his chieftainship. He was son and heir to Ndaba, and must have been born towards the end of the eighteenth century. He belonged to the Ama-Dlomo section of the tribe, which had usurped the place of the Ama-Hlanga. It was during his reign that the Ama-Qwati got a footing in his country. This tribe were a Minor House of the Ama-Xesibe. With the restlessness characteristic of most Bantu tribes they set out in search of a new home where they could develop as an independent tribe. They entered Tembuland and sought by force to seize a piece of the land, but Ngubencuka proved too strong for them. They then passed on to Basutoland, but not being made welcome retraced their steps into Tembuland again. This time they came as suppliants, and Ngubencuka granted them permission to settle in his country.

1828 saw the invasion of Tembuland by the Ama-Ngwana or Mfecane. The Qwatis were the first to feel the edge of the Ama-Ngwana spears and fled before them. Ngubencuka became seriously alarmed and asked assistance from the Colonial Government, and from the Gcalekas. This was given and the invasion crushed. Ngubencuka married a daughter of Faku, the Pondo chief. This was Nonesi, and she became his Great Wife, but she had no son. In accordance with the usual custom in such cases, a child from one of the other houses of the chief was installed in Nonesi's house as the prospective heir. This was *Mtirara*. During Ngubencuku's time the district of Queenstown was taken from the Bushmen by Bawana, a Tembu chief. He belonged to the Right-Hand house of Dlomo, and was consequently of considerable importance. His clan is called Ama-Tshatshu after Bawana's father, Tshatshu. After Bawana's death, his son, Mapasa, a man of hasty and passionate character, became chief of the Ama-Tshatshu. He was a source of constant annoyance to the Governor. During the War of the Axe, though professing to be neutral, he was assisting the Gaikas. He had no intention of involving himself in serious fighting, but was allured by the prospect of raiding cattle. This did not help him much, however, as all the cattle captured by him were confiscated by the Principal Chief, Mtirara, who handed them over to the Europeans. This act was not dictated by any lofty ideas of justice, but by the hope of enlisting the help of the whites in his own troubles with the tribes round about him.

In 1836, the year immediately following the death of Hintsa, the Xosa chief, Tembuland was entered by raiding parties of Bacas under Ncapayi, and later by a combined force of Bacas and Pondos under Faku. Large numbers of cattle were captured, and large numbers of Tembus shifted further inland in order to get away from the disturbed area.

These matters have already been referred to in the chapter dealing with the Bacas.

Mtirara died during the year preceding the war of Mlanjeni, at Quluqu. *Ngangelizwe* (or Qeya), the heir, was but a child at the time of his father's death, and a regent was appointed in the person of Joyi, a younger brother of Mtirara. Joyi's residence was first at the Rode ; then he shifted to the Tsitsa. Representative chiefs of the two great sections of the Tembu tribe, namely Bacela, of the Ama-Qiya or Ama-Hlanga, and Mqanqeni, of the Ama-Dlomo, went to Joyi to persuade him to leave Tsitsa and take up his residence at the Tyalara, the Great Place, where he would have the child-heir under his immediate personal supervision. An additional reason for this request was the threatened disturbance of the peace of the tribe through Joyi's presence at the Tsitsa, for a complaint had been made to these representatives by a section of Hlubis resident there, who refused to come under the control of Joyi. This so annoyed Joyi that he attacked the Hlubis, said to be under Ludidi, and compelled them to move on to other parts.

There seems to be a discrepancy between this traditional story of Ludidi's residence, and others which state that he was living at the Ngqungqu in the Mqanduli district when this attack was made by Joyi.

War between Joyi and Gqirana (1680).

The Tembus have proved to be the least warlike of all South African tribes. Tribal history is mostly composed of genealogy and war, but of the latter there is little to relate in connection with the

Tembus. Battles with other tribes there have been, but the Tembus have never distinguished themselves in these. In 1875, though the Tembus were responsible for the events which brought on the war of Nongxokozelo with the Gcalekas, they made no serious attempt at a stand, and the Gcalekas simply walked through their country. Menziwa's Fingoes, who were living in Tembuland, alone put up a fight, but were badly cut up by the Gcalekas. This is mentioned in the chapter dealing with Kreli's reign.

The battle to be mentioned here, between Joyi and Gqirana, otherwise Mditshwa, was of the usual character of Tembu battles. Gqirana was uncle to Mhlontlo. Owing to claims advanced by Gqirana (Mditshwa) to the chieftainship of the Pondomise, fighting took place, previous to the events about to be recorded, between these two chiefs, in which the rightful heir Mhlontlo successfully asserted his claim. As a result of this, Gqirana separated from Mhlontlo and went to reside on the west of the Umtata river, erecting kraals at Zimbane and Cicira. In consequence of mutual raiding of cattle between the Tembus and the Pondomise, Joyi chose to regard himself as the aggrieved party, though both were equally guilty. He, therefore, elected to bring this matter to the test of battle. Gqirana was quite pleased at this decision, and both made preparations for war.

Joyi moved across country in the direction of Gqirana's quarters at Zimbane. Gqirana, who was at the Cicira, hearing that the Tembus were approaching his home at the Zimbane, sent forward his forces to meet them. He arranged them in three divisions. The division on the right was under command of Gqirana himself ; the centre division was commanded by Jeco, son of Ndayi, the third being under a separate command. The Tembus were already in order of battle at Zimbane when the Pondomise came in sight of them.

The Pondomise centre under Jeco was the first to attack. The right under the chief Gqirana soon followed, and the third division almost simultaneously. Gqirana found himself opposite the Tembu left wing, immediately under command of Joyi and drove it back. Jeco and his force were for a time unable to make progress against the Tembus opposed to them. Noting, however, that the Tembu left was bending under Gqirana's attack, Jeco forced the assault more vigorously, and broke through the Tembu centre. Many Tembus fell here and more especially at a vlei called in memory of the event *icibi laba-Tembu* (the Tembus' vlei), which lay just behind the Tembu centre. The Tembus were driven in the direction of Qunu, where the victorious Pondomise gave up the pursuit.

While Joyi was being driven towards Qunu, other forces were assembling in lower Tembuland to assist Joyi, but came up too late to change the fortune of the day. These new forces were the AmaNqabe, Ama-Egebe, and Ama-Xesibe. On the day after the battle they advanced to Gqirana's head-quarters at Cicira, but found only burning huts, the Pondomise having evacuated their positions and gone away towards Tsolo. From that time Tsolo has remained the main position of Gqirana's (Mditshwa's) Pondomise.

FF

Ngangelizwe.

Ngangelizwe, Mtirara's heir, came of age in 1863. He was previously known by the name of Qeya, but, on attaining manhood and being appointed chief, he received a new name in supposed keeping with his new dignity. He was named Ngangeliswe. On his accession he found that the Ama-Qwati, who had been given land whereon to reside by his predecessors, were not submitting to the authority of the Tembu chiefs as they were expected to do. In order, therefore, to check their unruly behaviour, Ngangelizwe granted facilities to other alien tribes to reside in his country. Among others he admitted Fingoes under the chief Menziwa, and placed them on the east bank of the Bashee river, in the locality still occupied by them. Europeans were also granted land, with the same purpose in view, on the Umtata river. These were the nucleus round which the town of Umtata ultimately gathered.

Ngangelizwe conducted himself in a manner which caused grave dissatisfaction among his own people. In 1866 he married Nomkafulo, daughter of Kreli, the Paramount Chief of the Xosas ; her name as a chief's wife was *Novili*. She was the mother of Dalinyebo, late Principal Chief of the Tembus. Ngangelizwe treated her with the utmost cruelty. After five years of married life, during which Novili endured much suffering at the hands of her husband, she left him secretly and, by the help of Menziwa, the Fingo chief already referred to, managed to reach her father's place, her body a mass of wounds. Ngangelizwe was in very deed a brute in human form, incapable of controlling his temper, ready to take offence on the slightest provocation, and to inflict injury on the least annoyance. Kreli, though a thorough Native gentleman, was not a man to flout or trifle with. Ngangelizwe knowing this, and fearing the consequences of his brutality, did not wait until he heard that Kreli was arming to punish him, but immediately asked to be taken under Government protection. This was agreed to, and a magistrate, Mr. E. B. Chalmers, was sent to reside near Ngangelizwe. Seven months passed, from the time of the appointment of the magistrate, when Kreli collected an army with the intention of entering Tembuland and punishing Ngangelizwe for his treatment of Novili. The army was to be under the leadership of himself and his heir, Sigcawu. Before setting out, however, Kreli brought the matter of his daughter's treatment before the Colonial Government, and the following magistrates were appointed to look into the case, William Fynn and E. B. Chalmers. Judgment was given against Ngangelizwe, and a fine of forty head of cattle was imposed on him. The Gcalekas, much against their feelings, bowed to the judgment and for the time being stayed their army. Nevertheless, the Gcalekas were waiting for something to give them the opportunity they longed for to attack the Tembus. They stirred up the sleeping " dogs of war " by raiding Tembu cattle, and the Tembus retaliated in like manner, until, in 1872, Kreli crossed the lower Bashee with a strong force, and entered Tembuland. Little came of this move, for the Tembus refused to meet Kreli and secured the good offices of the Government on their behalf.

Nongxokozelo (1875).

We shall touch briefly on the war of Nongxokozelo, as the story has already been told elsewhere
(see chap. on Kreli). In 1875, Ngangelizwe brutally treated Nongxokozelo, the female attendant
who had accompanied Novili at the time of her
marriage, and remained in attendance on her mis-
tress until she took refuge with her father. Nongxokozelo was compelled to remain at the Tembu
court by the authority of Ngangelizwe. It is said
that the chief so cruelly used her that she lay at
death's door, and the unfeeling monster told
Ndevu, one of his servants, to finish her off with
his cudgel (*bunguza*), which he did. This occurred
during the winter of that year. Ngangelizwe
reported to the magistrate that she had been suffering for four days from headache, and from a
pain in her side (which is not unlikely considering
the treatment to which she had been subjected.)

Secret information of what had happened to the
poor girl reached Kreli, who dispatched two messengers to go and find out the truth of the matter.
They were also to conduct themselves as if unaware
of Nongxokozelo's death, and asked to be allowed
to see her. Ngangelizwe refused this request, but
at the same time he knew that Kreli's messengers
were not imposed upon by his excuses, and he
perceived that war would follow. When it became
evident that war was about to break out, the Fingo
chief, Menziwa, intimated his resolution to take
no part in the war. Ngangelizwe heard of this
and vowed vengeance against Menziwa, who,
realizing his danger, crossed the Bashee together
with his people and temporarily settled at Idutywa.
In crossing the Bashee, Menziwa sent over first

the women and children, the men fully armed remaining behind to cover the crossing, for a Tembu army was following them up. The Tembus, however, arrived at the Bashee when all the Fingoes were safely on the other side. They then retired, not desiring to enter hostile territory. The Government advised Kreli to refer the matter of Nongxokozelo to the ordinary court of law. Again Kreli yielded. The case was tried at Idutywa, by Messrs. J. Ayliff and W. Wright, two magistrates appointed by the Government to deal with it. Ngangelizwe was again found guilty and condemned to pay two hundred cattle and one hundred pounds.

The next matter to engage the attention of the authorities was the position of the Fingo chief, Menziwa, and his people, who had fled into the Idutywa district in order to escape from Ngangelizwe's vengeance for their declared intention to remain neutral in the event of hostilities between the Gcalekas and Tembus breaking out. It was decided that Menziwa be restored to his former position in Tembuland. With this in view, a body of mounted Frontier Police under Commandant Bowker was sent with Menziwa to escort him across the Bashee, and resettle him at the Mtentu, his former place of abode. These commotions, due to the wilful conduct of Ngangelizwe, and the realization on his part that the Gcalekas were determined to punish him, induced him to request the Government to definitely receive him as a subject.

One of Ngangalizwe's subjects, Dalasile, chief of the Ama-Qwati, stood out against coming under the wing of the Government, and Stokwe, chief of the Ama-Vundle, was of like mind. These chiefs were a constant source of annoyance to the Government from that time onwards, until their opposition culminated in their active participation in Hope's war (1881).

The Ama-Qwati War.

The Ama-Qwati have already been mentioned with the Ama-Xesibe, from whom they are derived. A few remarks may here be added regarding them as Tembu subjects. Because of their different origin they have never amalgamated with the Tembus but have maintained their separate identity. It has been related that, when they separated from the Xesibes, they entered Tembuland and tried to secure a footing in the country by force, but were unable to do so. They then crossed the Drakensberg into Basutoland, but were not made welcome. They came back on their tracks and re-entered Tembuland together with the Ama-Vundle, and were granted permission to settle in the country by Ngubencuka.

Native accounts state that the cause of war between the Ama-Qwati and the Government was the capture and imprisonment of the chief of the Ama-Tshatshu, a Tembu tribe or rather, clan, This chief was Gungubele. He had assisted Kreli in the War of Ngcayecibi, 1877-78, and for this was imprisoned. Sureties were required for the payment of a fine imposed upon him. These were secured in the persons of the following chiefs : Matanzima, Mbambonduna, and Siqungati, Tembu chiefs, and Dalasile of the Ama-Qwati, and also Stokwe of the Ama-Vundle.

The amount of the fine demanded was not forthcoming in full, hence Gungubele's continued imprisonment. Instead of paying off the whole amount, the sureties are said to have held that a sufficient sum had been paid, and that the chief should be liberated. This demand was not granted, and war followed.

The main part of the fighting which followed was in the Indwe district. Major Elliot, the Chief Magistrate, advised all Europeans in Qwati territory to withdraw, as well as those in neighbouring districts, and come into Umtata or retire to the Colony. Ngangelizwe, being asked by Major Elliot how he proposed to act in connection with these matters, replied that he favoured the Government. The Tembus, therefore, took no active part in the war. The Ama-Qwati were soon overcome and, after seven days of being harried from point to point, surrendered. They had previously sought to make common cause with the Pondomise whom they knew to be preparing for taking part in what is known as Hope's war. On the other hand the Pondomise were requested by Government to prevent the Ama-Qwati entering their territory, to which request Mhlontlo replied by asking for guns, which were ultimately used against the Government. Such is the Native story, but it might just be said that it differs in some points from the historical version : moreover, in the former, events which took place in 1878 are merged into those of 1881.

Dalindyebo.

In the last month (December 31st) of the year 1884, Ngangelizwe died leaving as his heir the eldest son of his Great Wife, Novili. The name by which he was known before his accession was *Aliva*

(Oliver ?), but when he was raised to the chieftainship he was given the name of *Dalindyebo*. This chief, above all his predecessors among Tembu chiefs, was respected by Europeans, not only because he was a loyal subject of the Government, but also because he was a man of considerable knowledge, character, and self-respect. He specially commended himself to that section of his people who were more enlightened and civilized than the majority. On the other hand, it is true that the conduct and qualities which secured for him the esteem of the more advanced, were just those which failed to secure for him the same deep love and respect from the uncivilized. Through what he was as a man and leader the Tembu tribe benefited greatly, as it obtained a position of security and assurance which it never had before.

Ama-Gubevu.

This small but important tribe should have found a place along with the Ama-Hlubi, or other Fingo tribes, though it is of Basuto origin. Before the days of Tshaka, and the break up of the Fingo tribes, the Ama-Gubevu, in consequence of having fought and been beaten by another Basuto tribe, crossed the Drakensberg mountains, entered Natal, and joined themselves to the Hlubis. The Gubevus were at that time under their chief, Meyi. Meyi had two sons, Sengana, his heir, and Gubevu, of the Right-Hand House. For some reason, the Ama-Gubevu separated from those of the superior house and established themselves as a separate tribe. During the dispersals of Tshaka's time, the Gubevus were uprooted and followed the unfortunate Fingoes down to Hintsa's country, and attached themselves to their old friends of happier days, the Hlubis. They are still identified with them, and reside alongside of them in the Toleni district near Ndabakazi. They are recognized as one of the most important fighting tribes among the Fingoes.

Gubevu genealogy is as follows.

(Gt. H.)	MEYI	(Rt. H.)	
Sengana		Gubevu	
Matomana		Saba	
Mtshaba		Nokala	(M. H.)
Pike		Kali	Bum
		Tiba (no issue)	Njatye
			Gwabini
			Faleni
			Eleki

Ama-Molo.

There is in Pondoland a peculiar tribe, the descendants of an alien race. Its tribal name is Ama-Mholo or Ama-Molo (the first *o* is pronounced with an aspirate). The progenitors of this tribe are described as men of a black race, having long black hair, and features of a different cast from those of the Bantu. Though these features are still evident in some members of the tribe, they are, as the writer saw them in 1924, gradually merging into those of the Bantu. The progenitors were three in number, two males and a female, who had been cast ashore on the Pondoland coast, from some wreck. Their names, according to Native pronunciation, were Bhayi, and Mera ; the name of the female, however, was not given. They were probably Malay or Indian, possibly natives of Madagascar. The story concerning them, as handed down by tradition, is as follows. On a certain day, in their own country, Bhayi, his wife, and two others named Tulwana and Pita, walked down to the shore near their home to bathe. While in the water, they were suddenly surrounded by white men, captured, and placed on board of a ship. In the course of the voyage the ship was wrecked on the coast of Pondoland, and the three mentioned were cast ashore. Two of the original party must have been lost, but another man, Mera, was washed ashore with them. Imagining that they could reach their own country by following the coast line eastwards, they walked for many days but lost all hope in the end and turned south. Reaching Pondoland they determined to settle among the Pondos. Bhayi's wife being childless he married a Pondo woman, by whom he had six sons, named Poto, Mngcolwana, Mnyuli, Mgareni and Falteni, the last two being twins, and finally, Nyango.

In 1920 the chief of the Ama-Mholo was Mxaga. The information given here was obtained from his principal son, Nwantsu. The tribe is resident at the mouth of the Mtakatyi river, in the Ngqeleni district.

The following is the genealogy of the Molos or Mholos:—

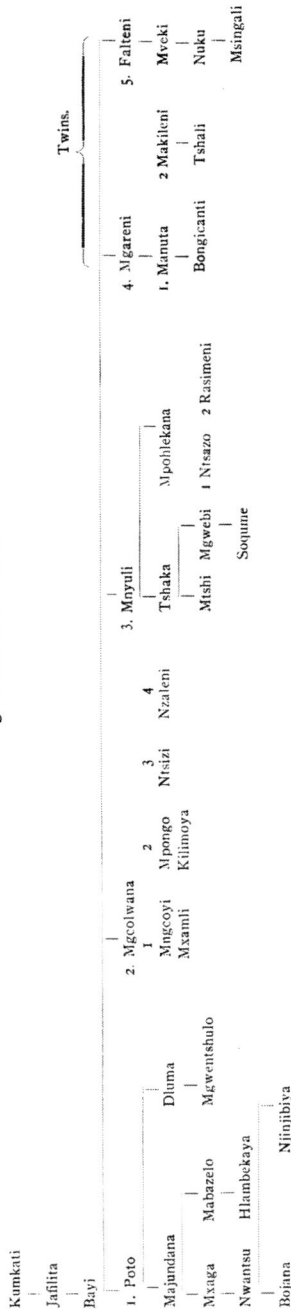

Ama-Mholos.

Kumkati

Jafilita

Bayi

1. Poto

Majundana — Dluma — Mgwentshulo

Mxaga — Mabazelo — Hlambekaya

Nwantsu

Bojana — Ninjibiya

2. Mgcolwana

1 Mngcoyi — Mxamli

2 Mpongo — Kilimoya

3 Ntsizi

4 Nzaleni

3. Mnyuli

Tshaka — Mgwebi — Mpohlekana

Mtshi — Soqune — 1 Ntsazo — 2 Rasimeni

Twins.

4. Mgareni

1. Manuta — Bongicanti

2 Makileni — Tshali

5. Falteni

Mveki — Nuku — Msingali

J. H. Soga.

To face the last page

The material originally positioned here is too large for reproduction in this reissue. A PDF can be downloaded from the web address given on page iv of this book, by clicking on 'Resources Available'.

Printed at the
Lovedale Institution Press, Lovedale C.P.

CPSIA information can be obtained at www.ICGtesting.com
Printed in the USA
BVOW03s2326031113

335309BV00001BA/6/P